Fodor's

MAUI

WELCOME TO MAUI

"Maui no ka oi" is what locals say—it's the best, the most, the top of the heap. To those who know Maui well, there are good reasons for the superlatives. The island's miles of perfect beaches, lush green valleys, and volcanic landscapes, as well as its historic villages, top-notch water sports, and stellar restaurants and resorts, have made it an international favorite. Maui is also home to rich culture and stunning ethnic diversity, as reflected in the island's wide range of food and traditional activities.

TOP REASONS TO GO

★ **Beaches:** From black-sand beauties to palm-lined strands, each beach is unique.

★ **Resorts:** Opulent spas, pools, gardens, and golf courses deliver pampering aplenty.

★ **Hawaiian Culture:** From hula to luau, you can experience Maui's diverse culture.

★ **Road to Hana:** This famed winding road offers stunning views of coast and ocean.

★ **Whale-Watching:** Humpback whales congregate each winter right off Maui's shores.

★ **Water Sports:** Surfing, snorkeling, and sailing are just a few top options.

Fodor's MAUI

Publisher: Amanda D'Acierno, *Senior Vice President*

Design: Tina Malaney, *Associate Art Director*; Erica Cuoco, *Production Designer*

Photography: Jennifer Arnow, *Senior Photo Editor*; Mary Robnett, *Photo Researcher*

Maps: Rebecca Baer, *Senior Map Editor*; Mark Stroud (Moon Street Cartography); David Lindroth, *Cartographers*

Production: Angela L. McLean, *Senior Production Manager*

Sales: Jacqueline Lebow, *Sales Director*

Marketing & Publicity: Heather Dalton, *Marketing Director*; Katherine Punia, *Publicity Director*

Business & Operations: Susan Livingston, *Senior Vice President, Strategic Business Planning*; Sue Daulton, *Vice President, Operations*

Fodors.com: Megan Bell, *Executive Director, Revenue & Business Development*; Yasmin Marinaro, *Senior Director, Marketing & Partnerships*

Copyright © 2017 by Fodor's Travel, a division of Penguin Random House LLC

Writers: Lehia Apana, Christie Leon, Heidi Pool

Editor: Eric Wechter and Douglas Stallings

Production Editor: Jennifer DePrima

17th Edition

ISBN 978-1-101-87996-2

ISSN 1559–0798

SPECIAL SALES

This book is available at special discounts for bulk purchases for sales promotions or premiums. For more information, e-mail specialmarkets@penguinrandomhouse.com.

PRINTED IN THE UNITED STATES OF AMERICA

10 9 8 7 6 5 4 3 2 1

CONTENTS

CONTENTS

ABOUT THIS GUIDE

Fodor's Recommendations

Everything in this guide is worth doing—we don't cover what isn't—but exceptional sights, hotels, and restaurants are recognized with additional accolades. **Fodor'sChoice★** indicates our top recommendations. Care to nominate a new place? Visit Fodors.com/contact-us.

Trip Costs

We list prices wherever possible to help you budget well. Hotel and restaurant price categories from **$** to **$$$$** are noted alongside each recommendation. For hotels, we include the lowest cost of a standard double room in high season. For restaurants, we cite the average price of a main course at dinner or, if dinner isn't served, at lunch. For attractions, we always list adult admission fees; discounts are usually available for children, students, and senior citizens.

Hotels

Our local writers vet every hotel to recommend the best overnights in each price category, from budget to expensive. Unless otherwise specified, you can expect private bath, phone, and TV in your room. For expanded hotel reviews visit Fodors.com.

Top Picks

★ Fodor'sChoice

Listings

- ✉ Address
- 📨 Branch address
- ☎ Telephone
- 📠 Fax
- 🌐 Website
- 📧 E-mail
- 🎟 Admission fee
- 🕒 Open/closed times
- [M] Subway
- ✥ Directions or Map coordinates

Hotels & Restaurants

- 🏨 Hotel
- 🛏 Number of rooms
- 🍽 Meal plans
- 🍴 Restaurant
- ✍ Reservations
- 👔 Dress code
- ▭ No credit cards
- [$] Price

Other

- ⇨ See also
- ☞ Take note
- ⛳ Golf facilities

Restaurants

Unless we state otherwise, restaurants are open for lunch and dinner daily. We mention dress code only when there's a specific requirement and reservations only when they're essential or not accepted.

Credit Cards

The hotels and restaurants in this guide typically accept credit cards. If not, we'll say so.

EUGENE FODOR

Hungarian-born Eugene Fodor (1905–91) began his travel career as an interpreter on a French cruise ship. The experience inspired him to write *On the Continent* (1936), the first guidebook to receive annual updates and discuss a country's way of life as well as its sights. Fodor later joined the U.S. Army and worked for the OSS in World War II. After the war, he kept up his intelligence work while expanding his guidebook series. During the Cold War, many guides were written by fellow agents who understood the value of insider information. Today's guides continue Fodor's legacy by providing travelers with timely coverage, insider tips, and cultural context.

EXPERIENCE MAUI

WHAT'S
WHERE

1 West Maui. This sunny leeward area with excellent beaches is ringed by upscale resorts and condominiums in areas such as Kaanapali and, farther north, Kapalua. Also on the coast is the busy, tourist-oriented town of Lahaina, a former whaling center with plenty of shops and good restaurants that's a base for snorkel and other tours.

2 South Shore. The leeward side of Maui's eastern half is what most people mean when they say "South Shore." This popular area is sunny and warm year-round; Kihei, a fast-growing town, and Wailea, a luxurious resort area with some outstanding hotels, are here. Notable beaches include Makena, mostly undeveloped and spectacular, and Wailea, fronting the resorts.

3 Central Maui. Between Maui's two mountain areas is Central Maui, home to the county seat of Wailuku and the commercial center of Kahului. Kahului Airport, Maui's main terminal, is here, along with convenient shopping malls and a good selection of reasonably priced restaurants. In addition, local museums such as the Bailey House provide good background on Maui's history.

4 Upcountry. Island residents have a name they use affectionately to describe the

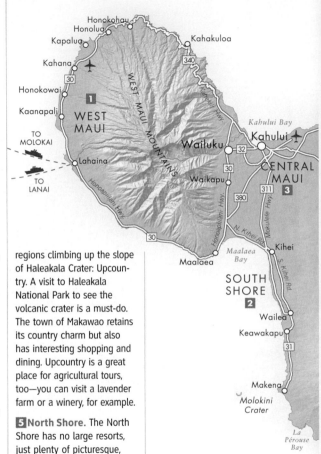

regions climbing up the slope of Haleakala Crater: Upcountry. A visit to Haleakala National Park to see the volcanic crater is a must-do. The town of Makawao retains its country charm but also has interesting shopping and dining. Upcountry is a great place for agricultural tours, too—you can visit a lavender farm or a winery, for example.

5 North Shore. The North Shore has no large resorts, just plenty of picturesque, laid-back small towns like Paia and Haiku—and great windsurfing action at Hookipa Beach. Baldwin Beach is a local favorite just off the highway. The towns are good spots for a break if you're heading out along the Road to Hana. Inland, this part of Maui is lush and wild.

6 **Road to Hana.** The island's windward northeastern side is largely one great rain forest, traversed by the stunning Road to Hana. Exploring this iconic, winding road with its dramatic coastal views can be the highlight of a trip. The tiny town of Hana preserves the slow pace of the past—if you want to escape from it all, consider an overnight stay here.

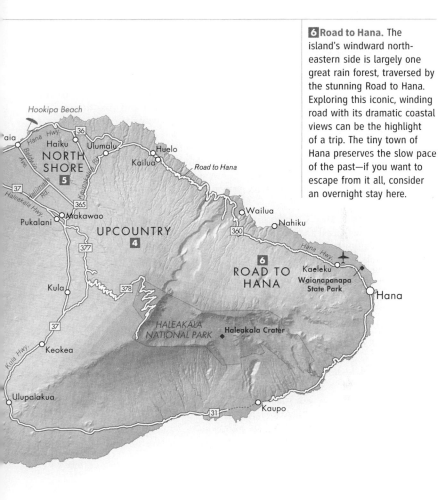

Hookipa Beach

'aia

Hana Hwy. 36

Baldwin Ave.

Haiku Ulumalu

Kailua Huelo

NORTH SHORE

5

Kaupakalua Rd.

Road to Hana

37

Haleakala Hwy.

Kailiili Rd.

365

Pukalani Makawao

377

UPCOUNTRY

4

Wailua

360 Nahiku

Hana Hwy.

6

ROAD TO HANA

Kaeleku

Waianapanapa State Park

Kula 378

HALEAKALA NATIONAL PARK ◆ Haleakala Crater

37

Kula Hwy. Keokea

Ulupalakua

31 Kaupo

Hana

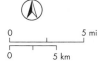

0 ————————— 5 mi

0 ————————— 5 km

MAUI PLANNER

When You Arrive

Most visitors arrive at Kahului Airport in Central Maui. A rental car is the best way to get from the airport to your destination. The major car-rental companies have desks at the airport and can provide a map and directions to your hotel. ■ TIP➔ Flights from the mainland tend to arrive around the same time, leading to long lines at car-rental windows. If possible, send one person to pick up the car while the others wait for the baggage.

Visitor Information

The Hawaii Visitors and Convention Bureau (HVCB) has general and vacation-planning information for Maui and all the Islands, and offers a free official vacation planner. The Maui Visitors & Convention Bureau website includes information on accommodations, sights, events, and itineraries.

Hawaii Visitors and Convention Bureau. ✉ *2270 Kalakaua Ave., Suite 801, Honolulu* ☎ *800/464–2924* ⊕ *www.gohawaii.com.*

Getting Here and Around

If you want to travel around on your own schedule, a rental car is a must on Maui. It's also one of your biggest trip expenses, especially given the price of gasoline—higher on Maui than on Oahu or the mainland. ⇨ *See Travel Smart for details of renting a car and driving.* If you need to ask for directions, try your best to pronounce the multivowel road names. Locals don't use (or know) highway route numbers and will respond with looks as blank as yours. Also, they will give you directions by the time it takes to get somewhere rather than by the mileage.

Island Driving Times

Driving from one point on Maui to another can take longer than the mileage indicates. It's 52 miles from Kahului

Airport to Hana, but the drive will take you about three hours if you stop to smell the flowers, which you certainly should do. As for driving to Haleakala, the 38-mile drive from sea level to the summit will take about two hours. The roads are narrow and winding; you must travel slowly. Kahului is the transportation hub—the main airport and largest harbor are here. Traffic on Maui's roads can be heavy, especially from 6 am–8:30 am and 3:30 pm–6:30 pm. Here are average driving times.

Kahului to Wailea	17 miles/30 mins
Kahului to Kaanapali	25 miles/45 mins
Kahului to Kapalua	36 miles/1 hr 15 mins
Kahului to Makawao	13 miles/25 mins
Kapalua to Haleakala	73 miles/3 hrs
Kaanapali to Haleakala	62 miles/2 hrs 30 mins
Wailea to Haleakala	54 miles/2 hrs 30 mins
Kapalua to Hana	88 miles/5 hrs
Kaanapali to Hana	77 miles/5 hrs
Wailea to Hana	69 miles/4 hrs 30 mins
Wailea to Lahaina	20 miles/45 mins
Kapalua to Lahaina	12 miles/20 mins

Island Hopping

If you have a week or more on Maui, you may want to set aside a day or two for a trip to Molokai or Lanai. Tour operators such as Trilogy offer day-trip packages to Lanai, which include snorkeling and a van tour of the island. Ferries are available to both islands and have room for your golf clubs and mountain bike. (The Molokai channel can be rough, so avoid ferry travel on a blustery day.)

If you prefer to travel to Molokai or Lanai by air, and you're not averse to flying on smaller prop planes, book with Mokulele Airlines for flights to Hana, Maui, and Molokai, or with Island Air for flights to Lanai (via Honolulu). (⇨ *See Air Travel under Getting Here and Around in Travel Smart.*)

Dining and Lodging on Maui

Hawaii is a melting pot of cultures, and nowhere is this more apparent than in its cuisines. From luau and plate lunches to sushi and teriyaki steak, there's no shortage of interesting flavors and presentations. Restaurant atmosphere varies, too, from casual local spots to elegantly decorated resort restaurants.

Whether you're looking for a quick snack or a multicourse meal, we can help you find the best eating experiences the island has to offer. Jump in and enjoy!

Choosing lodging is a tough decision, but fret not: our expert writers and editors have done most of the legwork.

To help narrow your choices, consider what type of property you'd like to stay at (big resort, quiet bed-and-breakfast, or condo rental) and what type of island climate you're looking for (beachfront strand or remote rain forest). We give you all the details you need to book a place that suits your style.

■ TIP➜ Reserve your room well in advance, and ask about discounts and packages. Hotel websites often have Internet-only deals.

Money Savers

There are ways to travel to paradise even on a budget.

Accommodations: No matter what the season, ask about deals—a free night after three or four or five paid nights, kids stay free, meal credits. Condos are less expensive and bigger than hotel rooms and are perfect for families or groups of friends. If you pass up the ocean view, you'll save money. In September, October, and May, many hotels offer reduced rates.

Food: Eat a big breakfast and skip lunch. You'll probably be sightseeing or at the beach anyway. It's easy to get by with a smoothie or fruit and yogurt. If you eat lunch out, go to that high-end restaurant. Lunch will be less expensive. Early evening "happy hour" deals are a great way to save money while sampling the chef's specialties. If you're staying in a condo, eat in or pack a picnic when you can.

Activities: Pick up free publications at the airport and at racks all over the island; many of them are filled with money-saving coupons. Activity desks—there are dozens around Kaanapali and Wailea as well as in Lahaina and Kihei—are good places to check on discounts if you're not booking in advance. However, advance booking will ensure you get the activity you want; sometimes you can save 10% or more if you book on outfitters' websites.

HAWAII TODAY

Hawaiian culture and tradition here have experienced a renaissance over the last few decades. There's a real effort to revive traditions and to respect history as the Islands go through major changes. New developments often have a Hawaiian cultural expert on staff to ensure cultural sensitivity and to educate newcomers.

Nonetheless, development remains a huge issue for all Islanders—land prices are still skyrocketing, putting many areas out of reach for locals. Traffic is becoming a problem on roads that were not designed to accommodate all the new drivers, and the Islands' limited natural resources are being seriously tapped. The government, although sluggish to respond at first, is trying to make development in Hawaii as sustainable as possible.

Sustainability

Although sustainability is an effective buzzword and authentic direction for the Islands' dining establishments, 90% of Hawaii's food and energy is imported. Most of the land was used for monocropping of pineapple or sugarcane, both of which have all but vanished. Sugarcane is now produced only on Maui, while pineapple production has dropped precipitously. Dole, once the largest pineapple company in Hawaii, closed its plants in 1991, and after 90 years, Del Monte stopped pineapple production in 2008. The next year, Maui Land and Pineapple Company also ceased its Maui Gold pineapple operation, although in early 2010 a group of executives took over one-third of the land and created a new company. The low costs of labor and transportation from Latin American and Southeast Asian pineapple producers are factors contributing to the industry's demise in Hawaii. But the Islands have perfected a sugar pineapple that is way less acidic than the usual ones. Although the imports have proved daunting, they have also set the stage for great agricultural change to be explored.

Back-to-Basics Agriculture

Emulating how the Hawaiian ancestors lived and returning to their simple ways of growing and sharing a variety of foods have become statewide initiatives. Hawaii has the natural conditions and talent to produce far more diversity in agriculture than it currently does.

The seed of this movement thrives through various farmers' markets and partnerships between restaurants and local farmers. Localized efforts such as the Hawaii Farm Bureau Federation are collectively aiding the organic and sustainable agricultural renaissance. From home-cooked meals to casual plate lunches to fine-dining cuisine, these sustainable trailblazers enrich the culinary tapestry of Hawaii and uplift the Islands' overall quality of life.

Tourism and the Economy

The $10 billion tourism industry represents a third of Hawaii's state income. Naturally, this dependency caused economic hardship when the financial meltdown of recent years affected tourists' ability to visit and spend. But the tourism industry has bounced back strong once again.

One way the industry has changed has been to adopt more eco-conscious practices, as many Hawaii residents feel that development shouldn't happen without regard for impact to local communities and their natural environment.

Belief that an industry based on the Hawaiians' *aloha* should protect, promote, and empower local culture and provide more entrepreneurial opportunities for local people has become more important to tourism businesses. More companies are incorporating authentic Hawaiiana in their programs and aim not only to provide a commercially viable tour but also to ensure that the visitor leaves feeling connected to his or her host. The concept of *kuleana*, a word for both privilege and responsibility, is upheld. Having the privilege to live in such a sublime place comes with the responsibility to protect it.

Sovereignty

Political issues of sovereignty continue to divide Native Hawaiians, who have formed myriad organizations, each operating with a separate agenda and lacking one collectively defined goal. Ranging from achieving complete independence to solidifying a nation within a nation, existing sovereignty models remain fractured and their future unresolved.

The introduction of the Native Hawaiian Government Reorganization Act of 2009 attempts to set up a legal framework in which Native Hawaiians can attain federal recognition and coexist as a self-governed entity. Also known as the Akaka Bill after former Senator Daniel Akaka of Hawaii, this bill has been presented before Congress and is still pending.

Rise of Hawaiian Pride

After the overthrow of the monarchy in 1893, a process of Americanization began. Traditions were duly silenced in the name of citizenship. Teaching the Hawaiian language was banned from schools, and children were distanced from their local customs.

But Hawaiians are resilient people, and with the rise of the civil rights movement they began to reflect on their own national identity, bringing an astonishing renaissance of the Hawaiian culture to fruition.

The people rediscovered language, hula, chanting, and even the traditional Polynesian arts of canoe building and wayfinding (navigation by the stars without use of instruments). This cultural resurrection is now firmly established in today's Hawaiian culture, with a palpable pride that exudes from Hawaiians young and old.

The election of President Barack Obama increased Hawaiian pride. The president's strong connection and commitment to Hawaiian values of diversity, spirituality, family, and conservation have restored confidence that Hawaii can inspire a more peaceful, tolerant, and environmentally conscious world.

The Arts

The Hawaiian Islands have inspired artistic expression from the time they were first inhabited. From ancient hula to digital filmmaking, the arts are alive and well. Honolulu is the artistic hub of the state. The Honolulu Museum of Art has an impressive permanent collection and hosts major exhibitions throughout the year. It comprises four locations including the spectacular Shangri La, the former home of heiress Doris Duke, filled with Islamic treasures. The Hawaii Theater in Honolulu—a restored art deco palace—stages theatrical productions, concerts, and films. The Maui Arts & Cultural Center (MACC) has a 1,200-seat theater for concerts, theatrical productions, and film, as well as an amphitheater and art gallery. Numerous art galleries thrive on the Islands.

MAUI
TOP ATTRACTIONS

Hike Haleakala

(A) Take time to trek down one of the trails into Haleakala National Park's massive bowl and see proof, at this dormant volcano, of how powerful the earth's exhalations can be. The cinder cones have beautiful swirls of subtle colors that can sparkle in the sunlight. You won't see a landscape like this anywhere, outside of visiting the moon. The barren terrain is deceptive, however—many of the world's rarest plants, birds, and insects live here.

Take the Road to Hana

(B) Spectacular views of waterfalls, sheer cliffs, lush forests, and the sparkling ocean are part of the pleasure of the twisting drive along the North Shore to tiny, timeless Hana in East Maui. The journey is the destination, but once you arrive, kick back and enjoy. Wave to pedestrians, "talk story" with locals in line at the Hasegawa store, and explore the multicolor beaches. An overnight stay here allows for the most

relaxed experience, though; a day trip is a big push. You may decide to drive just part of the way as an alternative.

Discover the Joy of Snorkeling

(C) Snorkeling is a must, either on your own with a buddy or on a snorkel cruise. Maui has snorkel boats of all sizes to take you to spots such as the Molokini Crater. Wherever you duck under, you'll be inducted into a mesmerizing world underwater. Slow down and keep your eyes open; even fish dressed in camouflage can be spotted when they snatch at food passing by. Some great spots to try right near the shore are Honolua Bay and Kekaa (known as Black Rock, it's in front of the Sheraton Maui) in West Maui; there are also good spots on the rocky fringes of Wailea's beaches on the South Shore.

Stretch Out on Makena

(D) This South Shore beauty is the sand dreams are made of: deep, golden, and pillowy. Don't be discouraged by the

crammed parking lots; there's more than enough room. Makena (Oneloa in Hawaiian) is still relatively wild. There are no hotels, minimarts, or public restrooms nearby—instead there's crystal-clear water, the occasional pod of dolphins, and drop-dead-gorgeous scenery (including the sunbathers). You can grab a fish taco and a drink at a nearby truck for a tasty lunch.

Buy Tropical Fruit at a Roadside Stand
(**E**) Your first taste of ripe guava or mango is something to remember. Delicious lychee, mangoes, star fruit, bananas, passion fruit, pineapple, and papaya can be bought on the side of the road with the change in your pocket. Go on, let the juice run down your chin. Farmers' markets are another place to seek out taste treats— just be sure to ask if what you crave is indeed local.

Try the Resorts and Spas
(**F**) Indulge your inner rock star at the posh, pampering resorts and spas around the island. Even if you don't stay the night, you can enjoy the opulent gardens, restaurants, art collections, and perfectly cordial staff. For pure relaxation, book a spa treatment from the extensive menus.

Escape to a Bed-and-Breakfast
(**G**) Being a shut-in isn't so bad at a secluded B&B. It's a sure way to get a taste of what it's like to live in paradise: trees hanging with ripe fruit outside your door, late-night tropical rainstorms, a wild chicken or two. Rather than blasting the air-conditioning in a hotel room, relax with the windows open in a plantation house designed to capture sea breezes.

Whale-Watch
(**H**) Maui is the cradle for hundreds of humpback whales that return every year from late November through April to frolic in the warm waters and give birth.

Watch a mama whale teach her 1-ton calf how to tail-wave. You can eavesdrop on them, too: book a tour boat with a hydrophone or just plunk your head underwater to hear the strange squeaks, groans, and chortles of the cetaceans. Tours are good, but you can also easily watch whales from the beach.

Listen to Hawaiian Music

(I) Before his untimely death in 1997, Israel Kamakawiwoole, or "IZ," woke the world to the sound of modern Hawaiian music. Don't leave without hearing it live. The Maui Arts & Cultural Center in Kahului has top Hawaiian entertainers regularly, and so do many island bars and restaurants. George Kahumoku Jr.'s Slack Key Show: Masters of Hawaiian Music concert series on Wednesday and Thursday night at the Napili Kai Beach Resort in West Maui is excellent. The Hawaiian Slack Key Guitar Festival (⊕ *www.slackkeyfestival.com*) features guest performers who play Hawaii's signature style.

Go Surfing on West Maui

(J) Feel the thrill of a wave rushing beneath your feet at any one of the beginner's breaks along Honoapiilani Highway. Ask local surf schools about the best locations for beginners and consider taking a lesson or two. You can bring surf wax home as a souvenir. Stand-up paddle surfing is popular now, too.

Attend the Old Lahaina Luau

(K) The Old Lahaina Luau has a warm heart—and seriously good *poke* (cubed raw tuna tossed with herbs and other seasonings). Tuck a flower behind your ear, mix a dab of *poi* (taro-root paste) with your *lomilomi* salmon (rubbed with onions and herbs), and you'll be living like a local. Different styles of hula are part of the performance; the fire dancers are not traditional, but they are thrilling. Reserve well in advance.

1

Tee Off in Paradise

(L) Spectacular views, great weather year-round, and challenging courses created by the game's top designers make Maui an inspiring place to play golf. The Kapalua Resort on West Maui and the Wailea resort courses on the South Shore offer memorable rounds. Ask about twilight fees to save some money.

Tour Upcountry

(M) Beach lovers might need some arm-twisting to head up the mountain for a day, but the views and the fresh-smelling countryside are ample reward. On the roads winding through ranchlands, crisp, high-altitude air is scented with eucalyptus and the fragrances of the forest. Stop for an agricultural tour and learn about where the island's bounty comes from; you can sample it, too.

Dig into Ono Kine Grinds

(N) "Ono kine grinds" is local slang for the delicious food you'll find at dozens of restaurants islandwide. Maui chefs take their work seriously, and they have good material to start with: sun-ripened produce and seafood caught the very same morning. Try a plate lunch—that reminder of the state's cultural mix—at a casual spot. Sample as many types of fish as you can and don't be shy: try it raw. And cool off with shave ice flavored with tropical fruit syrups.

Windsurf at Kanaha

(O) You might not be a water-sports legend, but that doesn't mean you can't give it a try. In the early morning, this renowned windsurfing spot by Kahului Airport is safe for beginners. Don't settle for the pond in front of your hotel—book a lesson at Kanaha and impress yourself by hanging tough where the action is.

MAUI'S TOP BEACHES

Ah, Maui's beaches: it's hard to single out just a few, because the island's strands are so varied. The leeward shores of West and South Maui have calm beaches and some great snorkeling, but experienced surfers and windsurfers gravitate to the windward (North Shore and East Maui) beaches that face the open ocean. Here are some favorites for different interests from around the island.

Best for Families

Baldwin Beach, the North Shore. The long, shallow, calm end closest to Kahului is safe even for toddlers—with adult supervision, of course.

Kamaole III, the South Shore. Sand, gentle surf, a playground, a volleyball net, and barbecues all add up to great family fun.

Napili Beach, West Maui. Kids will love the turtles that snack on the *limu* (seaweed) growing on the lava rocks. This sometimes crowded crescent-shape beach offers sunbathing, snorkeling, swimming, bodysurfing, and startling sunsets.

Best Offshore Snorkeling

Olowalu, West Maui. The water remains shallow far offshore, and there's plenty to see.

Ulua, the South Shore. It's beautiful and the kids can enjoy the tide pools while the adults experience the excellent snorkeling.

Best Surfing

Honolua Bay, West Maui. One bay over from Slaughterhouse (Mokuleia) Beach north of Kapalua you can find one of the best surf breaks in Hawaii.

Hookipa, the North Shore. This is the place to see great surfers and windsurfers: it's not for beginners or for swimmers, but Hookipa is great for experienced wave riders and also for anyone who wants to take in the North Shore scene.

Best Sunsets

Kapalua Bay, West Maui. The ambience here is as stunning as the sunset.

Keawakapu, the South Shore. Most active beachgoers enjoy this gorgeous spot before midafternoon, when the wind picks up, so it's never crowded at sunset.

Best for Seeing and Being Seen

Kaanapali Beach, West Maui. Backed by resorts, condos, and restaurants, this is not the beach for solitude. But the sand is soft, the waters are gentle, and the action varies from good snorkeling at Black Rock (Kekaa) to people-watching in front of Whalers Village—not for nothing is this section called "Dig Me Beach."

Wailea Beach, the South Shore. At this beach fronting the ultraluxurious Four Seasons and Grand Wailea resorts, you never know who might be hiding in that private cabana.

Best Setting

Makena (Oneloa), the South Shore. Don't forget the camera for this beauty, a state park away from the Wailea resort area. Finding this long, wide stretch of golden sand and translucent offshore water is worth the effort. The icing on the cake is that this long beach is never crowded. Use caution for swimming, because the steep onshore break can get big.

Waianapanapa State Park, East Maui. This rustic black-sand beach will capture your heart—it's framed by lava cliffs and backed by bright-green beach *naupaka* bushes. Ocean currents can be strong, so enjoy the views and cool off in one of two freshwater pools. Get an early start, because your day's destination is just shy of Hana.

WHEN TO GO

Long days of sunshine and fairly mild year-round temperatures make Hawaii, including Maui, an all-season destination. Most resort areas are at sea level, with average afternoon temperatures of 75°F–80°F during the coldest months of December and January; during the hottest months of August and September the temperature often reaches 90°F. Higher Upcountry elevations have cooler and often misty conditions. Only at mountain summits does it reach freezing.

Typically the weather on Maui is drier in summer (more guaranteed beach days) and rainier in winter (greener foliage, better waterfalls). Throughout the year, West Maui and the South Shore (the leeward areas) are the driest, sunniest areas on the island—that's why the resorts are there. The North Shore and East Maui and Hana (the windward areas) get the most rain, are densely forested, and abound with waterfalls and rainbows.

Many travelers head to the Islands in winter, especially during Christmas and spring break; room rates average 10%–15% higher during these times than the rest of the year. The best months for bargains are May, September, and October.

Seasonal Specialties

In winter Maui is *the* spot for whale-watching. Humpback whales start arriving in November, are in full force by February, and are gone by early May. The biggest North Shore waves show up in winter: kiteboarders and windsurfers get their thrills in the windy, late summer months.

Only-in-Hawaii Holidays

Hawaiians appreciate any occasion to celebrate; not only are Hawaiian holidays honored, so are those of the state's immigrant cultures. If you happen to be in the Islands on March 26 or June 11, you'll notice light traffic and busy beaches—these are state holidays. March 26 recognizes the birthday of Prince Jonah Kuhio Kalanianaole, a member of the royal line who spearheaded the effort to set aside homelands for Hawaiian people. June 11 honors the first islandwide monarch, Kamehameha the Great; locals drape his statues with lei and stage elaborate parades. May 1 isn't an official holiday, but it's Lei Day in Hawaii, when schools and civic groups celebrate the flower lei with lei-making contests and pageants. Statehood Day is celebrated on the third Friday in August (Admission Day was August 21, 1959). Most Japanese and Chinese holidays are widely observed. On Chinese New Year, in winter, homes and businesses sprout red good-luck mottoes and everybody eats *gau* (steamed pudding) and *jai* (vegetarian stew). Good Friday is a state holiday in spring, a favorite for picnics. Summertime is for Obon festivals at Buddhist temples and the July 4 Rodeo; the Maui County Fair and Aloha Festivals are in fall.

MAUI FOR KIDS AND FAMILIES

With dozens of adventures to take, discoveries to make, and loads of kid-friendly beaches, Maui is a blast for families with children. The entire family, parents included, will enjoy surfing, discovering a waterfall in the rain forest, and snorkeling with sea turtles. And there are organized activities for kids that will free parents' time for a few romantic beach strolls.

Choosing a Place to Stay

Resorts. All the big resorts make kids' programs a priority. When booking your room, ask about "kids eat free" deals and the number of kids' pools at the resort. Also check out the ages and sizes of groups in the children's programs and find out whether the cost of the programs includes lunch, equipment, and activities.

On the South Shore, the best bet for families is the Fairmont Kea Lani Maui, where the accommodations are spacious suites. Kids will love the beach right in front of the Mana Kai Maui on the island's south side. The Westin Maui Resort & Spa, with its long list of activity programs for kids and adults, is a good choice in the Kaanapali Resort. Also in West Maui, Napili Kai Beach Resort sits on a protected crescent of white-sand beach that is perfect for body boarding, playing in the water, and sunbathing.

Condos. Condo and vacation rentals are a fantastic value for families vacationing in Hawaii. You can cook your own food, which is much less expensive than eating out, and often easier, and you'll get twice the space of a hotel room for about a quarter of the price.

If you decide to go the condo route, be sure to ask about the size of the complex's pool (some try to pawn off a tiny soaking tub as a pool) and whether barbecues are available. One of the best parts of staying in your own place is having a sunset family barbecue by the pool or overlooking the ocean.

In West Maui all the Aston Hotels & Resorts properties, like Papakea Resort, offer children's packages, such as "Kids Stay, Play and Eat Free," and have a *keiki* (child) activity program that ranges from sand-castle building to sightseeing excursions.

On the South Shore, Kamaole Sands is a family favorite, with an excellent location right across from three beach parks that are good for swimming and have grassy fields for games and picnics.

Ocean Activities

Hawaii is all about getting your kids outside—away from video games. And who could resist the turquoise water, the promise of spotting dolphins or whales, and the fun of body boarding or surfing?

On the Beach. Most people like being in the water, but toddlers and school-age kids are often completely captivated. The swimming pool at your condo or hotel is always an option, but don't be afraid to hit the beach with a little one in tow. Certain beaches in Hawaii are nearly as safe as a pool—completely protected bays with pleasant white-sand beaches. As always, use your judgment, and heed all posted signs and lifeguard warnings.

The leeward side of Maui has many calm beaches to try. Good ones include Wailea Beach in front of the Grand Wailea and Four Seasons resorts and Kamaole beach parks on the South Shore. Napili Bay in West Maui is great for kids and also for body boarding. On the North Shore, at the Kahului end of Baldwin Beach Park, check out the shallow pool known as Baby Beach.

On the Waves. Surf lessons are a great idea for older kids, especially if Mom and Dad want a little quiet time. Beginner lessons are always on safe and easy waves and last anywhere from two to four hours.

The world-class waves of Maui's North Shore are best left to the pros. The gentle swells off West and South Maui are where several respected operators provides lessons designed for beginners. Big Kahuna Adventures will show you how to ride the waves in Kihei on the South Shore.

The Underwater World. If your kids are ready to try snorkeling, Hawaii is a great place to introduce them to the underwater world. Even without a mask and snorkel, they'll be able to see colorful fish, and they may also spot turtles and dolphins at many of the island's beaches.

It's easy (and inexpensive) to learn the basics and see amazing underwater life immediately at Kaanapali Beach in front of the Sheraton Maui on the island's west side. For guided snorkel tours that offer beginner instruction, try Trilogy Excursions' family-oriented day trip from Lahaina to Lanai, or Maui Classic Charters' half-day Molokini visits out of Maalaea Harbor.

Land Activities

In addition to beach experiences, Hawaii has rain forests, botanical gardens, an aquarium, and even petting zoos and even farms with hands-on activities that will keep your kids entertained and out of the sun for a day. Older kids (over 10) may be interested in a zipline adventure.

Central Maui abounds with activities for children, including the Alexander & Baldwin Sugar Museum with its interactive displays and the Maui Tropical Plantation's farm tram, historic locomotive engine, and introductory zipline course.

If the weather's not great for seeing marine life in the ocean, see it at the excellent Maui Ocean Center in Maalaea on the South Shore, where all manner of live marine creatures—including reef fish, sea turtles, manta rays, and sharks—swim behind glass. It's expensive, but kids (and adults) can learn a lot from the displays.

To discover all there is to know about Maui's biggest annual visitor, the humpback whale, children will enjoy the Hawaiian Islands Humpback Whale National Marine Sanctuary on the South Shore and the worthwhile free museum at Whalers Village shopping center in Kaanapali in West Maui.

After Dark

At nighttime, younger kids get a kick out of luau, and many of the shows incorporate young audience members, adding to the fun. Older kids might find it all a bit lame, but there are a handful of new shows in the Islands that are more modern, incorporating acrobatics and lively music.

We think the best luau is the Old Lahaina Luau, which takes place nightly on the oceanfront at the north end of Lahaina. The show is traditional, lively, and colorful; it will keep the whole family entertained. Book in advance to avoid disappointment; this is extremely popular.

THE HAWAIIAN ISLANDS

Oahu. The state's capital, Honolulu, is on Oahu; this is the center of Hawaii's economy and by far the most populated island in the chain—its roughly 1 million residents add up to more than 70% of the state's population. At 597 square miles, Oahu is the third largest island in the chain; the majority of residents live in or around Honolulu, so the rest of the island still fits neatly into the tropical, untouched vision of Hawaii. Situated southeast of Kauai and northwest of Maui, Oahu is a central location for island-hopping. Pearl Harbor, iconic Waikiki Beach, and surfing contests on the legendary North Shore are all here.

Maui. The second largest island in the chain, Maui is northwest of the Big Island and close enough to be visible from its beaches on a clear day. The island's 729 square miles are home to about 150,000 people but host more than 2 million tourists every year. With its restaurants and lively nightlife, Maui is the only island that competes with Oahu in terms of entertainment; its charm lies in the fact that although entertainment is available, Maui's towns still feel like island villages compared to the heaving modern city of Honolulu.

The Big Island. The Big Island has the second-largest population of the Islands (almost 190,000) but feels sparsely settled due to its size. It's 4,038 square miles and growing—all the other Islands could fit onto the Big Island and there would still be room left over. The southernmost island in the chain (slightly southeast of Maui), the Big Island is home to Kilauea, the most active volcano on the planet; it percolates within Volcanoes National Park, which draws nearly 3 million visitors every year.

Kauai. The northernmost island in the chain (northwest of Oahu), Kauai is, at approximately 622 square miles, the fourth-largest of all the Islands and the least populated of the larger Islands, with about 70,000 residents. Known as the Garden Isle, this island is home to lush botanical gardens as well as the stunning Napali Coast and Waimea Canyon. The island is a favorite with honeymooners and others wanting to get away from it all—lush and peaceful, it's the perfect escape from the modern world.

Molokai. North of Lanai and Maui, and east of Oahu, Molokai is Hawaii's fifth-largest island, encompassing 260 square miles. On a clear night, the lights of Honolulu are visible from Molokai's western shore. Molokai is sparsely populated, with about 7,300 residents, the majority of whom are Native Hawaiians. Most of the island's 79,000 annual visitors travel from Maui or Oahu to spend the day exploring its beaches, cliffs, and former leper colony on Kalaupapa Peninsula.

Lanai. Lying just off Maui's western coast, Lanai looks nothing like its sister Islands, with pine trees and deserts in place of palm trees and beaches. Still, the tiny 140-square-mile island is home to about 3,200 residents and draws an average of 75,000 visitors each year to two resorts (one in the mountains and one at the shore), both operated by Four Seasons, and the small, 11-room Hotel Lanai.

Hawaii's Geology

The Hawaiian Islands comprise more than just the islands inhabited and visited by humans. A total of 19 islands and atolls constitute the State of Hawaii, with a total landmass of 6,423.4 square miles.

The Islands are actually exposed peaks of a submersed mountain range called the

Hawaiian Ridge–Emperor Seamounts chain. The range was formed as the Pacific plate moves very slowly (around 32 miles every million years, or about as fast as your fingernails grow) over a hot spot in the Earth's mantle. Because the plate moves northwestwardly, the Islands in the northwest portion of the archipelago are older, which is also why they're smaller— they have been eroding longer and have actually sunk back into the sea floor.

The Big Island is the youngest, and thus the largest, island in the chain. It is built from five different volcanoes, including Mauna Loa, which is the largest mountain on the planet (when measured from the bottom of the sea floor). Mauna Loa and Kilauea are the only Hawaiian volcanoes still erupting with any sort of frequency. Mauna Loa last erupted in 1984; Kilauea has been continuously erupting since 1983.

Mauna Kea (Big Island), Hualalai (Big Island), and Haleakala (Maui) are all in what's called the post-shield-building stage of volcanic development—eruptions decrease steadily for up to a million years before ceasing entirely. Kohala (Big Island), Lanai (Lanai), and Waianae (Oahu) are considered extinct volcanoes, in the erosional stage of development; Koolau (Oahu) and West Maui (Maui) volcanoes are extinct volcanoes in the rejuvenation stage—after lying dormant for hundreds of thousands of years, they began erupting again, but only once every several thousand years.

There is currently an active undersea volcano to the south and east of the Big Island called Kamaehu that has been erupting regularly. If it continues its current pattern, it should breach the ocean's surface in tens of thousands of years.

Hawaii's Flora and Fauna

More than 90% of native Hawaiian flora and fauna are endemic (they evolved into unique species here), like the koa tree and the yellow hibiscus. Long-dormant volcanic craters are perfect hiding places for rare native plants. The silversword, a rare cousin of the sunflower, grows on Hawaii's three tallest peaks: Haleakala, Mauna Kea, and Mauna Loa, and nowhere else on Earth. Ohia trees— thought to be the favorite of Pele, the volcano goddess—bury their roots in fields of once-molten lava, and one variety sprouts ruby pom-pom-like lehua blossoms. The deep yellow petals of ilima (once reserved for royalty) are tiny discs, which make elegant lei.

But most of the plants you see while walking around aren't Hawaiian at all, and came from Tahitian, Samoan, or European visitors. Plumeria is ubiquitous; alien orchids run rampant on the Big Island; bright orange relatives of the ilima light up the mountains of Oahu. Although these flowers are not native, they give the Hawaiian lei their color and fragrance.

Hawaii's state bird, the nene goose, is making a comeback from its former endangered status. It roams freely in parts of Maui, Kauai, and the Big Island. Rare Hawaiian monk seals breed in the northwestern Islands. With only 1,500 left in the wild, you probably won't catch many lounging on the beaches, although they have been spotted on the shores of Kauai in recent years. Spinner dolphins and sea turtles can be found off the coast of all the Islands; and every year from November to April, the humpback whales migrate past Hawaii in droves.

HAWAIIAN PEOPLE AND THEIR CULTURE

By 2013, Hawaii's population was more than 1.3 million with the majority of residents living on Oahu. Ten percent are Hawaiian or other Pacific Islander, almost 40% are Asian American, 9% are Latino, and about 26% Caucasian. Nearly a fifth of the population lists two or more races, making Hawaii the most diverse state in the United States.

Among individuals 18 and older, about 89% finished high school, half attained some college, and 29% completed a bachelor's degree or higher.

The Role of Tradition

The kingdom of Hawaii was ruled by a spiritual class system. Although the *alii,* or chief, was believed to be the direct descendent of a deity or god, high priests (*kahuna*) presided over every aspect of life, including *kapu* (taboos), which strictly governed the commoners.

Each part of nature and ritual was connected to a deity: Kane was the highest of all deities, symbolizing sunlight and creation; Ku was the god of war; Lono represented fertility, rainfall, music, and peace; Kanaloa was the god of the underworld or darker spirits. Probably the most well known by outsiders is Pele, the goddess of fire.

The kapu not only provided social order, they also swayed the people to act with reverence for the environment. Any abuse was met with extreme punishment—often death—as it put the land and people's *mana,* or spiritual power, in peril.

Ancient deities play a huge role in Hawaiian life today—not just in daily rituals, but in the Hawaiians' reverence for their land. Gods and goddesses tend to be associated with particular parts of the land, and most of them are connected with many places, thanks to the body of stories built up around each.

One of the most important ways the ancient Hawaiians showed respect for their gods and goddesses was through the hula. Various forms of the hula were performed as prayers to the gods and as praise to the chiefs. Performances were taken very seriously, as a mistake was thought to invalidate the prayer, or even to offend the god or chief in question. Hula is still performed both as entertainment and as prayer; it is not uncommon for a hula performance to be included in an official government ceremony.

Who Are the Hawaiians Today?

To define the Hawaiians in a page, let alone a paragraph, is nearly impossible. Those considered to be indigenous Hawaiians are descendants of the ancient Polynesians who crossed the vast ocean and settled Hawaii. According to the government, there are Native Hawaiians or native Hawaiians (note the change in capitalization), depending on a person's background.

Federal and state agencies apply different methods to determine Hawaiian lineage, from measuring blood percentage to mapping genealogy. This has caused turmoil within the community, because it excludes many who claim Hawaiian heritage. It almost guarantees that, as races intermingle, even those considered Native Hawaiian now will eventually disappear on paper, displacing generations to come.

Modern Hawaiian Culture

Perfect weather aside, Hawaii might be the warmest place anyone can visit. The Hawaii experience begins and ends with *aloha,* a word that envelops love, affection, and mercy, and has become a salutation for hello and good-bye. Broken down, *alo* means "presence" and *ha* means "breath"—the presence of breath.

It's to live with love and respect for self and others with every breath. Past the manicured resorts and tour buses, aloha is a moral compass that binds all of Hawaii's people.

Hawaii is blessed with some of the most unspoiled natural wonders, and aloha extends to the land, or *aina*. Hawaiians are raised outdoors and have strong ties to nature. They realize as children that the ocean and land are the delicate sources of all life. Even ancient gods were embodied by nature, and this reverence has been passed down to present generations who believe in *kuleana,* their privilege and responsibility.

Hawaii's diverse cultures unfold in a beautiful montage of customs and arts—from music, to dance, to food. Musical genres range from slack key to *Jawaiian* (Hawaiian reggae) to *hapa-haole* (Hawaiian music with English words). From George Kahumoku's Grammy-worthy laid-back strumming to the late Iz Kamakawiwoole's "Somewhere over the Rainbow" to Jack Johnson's more mainstream tunes, contemporary Hawaiian music has definitely carved its ever-evolving niche.

The Merrie Monarch Festival celebrates more than 50 years of worldwide hula competition and education. The fine-dining culinary scene, especially in Honolulu, has a rich tapestry of ethnic influences and talent. But the real gems are the humble hole-in-the-wall eateries that serve authentic cuisines of many ethnic origins in one plate, a deliciously mixed plate indeed.

And perhaps the most striking quality in today's Hawaiian culture is the sense of family, or *ohana*. Sooner or later, almost everyone you meet becomes an uncle or auntie, and it is not uncommon for near-strangers to be welcomed into a home as a member of the family.

Until the last century, the practice of *hanai,* in which a family essentially adopts a child, usually a grandchild, without formalities, was still prevalent. While still practiced to a somewhat lesser degree, the *hanai,* which means to feed or nourish, still resonates within most families and communities.

How to Act Like a Local

Adopting local customs is a firsthand introduction to the Islands' unique culture. So live in T-shirts and shorts. Wear cheap rubber flip-flops, but call them slippers. Wave people into your lane on the highway, and, when someone lets you in, give them a wave of thanks in return. Never, ever blow your horn, even when the pickup truck in front of you is stopped for a long session of "talk story" right in the middle of the road.

Holoholo means to go out for the fun of it—an aimless stroll, ride, or drive. "Wheah you goin', braddah?" "Oh, *holoholo*." It's local speak for Sunday drive, no plan, it's not the destination but the journey. Try setting out without an itinerary. Learn to *shaka*: pinky and thumb extended, middle fingers curled in, waggle sideways. Eat white rice with everything. When someone says, "Aloha!" answer, "Aloha no!" ("And a real big aloha back to you"). And, as the locals say, "No make big body" ("Try not to act like you own the place").

TOP 10 HAWAIIAN FOODS TO TRY

Food in Hawaii is a reflection of the state's diverse cultural makeup and tropical location. Fresh seafood, organic fruits and vegetables, free-range beef, and locally grown products are the hallmarks of Hawaii regional cuisine. Its preparations are drawn from across the Pacific Rim, including Japan, the Philippines, Korea, and Thailand—and "local food" is a cuisine in its own right. Don't miss Hawaiian-grown coffee either, whether it's smooth Kona from the Big Island or coffee grown on other Islands.

Bento Box

The bento box gained popularity back in the plantation days, when workers toiled in the sugarcane fields. No one brought sandwiches to work then. Instead it was a lunch box with the ever-present steamed white rice, pickled *ume* (plum) to preserve the rice, and meats such as fried chicken or fish. Today, many stores sell prepackaged bentos or you may go to an *okazuya* (Japanese deli) with a hot buffet counter and create your own.

Crack Seed

There are dozens of varieties of crack seed in dwindling specialty shops and at the drugstores. Chinese call the preserved fruits and nuts *see mui,* but somehow the Pidgin English version is what Hawaiians prefer. Those who like hard candy and salty foods will love *li hing* mangoes and rock-salt plums, and those with an itchy throat will feel relief from the lemon strips. Peruse large glass jars of crack seed sold in bulk or smaller hanging bags—the latter make good gifts to give to friends back home.

Fresh Ahi or Tako Poke

There's nothing like fresh ahi or *tako* (octopus) *poke* to break the ice at a backyard party, except, of course, the cold beer handed to you from the cooler. The perfect *pupu, poke* (pronounced "poh-kay") is basically raw seafood cut into bite-sized chunks and mixed with everything from green onions to roasted and ground *kukui* nuts. Other variations include mixing the fish with chopped round onion, sesame oil, seaweed, and chili pepper water. *Shoyu* (the "local" name for soy sauce) is the constant. These days, grocery stores sell endless poke varieties such as kimchi crab; anything goes, from adding mayonnaise to *tobiko* (caviar). Fish lovers who want to take it to the next level order sashimi, the best cuts of ahi sliced and dipped in a mixture of shoyu and wasabi.

Manapua

Another savory snack is *manapua,* fist-size dough balls fashioned after Chinese *bao* (a traditional Chinese bun) and stuffed with fillings such as *char siu* (Chinese roast pork) and then steamed. Many mom-and-pop stores sell them in commercial steamer display cases along with pork hash and other dim sum. Modern-day fillings include curry chicken.

Malasadas

The Portuguese have contributed much to Hawaii cuisine in the form of sausage, soup, and sweetbread. But their most revered food is *malasadas,* hot, deep-fried doughnuts rolled in sugar. Malasadas are crowd-pleasers—buy them by the dozen, hot from the fryer, placed in brown paper bags to absorb the grease, or bite into gourmet malasadas at restaurants, filled with vanilla or chocolate cream.

Plate Lunch

It would be remiss not to mention the plate lunch as one of the most beloved dishes in Hawaii. It generally includes two scoops of sticky white rice, a scoop of macaroni or macaroni-potato salad, heavy on the mayo, and perhaps kimchi or *koko* (salted cabbage). There are countless choices of main protein such as chicken *katsu* (fried cutlet), fried mahimahi, and tomato. The king of all plate lunches is the Hawaiian plate. The main item is *laulau* (pork or fish wrapped in taro leaf) or *kalua* pig (cooked in an underground oven, or *imu*) and cabbage along with poi, *lomilomi* salmon (salmon-and-tomato salad), chicken long rice, and sticky white rice.

Saimin

The ultimate hangover cure and the perfect comfort food during Hawaii's mild winters, *saimin* ranks at the top of the list of local favorites. In fact, it's one of the few dishes deemed truly local, having been highlighted in cookbooks since the 1930s. Saimin is an Asian-style noodle soup so ubiquitous it's even on McDonald's menus statewide. In mom-and-pop shops, a large melamine bowl is filled with homemade *dashi,* or broth, and wheat-flour noodles and then topped off with strips of omelet, green onions, bright pink fish cake, and char siu or canned luncheon meat, such as SPAM. Add shoyu and chili pepper water, lift your chopsticks, and slurp away.

Shave Ice

Much more than just a snow cone, shave ice is what locals crave after a blazing day at the beach or a hot-as-Hades game of soccer. If you're lucky, you'll find a neighborhood store that hand-shaves the ice, but it's rare. Either way, the counter person will ask you first if you'd like ice cream and/or adzuki beans scooped into the bottom of the cone or cup. Then they shape the ice into a giant mound and add colorful fruit syrups. First-timers should order the rainbow, of course.

SPAM

Speaking of SPAM, Hawaii's most prevalent grab-and-go snack is SPAM *musubi.* Often displayed next to cash registers at groceries and convenience stores, the glorified rice ball is rectangular, topped with a slice of fried SPAM and wrapped in *nori* (seaweed). Musubi is a bite-size meal in itself. But just like sushi, the rice part hardens when refrigerated. So it's best to gobble it up right after purchase.

Hormel Company's SPAM actually deserves its own recognition—way beyond as a mere musubi topping. About 5 million cans are sold per year in Hawaii, and the Aloha State even hosts a festival in its honor. It's inexpensive protein and goes a long way when mixed with rice, scrambled eggs, noodles or, well, anything. The spiced luncheon meat gained popularity in World War II days, when fish was rationed. Gourmets and those with aversions to salt, high cholesterol, or high blood pressure may cringe at the thought of eating it, but SPAM in Hawaii is here to stay.

Tropical Fruits

Tropical fruits such as apple banana and strawberry papaya are plucked from trees in island neighborhoods and eaten for breakfast—plain or with a squeeze of fresh lime. Give them a try; the apple banana tastes somewhat like an apple, and the strawberry papaya's rosy flesh explains its name. Locals also love to add their own creative touches to exotic fruits. Green mangoes are pickled with Chinese five spice, and Maui Gold pineapples are topped with *li hing mui* (salty dried plum) powder (heck, even margarita glasses are rimmed with it). Green papaya is tossed in a Vietnamese salad with fish paste and fresh prawns.

ONLY IN HAWAII

Traveling to Hawaii is as close as an American can get to visiting another country while staying within the United States. There's much to learn and understand about the state's indigenous culture, the hundred years of immigration that resulted in today's blended society, and the tradition of aloha that has welcomed millions of visitors over the years.

Aloha Shirt

To go to Hawaii without taking an aloha shirt home is almost sacrilege. The first aloha shirts from the 1920s and 1930s—called "silkies"—were classic canvases of art and tailored for the tourists. Popular culture caught on in the 1950s, and they became a fashion craze. With the 1960s came more subdued designs, Aloha Friday was born, and the shirt became appropriate clothing for work, play, and formal occasions. Because of its soaring popularity, cheaper and mass-produced versions became available.

Hawaiian Quilt

Although ancient Hawaiians were already known to produce fine *kapa* (bark) cloth, the actual art of quilting originated from the missionaries. Hawaiians have created designs to reflect their own aesthetic, and bold patterns evolved over time. They can be pricey, because the quilts are intricately made by hand and can take years to finish. These masterpieces are considered precious heirlooms that reflect the history and beauty of Hawaii.

Hula

"Hula is the language of the heart, therefore the heartbeat of the Hawaiian people." —Kalakaua, the Merrie Monarch.

Thousands—from tots to seniors—devote hours each week to hula classes. All of these dancers need some place to show off their stuff, and the result is a network of hula competitions (generally free or very inexpensive) and free performances in malls and other public spaces. Many resorts offer hula instruction.

Luau

The luau's origin, which was a celebratory feast, can be traced back to the earliest Hawaiian civilizations. In the traditional luau, the taboo or *kapu* laws were very strict, requiring men and women to eat separately. Nevertheless, in 1819 King Kamehameha II broke the great taboo and shared a feast with women and commoners, ushering in the modern-era luau. Today, traditional luau usually commemorate a child's first birthday, graduation, wedding, or other family occasion. They also are a Hawaiian experience that most visitors enjoy, and resorts and other companies have incorporated the fire-knife dance and other Polynesian dances into their elaborate presentations.

Nose Flutes

The nose flute is an instrument used in ancient times to serenade a lover. For the Hawaiians, the nose is romantic, sacred, and pure. The Hawaiian word for kiss is *honi*. Similar to an Eskimo's kiss, the noses touch on each side sharing one's spiritual energy or breath. The Hawaiian term *ohe hano ihu* simply translates to "bamboo," from which the instrument is made; "breathe," because one has to gently breathe through it to make soothing music; and "nose," as it is made for the nose and not the mouth.

Popular Souvenirs

Souvenir shopping can be intimidating. There's a sea of island-inspired and often kitschy merchandise, so we'd like to give you a breakdown of popular and fun gifts that you might encounter and consider bringing home. If authenticity is important to you, be sure to check labels and ask shopkeepers. Museum shops are good places for authentic, Hawaiian-made souvenirs.

Fabrics. Purchased by the yard or already made into everything from napkins to bedspreads, modern Hawaiian fabrics make wonderful keepsakes.

Home accessories. Deck out your kitchen or dining room in festive luau style with bottle openers, pineapple mugs, tiki glasses, shot glasses, slipper and surfboard magnets, and salt-and-pepper shakers.

Lauhala products. *Lauhala* weaving is a traditional Hawaiian art. The leaves come from the *hala,* or *pandanus,* tree and are handwoven to create lovely gift boxes, baskets, bags, and picture frames.

Lei and shell necklaces. From silk or polyester flower lei to kukui or puka shell necklaces, lei have been traditionally used as a welcome offering to guests (although the artificial ones are more for fun, since real flowers are always preferable).

Spa products. Relive your spa treatment at home with Hawaiian bath and body products, many of them manufactured with ingredients found only on the Islands.

Vintage Hawaii. You can find vintage photos, reproductions of vintage postcards or paintings, heirloom jewelry, and vintage aloha wear in many specialty stores.

Slack-Key Guitar and the Paniolo

Kihoalu, or slack-key music, evolved in the early 1800s when King Kamehameha III brought in Mexican and Spanish vaqueros to manage the overpopulated cattle that had run wild on the Islands. The vaqueros brought their guitars and would play music around the campfire after work. When they left, supposedly leaving their guitars to their new friends, the Hawaiian *paniolo,* or cowboys, began to infuse what they learned from the vaqueros with their native music and chants, and so the art of slack-key music was born. Today, the paniolo culture thrives where ranchers have settled.

Traditional Canoe

Hawaii's ancestors voyaged across 2,500 miles from Polynesia on board a double-hulled canoe with the help of the stars, the ocean swells, and the flight pattern of birds. The creation of a canoe spanned months and involved many religious ceremonies by the *kahuna kalai waa,* or high priest canoe builder. In 1973, the Polynesian Voyaging Society was founded to rediscover and preserve this ancestral tradition. Since 1975, the group has built and launched the majestic *Hokulea* and *Hawaiiloa,* which regularly travel throughout the South Pacific. In 2014, *Hokulea* began a historic, three-year, around-the-world voyage.

Ukulele

The word *ukulele* literally translates to "the jumping flea" and came to Hawaii in the 1880s by way of the Portuguese and Spanish. Once a fading art form, today it brings international kudos as a solo instrument, thanks to tireless musicians and teachers who have worked hard to keep it by our fingertips.

One such teacher is Roy Sakuma. Founder of four ukulele schools and a legend in his own right, Sakuma and his wife, Kathy, produced Oahu's first Ukulele Festival in 1971. Since then, they've brought the tradition to the Big Island, Kauai, and Maui. The free event annually draws thousands of artists and fans from all over the globe.

THE HISTORY OF HAWAII

Hawaiian history is long and complex; a brief survey can put into context the ongoing renaissance of native arts and culture.

The Polynesians

Long before both Christopher Columbus and the Vikings, Polynesian seafarers set out to explore the vast stretches of the open ocean in double-hulled canoes. From western Polynesia, they traveled back and forth between Samoa, Fiji, Tahiti, the Marquesas, and the Society Isles, settling on the outer reaches of the Pacific, Hawaii, and Easter Island, as early as AD 300. The golden era of Polynesian voyaging peaked around AD 1200, after which the distant Hawaiian Islands were left to develop their own unique cultural practices and subsistence in relative isolation.

The Islands' symbiotic society was deeply intertwined with religion, mythology, science, and artistry. Ruled by an *alii*, or chief, each settlement was nestled in an *ahupuaa*, a pie-shaped land division from the uplands where the alii lived, through the valleys and down to the shores where the commoners resided. Everyone contributed, whether it was by building canoes, catching fish, making tools, or farming land.

A United Kingdom

When the British explorer Captain James Cook arrived in 1778, he was revered as a god. With guns and ammunition purchased from Cook, the Big Island chief, Kamehameha the Great, gained a significant advantage over the other alii. He united Hawaii into one kingdom in 1810, bringing an end to the frequent interisland battles that dominated Hawaiian life.

Tragically, the new kingdom was beset with troubles. Native religion was abandoned, and *kapu* (laws and regulations) were eventually abolished. The European explorers brought foreign diseases with them, and within a few short decades the Native Hawaiian population was decimated.

New laws regarding land ownership and religious practices eroded the underpinnings of precontact Hawaii. Each successor to the Hawaiian throne sacrificed more control over the island kingdom. As Westerners permeated Hawaiian culture, Hawaii became more riddled with layers of racial issues, injustice, and social unrest.

Modern Hawaii

In 1893, the last Hawaiian monarch, Queen Liliuokalani, was overthrown by a group of Americans and European businessmen and government officials, aided by an armed militia. This led to the creation of the Republic of Hawaii, and it became a U.S. territory for the next 60 years. The loss of Hawaiian sovereignty and the conditions of annexation have haunted the Hawaiian people since the monarchy was deposed.

Pearl Harbor was attacked in 1941, which pulled the United States immediately into World War II. Tourism, from its beginnings in the early 1900s, flourished after the war and naturally inspired rapid real estate development in Waikiki. In 1959, Hawaii officially became the 50th state. Statehood paved the way for Hawaiians to participate in the American democratic process, which was not universally embraced by all Hawaiians. With the rise of the civil rights movement in the 1960s, Hawaiians began to reclaim their own identity, from language to hula.

HAWAII AND THE ENVIRONMENT

Sustainability—it's a word rolling off everyone's tongues these days. In a place known as the most remote island chain in the world (check your globe), Hawaii relies heavily on the outside world for food and material goods—estimates put the percentage of food arriving on container ships as high as 90. Like many places, though, efforts are afoot to change that. And you can help.

Shop Local Farms and Markets

From Kauai to the Big Island, farmers' markets are cropping up, providing a place for growers to sell fresh fruits and vegetables. There is no reason to buy imported mangoes, papayas, avocadoes, and bananas at grocery stores, when the ones you'll find at farmers' markets are not only fresher but tastier, too. Some markets allow the sale of fresh-packaged foods—salsa, say, or smoothies—and the on-site preparation of food—like *laulau* (pork, beef, and fish or chicken with taro, or luau, leaves wrapped and steamed in *ti* leaves) or roasted corn on the cob—so you can make your run to the market a dining experience.

Not only is the locavore movement vibrantly alive at farmers' markets, but Hawaii's top chefs are sourcing more of their produce—and fish, beef, chicken, and cheese—from local providers as well. You'll notice this movement on restaurant menus featuring Kilauea greens or Hamakua tomatoes or locally caught mahimahi.

And although most people are familiar with Kona coffee farm tours on the Big Island, if you're interested in the growing Slow Food movement in Hawaii, you'll be heartened to know many farmers are opening up their operations for tours—as well as sumptuous meals.

Support Hawaii's Merchants

Food isn't the only sustainable effort in Hawaii. Buying local goods like art and jewelry, Hawaiian heritage products, crafts, music, and apparel is another way to "green up" the local economy. The County of Kauai helps make it easy with a program called **Kauai Made** (⊕ *www. kauaimade.net*), which showcases products made on Kauai, by Kauai people, using Kauai materials. Think of it as the Good Housekeeping Seal of Approval for locally made goods.

Then there are the crafty entrepreneurs who are diverting items from the trash heap by repurposing garbage. Take Oahu's **Muumuu Heaven** (⊕ *www.muumuuheaven. com*). They got their start by reincarnating vintage aloha apparel into hip new fashions.

Choose Green Tour Operators

Conscious decisions when it comes to island activities go a long way to protecting Hawaii's natural world. The **Hawaii Ecotourism Association** (⊕ *www.hawaiiecotourism. org*) recognizes tour operators for, among other things, their environmental stewardship. The **Hawaii Tourism Authority** (⊕ *www. hawaiitourismauthority.org*) recognizes outfitters for their cultural sensitivity. Winners of these awards are good choices when it comes to guided tours and activities.

WEDDINGS AND HONEYMOONS

There's no question that Hawaii is one of the country's foremost honeymoon destinations. Romance is in the air here, and the white, sandy beaches, turquoise water, swaying palm trees, balmy tropical breezes, and perpetual sunshine put people in the mood for love. It's easy to understand why Hawaii is fast becoming a popular wedding destination as well, especially as the cost of airfare is often discounted, new resorts and hotels entice visitors, and same-sex marriage is now legal in the state. A destination wedding is no longer exclusive to celebrities and the superrich. You can plan a traditional ceremony in a place of worship followed by a reception at an elegant resort, or you can go barefoot on the beach and celebrate at a luau. There are almost as many wedding planners in the Islands as real estate agents, which makes it oh-so-easy to wed in paradise, and then, once the knot is tied, stay and honeymoon as well.

The Big Day

Choosing the Perfect Place. When choosing a location, remember that you really have two choices to make: the ceremony location and where to have the reception, if you're having one. For the former, there are beaches, bluffs overlooking beaches, gardens, private residences, resort lawns, and, of course, places of worship. As for the reception, there are these same choices, as well as restaurants and even luau. If you decide to go outdoors, remember the seasons—yes, Hawaii has seasons. If you're planning a winter wedding outdoors, be sure you have a backup plan (such as a tent), in case it rains. Also, if you're planning an outdoor wedding at sunset—which is very popular—be sure you match the time of your ceremony to the time the sun sets at that time of year. If you choose an indoor spot, be sure to ask for pictures of the location when you're planning. You don't want to plan a pink wedding, say, and wind up in a room that's predominantly red. Or maybe you do. The point is, it should be your choice.

Finding a Wedding Planner. If you're planning to invite more than an officiant and your loved one to your wedding ceremony, seriously consider an on-island wedding planner who can help select a location, help design the floral scheme and recommend a florist as well as a photographer, help plan the menu and choose a restaurant, caterer, or resort, and suggest any Hawaiian traditions to incorporate into your ceremony. And more: Will you need tents, a cake, music? Maybe transportation and lodging? Many planners have relationships with vendors, providing packages—which mean savings.

If you're planning a resort wedding, most have on-site wedding coordinators; however, there are many independents around the Islands and even those who specialize in certain types of ceremonies—by locale, size, religious affiliation, and so on. A simple "Hawaii weddings" Google search will reveal dozens. What's important is that you feel comfortable with your coordinator. Ask for references and call them. Share your budget. Get a proposal—in writing. Ask how long they've been in business, how much they charge, how often you'll meet with them, and how they select vendors. Request a detailed list of the exact services they'll provide. If your idea of your wedding doesn't match their services, try someone else. If you can afford it, you might want to meet the planner in person.

Getting Your License. The good news about marrying in Hawaii is that there is no waiting period, no residency or citizenship requirement, and no blood test or shots are required. You can apply and pay the fee online; however, both the bride and groom must appear together in person before a marriage-license agent to receive the marriage license (the permit to get married). You'll need proof of age—the legal age to marry is 18. (If you're 19 or older, a valid driver's license will suffice; if you're 18, a certified birth certificate is required.) Upon approval, a marriage license is immediately issued and costs $60 (credit cards accepted online and in person; cash only accepted in person). After the ceremony, your officiant will mail the marriage certificate (proof of marriage) to the state. Approximately four months later, you will receive a copy in the mail. (For $10 extra, you can expedite this process; ask your marriage-license agent when you apply.) For more detailed information, visit ⊕ *marriage.ehawaii.gov.*

Also—this is important—the person performing your wedding must be licensed by the Hawaii Department of Health, even if he or she is a licensed officiant. Be sure to ask.

Wedding Attire. In Hawaii, basically anything goes, from long, formal dresses with trains to white bikinis. Floral sundresses are fine, too. For men, tuxedos are not the norm; a pair of solid-colored slacks with a nice aloha shirt is. In fact, tradition in Hawaii for the groom is a beautiful white aloha shirt (they do exist) with slacks or long shorts and a colored sash around the waist. If you're planning a wedding on the beach, barefoot is the way to go.

If you decide to marry in a formal dress and tuxedo, you're better off making your selections on the mainland and hand-carrying them aboard the plane. Yes, it can

be a pain, but ask your wedding-gown retailer to provide a special carrying bag. After all, you don't want to chance losing your wedding dress in a wayward piece of luggage.

Local Customs. The most obvious traditional Hawaiian wedding custom is the lei exchange in which the bride and groom take turns placing a lei around the neck of the other—with a kiss. Bridal lei are usually floral, whereas the groom's is typically made of *maile*, a green leafy garland that drapes around the neck and is open at the ends. Brides often also wear a *lei poo*—a circular floral headpiece. Other Hawaiian customs include the blowing of the conch shell, hula, chanting, and Hawaiian music.

The Honeymoon

Do you want champagne and strawberries delivered to your room each morning? A breathtaking swimming pool in which to float? A five-star restaurant in which to dine? Then a resort is the way to go. If, however, you prefer the comforts of a home, try a bed-and-breakfast. A small inn is also good if you're on a tight budget or don't plan to spend much time in your room. On the other hand, maybe you want your own private home in which to romp naked—or just laze around recovering from the wedding planning. Maybe you want your own kitchen so you can whip up a gourmet meal for your loved one. In that case, a private vacation-rental home is the answer. Or maybe a condominium resort. That's another beautiful thing about Hawaii: the lodging accommodations are almost as plentiful as the beaches, and there's one that will perfectly match your tastes and your budget.

LUAU: A TASTE OF HAWAII

The best place to sample Hawaiian food is at a backyard luau. Aunts and uncles are cooking, the pig is from a cousin's farm, the fish is from a brother's boat, and someone plinks a wistful tune on a ukulele.

The luau is such a special event that even locals have to angle for invitations. So unless you're tight with a local family, your choice is most likely between a commercial luau and a Hawaiian restaurant.

Some commercial luau are not particularly authentic; they offer little of the traditional diet and are more about umbrella drinks, spectacle, and fun.

For greater culinary authenticity, folksy experiences, and rock-bottom prices, try a Hawaiian restaurant. Most are located in anonymous storefronts in residential neighborhoods.

Much of what is known today as Hawaiian food would be foreign to a 16th-century Hawaiian. The precontact diet was simple and healthy—mainly raw and steamed seafood and

vegetables. Early Hawaiians used earth ovens and heated stones to cook seafood, taro, sweet potatoes, and breadfruit. They seasoned their food with sea salt and ground kukui nuts. Seaweed, fern shoots, sweet potato vines, coconut, banana, sugarcane, and select greens and roots rounded out the diet.

Immigrants added their favorites to the ti leaf–lined table, so now foods as disparate as salt salmon and chicken long rice have become Hawaiian—even though there is no salmon in Hawaii and long rice (cellophane noodles) is Chinese.

AT THE LUAU: KALUA PORK
The heart of any luau is the *imu*, the earth oven in which a whole pig is roasted. The preparation of an imu is an arduous affair for most families, who

tackle it only once a year or so for a baby's first birthday or at Thanksgiving, when many Islanders prefer to imu their turkeys. Commercial luau operations have it down to a science, however.

The Art of the Stone. The key to a proper imu is the *pohaku*, the stones. Imu cook by means of long, slow, moist heat released by special stones that can withstand a hot fire without exploding. Many Hawaiian families keep their imu stones in a pile in the backyard and pass them on through generations.

Pit Cooking. The imu makers first dig a pit about the size of a refrigerator, then lay down *kiawe* (mesquite) wood and stones, and build a white-hot fire that is allowed to burn itself out. The ashes are raked away, and the hot stones covered with banana and ti leaves. Well-wrapped in ti or banana leaves and a net of chicken wire, the pig is lowered onto the leaf-covered stones. *Laulau* (leaf-wrapped bundles of meats, fish, and taro leaves) may also be placed inside. Leaves—ti, banana, even ginger—cover the pig followed by wet burlap sacks (to create steam). The whole is topped with a canvas tarp and left to steam for the better part of a day.

Opening the Imu. This is the moment everyone waits for: The imu is unwrapped like a giant present and the imu keepers gingerly wrestle out the steaming pig. When it's unwrapped, the

meat falls moist and smoky-flavored from the bone.

Which Luau? Most resort hotels have luau on their grounds that include hula, music, and, of course, lots of food and drink. Each island also has at least one "authentic" luau.

MEA AI ONO: GOOD THINGS TO EAT

Laulau. Steamed meats, fish, and taro leaf in ti-leaf bundles: fork-tender, a medley of flavors; the taro resembles spinach.

Lomi Lomi Salmon. Salt salmon in a piquant salad or relish with onions and tomatoes.

Poi. A paste made of pounded taro root, poi may be an acquired taste, but it's a must-try during your visit.

Consider: The Hawaiian Adam is descended from *kalo* (taro). Young taro plants are called *keiki*, or children. Poi is the first food after mother's milk for many Islanders. *Ai*, the word for food, is synonymous with poi in many contexts.

Not only that, we love it. "There is no meat that doesn't taste good with poi," the old Hawaiians said. But you have to know how to eat it: with something rich or powerfully flavored.

ALL ABOUT LEI

Lei brighten every occasion in Hawaii, from birthdays to weddings to baptisms. Artisans weave flowers, ferns, and vines into gorgeous creations that convey an array of heartfelt messages.

"Welcome," "Congratulations," "Good luck," "Farewell," "Thank you," "I love you." When it's difficult to find the right words, a lei can express exactly the right sentiment.

Though lei are usually created from native flora, Niihau, the Forbidden Island, is famous for its exquisite tiny shells made into lei. Some of these shell lei can cost thousands of dollars and are often an exotic jewelry item. Lei are also sometimes constructed of paper, fish teeth, and even candy.

If you happen to be in the Islands around May 1, be sure to seek out the annual May Day celebrations at local schools and parks, because "May Day is Lei Day" in Hawaii. Not a Hawaiian tradition, Lei Day was the brainchild of poet Don Blanding in 1928. Happening during the full blossoming of spring flowers, May Day creations are a feast for the eyes.

WHERE TO BUY LEI

Most airports, supermarkets, and every florist shop in Hawaii sell lei. And you'll always find lei sellers at crafts fairs and outdoor festivals.

LEI ETIQUETTE

Lei are usually presented with a kiss on the cheek. To wear a closed lei, drape it over your shoulders, half in front and half in back. Open lei are worn around the neck, with the ends draped over the front in equal lengths.

Pikake, ginger, and other sweet, delicate blossoms are "feminine" lei. Men opt for cigar, crown flower, and ti leaf lei, which are sturdier and don't emit as much fragrance.

You shouldn't wear a lei before you give it to someone else. Hawaiians believe the lei absorbs your *mana* (spirit); if you give your lei away, you'll be giving away part of your essence.

TYPES OF LEI

Orchid. Growing wild on every continent except Antarctica, orchids comprise the largest family of plants in the world. Of the more than 20,000 species of orchids, only three are native to Hawaii—and they are very rare. The pretty lavender vanda you see hanging by the dozens at local lei stands has probably been imported from Thailand.

Maile. An endemic twining vine with a heady aroma, maile is sacred to Laka, goddess of the hula. In ancient times, dancers wore maile and decorated hula altars with it to honor Laka. Today, "open" maile lei usually are given to men. Instead of ribbon, interwoven lengths of maile are used at dedications of new businesses.

Ilima. Designated by Hawaii's Territorial Legislature in 1923 as the official flower of the island of Oahu, the golden ilima is so delicate it lasts for just a day. Five to seven hundred blossoms are needed to make one garland. Queen Emma, wife of King Kamehameha IV, preferred ilima over all other lei, which may have led

to the incorrect belief that they were reserved only for royalty.

Plumeria. Plumeria ranks among the most popular lei in Hawaii because it's fragrant, hardy, plentiful, inexpensive, and requires very little care. Although yellow is the most common color, you'll also find plumeria lei in shades of pink, red, orange, and "rainbow" blends.

Pikake. Favored for its fragile beauty and sweet scent, pikake was introduced from India. In lieu of pearls, many brides in Hawaii adorn themselves with long, multiple strands of white pikake. Princess Kaiulani enjoyed showing guests her beloved pikake and peacocks at Ainahau, her Waikiki home. Interestingly, *pikake* is the Hawaiian word for both the bird and the blossom.

Kukui. The *kukui* (candlenut) is Hawaii's state tree. Early Hawaiians strung the oily kukui nuts together and burned them for light. They also burned the nuts with oil to make an indelible dye and mashed roasted nuts to consume as a laxative. Kukui nut lei may not have been made until after Western contact, when the Hawaiians saw black beads from Europe and wanted to imitate them.

HULA: MORE THAN A FOLK DANCE

Hula has been called "the heartbeat of the Hawaiian people" and "the world's best known, most misunderstood dance." Both are true. Hula isn't just dance. It is storytelling. Today's Hawaii distinguishes between the traditional hula (*kahiko*) and modern hula (*auana*).

Called "an extension of a piece of poetry," hula integrates every important Hawaiian cultural practice: poetry, history, genealogy, craft, plant cultivation, martial arts, religion, and protocol. So when 19th-century Christian missionaries sought to eradicate a practice they considered depraved, they threatened more than just a folk dance.

With public performance outlawed and private hula practice discouraged, hula went underground for decades. The fragile verbal link by which culture was transmitted from teacher to student hung by a thread, as hula's practitioners were a secretive and protected circle.

As if that weren't bad enough, vaudeville, Broadway, and Hollywood got hold of the hula, giving it the glitz treatment in an unbroken line from "Oh, How She Could Wicky Wacky Woo" to "Rock-A-Hula Baby." Hula became shorthand for paradise: fragrant flowers, lazy hours, gorgeous beaches. Ironically, this development assured that hundreds of Hawaiians could make a living performing and teaching hula. Many danced *auana* (modern form) in performance, but taught *kahiko* (traditional), quietly, at home or in hula schools.

Today, language immersion programs have assured a new generation of proficient—and even eloquent—chanters, songwriters, and translators. Visitors can see more traditional hula than at any other time in the last 200 years.

ABOUT THE HULA

At backyard parties, hula is performed in bare feet and street clothes. But in performance, adornments play a key role, as do rhythm-keeping implements such as the *pahu* drum and the *ipu* (gourd).

In hula *kahiko* (traditional style), the usual dress is multiple layers of stiff fabric (often with a pellom lining, which most closely resembles *kapa*, the paperlike bark cloth of the Hawaiians). These wrap tightly around the bosom but flare below the waist to form a skirt. In precontact times, dancers wore only kapa skirts. Men traditionally wear loincloths.

Monarchy-period hula is performed in voluminous muumuu or high-necked muslin blouses and gathered skirts. Men wear white or gingham shirts and black pants.

In hula *auana* (modern), dress for women can range from grass skirts and strapless tops to contemporary tea-length dresses. Men generally wear aloha shirts, but sometimes don grass skirts over pants or even everyday gear.

SURPRISING HULA FACTS

Grass skirts are not traditional; workers from Kiribati (the Gilbert Islands) brought this custom to Hawaii.

Hula *mai* is a traditional hula form in praise of a noble's genitals; the power of the *alii* (royalty) to procreate gave *mana* (spiritual power) to the entire culture.

Hula students in old Hawaii adhered to high standards: scrupulous cleanliness, no sex, daily cleansing rituals, certain food prohibitions, and no contact with the dead. They were fined if they broke the rules.

WHERE TO WATCH HULA

If you're interested in "the real thing," there are annual hula festivals on each island. Check the individual island visitors' bureaus websites (⊕ *www. gohawaii.com*).

For total immersion, check out the weeklong Merrie Monarch Festival in Hilo in early Spring. *Halaus* (schools) from every island and from around the world compete with a common goal of preserving and promoting this sacred art form. If you can't make it to a festival and are in the Islands, check the local TV listings for festival coverage; it's an annual event that spellbinds many island residents.

There are plenty of other hula shows at resorts, lounges, and shopping centers. Ask your hotel concierge for performance information.

CRUISING THE HAWAIIAN ISLANDS

Cruising has become popular in Hawaii. Cruises are a comparatively inexpensive way to see all of Hawaii, and you'll save travel time by not having to check in at hotels and airports on each island. The limited amount of time in each port can be an argument against cruising, but you can make reservations for tours, activities, rental cars, and more aboard the cruise ship. This will also give you more time for sightseeing and shopping at ports.

The larger cruise lines such as Carnival, Princess, and Holland America offer itineraries of 10–16 days departing from the West Coast of the United States, most with stops at all the major Hawaiian Islands. Some cruise lines, such as Crystal, Cunard, and Disney, include ports in Hawaii on around-the-world cruises. All have plenty on board to keep you busy during the 4–5 days that you are at sea between the U.S. mainland and Hawaii.

Cruise ships plying the Pacific from the continental United States to Hawaii are floating resorts complete with pools, spas, rock-climbing walls, restaurants, nightclubs, shops, casinos, children's programs, and much more. Most hold thousands of passengers with an average staff-to-passenger ratio of three to one.

Prices for cruises are based on accommodation type: interior (no window, in an inside corridor); outside (includes a window or porthole); balcony (allows you to go outside without using a public deck); and suite (larger cabin, more amenities and perks). Passages start at about $1,000 per person for the lowest class accommodation (interior) and include room, on-board entertainment, and food. Ocean-view, balcony, and suite accommodations can run up to $6,500 and more per person.

Cruising to Hawaii

Carnival Cruises is great for families, with plenty of kid-friendly activities. Departing from Los Angeles or Vancouver, Carnival's "fun ships" show your family a good time, both on board and on shore (☎ 888/227–6482 ⊕ www.carnival.com). The grand dame of cruise lines, Holland America has a reputation for service and elegance. Their 14-day Hawaii cruises leave from and return to San Diego, with a brief stop at Ensenada (☎ 877/932–4259 ⊕ www.hollandamerica.com). More affordable luxury is what Princess Cruises offers. Although their prices seem a little higher, you get more bells and whistles on your trip (more affordable balcony rooms, more restaurants to choose from, personalized service) (☎ 800/774–6237 ⊕ www.princess.com).

Cruising within Hawaii

Norwegian Cruise Lines (⊕ www.ncl.com) is the only major operator to begin and end cruises in Hawaii. *Pride of Hawaii* (vintage America theme, family focus with lots of connecting staterooms and suites) offers a seven-day itinerary that includes stops on Maui, Oahu, the Big Island, and Kauai. This is the only ship to cruise Hawaii that does not spend days at sea visiting a foreign port, allowing you more time to explore destinations). Ocean conditions in the channels between islands can be a consideration when booking an interisland cruise on a smaller vessel such as the one operated by **Un-Cruise Adventures** (⊕ www.un-cruise.com)—a stately yacht accommodating only 36 passengers. This yacht's small size allows it to dock at less frequented islands such as Molokai and Lanai. The cruise is billed as "all inclusive"—your passage includes shore excursions, water activities, and a massage.

EXPLORING MAUI

Updated by
Lehia Apana

Those who know Maui well understand why it's earned all its superlatives. The island's miles of perfect beaches, lush green valleys, historic villages, top-notch water sports and outdoor activities, and amazing marine life have made it an international favorite. But nature isn't all Maui has to offer: it's also home to a wide variety of cultural activities, stunning ethnic diversity, and stellar restaurants and resorts.

Maui is much more than sandy beaches and palm trees; it's a land of water and fire. Puu Kukui, the 5,788-foot interior of the West Maui Mountains, also known as Mauna Kahalawai, is one of Earth's wettest spots—an annual rainfall of 400 inches has sculpted the land into impassable gorges and razor-sharp ridges. On the opposite side of the island, the blistering lava fields at Ahihi-Kinau receive scant rain. Just above this desertlike landscape, *paniolo* (cowboys) herd cattle on rolling, fertile ranchlands. On the island's rugged east side is the lush, tropical Hawaii of travel posters.

In small towns like Paia and Hana you can see remnants of the past mingling with modern-day life. Ancient *heiau* (platforms, often made of stone, once used as places of worship) line busy roadways. Old coral-and-brick missionary homes now house broadcasting networks. The antique smokestacks of sugar mills tower above communities where the children blend English, Hawaiian, Japanese, Chinese, Portuguese, Filipino, and more into one colorful language. Hawaii is a melting pot like no other. Visiting an eclectic mom-and-pop shop—such as Upcountry Makawao's Komoda Store and Bakery—can feel like stepping into another country, or back in time. The more you look here, the more you find.

At 729 square miles, Maui is the second-largest Hawaiian Island, but it offers more miles of swimmable beaches than any of its neighbors. Despite rapid growth over the past few decades, the local population still totals less than 200,000.

GEOLOGY

Maui is made up of two volcanoes, one now extinct and the other dormant but that erupted long ago, joined into one island. The resulting depression between the two is what gives the island its nickname, The Valley Isle. West Maui's 5,788-foot Puu Kukui was the first volcano to form, a distinction that gives that area's mountainous topography a more weathered look. The Valley Isle's second volcano is the 10,023-foot Haleakala, where desertlike terrain abuts tropical forests.

HISTORY

Maui's history is full of firsts—Lahaina was the first capital of Hawaii and the first destination of the whaling industry (early 1800s), which explains why the town still has that seafaring vibe. Lahaina was also the first stop for missionaries on Maui (1823). Although they suppressed aspects of Hawaiian culture, the missionaries did help invent the Hawaiian alphabet and built a printing press—the first west of the Rockies—that rolled out the news in Hawaiian, as well as, not surprisingly, Hawaii's first Bibles. Maui also boasts the first sugar plantation in Hawaii (1849) and the first Hawaiian luxury resort (1946), now called the Travaasa Hana.

ON MAUI TODAY

In the mid-1970s savvy marketers saw a way to improve Maui's economy by promoting The Valley Isle to golfers and luxury travelers. The ploy worked well; Maui's visitor count is about 2.5 million annually. Impatient traffic now threatens to overtake the ubiquitous aloha spirit, development encroaches on agricultural lands, and county planners struggle to meet the needs of a burgeoning population. But Maui is still carpeted with an eyeful of green, and for every tailgater there's a local on "Maui time" who stops for each pedestrian and sunset.

WEST MAUI

Separated from the remainder of the island by steep *pali* (cliffs), West Maui has a reputation for attitude and action. Once upon a time this was the haunt of whalers, missionaries, and the kings and queens of Hawaii. Today the main drag, Front Street, is crowded with T-shirt and trinket shops, art galleries, and restaurants. Farther north is Kaanapali, Maui's first planned resort area. Its first hotel, the Sheraton, opened in 1963. Since then, massive resorts, luxury condos, and a shopping center have sprung up along the white-sand beaches, with championship golf courses across the road. A few miles farther up the coast is the ultimate in West Maui luxury, the resort area of Kapalua. In between, dozens of strip malls line both the *makai* (toward the sea) and *mauka* (toward the mountains) sides of the highway. There are gems here, too, like Napili Bay and its jaw-dropping crescent of sand.

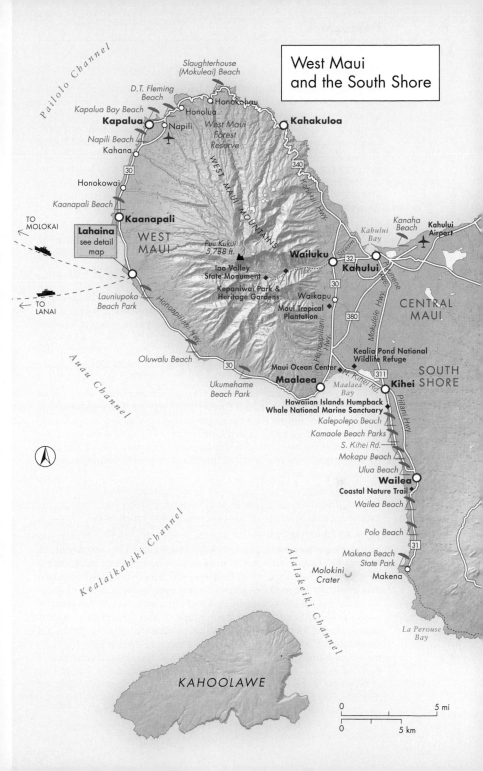

West Maui and the South Shore

Pailolo Channel

Slaughterhouse (Mokuleai) Beach

D.T. Fleming Beach

Honokohau

Kapalua Bay Beach

Honolua

Kapalua

Napili

Kahakuloa

Napili Beach

West Maui Forest Reserve

Kahana

30

Honokowai

WEST MAUI MOUNTAINS

340

Kahekili Hwy.

Iao Stream

Kahului Bay

Kanaha Beach

Kahului Airport

Kaanapali Beach

Kaanapali

TO MOLOKAI

Lahaina see detail map

WEST MAUI

Puu Kukui 5,788 ft.

Wailuku

32

Kahului

TO LANAI →

Iao Valley State Monument

Kepaniwai Park & Heritage Gardens

Waikapu

30

Launiupoko Beach Park

Honoapiilani Hwy.

30

380

CENTRAL MAUI

Maui Tropical Plantation

Oluwalu Beach

Kealia Pond National Wildlife Refuge

Auau Channel

Ukumehame Beach Park

Maui Ocean Center

Maalaea

N. Kihei Rd.

Maalaea Bay

311

Kihei

SOUTH SHORE

Honoapiilani Hwy.

Mokulele Hwy.

Piilani Hwy.

Hawaiian Islands Humpback Whale National Marine Sanctuary

Kalepolepo Beach

Kamaole Beach Parks

S. Kihei Rd.

Mokapu Beach

Ulua Beach

Kealaikahiki Channel

Wailea

Coastal Nature Trail

Wailea Beach

Polo Beach

Alalakeiki Channel

31

Makena Beach State Park

Makena

Molokini Crater

La Perouse Bay

KAHOOLAWE

0 — 5 mi

0 — 5 km

LAHAINA

27 miles west of Kahului; 4 miles south of Kaanapali.

Lahaina, a bustling waterfront town packed with visitors from around the globe, is considered the center of Maui. Some may describe Lahaina as tacky, with too many T-shirt vendors and not enough mom-and-pop shops, but this historic village houses some of Hawaii's most excellent restaurants, boutiques, cafés, and galleries. ■TIP→ If you spend Friday afternoon exploring Front Street, hang around for Art Night, when the galleries stay open late and offer entertainment, including artists demonstrating their work. A free gallery street map is available in Lahaina Visitor Center on the ground floor of the Old Lahaina Courthouse (648 Wharf Street).

Sunset cruises and other excursions depart from Lahaina Harbor. At the southern end of town an important archaeological site—Mokuula—is currently being researched, excavated, and restored. This was once a spiritual and political center, as well as home to Maui's chiefs.

GETTING HERE AND AROUND

It's about a 45-minute drive from Kahului Airport to Lahaina (take Route 380 to Route 30), depending on the traffic on this heavily traveled route. Traffic can be slow around Lahaina, especially 4–6 pm. Shuttles and taxis are available from Kahului Airport. The Maui Bus Lahaina Islander route runs from Queen Kaahumanu Center in Kahului to the Wharf Cinema Center on Front Street, Lahaina's main thoroughfare.

CRUISE TRAVEL TO LAHAINA

Visitors arriving by sea at Lahaina Harbor are greeted by the version of Hawaii seen in postcards. A former whaling port, Lahaina has a rich history, several informative museums, and flashy shops, art galleries, and restaurants. Lahaina Visitor Center in the Old Lahaina Courthouse is a good place to start your exploration, and any one of the staff members there can answer your questions or provide information on the best sites to visit.

Lahaina is relatively compact, with sandy beaches and creature comforts within walking distance. Taxi fares run $5–$15 in and around Lahaina. Famed Kaanapali Beach is a short 4½ miles away.

TOP ATTRACTIONS

Baldwin Home Museum. If you want some insight into 19th-century life in Hawaii, this informative museum is an excellent place to start. Begun in 1834 and completed the following year, the coral-and-stone house was originally home to missionary Dr. Dwight Baldwin and his family. The building has been carefully restored to reflect the period and many of the original furnishings remain: you can view the family's grand piano, carved four-poster bed, and most interestingly, Dr. Baldwin's dispensary. Also on display is the "thunderpot"—learn how the doctor single-handedly inoculated 10,000 Maui residents against smallpox. Admission includes a guided tour every half hour, or come Friday at 6 pm for a special candlelight tour. ⊠ *120 Dickenson St., Lahaina* ☎ *808/661–3262* ⊕ *www.lahainarestoration.org* ✎ *$7, includes admission to Wo Hing Museum* ☉ *Sat.–Thurs. 10–4, Fri. 10–8:30.*

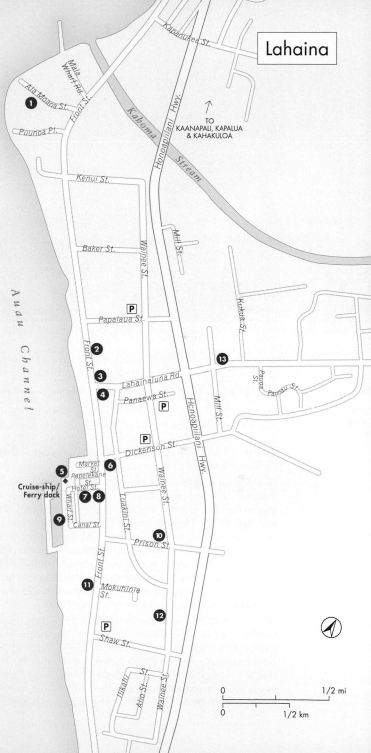

Lahaina

TO
KAANAPALI, KAPALUA
& KAHAKULOA

Auau Channel

Kahoma Stream

Honoapiilani Hwy

Kapanukea St.

Mala Wharf Rd. St.

Ata Moana St.

Front St.

Puunoa Pt.

Kenui St.

Baker St.

Wainee St.

Mill St.

Papalaua St.

Lahainaluna Rd.

Panaewa St.

Dickenson St.

Kukua St.

Pauoa St.

Pauaau St.

Market St.

Papelekane St.

Hotel St.

Wharf St.

Canal St.

Cruise-ship/
Ferry dock

Prison St.

Tuakini St.

Wainee St.

Honoapiilani Hwy.

Mill St.

Mokuhinia St.

Shaw St.

Ilikani St.

Alio St.

Wainee St.

0   1/2 mi

0   1/2 km

Once a whaling center, Lahaina Harbor bustles with tour boats, fishing vessels, and pleasure craft.

Banyan Tree. Planted in 1873, this massive tree is the largest of its kind in the United States and provides a welcome retreat and playground for visitors and locals, who rest and play music under its awesome branches. Many Lahaina festivals and weekend arts and craft fairs center on the Banyan Tree. ■ TIP→ **The Banyan Tree is a popular and hard-to-miss meeting place if your party splits up for independent exploring.** It's also a terrific place to be when the sun sets—mynah birds settle in here for a screeching symphony, which is an event in itself. ⊠ *Front St. between Hotel and Canal sts., Lahaina* ⊕ *www.lahainarestoration.org.*

Hale Paahao (Old Prison). Lahaina's jailhouse is a reminder of rowdy whaling days. Its name literally means "stuck-in-irons house," referring to the wall shackles and ball-and-chain restraints. The compound was built in the 1850s by convict laborers out of blocks of coral that had been salvaged from the demolished waterfront fort. Most prisoners were sent here for desertion, drunkenness, or reckless horse riding. Today, a wax figure representing an imprisoned old sailor tells his recorded tale of woe. There are also interpretive signs for the botanical garden and whale boat in the yard. ⊠ *Wainee and Prison Sts., Lahaina* ⊕ *lahainarestoration.org* ☞ *Free* ☉ *Daily 10–4.*

Holy Innocents' Episcopal Church. Built in 1927, this beautiful open-air church is decorated with paintings depicting Hawaiian versions of Christian symbols (including a Hawaiian Madonna and child), rare or extinct birds, and native plants. At the afternoon services, the congregation is typically dressed in traditional clothing from Samoa and Tonga. Anyone is welcome to slip into one of the pews, carved from native woods. Queen Liliuokalani, Hawaii's last reigning monarch, lived in a large grass house on this site as a child. ✉ *561 Front St., near Mokuhina St., Lahaina* ☎ *808/661–4202* ⊕ *www.holyimaui.org* ▱ *Free* ☉ *Daily 8–5.*

Fodor's Choice
★

Martin Lawrence Galleries. In business since 1975, Martin Lawrence displays the works of such world-renowned artists as Picasso, Erté, and Chagall in a bright and friendly gallery. Modern and pop-art enthusiasts will also find pieces by Keith Haring, Andy Warhol, and Japanese creative icon Takashi Murakami. ✉ *790 Front St., at Lahainaluna Rd., Lahaina* ☎ *808/661–1788* ⊕ *www.martinlawrence.com.*

Fodor's Choice
★

Old Lahaina Courthouse. The Lahaina Arts Society, Lahaina Vistor Center, and Lahaina Heritage Museum occupy this charming old government building in the center of town. Wander among the terrific displays and engage with an interactive exhibit about Lahaina's history, pump the knowledgeable visitor center staff for tips—be sure to ask for the walking-tour brochure covering historic Lahaina sites—and stop at the theater with a rotating array of films about everything from whales to canoes. Erected in 1859 and restored in 1999, the building has served as a customs and court house, governor's office, post office, vault and collector's office, and police court. On August 12, 1898, its postmaster witnessed the lowering of the Hawaiian flag when Hawaii became a U.S. territory. The flag now hangs above the stairway. ▪**TIP**➜ There's a public restroom in the building. ✉ *648 Wharf St., Lahaina* ☎ *808/667–9193 for Lahaina Visitor Center, 808/661–3262 for Lahaina Heritage Museum* ⊕ *www.lahainarestoration.org/old-lahaina-courthouse* ▱ *Free* ☉ *Daily 9–5.*

Fodor's Choice
★

Waiola Church and Wainee Cemetery. Immortalized in James Michener's *Hawaii,* the original church from the early 1800s was destroyed once by fire and twice by fierce windstorms. Repositioned and rebuilt in 1954, the church was renamed Waiola ("water of life") and has been standing proudly ever since. The adjacent cemetery was the region's first Christian cemetery and is the final resting place of many of Hawaii's most important monarchs, including Kamehameha the Great's wife, Queen Keopuolani, who was baptized during her final illness. ✉ *535 Wainee St., Lahaina* ☎ *808/661–4349* ⊕ *www.waiolachurch.org* ▱ *Free* ☉ *Weekdays 8–2, Sun. service at 9.*

Fodor's Choice
★

Wo Hing Museum. Smack-dab in the center of Front Street, this eye-catching Chinese temple reflects the importance of early Chinese immigrants to Lahaina. Built by the Wo Hing Society in 1912, the museum contains beautiful artifacts, historic photos displays of Dr. Sun Yat-sen, and a Taoist altar. Don't miss the films playing in the rustic theater next door—some of Thomas Edison's first films, shot in Hawaii circa 1898, show Hawaiian wranglers herding steer onto ships. Ask the docent for some star fruit from the tree outside, for the altar or for yourself. Note that the altar may be closed at certain times. ▪**TIP**➜ If you are in town in late January or early February, this museum hosts a nice Chinese New Year festival. ✉ *858 Front St., Lahaina* ☎ *808/661–5553* ⊕ *www.lahainarestoration.org* ▱ *$7, includes admission to Baldwin Home* ☉ *Daily 10–4.*

2

WORTH NOTING

Hauola Stone. Just visible above the tide is a gigantic stone, perfectly molded into the shape of a low-back chair and believed by Hawaiians to hold healing powers. It sits in the harbor, just off the land, where the sea and the underground freshwater meet. ✉ *Wharf and Papelekane sts., behind Lahaina Public Library, Lahaina* ⊕ *www.lahainarestoration.org* 🖾 *Free.*

Lahaina Galleries. Fine works of both national and international artists are displayed at this well-regarded gallery. Besides the space in Lahaina, there's a second location in The Shops at Wailea. Prices start at more than $2,000 for originals. ✉ *828 Front St., Lahaina* 🕾 *808/661–6284* ⊕ *www.lahainagalleries.com.*

> ### WALKING TOURS
>
> Lahaina's side streets are best explored on foot. Both the Baldwin Home and the Old Lahaina Courthouse offer free, self-guided, walking-tour brochures and maps. The Courthouse booklet is often recommended and includes more than 50 sites. The Baldwin Home brochure is less well known but, in our opinion, easier to follow; it details a short but enjoyable loop tour of the town.

Lahaina Harbor. For centuries, Lahaina has drawn ships of all sizes to its calm harbor: King Kamehameha's conquering fleet of 800 carved *koa* canoes gave way to Chinese trading ships, Boston whalers, United States Navy frigates, and, finally, a slew of pleasure craft. The picturesque harbor is the departure point for ferries headed to nearby islands, sailing charters, deep-sea fishing trips, and snorkeling excursions. It's also a port of call for cruise ships from around the world. ✉ *Wharf St., Lahaina* 🖾 *Free.*

Lahaina Jodo Mission. Established at the turn of the 20th century by Japanese contract workers, this Buddhist mission is one of Lahaina's most popular sites thanks to its idyllic setting and spectacular views across the channel. Although the buildings are not open to the public, you can stroll the grounds and enjoy glimpses of a 90-foot-high pagoda, as well as a great 3.5-ton copper and bronze statue of the Amida Buddha (erected in 1968). If you're in the vicinity at 8 on any evening, you may be able to hear the temple bell toll 11 times; the first three peals signifying Buddhist creeds, and the following representing the Noble Eightfold Path. ✉ *12 Ala Moana St., near Lahaina Cannery Mall, Lahaina* 🕾 *808/661–4304* 🖾 *Free.*

Pioneer Mill Smokestack. The former Pioneer Mill Company used this site to mill sugar back when Lahaina's main moneymaker was sugarcane. In 2010, the Lahaina Restoration Foundation restored the original smokestack—the tallest structure in Lahaina—and created a place for visitors to learn about the rich plantation history of West Maui. Take an interpretive walk around the smokestack along the landscaped grounds, then check out the refurbished locomotives that used to cart sugar between the fields and the mill. ✉ *275 Lahainaluna Rd., Lahaina* 🕾 *808/661–3262* ⊕ *www.lahainarestoration.org.*

KAANAPALI AND NEARBY

4 miles north of Lahaina.

As you drive north from Lahaina, the first resort community you reach is Kaanapali, a cluster of high-rise hotels framing a world-class white-sand beach. This is part of West Maui's famous resort strip and is a perfect destination for families and romance seekers wanting to be in the center of the action. A little farther up the road lie the condo-filled beach towns of Honokowai, Kahana, and Napili, followed by Kapalua. Each boasts its own style and flavor, though most rely on a low-key beach vibe for people wanting upscale vacation rentals. ⇨ *For details on specific beaches, see Chapter 3, Beaches.*

FUN THINGS TO DO IN WEST MAUI

- Get into the Hawaiian swing of things at the Old Lahaina Luau.

- Take a late-afternoon stroll on the beach fronting the Lahaina Jodo Mission.

- Make an offering at the Taoist altar in the Wo Hing Museum.

- Sail into the sunset from Lahaina Harbor.

- Attend the mynah birds' symphony beneath the Banyan Tree.

GETTING HERE AND AROUND

Shuttles and taxis are available from Kahului and West Maui airports. Resorts offer free shuttles between properties, and some hotels also provide complimentary shuttles into Lahaina. In the Maui Bus system the Napili Islander begins and ends at Whalers Village in Kaanapali and stops at most condos along the coastal road as far north as Napili Bay.

TOP ATTRACTIONS

Kaanapali. The theatrical look of Hawaii tourism—planned resort communities where luxury homes mix with high-rise hotels, fantasy swimming pools, and a theme-park landscape—began right here in the 1960s, when clever marketers built this sunny shoreline into a playground for the world's vacationers. Three miles of uninterrupted white-sand beach and placid water form the front yard of this artificial utopia, with its 40 tennis courts and two championship golf courses.

Located near the Sheraton Maui, this area in ancient times was known for its bountiful fishing (especially lobster) and its seaside cliffs. The sleepy fishing village was washed away by the wave of Hawaii's new economy: tourism. Puu Kekaa (today incorrectly referred to as Black Rock) was a *lele*, a place in ancient Hawaii believed to be where souls leaped from into the afterlife. ⊠ *Kaanapali.*

WORTH NOTING

Farmers' Market of Maui–Honokowai. From pineapples to corn, the produce at this West Maui open-air market is local and flavorful. Prices are good, too. Colorful tropical flowers and handcrafted items are also available. ⊠ *3636 Honoapiilani Hwy., across from Honokowai Park, Honokowai* ☎ *808/669–7004* ☉ *Mon., Wed., and Fri. 7–11 am.*

On the north end of West Maui, remote Kahakuloa is a reminder of Old Hawaii.

KAPALUA AND KAHAKULOA

Kapalua is 10 miles north of Kaanapali; 36 miles west of Kahului.

Upscale Kapalua is north of the Kaanapali resorts, past Napili, and is a hideaway for those with money who want to stay incognito. Farther along the Honoapiilani Highway is the remote village of Kahakuloa, a reminder of Old Hawaii.

GETTING HERE AND AROUND

Shuttles and taxis are available from Kahului and West Maui airports. The Ritz-Carlton, Kapalua, has a resort shuttle within the Kapalua Resort.

TOP ATTRACTIONS

Kahakuloa. The wild side of West Maui, this tiny village at the north end of Honoapiilani Highway is a relic of pre-jet-travel Maui. Remote villages similar to Kahakuloa were once tucked away in several valleys in this area. Many residents still grow taro and live in the old Hawaiian way. Driving this route is not for the faint of heart: the unimproved road weaves along coastal cliffs, and there are lots of blind curves; it's not wide enough for two cars to pass in places, so one of you (most likely you) will have to reverse on this nail-biter of a "highway." ⚠ **Watch out for stray cattle, roosters, and falling rocks.** True adventurers will find terrific snorkeling and swimming along this drive, as well as some good hiking trails, a labyrinth, and excellent banana bread. ✉ *Kahakuloa.*

QUICK
BITES
Julia's Best Banana Bread. Follow the signs in Kahakuloa village to this bright green roadside stand, which offers some of Maui's most delicious banana bread, coconut candy, passion fruit butter, taro chips, and other treats. The stand is open daily 9–5:30 or until the goodies are sold out. ⊠ *7465 Kahekili Hwy., Kahakuloa.*

2

Kapalua. Beautiful and secluded, Kapalua is West Maui's northernmost, most exclusive resort community. First developed in the late 1970s, the resort now includes the Ritz-Carlton, posh residential complexes, two golf courses, and the surrounding former pineapple fields. The area's distinctive shops and restaurants cater to dedicated golfers, celebrities who want to be left alone, and some of the world's richest folks. In addition to golf, recreational activities include hiking and snorkeling. Mists regularly envelop the landscape of tall Cook pines and rolling fairways in Kapalua, which is cooler and quieter than its southern neighbors. The beaches here, including Kapalua and D.T. Fleming, are among Maui's finest. ⊠ *Kapalua.*

QUICK
BITES
Honolua Store. In contrast to Kapalua's many high-end retailers, the old Honolua Store still plies the groceries and household goods it did in plantation times. Hefty plates of *ono* (delicious) local foods are served at the deli until 6:30 pm and best enjoyed on the wrap-around porch. The plate lunches are the quintessential local meal. ⊠ *502 Office Rd., Kapalua* ☎ *808/665–9105.*

SOUTH SHORE

Blessed by more than its fair share of sun, the southern shore of Haleakala was an undeveloped wilderness until the 1970s, when the sun worshippers found it. Now restaurants, condos, and luxury resorts line the coast from the world-class aquarium at Maalaea Harbor, through working-class Kihei, to lovely Wailea, a resort community rivaling its counterpart, Kaanapali, on West Maui. Farther south, the road disappears and unspoiled wilderness still has its way.

Because the South Shore includes so many fine beach choices, a trip here—if you're staying elsewhere on the island—is an all-day excursion, especially if you include a visit to the aquarium. Get active in the morning with exploring and snorkeling, then shower in a beach park, dress up a little, and enjoy the cool luxury of the Wailea resorts. At sunset, settle in for dinner at one of the area's many fine restaurants.

MAALAEA

13 miles south of Kahului; 6 miles west of Kihei; 14 miles southeast of Lahaina.

Pronounced "Mah- *ah*-lye- *ah*," this spot is not much more than a few condos, an aquarium, and a wind-blasted harbor (where there are tour boats)—but that's more than enough for some visitors. Humpback whales seem to think Maalaea is tops for meeting mates, and green sea turtles treat it like their own personal spa, regularly seeking appointments with cleaner wrasses in the harbor. Surfers revere this spot for "freight trains," reportedly the world's fastest waves.

A small Shinto shrine stands at the shore here, dedicated to the fishing god Ebisu Sama. Across the street, a giant hook often swings heavy with the sea's bounty, proving the worth of the shrine. At the end of Hauoli Street (the town's sole road), a small community garden is sometimes privy to traditional Hawaiian ceremonies. That's all, there's not much else—but the few residents here like it that way.

> ### FUN THINGS TO DO ON THE SOUTH SHORE
>
> ■ Witness the hammerheads feeding at the Maui Ocean Center.
>
> ■ Spike a volleyball at Kalama Park (⇨ see Beaches, Chapter 3).
>
> ■ Observe the green sea turtles while snorkeling at Ulua beach.
>
> ■ Take a surf lesson.
>
> ■ Decipher whale song at the Hawaiian Islands Humpback Whale National Marine Sanctuary.
>
> ■ Sink into Makena's soft sand.

GETTING HERE AND AROUND
To reach Maalaea from Kahului Airport, take Route 380 to Route 30. The town is also a transfer point for many Maui Bus routes.

TOP ATTRACTIONS
Maalaea Small Boat Harbor. With so many good reasons to head out onto the water, this active little harbor is quite busy. Many snorkeling and whale-watching excursions depart from here. There was a plan to expand the facility, but surfers argued that would have destroyed their surf breaks. In fact, the surf here is world-renowned. The elusive spot to the left of the harbor, called "freight train," rarely breaks, but when it does, it's said to be the fastest anywhere. Shops, restaurants, and a museum front the harbor. ⊠ *101 Maalaea Boat Harbor Rd., off Honoapiilani Hwy., Maalaea.*

FAMILY
Fodor's Choice
★

Maui Ocean Center. You'll feel as though you're walking from the seashore down to the bottom of the reef at this aquarium, which focuses on creatures of the Pacific. Vibrant exhibits let you get close to turtles, rays, sharks, and the unusual creatures of the tide pools; allow two hours or so to explore it all. It's not an enormous facility, but it does provide an excellent (though pricey) introduction to the sea life that makes Hawaii special. The center is part of a complex of retail shops and restaurants overlooking the harbor. Enter from Honoapiilani Highway as it curves past Maalaea Harbor. ■TIP➔ The Ocean Center's gift shop is one of the best on Maui for artsy souvenirs and toys. ⊠ *192 Maalaea Rd., off Honoapiilani Hwy., Maalaea* ☎ *808/270-7000* ⊕ *www.mauioceancenter.com* ⊠ *$25.95* ⊗ *Sept.–June, daily 9–5; July and Aug., daily 9–6.*

KIHEI

9 miles south of Kahului; 20 miles east of Lahaina.

Traffic lights and shopping malls may not fit your notion of paradise, but Kihei offers dependably warm sun, excellent beaches, and a front-row seat to marine life of all sorts. Besides all the sun and sand, the town's relatively inexpensive condos and excellent restaurants make this a home base for many Maui visitors.

County beach parks, such as Kamaole I, II, and III, have lawns, showers, and picnic tables. ■ TIP➜ Remember: beach park or no beach park, the public has a right to the entire coastal strand but not to cross private property to get to it.

GETTING HERE AND AROUND

Kihei is a 20-minute ride south of Kahului once you're past the heavy traffic on Dairy Road and are on the four-lane Mokulele Highway (Route 311).

TOP ATTRACTIONS

FAMILY

Fodor'sChoice

★

Hawaiian Islands Humpback Whale National Marine Sanctuary. This nature center sits in prime humpback-viewing territory beside a restored ancient Hawaiian fish pond. Whether the whales are here or not, the education center is a great stop for youngsters curious to know more about underwater life, and for anyone eager to gain insight into the cultural connection between Hawaii and its whale residents. Interactive displays and informative naturalists explain it all, including the sanctuary that acts as a breeding ground for humpbacks. Throughout the year, the center hosts activities that include talks, labs, and volunteer opportunities. The sanctuary itself includes virtually all the waters surrounding the archipelago. ■ TIP➜ Just outside the visitor center is the ancient Koieie fish pond; it is a popular place for locals to bring their children to wade in the water. ⊠ *726 S. Kihei Rd., Kihei* ☎ *808/879–2818, 800/831–4888 (toll-free)* ⊕ *www.hawaiihumpbackwhale.noaa. gov* ⌂ *Free* ۞ *Weekdays 10–3.*

FAMILY

Kealia Pond National Wildlife Refuge. Natural wetlands have become rare in the Islands, so the 700 acres of this reserve attract migratory birds, such as osprey and long-legged stilts that casually dip their beaks into the shallow waters as traffic shuttles by. It is also home to other wildlife. Interpretive signs on the boardwalk, which stretches along the coast by North Kihei Road, explain the journey of the endangered hawksbill turtles and how they return to the sandy dunes year after year. The main entrance to the reserve is on Mokulele Highway. A visitor center provides a good introduction. ⊠ *Mokulele Hwy., mile marker 6, Kihei* ☎ *808/875–1582* ⊕ *www.fws.gov/kealiapond* ⌂ *Free* ۞ *Weekdays 7:30–4.*

WORTH NOTING

Farmers' Market of Maui–Kihei. Tropical flowers, tempting produce, massive avocados, and locally made preserves, banana bread, and crafts are among the bargains at this South Shore market in the west end of Kihei, next to the ABC Store. ⊠ *61 S. Kihei Rd., Kihei* ☎ *808/875–0949* ۞ *Mon.–Thurs. 8–4, Fri. 8–5.*

WAILEA AND FARTHER SOUTH

15 miles south of Kahului, at the southern border of Kihei.

The South Shore's resort community, Wailea is slightly quieter and drier than its West Maui sister, Kaanapali. Many visitors cannot pick a favorite, so they stay at both. The luxury of the resorts (borderline excessive) and the simple grandeur of the coastal views make the otherwise stark landscape an outstanding destination. Take time to stroll the coastal beach path; a handful of perfect little beaches, all with public access, front the resorts.

The first two resorts were built here in the late 1970s. Soon a cluster of upscale properties sprang up, including the Four Seasons Resort Maui at Wailea and the Fairmont Kea Lani. Check out the Grand Wailea Resort's chapel, which tells a Hawaiian love story in stained glass.

GETTING HERE AND AROUND

From Kahului Airport, take Route 311 (Mokulele Highway) to Route 31 (Piilani Highway) until it ends in Wailea. Shuttles and taxis are available at the airport. If you're traveling by Maui Bus, the Kihei Islander route runs between The Shops at Wailea and Queen Kaahumanu Center in Kahului. There's a resort shuttle, and a paved shore path goes between the hotels.

WORTH NOTING

Coastal Nature Trail. A 1.5-mile-long paved beach walk allows you to stroll among Wailea's prettiest properties, restaurants, and rocky coves. The trail teems with joggers in the morning hours. The makai is landscaped with rare native plants like the silvery *hinahina*, named after the Hawaiian moon goddess. In winter, keep an eye out for whales. The trail is accessible from Polo Beach as well as from the many Wailea beachfront resorts. ⊠ *Wailea Beach, Wailea Alanui Dr., south of Grand Wailea Resort, Wailea.*

CENTRAL MAUI

Kahului, where you most likely landed when you arrived on Maui, is the industrial and commercial center of the island. West of Kahului is Wailuku, the county seat since 1950 and the most charming town in Central Maui, with some good, inexpensive restaurants. Outside these towns are attractions ranging from museums and historic sites to gardens.

You can combine sightseeing in Central Maui with some shopping at the Queen Kaahumanu Center, Maui Mall, and Maui Marketplace. This is one of the best areas on the island to stock up on groceries and supplies, thanks to major retailers including Walmart, Kmart, and Costco. Note that grocery prices are much higher than on the mainland.

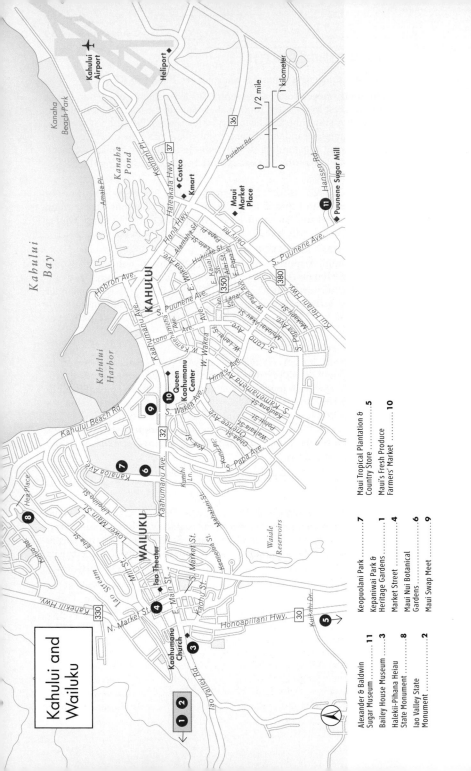

Kahului and Wailuku

Kahului Bay

Kanaha Beach Park

Kahului Airport

Heliport

Kanaha Pond

Costco

Kmart

Maui Market Place

Puunene Sugar Mill **11**

1/2 mile

1 kilometer

36

37

KAHULUI

Hobron Ave.

Kaahumanu Ave.

Hana Hwy.

S. Puunene Ave.

350

380

Kahului Harbor

Kahului Beach Rd.

Queen Kaahumanu Center **10**

9

7

6

32

WAILUKU

Kaahumanu Ave.

Iao Theater

Kaahumanu Church

Lower Main St.

N. Market St.

Iao Valley Rd.

Kahekili Hwy.

330

Honoapiilani Hwy.

30

8

4

3

5

Waiale Reservoirs

1 2

KAHULUI

3 miles west of Kahului Airport; 9 miles north of Kihei; 31 miles east of Kaanapali; 51 miles west of Hana.

With the island's largest airport and commercial harbor, Kahului is Maui's commercial hub. But it also offers plenty of natural and cultural attractions. The town was developed in the early 1950s to meet the housing needs of the large sugarcane interests here, specifically those of Alexander & Baldwin. The company was tired of playing landlord to its many plantation workers and sold land to a developer who promised to create affordable housing. The scheme worked and "Dream City," the first planned city in Hawaii, was born.

FUN THINGS TO DO IN CENTRAL MAUI

■ Unwind to slack-key guitar at a Maui Arts & Cultural Center concert.

■ Marvel at the indigenous plant life at Maui Nui Botanical Gardens.

■ Pick your way through Iao Valley's guava and ginger forest.

■ Imagine mastering the ancient weapons at the Bailey House Museum.

■ Boost your fortune with a pair of foo dogs purchased on Market Street.

GETTING HERE AND AROUND

From the airport, take Keolani Place to Route 36 (Hana Highway), which becomes Kaahumanu Avenue, Kahului's main drag. Run by Maui Bus, the Kahului Loop route traverses all of the town's major shopping centers; the fare is $2.

CRUISE TRAVEL TO KAHULUI

Most visitors who arrive on Maui by sea will dock at Kahului Harbor. Although this area is more commercial hub than tourist attraction, it's a convenient and central place to begin your explorations. Because many attractions are spread far apart, your best bet is to reserve a car from one of the many rental companies stationed at Kahului Airport, 2.2 miles down the road.

For taxi travel in and around Kahului, expect to pay around $5–$10. Travelers on a tight budget can walk or catch a taxi 1½ miles from the harbor to the island's largest mall, Queen Kaahumanu Center. This is the central hub of the Maui Bus, and a starting point for buses headed to the more desirable tourist towns of Kihei and Lahaina; the cost is $2 per ride or $4 for a day pass.

TOP ATTRACTIONS

Alexander & Baldwin Sugar Museum. Maui's largest landowner, A&B was one of the "Big Five" companies that spearheaded the planting, harvesting, and processing of sugarcane. At this museum, historic photos, artifacts, and documents explain the introduction of sugarcane to Hawaii. Exhibits reveal how plantations brought in laborers from other countries, forever changing the Islands' ethnic mix. Although Hawaiian cane sugar is now being supplanted by cheaper foreign versions—as well as by sugar derived from inexpensive sugar beets—the crop was for many years the mainstay of the local economy. You can find the museum in a small, restored plantation manager's house across the street from the post office and the still-operating sugar refinery, where smoke billows up when cane is being processed. Their gift shop sells excellent sugar, coffee, and a selection of history books. ⊠ *3957 Hansen Rd., Puunene* ☎ *808/871–8058* ⊕ *www.sugarmuseum.com* 🖾 *$7* ⊙ *Daily 9:30–4:30; last admission at 4.*

FAMILY **Maui Nui Botanical Gardens.** Hawaiian and Polynesian species are cultivated at this fascinating seven-acre garden, including Hawaiian bananas; local varieties of sweet potatoes and sugarcane; and native poppies, hibiscus, and *anapanapa*, a plant that makes a natural shampoo when rubbed between your hands. Reserve ahead for the weekly ethnobotany tours. Self-guided tour booklets and an audio tour wand is included with admission, and a docent tour is $10 (and must be arranged in advance). ⊠ *150 Kanaloa Ave., Kahului* ☎ *808/249–2798* ⊕ *www.mnbg.org* 🖾 *$5* ⊙ *Mon.–Sat. 8–4.*

WORTH NOTING

Halekii-Pihana Heiau State Monument. Stand here at either of the two *heiau* (ancient Hawaiian stone platforms once used as places of worship) and imagine the chief of Maui surveying his domain. That's what Kahekili, Maui's last chief, did and so did Kamehameha the Great after he defeated Kahekili's soldiers. Today the view is most instructive. The suburban community behind you is all Hawaiian Homelands—property owned solely by native Hawaiians. ⊠ *End of Hea Pl., off Kuhio Pl., Kahului* ☎ *808/984–8109* ⊕ *www.hawaiistateparks.org* 🖾 *Free* ⊙ *Daily 7:45–4:30.*

Maui Swap Meet. Even locals get up early to go to the Maui Swap Meet for fresh produce and floral bouquets. Hundreds of stalls sell everything from quilts to didgeridoos. Enter the parking lot from the traffic light at Kahului Beach Road. ⊠ *University of Hawaii Maui, 310 Kaahumanu Ave., Kahului* ☎ *808/244–3100* ⊕ *www.mauiexposition. com* ⊙ *Sat. 7–1.*

Maui's Fresh Produce Farmers' Market. Local purveyors showcase their fruits, vegetables, orchids, and crafts in the central courtyard at the Queen Kaahumanu Center. If "strictly local" is critical to you, it's a good idea to ask about the particular produce or flowers or whatever you want to purchase. ⊠ *Queen Kaahumanu Center, 275 W. Kaahumanu Ave., Kahului* ☎ *808/877–4325* ⊙ *Tues., Wed., and Fri. 8–4.*

WAILUKU

4 miles west of Kahului; 12 miles north of Kihei; 21 miles east of Lahaina.

Wailuku is peaceful now—although it wasn't always so. Its name means Water of Destruction, after the fateful battle in Iao Valley that pitted King Kamehameha the Great against Maui warriors. Wailuku was a politically important town until the sugar industry began to decline in the 1960s and tourism took hold. Businesses left the cradle of the West Maui Mountains and followed the new market (and tourists) to

2

the shores. Wailuku houses the county government but has the feel of a town that's been asleep for several decades.

The shops and offices now inhabiting Market Street's plantation-style buildings serve as reminders of a bygone era, and continued attempts at "gentrification," at the very least, open the way for unique eateries, shops, and galleries. Drop by on the first Friday of the month for First Friday, when Market Street is closed to traffic and turns into a festival with live music, performances, food, and more.

GETTING HERE AND AROUND

Heading to Wailuku from the airport, Hana Highway turns into Kaahumanu Avenue, the main thoroughfare between Kahului and Wailuku. Maui Bus system's Wailuku Loop stops at shopping centers, medical facilities, and government buildings; the fare is $2.

TOP ATTRACTIONS

Fodor'sChoice ★ **Bailey House Museum.** This repository of the largest and best collection of Hawaiian artifacts on Maui includes objects from the sacred island of Kahoolawe. Erected in 1833 on the site of the compound of Kahekili (the last ruling chief of Maui), the building was occupied by the family of missionary teachers Edward and Caroline Bailey until 1888. Edward Bailey was something of a Renaissance man: not only a missionary, but also a surveyor, a naturalist, and an excellent artist. The museum contains missionary-period furniture and displays a number of Bailey's landscape paintings, which provide a snapshot of the island during his time. The grounds include gardens with native Hawaiian plants and a fine example of a traditional canoe. The gift shop is one of the best sources on Maui for items that are actually made in Hawaii. ⊠ *2375A Main St., Wailuku* ☎ *808/244–3326* ⊕ *www.mauimuseum.org* ✉ *$7* ⊙ *Mon.–Sat. 10–4.*

Fodor'sChoice ★ **Iao Valley State Monument.** When Mark Twain saw this park, he dubbed it the Yosemite of the Pacific. Yosemite it's not, but it is a lovely deep valley with the curious **Iao Needle,** a spire that rises more than 2,000 feet from the valley floor. You can walk from the parking lot across Iao Stream and explore the thick, junglelike topography. This park has some lovely short strolls on paved paths, where you can stop and meditate by the edge of a stream or marvel at the native plants. Locals come to jump from the rocks or bridge into the stream—this isn't recommended. Mist often rises if there has been a rain, which makes being here even more magical. Be aware that this area is prone to flash flooding; if it's been raining, stay out of the water. Parking is $5, when an attendant is present. ⊠ *Western end of Rte. 32, Wailuku* ⊕ *www.hawaiistateparks.org* ✉ *$5 per car* ⊙ *Daily 7–7.*

FAMILY **Kepaniwai Park & Heritage Gardens.** Picnic facilities dot the landscape of this county park, a memorial to Maui's cultural roots. Among the interesting displays are an early-Hawaiian *hale* (house), a New England–style saltbox, a Portuguese-style villa with gardens, and dwellings from such other cultures as China and the Philippines. Next door, the **Hawaii Nature Center** has excellent interactive exhibits and pathways for hikes that are easy enough for children.

The peacefulness here belies the history of the area. In 1790, King Kamehameha the Great from the Island of Hawaii waged a successful and bloody battle against Kahekili, the son of Maui's chief. An earlier battle at the site had pitted Kahekili himself against an older Hawaii Island chief, Kalaniopuu. Kahekili prevailed, but the carnage was so great that the nearby stream became known as Wailuku (Water of Destruction), and the place where fallen warriors choked the stream's flow was called Kepaniwai (Damming of the Waters). ⊠ *870 Iao Valley Rd., Wailuku* ⬛ *Free* ☉ *Daily 7–7.*

Market Street. An idiosyncratic assortment of shops makes Wailuku's Market Street a delightful place for a stroll. Brown-Kobayashi and the Bird of Paradise Unique Antiques are the best shops for interesting collectibles and furnishings. Wailuku Coffee Company holds works by local artists and occasionally offers live entertainment in the evening. On the first Friday of every month Market Street closes to traffic (5:30–9) for Wailuku's First Friday celebration; festivities begin at 6, and the fun includes street vendors, live entertainment, and food. ⊠ *Market St., Wailuku* ⊕ *www.mauifridays.com.*

WORTH NOTING

FAMILY **Keopuolani Park.** Originally named Maui Central Park, Keopuolani Park got its name after schoolchildren argued before the county council that it be named for Hawaii's most revered queen, who was born near here and was forced to flee across the mountains before the arrival of Kamehameha the Great's army. This 101-acre park includes seven playing fields and a running path, gym, pool, skate park, and grass amphitheater. ⊠ *Kanaloa Ave., Wailuku* ☉ *Daily 7–7.*

FAMILY **Maui Tropical Plantation & Country Store.** When Maui's cash crop declined in importance, a group of visionaries opened an agricultural theme park on the site of this former sugarcane field. The 60-acre preserve offers a 40-minute tram ride with informative narration that covers the growing process and plant types. Children will enjoy such hands-on activities as coconut husking. Also here are an art gallery, a restaurant, and a store specializing in "Made in Maui" products. Don't leave without checking out the Kumu Farms stand, which offers seasonal organic produce and some of the tastiest papayas around. ⊠ *1670 Honoapiilani Hwy., Waikapu* ☎ *808/270–0333* ⊕ *www.mauitropicalplantation.com* ⬛ *Free, tram ride $20* ☉ *Daily 9–5.*

HALEAKALA NATIONAL PARK

41 miles southeast of Wailuku; 28 miles southeast of Pukalani.

From the Tropics to the Moon! Two hours, 38 miles, 10,023 feet—those are the unlikely numbers involved in reaching Maui's highest point, the summit of the volcano Haleakala. Nowhere else on earth can you drive from sea level (Kahului) to 10,023 feet (the summit) in only 38 miles. Haleakala Crater is the centerpiece of the park, though it's not actually a crater; technically, it's an erosional valley, flushed out by water pouring from the summit through two enormous gaps. The mountain has terrific camping and hiking, including a trail that loops through the crater, but

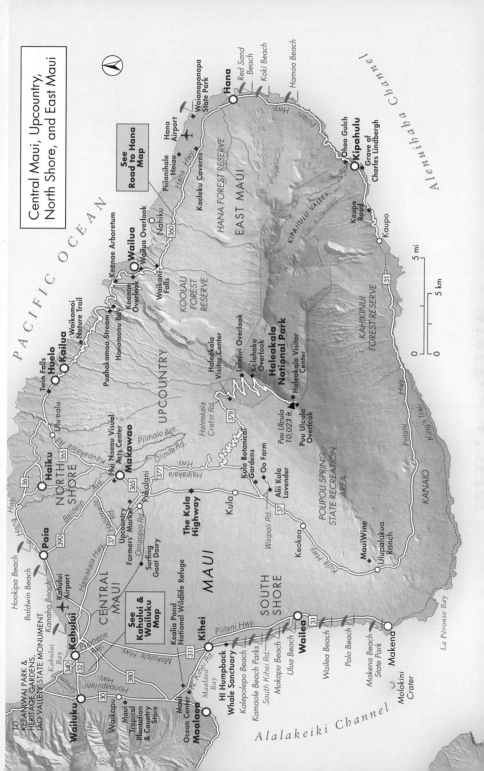

Central Maui, Upcountry,
North Shore, and East Maui

PACIFIC OCEAN

See
Road to Hana
Map

Twin Falls
Huelo
Kailua
Waikamoi
Nature Trail
Puohokamoa Stream
Honomanu Bay
Keanae Arboretum
Wailua Overlook
Wailua
Keanae
Overlook
Waikani
Falls
Nahiku

Piilanihale
Heiau
Hana Airport
Kaeleku Caverns
HANA FOREST RESERVE
EAST MAUI
Red Sand Beach
Koki Beach
Hamoa Beach
Hana
Waianapanapa State Park

Oheo Gulch
Kipahulu
Grave of
Charles Lindbergh
Kaupo
Road
Kaupo

KIPAHULU VALLEY

KOOLAU
FOREST
RESERVE

KAHIKINUI
FOREST RESERVE

Alenuihaha Channel

Ulu malu
Haiku
Ho'omau Rd.
Hi'i Noeau Visual
Arts Center
Makawao
Pukalani
Upcountry
Farmers' Market
Omaopio Rd.
Surfing
Goat Dairy
NORTH
SHORE
Baldwin Ave.
Haleakala Hwy.
Paia
Hookipa Beach
Baldwin Beach
Kahului Airport
Kahului
Kanaha Beach
Kabului Bay
Kaahumanu Ave.
Puunene Ave.
CENTRAL
MAUI

Olinda Rd.
Piiholo Ave.
Haleakala
Crater Rd.
UPCOUNTRY

Haleakala
Visitor Center
Leleiwi Overlook
Kolahaku
Overlook
Haleakala Visitor
Center
Haleakala
National Park

Puu Ulaula
10,023 ft.
Puu Ulaula Overlook

POLIPOLI SPRING
STATE RECREATION
AREA

KANAIO

Kula Botanical
Gardens
Oo Farm
Alii Kula
Lavender
Kula
The Kula
Highway
Keokea
MauiWine
Ulupalakua Ranch
Waipoli Rd.
King's Trail
Piilani Hwy.

Pilani Hwy.
Kula Hwy.

See
Kahului &
Wailuku Map

Kealia Pond
National Wildlife Refuge
Kihei
Piilani Hwy.
HI Humpback
Whale Sanctuary
Maalaea
Bay
Kalepolepo Beach
Kamaole Beach Parks
South Kihei Rd.
Mokapu Beach
Ulua Beach
Wailea
Wailea Beach
Polo Beach
Makena Beach
State Park
Makena
Molokini
Crater

SOUTH
SHORE

MAUI

Maui
Ocean Center
Maalaea

Maui Tropical
Plantation &
Country Store
Waikapu
Wailuku
TO
KEPANIWAI PARK &
HERITAGE GARDENS,
IAO VALLEY STATE MONUMENT

Iao
Stream
Honoapiilani Hwy.
Mokulele Hwy.
N. Kihei Rd.
Maalaea Rd.

Alalakeiki Channel

La Pérouse Bay

5 mi
5 km

the chance to witness this unearthly landscape is reason enough for a visit. Another section of the park, Oheo Gulch in Kipahulu, can only be reached via the Road to Hana.

Exploring Haleakala Crater is one of the best hiking experiences on Maui. The volcanic terrain offers an impressive diversity of colors, textures, and shapes—almost as if the lava has been artfully sculpted. The barren landscape is home to many plants, insects, and birds that exist nowhere else on earth and have developed intriguing survival mechanisms, such as the sun-reflecting, hairy leaves of the silversword, which allow it to survive the intense climate.

Fodor's Choice ★ **Haleakala National Park.** Nowhere else on Earth can you drive from sea level to 10,023 feet in only 38 miles. And what's more shocking: in that short vertical ascent to the summit of the volcano Haleakala you'll journey from lush, tropical island landscape to the stark, moonlike basin of the volcano's enormous, otherworldly crater.

Established in 1916, Haleakala National Park covers an astonishing 33,222 acres, with the Haleakala Crater as its centerpiece. There's terrific hiking, including trails for one-hour, four-hour, eight-hour, and overnight hikes, one of which goes through the Waikamoi Cloud Forest on Monday and Thursday only and requires reservations (call the park line no more than a week in advance). No other hikes require reservations. There is also on-site camping.

■TIP→ Before you head up Haleakala, call for the latest weather conditions. Extreme gusty winds, heavy rain, and even snow in winter are not uncommon. Because of the high altitude, the mountaintop temperature is often as much as 30°F cooler than that at sea level, so bring a jacket.

There's a $15-per-car fee to enter the park, good for three days. Hold on to your receipt—it can also be used at Oheo Gulch in Kipahulu. Once inside the park, stop at the **Park Headquarters** to learn about the volcano's history, and pick up trail maps (and memorabilia, if you please) at the gift shop. Campers and hikers must check in here.

What's in store for you as you make your ascent:

The **Leleiwi Overlook** is at about the 8,800-foot level and offers you your first awe-inspiring view of the crater. The small hills in the basin are cinder cones (*puu* in Hawaiian). If you're here in the late afternoon, it's possible you'll see yourself reflected on the clouds and encircled by a rainbow—a phenomenon called the Brocken Specter. Don't wait long for this, because it's not a daily occurrence.

At 9,000 feet, at **Kalahaku Overlook,** the famous silversword plant grows in the desertlike landscape. This endangered beauty grows only here and at the Big Island's two peaks. When it reaches maturity it sends forth a 3- to 8-foot-tall stalk with several hundred tiny sunflowers. It blooms once, then dies.

Haleakala Visitor Center, at 9,740 feet, has exhibits inside and a trail that leads to White Hill—a short, easy walk with even better views of the valley.

The highest point on Maui is the **Puu Ulaula Overlook,** at the 10,023-foot summit. Here, a glass-enclosed lookout provides a 360-degree view. The building is open 24 hours a day and has the best sunrise view. The *Maui News* posts the hour of sunrise, which falls between 5:45 and 7 am, depending on the time of year. Bring blankets or hotel towels to stay warm on the cold and windy summit. On a clear day you can see the islands of Molokai, Lanai, Kahoolawe, and the Big Island; on a *really* clear day you can even spot Oahu glimmering in the distance.

■ TIP→ The air is thin at 10,000 feet. Don't be surprised if you feel a little breathless while walking around the summit. Take it easy and drink lots of water. Anyone who has been scuba diving within the last 24 hours should not make the trip up Haleakala. ⊠ *Haleakala Crater Rd., Makawao* ☎ *808/572–4400, 866/944–5025 for weather conditions* ⊕ *www.nps.gov/hale* ⊠ *$15 per car* ☉ *Park 24 hrs; park headquarters daily 8–3:45; Haleakala Visitor Center daily 6–3.*

UPCOUNTRY

The west-facing upper slope of Haleakala is considered "Upcountry" by locals and is a hidden gem by most accounts. Although this region is responsible for most of Maui's produce—lettuce, tomatoes, strawberries, sweet Maui onions, and more—it is also home to innovators, renegades, artists, and some of Maui's most interesting communities. It may not be the Maui of postcards, but some say this is the real Maui and is well worth at least a day or two of exploring.

Upcountry is also fertile ranch land; cowboys still work the fields of the historic 18,000-acre Ulupalakua Ranch and the 30,000-acre Haleakala Ranch. ■ TIP→ Take an agricultural tour and learn more about the island's bounty. Lavender and wine are among the offerings. Up here cactus thickets mingle with purple jacaranda, wild hibiscus, and towering eucalyptus trees. Keep an eye out for *pueo,* Hawaii's native owl, which hunts these fields during daylight hours.

A drive to Upcountry Maui from Wailea (South Shore) or Kaanapali (West Maui) can be an all-day outing if you take the time to visit Maui's Winery and the tiny but entertaining town of Makawao. You may want to cut these side trips short and combine your Upcountry tour with a visit to Haleakala National Park (⇨ *see Haleakala National Park feature*)—it's a Maui must-see/do. If you leave early enough to catch the sunrise from the summit of Haleakala, you should have plenty of time to explore the mountain, have lunch in Kula or at Ulupalakua Ranch, and end your day with dinner in Makawao.

THE KULA HIGHWAY

15 miles east of Kahului; 44 miles east of Kaanapali; 28 miles east of Wailea.

Kula: most Mauians say it with a hint of a sigh. Why? It's just that much closer to heaven. On the broad shoulder of Haleakala, this is blessed country. From the Kula Highway most of Central Maui is visible—from the lava-scarred plains of Kanaio to the cruise ship–lighted waters of Kahului Harbor. Beyond the central valley's sugarcane fields, the plunging profile of the West Maui Mountains can be seen in its entirety, wreathed in ethereal mist. If this sounds too dramatic a description, you haven't been here yet. These views, coveted by many, continue to drive real-estate prices further skyward. Luckily, you can still have them for free—just pull over on the roadside and inhale the beauty. Explore it for yourself on some of the area's agricultural tours.

GETTING HERE AND AROUND

From Kahului, take Route 37 (Haleakala Highway), which runs into Route 377 (Kula Highway). Upper and Lower Kula highways are both numbered 377, but join each other at two points.

TOP ATTRACTIONS

Alii Kula Lavender. Make time for tea and a scone at this lavender farm with a falcon's view: it's *the* relaxing remedy for those suffering from too much sun, shopping, or golf. Knowledgeable guides lead tours through winding paths of therapeutic lavender varieties, protea, and succulents. The gift shop is stocked with many locally made lavender products, such as brownies, moisturizing lotions, and fragrant sachets. Make a reservation in advance for the walking tours. If you don't make it to the farm, there's also an Alii Kula Lavender gift shop in Paia town. ⊠ *1100 Waipoli Rd., Kula* ☎ *808/878–3004* ⊕ *www.aklmaui.com* ⊠ *$3, walking tours $12 (reservations recommended)* ⊗ *Daily 9–4.*

Fodor's Choice
★
MauiWine. Tour Maui's only winery and its historic grounds, the former Rose Ranch, for a chance to learn about its history and to sample such wines as Ulupalakua Red and Upcountry Gold. The King's Cottage tasting room is a cottage built in the late 1800s for the frequent visits of King Kalakaua. The cottage also contains the **Ulupalakua Ranch History Room,** which tells colorful stories of the ranch's owners, the paniolo tradition that developed here, and Maui's polo teams. The winery's top seller, naturally, is the pineapple wine, Maui Blanc. Complimentary tastings of the pineapple and sparkling wines are available all day. The old Ranch Store across the road may look like a museum, but in fact it's an excellent pit stop. The elk burgers are fantastic. ⊠ *Ulupalakua Ranch, 14815 Piilani Hwy., Kula* ☎ *808/878–6058* ⊕ *www.mauiwine. com* ⊠ *Free* ⊗ *Daily 10–5:30; tours at 10:30, 1:30, and 3:30.*

Fodor's Choice
★
Oo Farm. About a mile from Alii Kula Lavender are 8 acres of organic salad greens, herbs, vegetables, coffee, cocoa, fruits, and berries—all of it headed directly to restaurants in Lahaina. Oo Farm is owned and operated by the restaurateurs responsible for some of Maui's finest dining establishments, and more than 300 pounds of its produce end up on diners' plates every week. Reserve a space for the midday tours, which include an informational walk around the pastoral grounds and an alfresco lunch prepared by an on-site chef. Cap off the experience with house-grown, -roasted, and -brewed coffee, and some of the yummiest chocolate in the state. Reservations are necessary. ⊠ *651 Waipoli Rd., Kula* ☎ *808/667–4341 for reservations only* ⊕ *www.oofarm.com* ⊠ *Lunch tours from $58* ⊗ *Mon.–Thurs. 10:30–2.*

WORTH NOTING

Keokea. More of a friendly gesture than a town, this tiny outpost is the last bit of civilization before Kula Highway becomes a winding back road. A coffee tree pushes through the sunny deck at Grandma's Maui Coffee, the morning watering hole for Maui's cowboys who work at Ulupalakua or Kaupo Ranch. Keokea Gallery next door sells cool, quirky artwork. And two tiny stores—Fong's and Ching's—are testament to the Chinese immigrants who settled the area in the late 19th century. ∎TIP➜ **The only restroom for miles is in the public park, and the view makes stretching your legs worth it.** ⊠ *Kula.*

Kula Botanical Gardens. This well-kept garden has assimilated itself naturally into its craggy 8-acre habitat. There are 2,500 species of plants and trees here, including native koa (prized by woodworkers) and *kukui* (the state tree, a symbol of enlightenment). There is also a good selection of proteas, the flowering shrubs that have become a signature flower crop of Upcountry Maui. A flowing stream feeds into a koi pond, nene and ducks can be viewed, and a paved pathway—which is stroller- and wheelchair-friendly—meanders throughout the grounds. ⊠ *638 Kekaulike Hwy., Kula* ☎ *808/878–1715* ⊕ *www.kulabotanicalgarden.com* ⊠ *$10* ⊗ *Daily 9–4.*

FAMILY **Surfing Goat Dairy.** It takes goats to make goat cheese, and they've got plenty of both at this 42-acre farm. Tours range from "casual" to "grand," and any of them delight kids as well as adults. If you have the time, the "Evening Chores and Milking Tour" is educational and fun. The owners make more than two dozen kinds of goat cheese, from the plain, creamy Udderly Delicious to more exotic varieties that include tropical ingredients. All are available in the dairy store, along with gift baskets and even goat-milk soaps. ⊠ *3651 Omaopio Rd., Kula* ☎ *808/878–2870* ⊕ *www.surfinggoatdairy.com* ⊠ *Free, tours $12–$28* ⊗ *Mon.–Sat. 9–5, Sun. 9–2.*

Fodor's Choice **Upcountry Farmers' Market.** Most of Maui's produce is grown Upcountry, ★ which is why everything is fresh at this outdoor market at the football field parking lot in Kulamalu Town Center. Vendors offer fruits, vegetables, flowers, jellies and breads, plus exotic finds like venison, kimchi, and macadamia nuts. Reflecting the island's cultural melting pot, prepared food offerings include Korean, Indian, and Thai dishes. There's also a nice selection of vegan and raw food. Go early, as nearly everything sells out. ⊠ *55 Kiopaa St., near Longs Drugs, Pukalani* ⊕ *www.upcountryfarmersmarket.com* ⊗ *Sat. 7–11 am.*

FUN THINGS TO DO UPCOUNTRY

∎ Nibble lavender scones with a view of the Valley Isle at Alii Kula Lavender Farm.

∎ Open the car windows wide and breathe in the fresh, cool country air.

∎ Taste pineapple wine at Maui's winery.

∎ Sit on the wraparound porch at Haliimaile General Store and sip wine while you search for rainbows.

∎ Watch a plein air painter work on the grounds at the Hui Noeau Visual Arts Center in Makawao.

2

MAKAWAO

10 miles east of Kahului; 10 miles southeast of Paia.

At the intersection of Baldwin and Makawao avenues, this once-tiny town has managed to hang on to its country charm (and eccentricity) as it has grown in popularity. Its good selection of specialized shops makes Makawao a fun place to spend some time.

The district was originally settled by Portuguese and Japanese immigrants who came to Maui to work the sugar plantations and then moved Upcountry to establish small farms, ranches, and stores. Descendants now work the neighboring Haleakala and Ulupalakua ranches. Every July 4 weekend the paniolo set comes out in force for the Makawao Rodeo.

The crossroads of town—lined with shops and down-home eateries—reflects a growing population of people who came here just because they liked it. For those seeking greenery rather than beachside accommodations, there are secluded bed-and-breakfasts around the town.

GETTING HERE AND AROUND

To get to Makawao by car, take Route 37 (Haleakala Highway) to Pukalani, then turn left on Makawao Avenue. You can also take Route 36 (Hana Highway) to Paia and make a right onto Baldwin Avenue. Either way takes you to the heart of Makawao.

TOP ATTRACTIONS

Fodor's Choice
★
Hui Noeau Visual Arts Center. The grande dame of Maui's visual arts scene, "the Hui" hosts exhibits that are always satisfying. Located just outside Makawao, the center's main building is an elegant two-story Mediterranean-style villa designed in 1917 by the defining Hawaii architect of the era, C.W. Dickey. Explore the grounds, sample locally made products, and learn about exceptional plant species during a tour held Monday and Wednesday at 10 am; it costs $12. A self-guided tour booklet is available for $6. ⊠ *2841 Baldwin Ave., Makawao* 🕾 *808/572–6560* ⊕ *www.huinoeau.com* ✉ *Free* ⊗ *Mon.–Sat. 9–4.*

QUICK
BITES
Komoda Store and Bakery. One of Makawao's landmarks is Komoda Store and Bakery, a classic mom-and-pop shop that has changed little in three-quarters of a century. If you arrive early enough, you can get an incredible "stick" doughnut or a delicious cream puff. The store daily makes hundreds, but sells out of them every day. ⊠ *3674 Baldwin Ave., Makawao* 🕾 *808/572–7261.*

NORTH SHORE

Blasted by winter swells and wind, Maui's North Shore draws watersports thrill seekers from around the world. But there's much more to this area of Maui than coastline. Inland, a lush, waterfall-fed Garden of Eden beckons. In forested pockets, wealthy hermits have carved out a little piece of paradise for themselves.

North Shore action centers on the colorful town of Paia and the windsurfing mecca of Hookipa Beach. It's a far cry from the more developed resort areas of West Maui and the South Shore. Paia is also a starting point for one of the most popular excursions in Maui, the Road to Hana. Waterfalls, phenomenal views of the coast and the ocean, and lush rain forest are all part of the spectacular 55-mile drive into East Maui.

PAIA

Fodor's Choice
★

9 miles east of Kahului; 4 miles west of Haiku.

At the intersection of Hana Highway and Baldwin Avenue, Paia has eclectic boutiques that supply everything from high fashion to hemp-oil candles. Some of Maui's best shops for surf trunks, Brazilian bikinis, and other beachwear are here. Restaurants provide excellent people-watching opportunities and an array of dining and takeout options from flatbread to fresh fish. The abundance is helpful because Paia is the last place to snack before the pilgrimage to Hana and the first stop for the famished on the return trip.

This little town on Maui's North Shore was once a sugarcane enclave, with a mill, plantation camps, and shops. The old sugar mill finally closed, but the town continues to thrive. In the 1970s Paia became a hippie town, as dropouts headed for Maui to open boutiques, galleries, and unusual eateries. In the 1980s windsurfers—many of them European—discovered nearby Hookipa Beach and brought an international flavor to Paia. Today this historic town is hip and happening.

GETTING HERE AND AROUND

Route 36 (Hana Highway) runs directly though Paia; 4 miles east of town, follow the sign to Haiku, a short detour off the highway. You can take the Maui Bus from the airport and Queen Kaahumanu Shopping Center in Kahului to Paia and on to Haiku.

TOP ATTRACTIONS

There's no better place on this or any other island to watch the world's finest windsurfers and kiteboarders in action than **Hookipa Beach.** They know the five different surf breaks there by name. Unless it's a rare day without wind or waves, you're sure to get a show. Note that it's not safe to park on the shoulder outside this beach. Use the ample parking lot at the county park entrance.

QUICK
BITES

Mana Foods. This North Shore's natural-foods store has an inspired deli with hot and cold items. ⊠ *49 Baldwin Ave., Paia* ☏ *808/579–8078* ⊕ *www. manafoodsmaui.com.*

HAIKU

13 miles east of Kahului; 4 miles east of Paia.

At one time this area centered on a couple of enormous pineapple canneries. Both have been transformed into rustic warehouse malls. Because of the post office next door, Old Haiku Cannery earned the title of town center. Here you can try eateries offering everything from plate lunches to vegetarian dishes to juicy burgers and fantastic sushi. Follow windy Haiku Road to Pauwela Cannery, the other defunct factory-turned-hangout. This jungle hillside is a maze of flower-decked roads that seem to double back on themselves.

GETTING HERE AND AROUND

Haiku is a short detour off Hana Highway (Route 36) just past Hookipa Beach Park on the way to Hana. Haiku Road turns into Kokomo Road at the post office.

ROAD TO HANA

The Road to Hana is a 55-mile journey into the unspoiled heart of Maui. Tracing a centuries-old path, the road begins as a well-paved highway in Kahului and ends in the tiny, rustic town of Hana on the island's rain-gouged windward side, spilling into a backcountry rarely visited by humans. Many travelers venture beyond Hana to **Oheo Gulch** in East Maui, where one can cool off in basalt-lined pools and waterfalls.

This drive is a Hawaii pilgrimage for those eager to experience what glossy magazines consider the "real" Hawaii. To most, the lure of Hana is its timelessness, and paired with the spectacular drive (which brings to life the old adage: the journey *is* the destination), this is one of Hawaii's best experiences. The Road to Hana is undoubtedly one of the most beautiful drives on the planet.

> **FUN THINGS TO DO ON THE NORTH SHORE**
>
> ■ Buy a teeny-weeny Maui Girl bikini in Paia.
>
> ■ Watch windsurfers somersault over waves at Hookipa.
>
> ■ Rub elbows with yogis and tow-in surfers at Anthony's Coffee Company.
>
> ■ Dig into a fish sandwich and fries at the Paia Fish Market.
>
> ■ Head out on the awesome Road to Hana, ending up in the tiny East Maui town.

The challenging part of the road takes only an hour and a half, but the drive begs to be taken at a leisurely pace. You'll want to slow the passage of time to take in foliage-hugged ribbons of road and roadside banana-bread stands, to swim beneath a waterfall, and to inhale the lush Maui tropics in all its glory. You'll also want to stop often and let the driver enjoy the view, too.

HUELO, KAILUA, AND NEARBY

10 miles east of Haiku.

As the Road to Hana begins its journey eastward, the slopes get steeper and the Pacific Ocean pops into view. The first waterfall you see, Twin Falls, is around mile marker 2, and farther up the road is the Koolau Forest Reserve. Embedded in the forest are two townships, Huelo and Kailua, both of which are great places to pull over and take in the dramatic landscape.

TIPS ON DRIVING THE ROAD TO HANA

If you're prone to motion sickness be aware that the Road to Hana has a fair share of twists and turns. Drive with your window down to allow in the fresh air—tinged with the aroma of guava and ginger.

With short stops, the drive from Paia to Hana should take you between two and three hours one-way. Lunching in Hana, hiking, and swimming can easily turn the round trip into a full-day outing, especially if you continue past Hana to the Oheo Gulch and Kipahulu. If you go that far, you might consider continuing around the "back side" for the return trip. The scenery is completely different, and you'll end up in beautiful Upcountry Maui.

Because there's so much scenery to take in—including abundant waterfalls and beaches—we recommend staying overnight in Hana. It's worth taking time to enjoy the full experience without being in a hurry. Try to plan your trip for a day that promises fair, sunny weather—although the drive can be even more beautiful when it's raining, the roads become more hazardous.

During high season (January–March and summer), the Road to Hana tends to develop trains of cars, with everyone in a line of six or more driving as slowly as the first car. The solution: leave early (dawn) and return late (dusk). If you find yourself playing the role of locomotive, pull over and let the other drivers pass. You can also let someone else take the turns for you—several companies offer van tours.

BASIC ROAD TIPS

■ Common courtesy in Hawaii dictates that slower drivers should pull over for faster drivers. Please don't try to zoom through this winding road.

■ When approaching one-lane bridges, it is local custom for about five cars to go in one direction at a time. If you happen to be the sixth car, stop before entering the bridge and let drivers traveling in the other direction pass.

■ Instead of stopping in the middle of the road, or a bridge, to snap photos, park at a turnoff and carefully walk back to the waterfall to take your photos.

■ Although rain makes the drive more beautiful, with gushing waterfalls and rainbows, it also makes the roads slick. Drive slowly and cautiously on wet roads.

■ Just after Haiku the mile markers start at zero again.

GETTING HERE AND AROUND

Just after Haiku, the mile markers on the Hana Highway change back to 0. The towns of Huelo and Kailua are at mile markers 5 and 6. To reach the townships, follow the signs toward the ocean side of the road.

TOP ATTRACTIONS

The following sites are arranged geographically by mile marker en route to Hana.

Twin Falls. Keep an eye out for the Twin Falls Fruit Stand just after mile marker 2 on the Hana Highway. Stop here and treat yourself to some fresh sugarcane juice. If you're feeling adventurous, follow the path

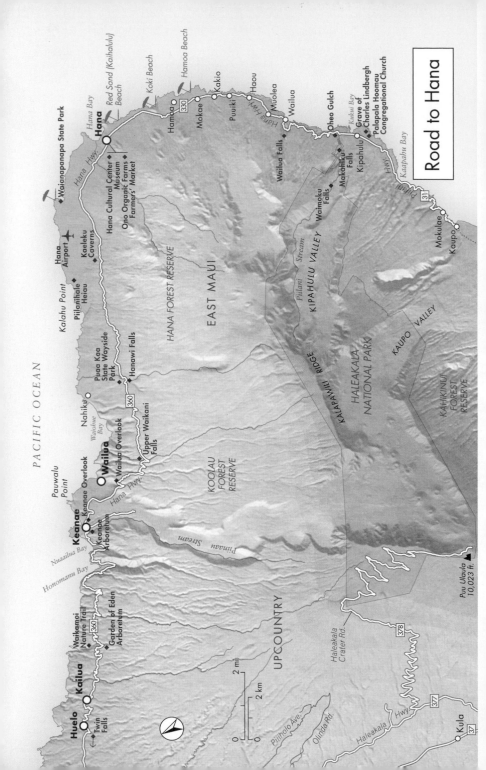

Road to Hana

PACIFIC OCEAN

EAST MAUI

HANA FOREST RESERVE

KOOLAU FOREST RESERVE

HALEAKALA NATIONAL PARK

KIPAHULU VALLEY

KALAPAWILI RIDGE

KAUPO VALLEY

KAHIKINUI FOREST RESERVE

UPCOUNTRY

Huelo

Kailua

Keanae

Wailua

Hana

Twin Falls

Waikamoi Nature Trail

Garden of Eden Arboretum

Keanae Arboretum

Keanae Overlook

Wailua Overlook

Upper Waikani Falls

Hanawi Falls

Puaa Kaa State Wayside Park

Nahiku

Piilanihale Heiau

Kalahu Point

Kaeleku Caverns

Hana Airport

Waianapanapa State Park

Hana Cultural Center Museum

Ono Organic Farms Farmers' Market

Pauwalu Point

Honomanu Bay

Nuaailua Bay

Waiohue Bay

Pi'inaau Stream

Piilani Stream

Red Sand (Kaihalulu) Beach

Koki Beach

Hamoa Beach

Hana Bay

Hamoa

Mokae

Puuiki

Kakio

Haou

Muolea

Wailua

Wailua Falls

Makahiku Falls

Waimoku Falls

Oheo Gulch

Grave of Charles Lindbergh

Palapala Hoomau Congregational Church

Kipahulu

Kaapahu Bay

Kukui Bay

Mokulae

Kaupo

Puu Ulaula 10,023 ft.

Haleakala Crater Rd.

Piiholo Ave.

Olinda Rd.

Haleakala Hwy

Kula

Hana Hwy

Hana Hwy

360

360

330

31

37

378

37

2 mi

2 km

0

beyond the stand to the paradisiacal waterfalls known as Twin Falls. Although it's still private property, the "no trespassing" signs have been replaced by colorfully painted arrows pointing toward the easily accessible falls. Several deep, emerald pools sparkle beneath waterfalls and offer excellent swimming and photo opportunities. In recent years, this natural attraction has become a tourist hot spot. Although the attention is well deserved, those who wish to avoid crowds may want to keep driving. ⊠ *Hana Hwy., past mile marker 2, Haiku-Pauwela.*

Huelo. When you see the colorful mailboxes on the makai of the road around mile marker 5 on the Hana Highway, follow the windy road to the rural area of Huelo—a funky community that includes a mix of off-the-grid inhabitants and vacation rentals. The town features two picturesque churches, one of which is Kaulanapueo Church, constructed in 1853 out of coral blocks. If you linger awhile, you may meet local residents and learn about a rural lifestyle you might not have expected to find on the Islands. The same can be said for nearby Kailua (mile marker 6). ■ TIP➔ When you're back up on Hana Highway, pull into the **Huelo Lookout Fruit Stand** for yummy smoothies and killer views of the Pacific below. ⊠ *Hana Hwy., near mile marker 5, Huelo.*

Waikamoi Nature Trail. Slightly after the town of Huelo, the Hana Highway enters the Koolau Forest Reserve. Vines wrap around street signs, and waterfalls are so abundant that you don't know which direction to look. A good start is between mile markers 9 and 10, where the Waikamoi Nature Trail sign beckons you to stretch your car-weary limbs. A short (if muddy) trail leads through tall eucalyptus trees to a coastal vantage point with a picnic table. Signage reminds visitors: "Quiet, Trees at Work" and "Bamboo Picking Permit Required." *Awapuhi*, or Hawaiian shampoo ginger, sends up fragrant shoots along the trail. ■ TIP➔ The area has picnic tables and a restroom. ⊠ *Hana Hwy., between mile markers 9 and 10.*

KEANAE, WAILUA, AND NEARBY

13 miles east of Kailua.

Officially, Keanae is the halfway point to Hana, but for many, this is where the drive offers the most rewarding vistas. The greenery seems to envelop the skinny road, forcing drivers to slow to a crawl as they "ooh" and "aah" at the landscape. Keanae itself isn't much of a stunner—save the banana-bread shack at the bottom of the road—but the scenery as your car winds through these tropics makes the white-knuckle parts of the drive worth it. Around the village of Wailua, one of the most fiercely native Hawaiian regions on the island, there seem to be waterfalls at every turn.

TOP ATTRACTIONS

The following sites are arranged geographically by mile marker en route to Hana.

Garden of Eden Arboretum. Just beyond mile marker 10 on the Hana Highway, the Garden of Eden Arboretum offers interpretive trails through 26 acres of manicured gardens. Anyone with a green thumb will appreciate the care and attention given to the more than 500 varieties of tropical plants—many of them native. Trails lead to the lovely Puohokamoa Falls, and provide a glimpse into the botanical wonders that thrive in this lush region. ■ TIP→ **If it has rained recently, Waikamoi Falls (also near mile marker 10) provides a chilly pool for swimming.** ✉ *10600 Hana Hwy., Haiku-Pauwela* ☎ *808/572–9899* ⊕ *www.mauigardenofeden.com* ✉ *$15* ☉ *Daily 8–4.*

Keanae Arboretum. Here you can add to your botanical education or enjoy a challenging hike into the forest. Signs help you learn the names of the many plants and trees now considered native to Hawaii. The meandering Piinaau Stream adds a graceful touch to the arboretum and provides a swimming pond. You can take a fairly rigorous hike from the arboretum if you can find the trail at one side of the large taro patch. Be careful not to lose the trail once you're on it. A lovely forest waits at the end of the 25-minute hike. ✉ *Hana Hwy., mile marker 17, Keanae* ✉ *Free* ☉ *Daily (recommended to visit only during daylight hrs).*

Keanae Overlook. Near mile marker 17 along the Hana Highway, you can stop at the Keanae Overlook. From this observation point you can take in the quiltlike effect the taro patches create against the dramatic backdrop of the ocean. In the other direction there are awesome views of Haleakala through the foliage. This is a great spot for photos. ✉ *Hana Hwy., near mile marker 17, Keanae.*

Upper Waikani Falls. Although not necessarily bigger or taller than the other falls along the Hana Highway, these are the most dramatic—some say the best—falls you'll find in East Maui. That's partly because the water is not diverted for sugar irrigation. The taro farmers in Wailua need all the runoff. To access the falls, park a half mile beyond mile marker 19, and follow the trail on the Hana side of the bridge to the 70-foot waterfalls. ■ TIP→ **This is a particularly good spot for photos.** ✉ *Hana Hwy., past mile marker 19, Wailua (Maui County).*

Wailua Overlook. From the parking lot on the side of the Hana Highway near mile marker 21, you can see Wailua Canyon in one direction and Wailua Village in the other. Photos are spectacular in the morning light of the verdant expanse below. Also from your perch, you can see Wailua Village's landmark 1860 church, which was allegedly constructed of coral that washed up onto the shore during a storm. ✉ *Hana Hwy., near mile marker 21, Wailua (Maui County).*

Puaa Kaa State Wayside Park. Many believe the stretch of landscape between mile markers 19 and 25 of the Hana Highway contain the most picturesque waterfalls on Maui. While there are stunning waterfalls in all directions, perhaps the loveliest is about a half mile beyond mile marker 22. The series of waterfalls gushing into a pool below will have you snapping screen savers. To get here, park at the turnoff just over the bridge and then carefully walk west across the bridge to the waterfalls. There are hiking trails that snake up the mountain, but they are muddy and slightly dangerous. ■ TIP→ **Usually in the parking lot by the waterfalls, a couple of flatbed trucks are loaded with crafts and fruit breads for sale. Look around for Dave's banana-bread truck; it's some of the best on the island.** ✉ *Hana Hwy., Wailua (Maui County)* ✛ *½ mile past mile marker 22.*

TREASURES ALONG THE ROAD TO HANA

The entire Road to Hana features postcard-worthy views. You'll be craning your neck to take in the lush landscape that seems to swallow your car, and every turnoff offers another striking photo opportunity, each one seemingly better than the last. However, there are some pit stops you'll kick yourself for skipping.

For jaw-dropping views, pull into the **Huelo Point Lookout** near mile marker 5, order a smoothie, and drink in the expanse of the Pacific Ocean and the historic Huelo township below.

If you are a banana-bread fan, be sure to stop in the small community of Keanae for some of the best loaves you're likely to try at the **Keanae Landing Fruit Stand.** Just be sure to arrive early, since the stand sells out frequently.

A half mile past mile marker 19, take a quick look toward the mountain to glimpse **Three Bears Falls**, also known as **Upper Waikani Falls.** There is a short trail to access this trio of gushers; just be sure that your shoes can handle the muddy terrain.

The waterfalls of **Puaa Kaa State Wayside Park** will likely be the backdrop for your holiday cards this year. From here you can embark on a muddy and rigorous hike into the rain forest to spot waterfalls spilling into pools. Wear durable hiking boots and bring extra clothes, as this trail will leave you covered in mud.

At mile marker 24, **Hanawi Falls** is another picturesque spot. The safest way to see the falls is on the bridge, so use caution.

At mile marker 31, turn onto Ulaino Road to explore the vast cave network of **Kaeleku Caverns.** Afterward, make your way to nearby **Piilanihale Heiau**, a beautiful 16th-century temple. While there, you can also amble through the lovely Kahanu Garden.

Near mile marker 32 you should carve out time to hike the 3-mile trail from **Waianapanapa State Park** to **Hana Bay**. You'll scramble over lava rock and along a stunning coastline rarely seen by travelers.

After you arrive in Hana, motor straight to **Hamoa Beach**, one of Hawaii's most beautiful strands. But the road does not end in Hana. In fact, for many travelers, the payoff comes at **Oheo Gulch's** abundant hiking trails—don't miss the inland hike through the bamboo forest. After you're done, you can travel a mile past Oheo Gulch and pay your respects at the grave of Charles Lindbergh.

Hanawi Falls. At mile marker 24 of the Hana Highway, just as you approach the bridge, look toward the mountains to catch a glimpse of Hanawi Falls. This lush spring-fed stream travels 9 miles to the ocean, and the waterfalls are real crowd-pleasers, even when rains have been light. The best views are from the bridge. ⚠ It is not safe to hike to the falls. ⊠ *Hana Hwy., near mile marker 24, Keanae.*

TROPICAL DELIGHTS

The drive to Hana wouldn't be as enchanting without a stop or two at one of the countless fruit and flower (and banana bread) stands by the highway. Every so often a thatch hut tempts passersby with apple bananas (a smaller, firmer variety), *lilikoi* (passion fruit), avocados, or star fruit just plucked from the tree. Leave a few dollars in the can for the folks who live off the land. Huge bouquets of tropical flowers are available for a handful of change, and some farms will ship.

One standout is **Keanae Landing Fruit Stand,** in the blink-and-you'll-miss-it community of Keanae. This legendary banana-bread shop is just past the coral-and-lava-rock church. Aunty Sandy's sweet loaves lure locals and tourists alike, but be sure to arrive early, because once the stand runs out, you'll have to scurry back up the main road to the **Halfway to Hana Fruit Stand** to find a tasty replacement.

HANA AND NEARBY

15 miles east of Keanae.

Even though the "town" is little more than a gas station, a post office, and a general store, the relaxed pace of life that Hana residents enjoy will likely have you in its grasp. Hana is one of the few places where the slow pulse of the island is still strong. The town centers on its lovely circular bay, dominated on the right-hand shore by a *puu* (volcanic cinder cone) called Kauiki. A short trail here leads to a cave, the birthplace of Queen Kaahumanu. Two miles beyond town, another puu presides over a loop road that passes Hana's two best beaches—Koki and Hamoa. The hill is called Ka Iwi O Pele (Pele's Bone). Off-shore here, at tiny Alau Island, the demigod Maui supposedly fished up the Hawaiian Islands.

Although sugar was once the mainstay of Hana's economy, the last plantation shut down in the 1940s. In 1946 rancher Paul Fagan built the Hotel Hana-Maui (now the Travassa Hana) and stocked the surrounding pastureland with cattle. Now it's the ranch and its hotel that put food on most tables. It's pleasant to stroll around this beautifully rustic property. In the evening, while local musicians play in the lobby bar, their friends jump up to dance hula. The cross you can see on the hill above the hotel was put there in memory of Fagan.

TOP ATTRACTIONS

The following sites are arranged geographically by mile marker en route to Hana.

Kaeleku Caverns. If you're interested in spelunking, take the time to explore Kaeleku Caverns (aka Hana Lava Tube), just after mile marker 31 on the Hana Highway. The site is a mile down Ulaino Road. The friendly folks at the cave give a brief orientation and promptly send nature enthusiasts into Maui's largest lava tube, accented by colorful underworld formations. You

can take a self-guided, 30- to 40-minute tour daily 10:30–4 for $11.95 per person. LED flashlights are provided. ✉ *Ulaino Rd., off Hana Hwy., Hana* ☎ *808/248–7308* ⊕ *www.mauicave.com* ⊘ *Daily 10:30–4.*

Piilanihale Heiau. This temple was built for a great 16th-century Maui king named Piilani and his heirs. Hawaiian families continue to maintain and protect this sacred site as they have for centuries, and they have not been eager to turn it into a tourist attraction. However, there is now a brochure, so you can tour the property yourself, including the 122-acre **Kahanu Garden,** a federally funded research center focusing on the ethnobotany of the Pacific. ✉ *650 Ulaino Rd., Hana* ✛ *To get here, turn left onto Ulaino Rd. at Hana Hwy. mile marker 31; the road turns to gravel; continue 1½ miles* ☎ *808/248–8912* ⊕ *www.ntbg.org* ✉ *$10* ⊘ *Weekdays 9–4., Sat. 9–2; guided tours weekdays (call for hrs; reservations required).*

Fodor's Choice
★ **Waianapanapa State Park.** Home to one of Maui's only black-sand beaches and freshwater caves for adventurous swimmers to explore, this park is right on the ocean. It's a lovely spot to picnic, hike, or swim. To the left you'll find the volcanic sand beach, picnic tables, and cave pools; to the right is an ancient trail that snakes along the ocean past blowholes, sea arches, and archaeological sites. The tide pools here turn red several times a year. Scientists say it's explained by the arrival of small shrimp, but legend claims the color represents the blood of Popoalaea, said to have been murdered in one of the caves by her husband, Chief Kakae. In either case, the dramatic landscape is bound to leave a lasting impression. ■TIP➔ **With a permit, you can stay in a state-run cabin for a steal. It's wise to book a year in advance as these rustic spots book up quickly.** ✉ *Hana Hwy., near mile marker 32, Hana* ☎ *808/984–8109* ⊕ *www.hawaiistateparks.org* ✉ *Free.*

Hana Cultural Center Museum. If you're determined to spend some time and money in Hana after the long drive along the Hana Highway, head to the Hana Cultural Center Museum in the center of town. Besides operating a well-stocked gift shop, it displays artifacts, quilts, a replica of an authentic *kauhale* (an ancient Hawaiian living complex, with thatch huts and food gardens), as well as other Hawaiiana. The knowledgeable staff can explain it all to you. ✉ *4974 Uakea Rd., Hana* ☎ *808/248–8622* ⊕ *www.hanaculturalcenter.org* ✉ *$3* ⊘ *Weekdays 10–4.*

Ono Organic Farms Farmers' Market. The family-owned Ono Farms offers certified organic produce at this roadside market at an old gas station—the only one in Hana. Depending on the season, you'll find such unusual delicacies as *rambutan* (resembling grapes), jackfruit (tastes like bananas), and lilikoi. ✉ *Hana Hwy., near Hasegawa General Store, Hana* ☎ *808/248–7779* ⊕ *www.onofarms.com* ⊘ *Daily 10–6.*

EAST MAUI

East Maui defies definition. Part hideaway for renegades, part escape for celebrities, this funky stretch of Maui surprises at every turn. You might find a smoothie shop that powers your afternoon bike ride, or a hidden restaurant–artist gathering off a backcountry road serving organic cuisine that could have been dropped in from San Francisco. Farms are abundant, and the dramatic beauty seems to get better the farther you get from Hana. This route leads through stark ocean vistas rounding the back side of Haleakala and into Upcountry. If you plan to meander this way, be sure to check the weather and road conditions.

2

KIPAHULU AND NEARBY

11 miles east of Hana.

Most know Kipahulu as the resting place of Charles Lindbergh. Kipahulu devotes its energy to staying under the radar. There is not much for tourists, save an organic farm, a couple of cafés, and astounding natural landscapes. Maui's wildest wilderness might not beg for your tourist dollars, but it is a tantalizing place to escape just about everything.

GETTING HERE AND AROUND

To access Kipahulu from Hana, continue on Hana Highway, also known as 330, for 11 miles southeast. You can also reach the area from Upcountry's Highway 37, which turns into Highway 31, though this route can take up to two hours and is a bit rough on your rental car.

TOP ATTRACTIONS

Fodor's Choice ★ **Oheo Gulch.** One branch of Haleakala National Park runs down the mountain from the crater and reaches the sea here, 10 miles past Hana at mile marker 42 on the Hana Highway, where a basalt-lined stream cascades from one pool to the next. Some tour guides still incorrectly call this area Seven Sacred Pools, but in truth there are more than seven, and they've never been considered sacred. You can park here and walk to the lowest pools for a cool swim. The place gets crowded, though, because most people who drive the Hana Highway make this their last stop. It's best to get here early to soak up the solace of these waterfalls. If you enjoy hiking, go up the stream on the 2-mile hike to **Waimoku Falls.** The trail crosses a spectacular gorge, then turns into a boardwalk that takes you through an amazing bamboo forest. You can pitch a tent in the grassy campground down by the sea. ■**TIP→ The $10 parking fee is good for three days and includes entry to Haleakalā Volcano.** ✉ *Piilani Hwy., 10 miles south of Hana, Hana.*

Grave of Charles Lindbergh. Many people travel the mile past Oheo Gulch to see the grave of Charles Lindbergh. The world-renowned aviator chose to be buried here because he and his wife, writer Anne Morrow Lindbergh, spent a lot of time living in the area in a home they'd built. He was buried here in 1974, next to Palapala Hoomau Congregational Church. The simple one-room church sits on a bluff over the sea, with the small graveyard on the ocean side. Since this is a churchyard, be considerate and leave everything exactly as you found it. Next to the churchyard on the ocean side is a small county park, a good place for a peaceful picnic. ⊠ *Palapala Hoomau Congregational Church, Piilani Hwy., Kipahulu.*

Kaupo Road. Also called Piilani Highway, this road winds through what locals say is one of the last parts of real Maui. It goes all the way around Haleakala's "back side" through Ulupalakua Ranch and into Kula. The desertlike area, with its grand vistas, is unlike anything else on the island, but some of the road is in bad shape, sometimes impassable in winter, and parts of it are unpaved. Car-rental agencies call it off-limits for their passenger cars, and no emergency assistance is available. The small communities around East Maui cling tenuously to the old ways—please be respectful of that if you do pass this way. Between Kipahulu and Kula may be a mere 38 miles, but the twisty road makes the drive take up to two hours. ■TIP➜ Fill up on gas and food, as the only stop out here is Kaupo Store, which hawks a few pricey necessities.

3

BEACHES

Visit Fodors.com for advice, updates, and bookings

Updated by
Heidi Pool

Of all the beaches on the Hawaiian Islands, Maui's are some of the most diverse. You can find the pristine, palm-lined shores you've always dreamed of, with clear and inviting waters the color of green sea glass, and you can also discover rich black-sand beaches, craggy cliffs with surging whitecaps, and year-round sunsets that quiet the soul. As on the other islands, all of Maui's beaches are public—but that doesn't mean it's not possible to find a secluded cove where you can truly get away from the world.

The island's leeward shores (West Maui and the South Shore) have the calmest, sunniest beaches. Hit the beach early, when the aquamarine waters are calm as bathwater. In summer, afternoon winds can be a sandblasting force and can chase away even the most dedicated sun-bathers. From November through May, these beaches are also great spots to watch the humpback whales that spend winter and early spring in Maui's waters.

Windward shores (the North Shore and East Maui) are for the more adventurous. Beaches face the open ocean rather than other islands, and tend to be rockier and more prone to powerful swells. This is particularly true in winter, when the North Shore becomes a playground for big-wave riders and windsurfers. Don't let this keep you away, however; some of the island's best beaches are those slivers of volcanic sand found on the windward shore.

In terms of beach gear, Maui is the land of plenty when it comes to stores stocked full of body boards and beach mats. Look for Longs Drugs (in Kihei, Kahului, Lahaina, Pukalani, and Wailuku) or the ABC Stores (in Kaanapali, Lahaina, Kihei, and elsewhere) for sunscreen, shades, towels, umbrellas, and more. If you want better deals and don't mind the drive into town, look for Kmart, Target, or Walmart in Kahu-lui. For more extensive gear, check out Sports Authority in Kahului. Equipment rentals are available at shops and resorts, too.

WEST MAUI

The beaches in West Maui are legendary for their glittering aquamarine waters backed by long stretches of golden sand. Reef fronts much of the western shore, making the underwater panorama something to behold. A few tips: parking can be challenging in resort areas; look for the blue "Shoreline Access" signs to find limited parking and a public path to the beach; and watch out for *kiawe* thorns when you park off-road, because they can puncture tires—and feet.

There are a dozen roadside beaches to choose from on Route 30, of which we like these best.

3

LAHAINA

FAMILY **Launiupoko Beach Park.** This is the beach park of all beach parks: both a surf break and a beach, it offers a little something for everyone with its inviting stretch of lawn, soft white sand, and gentle waves. The shoreline reef creates a protected wading pool, perfect for small children. Outside the reef, beginner surfers will find good longboard rides. From the long sliver of beach (good for walking), you can enjoy superb views of neighbor islands, and, landside, of deep valleys cutting through the West Maui Mountains. Because of its endless sunshine and serenity—not to mention such amenities as picnic tables and grills—Launiupoko draws a crowd on the weekends, but there's space for everyone (and overflow parking across the street). **Amenities:** parking (no fee); showers; toilets. **Best for:** sunset; surfing; swimming; walking. ⊠ *Rte. 30, mile marker 18, Lahaina.*

Olowalu. More an offshore snorkel and stand-up paddling spot than a beach, Olowalu is also a great place to watch for turtles and whales in season. The beach is literally a pullover from the road, which can make for some unwelcome noise if you're looking for quiet. The entrance can be rocky (reef shoes help), but if you've got your snorkel gear it's a 200-yard swim to an extensive and diverse reef. Shoreline visibility can vary depending on the swell and time of day; late morning is best. Except for during a south swell, the waters are usually calm. A half mile north of mile marker 14 you can find the rocky surf break, also called Olowalu. Snorkeling here is along pathways that wind among coral heads. Note: this is a local hangout and can be unfriendly at times. **Amenities:** none. **Best for:** snorkeling; stand-up paddling. ⊠ *Rte. 30, mile marker 14, south of Olowalu General Store, Olowalu.*

Puamana Beach Park. This is both a friendly beach park and a surf spot for mellow, longboard rides. With a narrow, sandy beach and a grassy area with plenty of shade, it offers mostly calm swimming conditions and a good view of neighboring Lanai. Smaller than Launiupoko, this beach park tends to attract locals looking to surf and barbecue; it has picnic tables and grills. **Amenities:** parking (no fee); showers; toilets. **Best for:** sunset; surfing; swimming. ⊠ *Rte. 30, ¼ mile south of Lahaina, Lahaina.*

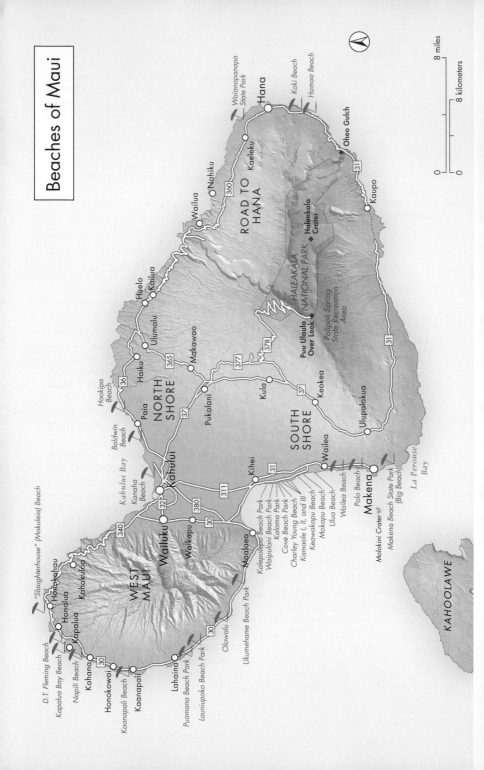

Beaches of Maui

WEST MAUI

NORTH SHORE

SOUTH SHORE

ROAD TO HANA

HALEAKALA NATIONAL PARK

KAHOOLAWE

"Slaughterhouse" (Mokuleia) Beach
D.T. Fleming Beach
Kapalua Bay Beach
Napili Beach
Honokahau
Honolua
Kapalua
Kahakuloa
Kahana
Honokowai
Kaanapali Beach
Kaanapali
Lahaina
Puamana Beach Park
Launiupoko Beach Park
Olowalu
Ukumehame Beach Park

Hookipa Beach
Baldwin Beach
Kahului Bay
Kanaha Beach
Paia
Haiku
Makawao
Pukalani
Kula
Keokea
Ulupalakua

Wailuku
Waikapu
Maalea
Kihei
Wailea Beach
Polo Beach
Wailea
Ulua Beach
Mokapu Beach
Keawakapu Beach
Kamaole I, II, and III
Charley Young Beach
Cove Beach Park
Kalama Park
Waipulani Beach Park
Kalepolepo Beach Park
Makena
Molokini Crater
Makena Beach State Park [Big Beach]
La Perouse Bay

Huelo
Ulumalu
Kailua
Nahiku
Wailua
Kaeleku
Hana
Waianapanapa State Park
Koki Beach
Hamoa Beach
Oheo Gulch
Kaupo

Haleakala Crater
Puu Ulaula Over Look
Polipoli Spring State Recreation Area

340
32
380
30
36
365
37
378
377
37
311
31
31
31
30
30
360

8 miles
8 kilometers

Ukumehame Beach Park. This popular park is also known as Thousand Peaks, because there's barely a break between each wave. Beginner to intermediate surfers say it's a good spot to longboard or body board. It's easy entry into the water, and you don't have to paddle out far. The beach itself leaves something to be desired, because it's more dead grass than sand, but there is some shade, mostly from thorny kiawe trees; footwear is a good idea. Portable toilets are available, along with picnic tables and grills. **Amenities:** parking (no fee); toilets. **Best for:** surfing. ⌧ *Rte. 30, near mile marker 12, Olowalu.*

> ### FREE BEACH ACCESS
>
> All of the island's beaches are free and open to the public—even those that grace the backyards of fancy hotels. Some of the prettiest beaches are often hidden by buildings; look for the blue "Shoreline Access" signs that indicate public rights-of-way through condominiums, resorts, and other private properties.

3

KAANAPALI AND NEARBY

Kaanapali Beach. If you're looking for quiet and seclusion, this is not the beach for you. But if you want lots of action, spread out your towel here. Stretching from the northernmost end of the Sheraton Maui Resort & Spa to the Hyatt Regency Maui Resort & Spa at its southern tip, Kaanapali Beach is lined with resorts, condominiums, restaurants, and shops. The center section in front of Whalers Village, also called "Dig Me Beach," is one of Maui's best people-watching spots: windsurfers, stand-up paddleboarders, and folks in catamarans head out from here, while others take in the scenery. A cement pathway weaves along the length of this 3-mile-long beach, leading from one astounding resort to the next.

The drop-off from Kaanapali's soft, sugary sand is steep, but waves hit the shore with barely a rippling slap. The northern section, known as Kekaa, was, in ancient Hawaii, a *lele,* or jumping-off place for spirits. It's easy to get into the water from the beach to enjoy the prime snorkeling among the lava-rock outcroppings. ■TIP→ Strong rip currents are often present near Kekaa; always snorkel with a companion.

Throughout the resort, blue "Shoreline Access" signs point the way to a few free-parking stalls and public rights-of-way to the beach. Kaanapali Resort public beach parking can be found between the Hyatt and the Marriott, between the Marriott and the Kaanapali Alii, next to Whalers Village, and at the Sheraton. You can park for a fee at most of the large hotels and at Whalers Village. The merchants in the shopping village will validate your parking ticket if you make a purchase. **Amenities:** parking (no fee); showers; toilets. **Best for:** snorkeling; sunset; swimming; walking. ⌧ *Honoapiilani Hwy., follow any of 3 Kaanapali exits, Kaanapali.*

FAMILY

Fodor's Choice

★

Napili Beach. Surrounded by sleepy condos, this round bay is a turtle-filled pool lined with a sparkling white crescent of sand. Sunbathers love this beach, which is also a terrific sunset spot. The shore break is steep but gentle, so it's great for body boarding and body surfing. It's easy to keep an eye on kids here as the entire bay is visible from everywhere. The beach is right outside the Napili Kai Beach Resort, a popular little resort for honeymooners, only a few miles south of Kapalua. **Amenities:** showers; toilets. **Best for:** sunset; surfing; swimming. ⊠ *5900 Lower Honoapiilani Hwy., look for Napili Pl. or Hui Dr., Napili.*

KAPALUA AND KAHAKULOA

D.T. Fleming Beach. Because the current can be quite strong, this charming, mile-long sandy cove is better for sunbathing than for swimming or water sports. Still, it's one of the island's most popular beaches. It's a perfect spot to watch the spectacular Maui sunsets, and there are picnic tables and grills. Part of the beach runs along the front of the Ritz-Carlton, Kapalua—a good place to grab a cocktail and enjoy the view. **Amenities:** lifeguards; parking (no fee); showers; toilets. **Best for:** sunset; walking. ⊠ *Rte. 30, 1 mile north of Kapalua, Kapalua.*

Fodor's Choice **Kapalua Bay Beach.** Over the years Kapalua has been recognized as one
★ of the world's best beaches, and for good reason: it fronts a pristine bay that is good for snorkeling, swimming, and general lazing. Just north of Napili Bay, this lovely, sheltered shore often remains calm late into the afternoon, although currents may be strong offshore. Snorkeling is easy here, and there are lots of colorful reef fish. This popular area is bordered by the Kapalua Resort, so don't expect to have the beach to yourself. Walk through the tunnel from the parking lot at the end of Kapalua Place to get here. **Amenities:** parking (no fee); showers; toilets. **Best for:** snorkeling; sunset; swimming. ⊠ *Rte. 30, turn onto Kapalua Pl., Kapalua.*

"Slaughterhouse" (Mokuleia) Beach. The island's northernmost beach is part of the Honolua-Mokuleia Marine Life Conservation District. "Slaughterhouse" is the surfers' nickname for what is officially Mokuleia. Weather permitting, this is a great place for body surfing and sunbathing. Concrete steps and a green railing help you get down the cliff to the sand. The next bay over, Honolua, has no beach but offers one of the best surf breaks in Hawaii. Competitions are often held there; telltale signs are cars pulled off the road and parked in the old pineapple field. **Amenities:** none. **Best for:** sunset; surfing. ⊠ *Rte. 30, mile marker 32, Kapalua.*

SOUTH SHORE

Sandy beach fronts nearly the entire southern coastline of Maui. The farther south, the better the beaches get. Kihei has excellent beach parks in town, with white sand, plenty of amenities, and paved parking lots. Good snorkeling can be found along the beaches' rocky borders. As good as Kihei is, Wailea is better. The beaches are cleaner, and the views more impressive. You can take a mile-long walk on a shore path from Ulua to near Polo Beach. Look for blue "Shoreline Access" signs for parking along the main thoroughfare, Wailea Alanui Drive. ■**TIP→** Break-ins have been reported at many parking lots, so don't leave valuables in the car. As you head to Makena, the terrain gets wilder; bring lunch, water, and sunscreen.

BEACH SAFETY ON MAUI

Hawaii's beautiful beaches can be dangerous at times due to large waves and strong currents. The state rates wave hazards using three signs: a yellow square (caution), a red stop sign (high hazard), and a black diamond (extreme hazard). Signs are posted and updated three times daily or as conditions change.

Generally, North Shore beaches (including Slaughterhouse and D.T. Fleming on the west side of the island) can be rough in the winter and not good for swimming or beginner-level water sports. On the south side, Kona storms (which usually occur in winter) can cause strong rip currents and powerful shore breaks.

Swim only when there's a normal caution rating, never swim alone, and don't dive into unknown water or shallow breaking waves. If you're unable to swim out of a rip current, tread water and wave your arms in the air to signal for help.

Even in calm conditions, there are other dangerous things in the water to be aware of, including razor-sharp coral, jellyfish, eels, and the occasional shark. Jellyfish cause the most ocean injuries, and signs are posted along beaches when they're present. Box jellyfish swarm to Hawaii's leeward shores 9–10 days after a full moon. Portuguese man-of-wars are usually found when winds blow from the ocean onto land. Reactions to a sting are usually mild (burning sensation, redness); however, in some cases they can be severe (breathing difficulties). If you are stung, pick off the tentacles, rinse the affected area with water, and apply ice. Seek first aid from a lifeguard if you experience severe reactions.

According to state sources, the chances of getting bitten by a shark in Hawaiian waters are low. To reduce your shark-attack risk:

■ Swim, surf, or dive with others at beaches patrolled by lifeguards.

■ Avoid swimming at dawn, dusk, and night.

■ Don't enter the water if you have open wounds or are bleeding.

■ Avoid murky waters, harbor entrances, areas near stream mouths, channels, or steep drop-offs.

■ Don't wear high-contrast swimwear or shiny jewelry.

■ If you spot a shark, leave the water quickly and calmly.

KIHEI

Charley Young Beach. This secluded 3-acre park sits off the main drag in a residential area. The sand is soft and smooth, with a gentle slope into the ocean. A cloister of lava rocks shelters the beach from heavy afternoon winds, creating a mellow spot in which to laze around. The usually gentle waves make for good swimming and you can find interesting snorkeling along the rocks on the north end. From South Kihei Road, turn onto Kaiau Street, just north of Kamaole I. **Amenities:** parking (no fee); showers; toilets. **Best for:** snorkeling; swimming. ⊠ *Kaiau St., Kihei.*

Cove Beach Park. Go to the Cove if you want to learn to surf or stand-up paddle. All the surf schools are here in the morning, pushing longboard

Sheltered Kapalua Bay Beach is ideal for snorkeling and swimming.

beginners onto the bunny-slope waves. For spectators there's a grassy area with some shade—and a tiny blink of a beach. If you aren't here to learn to surf, don't bother. The water is sketchy at best and plenty of other beaches are better. **Amenities:** parking (no fee); showers; toilets. **Best for:** stand-up paddling; surfing. ⊠ *S. Kihei Rd., turn onto Ili Ili Rd., Kihei.*

FAMILY **Kalama Park.** Stocked with grills and picnic pavilions, this 36-acre beach park with plenty of shade is great for families and sports lovers. With its extensive lawns and sports fields, the park welcomes volleyball, baseball, and tennis players, and even has a playground, skateboard park, and a roller hockey rink. The beach itself is all but nonexistent, but swimming is fair—though you must brave the rocky steps down to the water. If you aren't completely comfortable with this entrance, stick to the burgers and bocce ball. **Amenities:** parking (no fee); showers; toilets. **Best for:** partiers. ⊠ *S. Kihei Rd., across from Kihei Kalama Village, Kihei.*

Kalepolepo Beach Park. This tiny beach is the site of the ancient Kalepolepo Village, the prized property of King Kamehameha III in the 1850s. Here the *makaainana* (commoners) farmed, fished, and raised taro. Today, community stewards work to restore the ancient pond. The park has lots of shady trees and stays pretty quiet; however, the beach is only a sprinkling of sand, and swimming in the often-murky waters isn't recommended. Kaleopolepo is just south of Hawaiian Islands Humpback Whale National Marine Sanctuary. A portable toilet is available, and there are picnic tables and grills. **Amenities:** parking (no fee); showers; toilets. **Best for:** solitude. ⊠ *726 S. Kihei Rd., Kihei.*

SUN SAFETY ON MAUI

Hawaii's weather—seemingly never-ending warm, sunny days with gentle trade winds—can be enjoyed year-round with good sun sense. Because of Hawaii's subtropical location, the length of daylight here changes little throughout the year. The sun is particularly strong, with a daily UV average of 14.

The Hawaii Dermatological Society recommends these sun safety tips:

■ Plan your beach, golf, hiking, and other outdoor activities for the early morning or late afternoon, avoiding the sun between 10 am and 4 pm.

■ Apply a broad-spectrum sunscreen with a sun protection factor (SPF) of at least 15. Hawaii lifeguards use sunscreens with an SPF of 30. Cover areas that are most prone to burning like your nose, shoulders, tops of feet, and ears. And don't forget your lips.

■ Apply sunscreen at least 30 minutes before you plan to be outdoors, and reapply every two hours, even on cloudy days.

■ Wear light, protective clothing, such as a long-sleeve shirt and pants, broad-brimmed hat, and sunglasses.

■ Stay in the shade whenever possible—especially on the beach—by using an umbrella.

■ Children need extra protection from the sun. Apply sunscreen frequently and liberally on children and minimize their time in the sun. Sunscreen is not recommended for children under the age of six months.

FAMILY **Kamaole I, II, and III.** Three steps from South Kihei Road are three golden stretches of sand separated by outcroppings of dark, jagged lava rocks. You can walk the length of all three beaches if you're willing to get your feet wet. The northernmost of the trio, Kamaole I (across from the ABC Store—important to know if you forget your sunscreen) offers perfect swimming and an active volleyball court. There's also a great lawn, where you can spread out at the south end of the beach. Kamaole II is nearly identical except for the lawn, but there is no parking lot. The last beach, the one with all the people on it, is Kamaole III, perfect for throwing a disk or throwing down a blanket. This is a great family beach, complete with a playground, barbecue grills, kite flying, and, frequently, rented inflatable castles—a must at birthday parties for cool kids.

Locally—and quite disrespectfully, according to native Hawaiians—known as "Kam" I, II, and III, all three beaches have great swimming and lifeguards. In the morning the water can be as still as a lap pool. Kamaole III offers terrific breaks for beginning body surfers. **Amenities:** lifeguards; parking (no fee); showers; toilets. **Best for:** surfing; swimming; walking. ⊠ *S. Kihei Rd. between Alii Ke Alanui and Hale Kamaole Condominums, Kihei.*

Keawakapu Beach. Everyone loves Keawakapu, with its long stretch of golden sand, near-perfect swimming, and views of Puu Olai cinder cone. It's great fun to walk or jog this beach south into Wailea, as it's lined with over-the-top residences. It's best here in the morning—the winds pick up in the afternoon (beware of sandstorms). Keawakapu has

Catching a wave close to shore can give you an exciting ride.

three entrances: one is at the Mana Kai Maui resort (look for the blue "Shoreline Access" sign); the second is directly across from the parking lot on Kilohana Street (the entrance is unmarked); and the third is at the dead end of Kihei Road. Toilets are portable. **Amenities:** parking (no fee); showers; toilets. **Best for:** sunset; swimming; walking. ⊠ *S. Kihei Rd. near Kilohana St., Kihei.*

Waipuilani Park. Fronting the Maui Sunset Resort, Waipuilani Park is a spectacular place to sunbathe, relax, or picnic on golf course–grade grass. You can swim here, but water can be murky. A small beach hides behind the dunes, although it's usually speckled with seaweed and shells. This park often hosts local activities, such as volleyball and croquet, and it attracts many dog lovers. There are tennis courts, too. Although the park can be crowded, it's still a perfect place to watch the sunset. **Amenities:** parking (no fee); toilets. **Best for:** partiers; sunset. ⊠ *W. Waipuilani Rd. off South Kihei Rd., Kihei.*

WAILEA

Fodor'sChoice **Makena Beach State Park (Big Beach).** Locals successfully fought to turn ★ Makena—one of Hawaii's most breathtaking beaches—into a state park. This stretch of deep golden sand abutting sparkling aquamarine water is 3,000 feet long and 100 feet wide. It's often mistakenly referred to as Big Beach, but natives prefer its Hawaiian name, Oneloa. Makena is never crowded, no matter how many cars cram into the lots. The water is fine for swimming, but use caution. ■TIP→ **The shore drop-off is steep, and swells can get deceptively big.** Despite the infamous

"Makena cloud," a blanket that rolls in during the early afternoon and obscures the sun, it seldom rains here. For a dramatic view of the beach, climb Puu Olai, the steep cinder cone near the first entrance you pass if you're driving south. Continue over the cinder cone's side to discover "Little Beach"—clothing-optional by popular practice, although this is technically illegal. On Sunday, free spirits of all kinds crowd Little Beach's tiny shoreline for a drumming circle and bonfire. Little Beach has the island's best body surfing (no pun intended). Skim boarders catch air at Makena's third entrance, which is a little tricky to find (it's just a dirt path with street parking). **Amenities:** lifeguards; parking (no fee); toilets. **Best for:** surfing; swimming; walking. ⊠ *Off Wailea Alanui Dr., Makena* ⊕ *www.hawaiistateparks.org.*

FAMILY **Mokapu and Ulua.** Look for a little road and public parking lot near the Wailea Beach Marriott Resort & Spa if you are heading to Mokapu and Ulua beaches. Although there are no lifeguards, families love this place. Reef formations create tons of tide pools for kids to explore, and the beaches are protected from major swells. Snorkeling is excellent at Ulua, the beach to the left of the entrance. Mokapu, to the right, tends to be less crowded. **Amenities:** parking (no fee); showers; toilets. **Best for:** snorkeling; swimming. ⊠ *Wailea Alanui Dr., north of Wailea Marriott, Wailea.*

Polo Beach. Small and secluded, this crescent fronts the Fairmont Kea Lani. Swimming and snorkeling are great here, and it's a good place to whale watch. As at Wailea Beach, private umbrellas and chaise lounges occupy the choicest real estate, but there's plenty of room for you and your towel. There's a nice grass picnic area, although it's a considerable distance from the beach. The pathway connecting the two beaches is a great spot to jog or to take in awesome views of nearby Molokini and Kahoolawe. Rare native plants grow along the ocean, or *makai,* side of the path—the honey-sweet-smelling one is *naio,* or false sandalwood. **Amenities:** parking (no fee); showers; toilets. **Best for:** snorkeling; swimming. ⊠ *Kaukahi St., south of Fairmont Kea Lani entrance, Wailea.*

Wailea Beach. A road near the Grand Wailea Resort takes you to Wailea Beach, a wide, sandy stretch with snorkeling and swimming. If you're not a guest at the Grand Wailea or Four Seasons, the cluster of private umbrellas and chaise longues can be a little annoying, but the calm, unclouded waters and soft, white sand more than make up for this. From the parking lot, walk to the right to get to the main beach; to the left is another, smaller section that fronts the Four Seasons. There are picnic tables and grills away from the beach. **Amenities:** parking (no fee); showers; toilets. **Best for:** snorkeling; swimming. ⊠ *Wailea Alanui Dr., south of Grand Wailea Resort entrance, Wailea.*

NORTH SHORE

Many of the people you see jaywalking in Paia sold everything they owned to come to Maui and live a beach bum's life. Beach culture abounds on the North Shore. But these folks aren't sunbathers; they're big-wave riders, windsurfers, or kiteboarders, and the North Shore is their challenging sports arena. Beaches here face the open ocean and tend to be rougher and windier than beaches elsewhere on Maui—but don't let that scare you off. On calm days the reef-speckled waters are truly beautiful and offer a quieter and less commercial beachgoing experience than the leeward shore. Be sure to leave your car in a paved parking area so that it doesn't get stuck in soft sand.

PAIA AND KAHULUI

FAMILY **Baldwin Beach.** A local favorite, this big stretch of comfortable golden sand is a good place to stretch out, jog, or swim, although the waves can sometimes be choppy and the undertow strong. Don't be alarmed by those big brown blobs floating beneath the surface; they're just pieces of seaweed awash in the surf. You can find shade along the beach beneath the ironwood trees, or in the large pavilion, regularly used for local parties and community events. There are picnic tables and grills as well.

The long, shallow pool at the Kahului end of the beach is known as Baby Beach. Separated from the surf by a flat reef wall, this is where ocean-loving families bring their kids (and sometimes puppies) to practice a few laps. Take a relaxing stroll along the water's edge from one end of Baldwin Beach to Baby Beach and enjoy the scenery. The view of the West Maui Mountains is hauntingly beautiful. **Amenities:** lifeguard; parking (no fee); showers; toilets. **Best for:** swimming; walking. ⊠ *Hana Hwy., 1 mile west of Baldwin Ave., Paia.*

Fodor'sChoice **Hookipa Beach.** To see some of the world's finest windsurfers, hit this ★ beach along the Hana Highway. It's also one of Maui's hottest surfing spots, with waves that can reach 20 feet. Hookipa is not a good swimming beach, nor the place to learn windsurfing, but it's great for hanging out and watching the pros. There are picnic tables and grills. Bust out your telephoto lens at the cliffside lookout to capture the aerial acrobatics of board sailors and kiteboarders. **Amenities:** lifeguard; parking (no fee); showers; toilets. **Best for:** surfing; windsurfing. ⊠ *Rte. 36, 2 miles east of Paia, Paia.*

Kanaha Beach. Windsurfers, kiteboarders, joggers, and picnicking families like this long, golden strip of sand bordered by a wide grassy area with lots of shade. The winds pick up in the early afternoon, making for the best kiteboarding and windsurfing conditions—if you know what you're doing, that is. The best spot for watching kiteboarders is at the far left end of the beach. **Amenities:** lifeguard; parking (no fee); showers; toilets. **Best for:** kiteboarding; walking; windsurfing. ⊠ *Amala Pl., Kahului ✛ From Kaahumanu Ave., turn makai onto Hobron St., then right onto Amala Pl. Drive just over a mile through an industrial area and take any of 3 entrances into Kanaha.*

The black sand of small Waianapanapa State Park on the Road to Hana is made up of volcanic pebbles. You can swim here or hike a memorable coastal path past sea arches and blowholes.

ROAD TO HANA

East Maui's and Hana's beaches will literally stop you in your tracks—they're that beautiful. Black sand stands out against pewter skies and lush tropical foliage, creating picture-perfect scenes that seem too breathtaking to be real. Rough conditions often preclude swimming, but that doesn't mean you can't explore the shoreline.

HANA AND EAST MAUI

Hamoa Beach. Why did James Michener describe this stretch of salt-and-pepper sand as the most "South Pacific" beach he'd come across, even though it's in the North Pacific? Maybe it was the perfect half-moon shape, speckled with the shade of palm trees. Perhaps he was intrigued by the jutting black coastline, often outlined by rain showers out at sea, or the pervasive lack of hurry he felt here. Whatever it was, many still feel the lure. The beach can be crowded, yet it is nonetheless relaxing. Early mornings and late afternoons are best for swimming. At times the churning surf might intimidate swimmers, but the body surfing can be great. Hamoa is half a mile past Koki Beach on Haneoo Loop Road, 2 miles south of Hana town. **Amenities:** toilets. **Best for:** surfing; swimming. ⊠ *Haneoo Loop Rd., Hana.*

Koki Beach. You can tell from the trucks parked alongside the road that this is a favorite local surf spot. ■ **TIP➔ Watch conditions before swimming or body surfing, as rip currents can be mean.** Look for awesome views of the rugged coastline and a sea arch on the left end. *Iwa,* or white-throated frigate birds, dart like pterodactyls over the offshore Alau Islet. **Amenities:** none. **Best for:** surfing. ⊠ *Haneoo Loop Rd., 2 miles south of Hana town, Hana.*

Fodor's Choice **Waianapanapa State Park.** This black volcanic-pebble beach fringed with ★ green beach vines and palms will remain in your memory long after your visit. Swimming here is both relaxing and invigorating. Strong currents bump smooth stones up against your ankles, while seabirds flit above a black, jagged sea arch, and fingers of white foam rush onto the beach. There are picnic tables and grills. At the edge of the parking lot, a sign tells you the sad story of a doomed Hawaiian princess. Stairs lead through a tunnel of interlocking Polynesian *hau* (a native tree) branches to an icy cave pool—the secret hiding place of the ancient princess (you can swim in this pool, but beware of mosquitoes). In the other direction a dramatic 3-mile coastal path continues past sea arches, blowholes, cultural sites, and even a ramshackle fishermen's shelter, all the way to Hana town. **Amenities:** parking (no fee); showers; toilets. **Best for:** swimming; walking. ⊠ *Hana Hwy., near mile marker 32, Hana* ☎ *808/984–8109* ⊕ *www.hawaiistateparks.org.*

WHERE TO EAT

Updated by
Lehia Apana

For a place the size of Maui, there's a lot going on when it comes to the dining scene, from ethnic holes-in-the-wall to stunningly appointed hotel dining rooms, and from seafood trucks to oceanfront fish houses with panoramic views. Much of the food is excellent, but some of it is overpriced and touristy. If you're coming from a "food destination" city, you may have to adjust your expectations.

Follow the locavore trend, and at casual and fine-dining restaurants choose menu items made with products that are abundant on the island, like local fish, onions, avocados, cabbage, broccoli, asparagus, hydroponic tomatoes, myriad herbs, salad greens, *kalo* (taro), bananas, papaya, guava, *lilikoi* (passion fruit), coconut, mangoes, strawberries, and Maui pineapple. You can also look for treats grown on neighboring islands, such as mushrooms, purple sweet potatoes, and watermelon.

"Local food," a specific and official cuisine designated as such in the 1920s, is an amalgam of foods brought by the ethnic groups that have come here since the mid-1800s and also blended with the foods native Hawaiians have enjoyed for centuries. Dishes to try include *lomilomi* salmon, *laulau*, *poi*, Portuguese bean soup, *kalbi* ribs, chicken *katsu*, chow fun, hamburger steak, and macaroni salad. For a food adventure, take a drive into Central Maui and have lunch or dinner at one of the "local" spots recommended here. Or get even more adventurous and take a drive around Wailuku or Kahului and find your own hidden gem—there are plenty out there.

MAUI DINING PLANNER

WITH KIDS

Hawaii is an extremely kid-friendly place. The vibe is casual, and even the fancy restaurants have a menu for *keiki* (children), usually along with a box of crayons or other diversion tucked away somewhere. Some of the hotel restaurants feature cute-as-a-button "knee-high buffets" for the kids. Take advantage of local treats and experiences such as shave ice and a luau.

SMOKING

Smoking is prohibited in all Hawaii restaurants and bars, including on patios and other outdoor dining areas.

RESERVATIONS

Maui is one of the most popular vacation destinations in the world. It's always best to make reservations in advance, especially if you're traveling in a group of four or more. If you're determined to go to places like Mama's Fish House or the Old Lahaina Luau, you should make reservations as far in advance as possible. Most other places will do their best to accommodate you, even at the last minute.

WHAT TO WEAR

Casual clothing works for just about every restaurant on Maui. For dinner at hotels and other upscale restaurants, it's nice to see men in shirts with collars and women in evening resort wear, but nothing dressier is required anywhere. Bring a sweater or cover-up in winter months—many restaurants are open-air and can be breezy.

HOURS AND PRICES

Restaurants on Maui are busiest from 5 to 7, the early-bird-special hours and sunset time. By 8:30 many dining rooms are quiet, and by 10 most are closed. Places with popular bars and karaoke usually keep the kitchens open, too, but serve a limited menu. Unfortunately, many hotel restaurants are expensive and not very good; the best are listed here. To dine well on the cheap, look for coupons in the *Maui News,* found mostly in the "Maui Scene" section on Thursday, or check online for coupons at sites such as ⊕ *www.originalcouponbook.com.* Or go into Central Maui and enjoy the great ethnic restaurants where locals eat. Many upscale restaurants offer discounts of up to 50% during slow months (September–November). As for tipping, 18%–20% is considered standard for high-quality service.

WHAT IT COSTS			
$	$$	$$$	$$$$
Restaurants	under $18	$18–$26	$27–$35	over $35

Restaurant prices are the average cost of a main course at dinner or, if dinner is not served, at lunch.

WEST MAUI

Beautiful West Maui encompasses the area from tiny Olowalu, with its famous mom-and-pop Olowalu General Store, full of local-style *bentos* (box lunches), all the way north to the ritzy Kapalua Resort, with its glitzy (some say tired) annual wine-and-food festival. In between are Lahaina, the historic former capital of Hawaii, with its myriad restaurants on and off Front Street, and the resort area of Kaanapali. Have some fun checking out restaurants in the nooks and crannies of Kahana, Honokowai, and Napili, north of Kaanapali. All over the west side you'll find a rainbow of cuisines in just about every price category.

MAUI'S FOOD TRUCKS: MOVABLE FEASTS

As in so many other places, food-truck culture is taking hold on Maui, but don't expect to find well-equipped, customized trucks like the ones you see on the Food Network. Most have no websites, Twitter accounts, or Facebook pages; some don't even have phones. And many have irregular days and hours of operation. So just take a chance and consider it an adventure. You can also follow @FoodTrucksMaui on Twitter, or check 🌐 *Facebook.com/FoodTrucksOnMaui*, for the latest information.

A group of trucks has formed a sort of food court by the harbor on Kahului Beach Road opposite the Maui Arts & Cultural Center (1 Cameron Way, Kahului). The best of these is the **Geste Shrimp Truck**, which serves four different preparations of shrimp with sides of crab, mac salad, and rice. Hours are generally Tuesday–Saturday 10:30–5:30.

OLOWALU

$ AMERICAN 🍴 **Leoda's Kitchen and Pie Shop.** Slow down as you drive through the little roadside village of Olowalu, about 15 minutes before Lahaina town if you're coming from the airport, so you don't miss this adorable farmhouse-chic restaurant and pie shop, where everything is prepared with care. Old photos of the area, distressed wood, and muted colors set the mood. Try the signature ahi Benedict for breakfast. For lunch, have a sandwich or a burger with Kula onions. A rotating menu of nightly dinner specials offers comfort food at its best. All the breads are homemade and excellent, and most ingredients are sourced locally. Don't get too full: you must try the pie—the banana cream is out of this world, or dig into the Olowalu lime pie. [$] *Average main: $15* ✉ *820 Olowalu Village Rd., Olowalu* ☎ *808/662–3600* 🌐 *www.leodas.com.*

$ HAWAIIAN 🍴 **Olowalu General Store.** A Maui landmark for almost seven decades, one of the island's last true mom-and-pops is best known for its hot dogs, homemade Spam *musubi* (a slice of Spam on top of a block of rice, all wrapped in nori), and boiled peanuts. Don't overlook the plate lunches—Kalua pork, teriyaki chicken, and Korean teriyaki beef are best sellers—or the burgers. Full, local-style, hearty breakfast plates that include juice or soda are just $5.99. There are also smoothies, scoops of Maui's own Roselani Ice Cream in eight tropical flavors, and a wide selection of shave ice flavors. [$] *Average main: $8* ✉ *820 Olowalu Village Rd., Olowalu* ☎ *808/667–2883* 🕒 *No dinner.*

LAHAINA

$ HAWAIIAN 🍴 **Aloha Mixed Plate.** From the wonderful folks who bring you Maui's best luau—the Old Lahaina Luau—comes this casual, multiaward-winning, oceanfront eatery. If you've yet to indulge in a "plate lunch" (a protein—usually in an Asian-style preparation—two scoops of rice, and a scoop of macaroni salad), this is a good place to try one. The menu features fresh local fish preparations, lots of local produce, and such favorites as saimin, laulau, shoyu chicken, kalua pork, and poi from

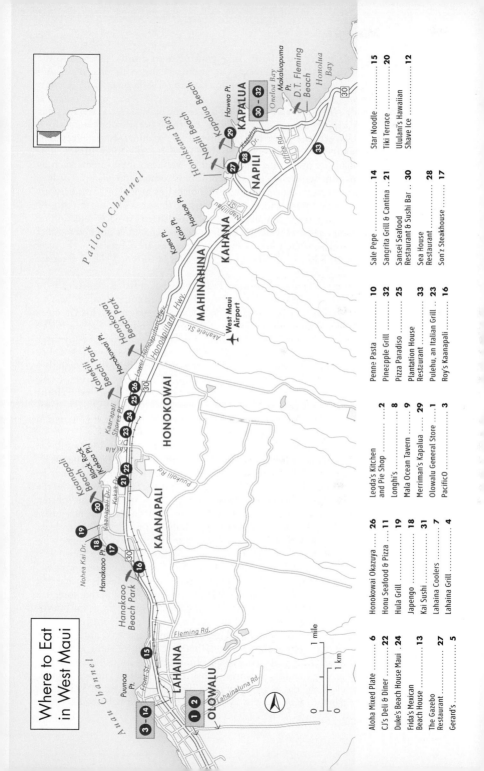

Where to Eat in West Maui

the restaurant's own farm. Take your plate to a table so close to the ocean you just might get wet. Oh, and don't forget the mai tai! [$] *Average main: $10* ✉ *1285 Front St., Lahaina* ☎ *808/661–3322* 🌐 *www.alohamixedplate.com.*

$$$ MEXICAN FUSION 🍴 **Frida's Mexican Beach House.** No matter the cuisine, serial restaurateur Mark Ellman always delivers. This, his third oceanfront eatery along Front Street (the other two are literally next door), is no exception. The setting is reason enough to dine here, but the food attracts diners all on its own. You'll find familiar Mexican menu items such as huevos rancheros and chiles rellenos, plus some Latin-inspired dishes, but adventurous diners who try such dishes as grilled Spanish octopus are rewarded with exotic and surprising flavors. The more than 40 varieties of tequila dominate the bar, and there's a wide selection of cocktails, beer, and wine. An open-floor dining area is situated parallel to the ocean, which means every seat scores an ocean view. [$] *Average main: $34* ✉ *1287 Front St., Lahaina* ☎ *808/661–1278* 🌐 *www.fridasmaui.com.*

$$$$ FRENCH Fodor's Choice ★ 🍴 **Gerard's.** Classically trained French chef Gerard Reversade, who started as an apprentice in acclaimed Paris restaurants when he was just 14, has for more than three decades remained true to his Gascony roots. His exacting standards—in the dining room as well as in the kitchen—have always been the hallmarks of his charming eponymous restaurant. He cooks *his* way, utilizing island ingredients in such dishes as escargots *forestière* (with garlic and mushrooms), chilled cucumber soup, and the ahi tartare with taro chips. The wine list is first-class, and the dessert list is extensive. Floral fabrics and white tablecloths evoke a French country inn. The service here is impeccable. [$] *Average main: $45* ✉ *The Plantation Inn, 174 Lahainaluna Rd., Lahaina* ☎ *808/661–8939* 🌐 *www.gerardsmaui.com* 🕒 *No lunch.*

$$$$ ECLECTIC 🍴 **Honu Seafood & Pizza.** Celebrity chef Mark Ellman and Judy Ellman have introduced another excellent restaurant to the Maui dining scene. This oceanfront fish house and pizza restaurant is right next door to their popular Mala Ocean Tavern. Much of the seafood comes from the East Coast and Pacific Northwest: clams, crabs, mussels, and lobster. The pizzas are cooked in a wood-fired brick oven (is there any other way?). The wine and cocktail lists are fabulous. Judy designed the sleek, bright interior with white walls, abundant use of wood, and large windows showcasing an unparalleled ocean view. [$] *Average main: $36* ✉ *1295 Front St., Lahaina* ☎ *808/667–9390* 🌐 *www.honumaui.com.*

$$ AMERICAN 🍴 **Lahaina Coolers.** It's been a popular, casual spot with locals since it first opened—several owners ago—in 1989, and to be around that long, it's got to be doing something right. You can get everything from huevos rancheros to local-style fried rice at breakfast; plate lunches, salads, wraps, and more for lunch; and fresh fish, chicken, steak, and pasta for dinner. If that's not enough for you, there are separate pizza, pupu, and bar menus. In the truest sense of the phrase, there's something for everyone. Since this restaurant buys its fish from Lahaina Harbor anglers, the catch of the day is always a good bet. [$] *Average main: $23* ✉ *180 Dickenson St., Lahaina* ☎ *808/661–7082* 🌐 *www.lahainacoolers.com.*

$$$$ AMERICAN 🍴 **Lahaina Grill.** At the top of many "best restaurants" lists, this expensive, upscale bistro is about as fashionably chic as it gets on Maui. The food and service are consistently excellent and the place is abuzz with beautiful people every night of the week. The Cake Walk (servings of Kona lobster crab cake, sweet Louisiana rock-shrimp cake, and seared ahi cake), toy-box tomato salad, and Kona-coffee-roasted rack of lamb are a few of the classics customers demand. Newer items include Marcho Farms center-cut all-natural veal osso bucco and seared lion-paw scallops. The full menu—including dessert—is available at the bar. The interior is as pretty as the patrons. [$] *Average main: $45* ✉ *127 Lahainaluna Rd., Lahaina* ☎ *808/667–5117* 🌐 *www.lahainagrill.com* 🕒 *No lunch.*

$$$ ITALIAN 🍴 **Longhi's.** A Lahaina landmark created by Bob Longhi ("a man who loves to eat") Longhi's has been serving pasta and other Italian fare to throngs of visitors since 1976. Although Bob's children run the restaurants now, his influence is still strong. Many of the classic dishes on the menu are his: prawns Venice, steak Longhi, and the signature lobster Longhi for two. The wine list is award-winning and gigantic. There are two spacious, open-air dining levels. Breakfast pastries are made in-house. **■TIP→ Before the rest of Lahaina (or Wailea) wakes up, have yourself a cup of freshly squeezed orange juice and some good, strong coffee to start the day.** There's a second Maui restaurant at The Shops at Wailea. [$] *Average main: $34* ✉ *888 Front St., Lahaina* ☎ *808/667–2288* 🌐 *www.longhis.com.*

$$$ MODERN HAWAIIAN Fodor's Choice ★ 🍴 **Mala Ocean Tavern.** Chef-owner Mark Ellman started Maui's culinary revolution of the late '80s with his restaurant Avalon, and Mala is a more than satisfactory successor. The place is adorable; the best tables are on the lanai, which actually juts out over the water. The menu reflects Mark's and his wife Judy's world travels with dishes influenced by the Middle East, the Mediterranean, Italy, Bali, and Thailand. Every item on the menu is delicious, and there's a focus on ingredients that promote local sustainability. The cocktails and wine list are great, too. Another location of Mala is at the Wailea Beach Marriott Resort, but the Lahaina original is highly recommended. [$] *Average main: $30* ✉ *1307 Front St., Lahaina* ☎ *808/667–9394* 🌐 *www.malaoceantavern.com.*

$$$$ MODERN HAWAIIAN 🍴 **Pacific'O.** Sophisticated outdoor dining on the beach (yes, truly *on* the beach) and creative Island cuisine using local, fresh-caught fish and greens and veggies grown in the restaurant's own Upcountry Oo Farm (and, quite possibly, picked that very morning)—this is the Maui dining experience you've been dreaming about. Start with the award-winning appetizer of prawn and basil wontons, move on to any of the fantastic fresh fish dishes, and for dessert, finish with the banana pineapple *lumpia* served hot with homemade ice cream. [$] *Average main: $38* ✉ *505 Front St., Lahaina* ☎ *808/667–4341* 🌐 *www.pacificomaui.com.*

$ ITALIAN 🍴 **Penne Pasta.** A couple of blocks off Front Street in Lahaina, this small restaurant packs a powerhouse of a menu with pizza, pastas, salads, and sandwiches. Heaping plates of reasonably priced, flavorful food make this low-key place a perfect alternative to an expensive night at the resort. House favorites include the cheesy baked penne in tomato cream sauce, and the linguine in clam sauce with lemon butter. There are nightly specials like the osso buco on Wednesday, made with lamb instead of veal and served with fettuccine and salad. Two can easily split a salad and entrée and leave completely sated. [$] *Average main: $12* ✉ *180 Dickenson St., Lahaina* ☎ *808/661–6633.*

$$ ITALIAN 🍴 **Sale Pepe.** Aromas from a wood-fired oven lure you into this cozy Italian restaurant set just off of Front Street, and the extensive wine list tempts you to stay awhile. Quality is paramount here, and it's clear that no shortcuts are taken. Proof: the flour, mozzarella, San Marzano tomatoes, and olive oil are imported directly from Italy, and the chef-owner Michele Bari (also from Italy) honed his skills at the prestigious Scuola Italiana Pizzaioli (International School of Pizza) in Venice. Favorites include the salumi plate served with house-made foccacia, the creamy risotto with pomodoro sauce and the kale and sausage pasta. The desserts change regularly—if you're lucky, the addictive tiramisù will be on the menu. [$] *Average main: $22* ✉ *878 Front St., Units 7 and 8, Lahaina* ☎ *808/667–7667* 🌐 *www.salepepemaui.com.*

$$ ASIAN Fodor's Choice ★ 🍴 **Star Noodle.** In the very short time since it opened this wonderful spot has become one of Maui's best restaurants. It's way up above the highway in a light industrial park, but don't be discouraged by the location. Take the drive, so you can discover a hip place and a welcoming staff who know the meaning of "aloha." There's a communal table in the center of the room, smaller tables around the perimeter, and tall chairs for those who like to eat at a bar. Menu-musts include the Ahi Avo, pan-roasted brussels sprouts with bacon and kimchi purée, and any of the noodle dishes, especially the Lahaina fried soup (fat chow fun, pork, bean sprouts). The cocktail list is fabulous and the Stargarita—a citrus-spiked take on a margarita—earns its "star" moniker. [$] *Average main: $18* ✉ *286 Kupuohi St., Lahaina* ☎ *808/667–5400* 🌐 *www.starnoodle.com.*

$ CAFÉ Fodor's Choice ★ 🍴 **Ululani's Hawaiian Shave Ice.** Nothing says you've arrived in Hawaii like a mound of fluffy ice drenched in rainbow-color syrups. Ululani's has upgraded this simple treat to gourmet proportions, with superfine ice shavings and homemade syrups in exotic flavors. Local favorites include guava, *li hing mui* (which is a savory-sweet plum flavor), and mango—though not necessarily as a combo. Fun add-ons like sweet adzuki beans and mochi balls complete the frosty experience. Expect long lines on most days. When you do make it to the counter, friendly service is just about guaranteed. The original location is in Lahaina (there are two now, both on Front Street), but there are also branches in Kihei, Wailuku, Kahului, and at the Hyatt Regency Maui in Kaanapali so satisfying that sweet tooth is a short drive away from wherever you are. [$] *Average main: $5* ✉ *819 Front St., Lahaina* ☎ 🌐 *www.ululanisshaveice.com.*

KAANAPALI AND HONOKAWAI

KAANAPALI

$ AMERICAN 🍴 **CJ's Deli & Diner.** Chef Christian Jorgensen left fancy hotel kitchens behind to open a casual place serving simple, delicious food at reasonable prices. The mango-glazed ribs, burgers, and classic reuben sandwich are all good choices, and the pineapple fried rice is *ono* (delicious); just order and pick up at the counter, and take your food to a table. If you're traveling to Hana or the Haleakala crater, buy a box lunch and you're set. If you're staying in a condo, the "Chefs to Go" service is a great alternative to picking up fast food (run-of-the-mill and usually lousy). Everything is prepped and comes with easy cooking instructions. And if you decide, even on the spur of the moment, that Maui is a nice place for a wedding, CJ's can cater it. $ *Average main: $12* ✉ *Fairway Shops, 2580 Kekaa Dr., Kaanapali* ☎ *808/667–0968* ⊕ *www.cjsmaui.com.*

$$$
MODERN
HAWAIIAN

✗ **Duke's Beach House Maui.** The spot's the thing—the view is amazing—at this casual eatery just steps from the beach on the grounds of the Honua Kai Resort & Spa. The food is reliable, the style all surfer-dudes and little grass shacks, and the signature cocktails big and pineapple-garnished. The fresh fish is a good bet, and you'll know from the aroma when you enter that there are burgers on the grill. Kimo's original hula pie is reason enough to come. You can buy the cool retro plate on which it's served for $20. $ *Average main: $28* ✉ *Honua Kai Resort & Spa, 130 Kai Malina Pkwy., Kaanapali* ☎ *808/662–2900* ⊕ *www. dukesmaui.com.*

4

$$$
MODERN
HAWAIIAN
FAMILY

✗ **Hula Grill.** A bustling and family-oriented spot on Kaanapali Beach at Whalers Village shopping center, this restaurant designed to look like a sprawling '30s beach house represents a partnership between TS Restaurants group and Hawaii Regional Cuisine pioneer chef Peter Merriman. It serves large dinner portions with an emphasis on fresh local fish—try the macadamia-nut crusted catch, fire-grilled ahi steak, or coconut seafood chowder. Just in the mood for an umbrella-adorned cocktail and some pupu? Go to the Barefoot Bar, where you can wiggle your toes in the sand while you sip. The beach is nicknamed "Dig Me"—you'll understand why after just a few moments. $ *Average main: $29* ✉ *Whalers Village, 2435 Kaanapali Pkwy., Kaanapali* ☎ *808/667–6636* ⊕ *www.hulagrillkaanapali.com.*

$$$$
ASIAN

✗ **Japengo.** This nicely appointed open-air restaurant gives hotel dining a better name. The ocean views are stunning, and the gentle trade winds cool the night air. The glassed-in sushi bar is gorgeous. But it's the food that makes Japengo worth a visit. The award-winning sashimi-style hamachi and watermelon is delicious, while the fresh local fish is well prepared and perfectly accompanied. Many dishes are offered in half-portions at half-price, the better to taste more of the creative menu. Perhaps most surprising are the desserts, which are crazy good. Even if dessert translates for you to "chocolate," the flaming piña colada crème here will change your mind forever. $ *Average main: $38* ✉ *Hyatt Regency Maui Resort & Spa, 200 Nohea Kai Dr., Kaanapali* ☎ *808/667–4909* ⊕ *www.japengomaui.com* ☽ *No lunch.*

$$$
ITALIAN

✗ **Pulehu, an Italian Grill.** This restaurant proves that good food doesn't need to be complicated, using many local Maui products to do what the Italians do best: craft simple, delicious food that lets the ingredients shine. Must-haves include the ahi carpaccio, seared scallops with smoked pork belly, and the deconstructed tiramisu. The wine list is excellent. In addition to the great food and drink, the service is stellar and the glassed-in exhibition kitchen provides an eyeful of culinary entertainment. $ *Average main: $32* ✉ *The Westin Kaanapali Ocean Resort Villas, 6 Kai Ala Dr., Kaanapali* ☎ *808/667–3254* ⊕ *www. pulehurestaurantmaui.com* ☽ *Closed Tues. and Wed.*

$$$$ MODERN HAWAIIAN Fodor's Choice ★

🍴 **Roy's Kaanapali.** Roy Yamaguchi is a James Beard Award–winning chef and the granddaddy of East-meets-West cuisine. He has restaurants all over the world, but his eponymous Maui restaurant was one of the first, and it's still one of the best. It's loud and brassy with a young vibe, but even if the atmosphere isn't quite your thing, come for the food. Signatures like fire-grilled, Szechuan-spiced baby back pork ribs, Roy's original blackened ahi tuna, hibachi-style grilled salmon, and the to-die-for hot chocolate soufflé have been on the menu from the beginning, and with good reason. Roy's wine list is exceptionally user-friendly. The service here is welcoming and professional. [$] *Average main: $36* ✉ *2990 Kaanapali Pkwy., Kaanapali* ☎ *808/669–6999* 🌐 *www.roysrestaurant.com.*

$$$ MEXICAN

🍴 **Sangrita Grill & Cantina.** The menu categories at Sangrita may be familiar, but the authentic ingredients and deep flavors are new. The guacamoles and salsas—all house-made from scratch—come with a bottomless basket of corn and flour chips. The carnitas braised in duck fat are stellar, and the avocado fries with cilantro pesto aïoli are addictive accompaniments. Seafood fanatics will love the chipotle-steamed mussles and octopus carpaccio. Save room for the unique flan for dessert. The cocktails prominently feature tequila and mezcal, and the wine list is affordable. The partially painted wooden tables and chairs are intriguing, and the service is delightful. [$] *Average main: $30* ✉ *Fairway Shops, 2580 Kekaa Dr., Kaanapali* ☎ *808/662–6000* 🌐 *www.sangritagrill.com.*

$$$$ STEAKHOUSE

🍴 **Son'z Steakhouse.** If you're celebrating a special occasion and want to splurge, this just might be the place for you. You'll descend a grand staircase into an amber-lighted dining room with soaring ceilings and a massive artificial lagoon complete with swans, ducks, waterfalls, and tropical gardens. Chef Geno Sarmiento's classic steakhouse menu features favorites like the bone-in ribeye and prime New York strip, and gigantic à la carte options big enough for two. Lighter appetites can choose from several chicken and fish dishes, including the must-try blackened ahi starter. The restaurant claims one of the largest wine cellars in Hawaii, with 1,500 bottles. [$] *Average main: $40* ✉ *Hyatt Regency Maui, 200 Nohea Kai Dr., Kaanapali* ☎ *808/667–4506* 🌐 *www.sonzrestaurant.com* 🕒 *No lunch.*

$$ MODERN HAWAIIAN

🍴 **Tiki Terrace.** Executive chef Tom Muromoto is a local boy who loves to cook modern, upscale Hawaiian food. He augments the various fresh fish dishes on his menu with items influenced by Hawaii's ethnic mix. This casual, open-air restaurant is the only place on Maui—maybe in Hawaii—where you can have a Native Hawaiian combination plate that is as healthful as it is authentic. Sunday brunch, complete with strolling Hawaiian musicians and hula dancers, is renowned here; and if you're around for any holiday, chow down at the amazing holiday brunch buffets. [$] *Average main: $26* ✉ *Kaanapali Beach Hotel, 2525 Kaanapali Pkwy., Kaanapali* ☎ *808/667–0124* 🌐 *www.kbhmaui.com* 🕒 *No lunch.*

HONOKAWAI

$ ✕ **Honokowai Okazuya.** Sandwiched between a dive shop and a salon
ECLECTIC in a nondescript mini strip mall, this small place has only a few stools
and a couple of tables outside, but it's fast and the food is consistently
good—all it takes to keep the place filled with locals. The beef black
bean chow fun and the mahimahi with lemon capers are the top-selling
favorites. There's plenty more, including vegetarian and lighter fare such
as Grandma's spicy tofu, egg fu yung, and even a veggie burger. This
isn't a good option for a late lunch, because it's closed 2:30–4:30. $ *Average main: $12 ✉ 3600-D Lower Honoapiilani Hwy., Honokowai
☎ 808/665–0512 ▭ No credit cards ⊗ Closed Sun.*

$ ✕ **Pizza Paradiso.** When it opened in 1995, this was an over-the-counter
ITALIAN pizza place. It has evolved over the years into a local favorite, serving
Italian, Mediterranean, and Middle Eastern comfort food as well as
pizza. The pies are so popular because of the top ingredients—100%
pure Italian olive oil and Maui produce whenever possible. The menu
also features gyros, falafel, grilled fish, rôtisserie chicken, and tiramisù.
$ *Average main: $14 ✉ Honokowai Marketplace, 3350 Lower Honoapiilani Rd., Honokowai ☎ 808/667–2929 ⊕ www.pizzaparadiso.com.*

KAPALUA AND NEARBY

NAPILI

$ ✕ **The Gazebo Restaurant.** Breakfast is the reason to seek out this res-
DINER taurant located poolside at the Napili Shores Resort. The ambience is
a little funky but the oceanfront setting and views are spectacular—
including the turtle, spinner dolphin, and, in winter, humpback-whale
sightings. The food is standard diner fare and portions are big. Many
folks think the Gazebo serves the best pancakes in West Maui. Have
them with pineapple, bananas, macadamia nuts, or white chocolate
chips, or make up your own combination. You will almost certainly
have to wait for a table, sometimes for quite a while, but at least it's a
pleasant place to do so. $ *Average main: $11 ✉ Napili Shores Maui,
5315 Lower Honoapiilani Hwy., Napili ☎ 808/669–5621 ⊗ No dinner.*

$$$ ✕ **Sea House Restaurant.** Built in the 1960s at the Napili Kai Beach
SEAFOOD Resort, before there were laws forbidding construction so close to the
beach, this restaurant is literally footsteps away from gorgeous Napili
Bay. Wear your beach wrap to breakfast and enjoy the signature oven-
baked pancakes or Molokai sweet potato egg frittata. For dinner, start
with the award-winning *poke* (raw fish) nachos and move on to spice-
crusted ahi. The menu also offers other fish from Hawaiian waters and
fresh local produce. Portions are generous. Folks who are gluten-free
will find excellent choices here. $ *Average main: $32 ✉ Napili Kai
Beach Resort, 5900 Lower Honoapiilani Rd., Napili ☎ 808/669–1500
⊕ www.seahousemaui.com.*

KAPALUA

$$$ ✕ **Kai Sushi.** For a quiet, light dinner, or to meet friends for a cock-
JAPANESE tail and some ultrafresh sushi, head to this handsome restaurant on
the lobby level of the Ritz-Carlton, Kapalua. You have your choice of
sushi, sashimi, and a list of rolls. The especially good Kai special roll

4

combines spicy tuna, yellowtail, and green onion. In keeping with the hotel's commitment to the culture, the restaurant's design was inspired by the story of Native Hawaiians' arrival by sea; the hand-carved ceiling beams resemble outrigger canoes. $ *Average main: $30* ⊠ *The Ritz-Carlton, Kapalua, 1 Ritz-Carlton Dr., Kapalua* ☎ *808/669–6200* ⊕ *www.ritzcarlton.com/kapalua* ⊗ *Closed Tues. and Wed. No lunch.*

$$$$
MODERN
HAWAIIAN
Fodor'sChoice
★

✕ **Merriman's Kapalua.** Perched above the postcard-perfect Kapalua Bay, this is the place to impress your date. An opulent dining area sets the mood for an equally lavish meal. Chef Peter Merriman highlights the islands' bounty, using fresh seafood and ingredients from local farms. With so many tempting creations, consider the duo option, which features two smaller-size entrées on one plate. You can't go wrong with the macadamia nut–crusted monchong or the roasted Jidori chicken. Gluten-free diners will be impressed with the selection as well. Save room for the toasted coconut crème brûlèe, then complete the experience at the restaurant's oceanfront lounge and fire pit. $ *Average main: $40* ⊠ *One Bay Club Pl., Kapalua* ☎ *808/669–6400* ⊗ *No lunch* ⚑ *Reservations essential.*

$$$$
MODERN
HAWAIIAN

✕ **Pineapple Grill.** High on the hill overlooking the Kapalua resort, this casual restaurant offers ocean, mountain, and resort views. The kitchen crew makes good use of the island's bounty, with dishes featuring greens and vegetables from Waipoli and Nalo farms, locally and sustainably caught fish, Maui pineapple, and Roselani ice cream. Menu item descriptions detail where almost every ingredient is sourced. $ *Average main: $38* ⊠ *200 Kapalua Dr., Kapalua* ☎ *808/669–9600* ⊕ *www.cohnrestaurants.com.*

$$$$
MODERN
HAWAIIAN

✕ **Plantation House Restaurant.** It's a bit of a drive, but when you get there you'll find a beautiful and comfortable restaurant with expansive views of the ocean below and the majestic mountains above. Chef JoJo Vasquez, who is known for local sourcing of as many ingredients as possible, calls his cuisine "Hawaiian Eclectic." $ *Average main: $40* ⊠ *Plantation Course Clubhouse, 2000 Plantation Club Dr., Kapalua* ☎ *808/669–6299* ⊕ *www.theplantationhouse.com.*

$$
ASIAN
Fodor'sChoice
★

✕ **Sansei Seafood Restaurant & Sushi Bar.** If you are a fish or shellfish lover, then this is the place for you. One of the most wildly popular restaurants in Hawaii with locations on three islands, Sansei takes sushi, sashimi, and contemporary Japanese food to a new level. Favorite dishes include the mango-and-crab-salad handroll, panko-crusted-ahi sashimi roll, Asian shrimp cake, Japanese calamari salad, and Dungeness crab ramen with Asian-truffle broth. There are great deals on sushi and small plates for early birds and night owls. This busy restaurant has several separate dining areas, a sushi bar, and a bar area, but the focus is squarely on excellent food and not the ambience. There's another branch in Kihei Town Center (*1881 S. Kihei Rd.; 808/879–0004*). $ *Average main: $26* ⊠ *600 Office Rd., Kapalua* ☎ *808/669–6286* ⊕ *www.sanseihawaii.com* ⊗ *No lunch.*

SOUTH SHORE

South Maui's dining scene begins at Maalaea Harbor and wends its way through the beach towns of Kihei and Wailea. There are plenty of casual, relatively inexpensive eateries along the way—until you reach Wailea, where most of the dining is pricey. Some of it, fortunately, is worth it.

In addition to the restaurants listed in this section, you can find branches of Mala Ocean Tavern (here called Mala Wailea) and Longhi's in this area; for reviews of these establishments, see the West Maui section.

4

KIHEI AND NORTH (MAALAEA)

KIHEI

$$$ ECLECTIC

🍴 **Cuatro.** Chef-owner Eric Arbogast has admirably turned this tiny space tucked into a corner of a strip mall into a comfortable restaurant serving well-prepared, delicious food. Signature dishes include spicy tuna nachos, Togarashi seared ahi, fresh local fish (prepared nightly in at least four different ways), Asian-style marinated grilled steak, and South of the Border–style marinated pork. The wine list is user-friendly, and the service is welcoming. [$] *Average main: $27* ✉ *Kihei Town Center, 1881 S. Kihei Rd., Kihei* ☎ *808/879–1110* 🌐 *www.cuatro808.com* 🕒 *No lunch.*

$ AMERICAN Fodor's Choice ★

🍴 **Kihei Caffe.** This small, unassuming place across the street from Kalama Beach Park has a breakfast menu that runs the gamut from healthy yogurt-filled papaya to the local classic, *loco moco*—two eggs, ground beef patty, rice, and brown gravy—and everything in between. And the best thing about it is that the breakfast menu is served all day long. Prices are extremely reasonable and it's a good spot for people-watching. This is a popular place with locals, so you may have to wait for a table, depending on the time and day. [$] *Average main: $8* ✉ *1945 S. Kihei Rd., Kihei* ☎ *808/879–2230* 🌐 *www.kiheicaffe.com* 🕒 *No dinner.*

$$ INDIAN

🍴 **Monsoon India.** Here you can enjoy a lovely ocean view while feasting on authentic Indian cuisine. Appetizers like *papadum* chips and samosas are served with homemade chutneys. There are 10 breads—naan and more—that come hot from the tandoori oven, along with six mix-and-match curries, lots of vegetarian selections, kebabs, and biryanis. There's live music on Friday and Saturday evenings and a popular Sunday brunch buffet. [$] *Average main: $20* ✉ *Menehune Shores, 760 S. Kihei Rd., Kihei* ☎ *808/875–6666* 🌐 *www.monsoonindiamaui.com* 🕒 *No lunch Mon. and Tues.*

$$ MEXICAN

🍴 **Roasted Chiles.** This family-run restaurant serves authentic flavors from Mexico City and other regions of Mexico. In fact, just about everything in the place has been brought directly from Mexico, including the furniture, paintings, and artisanal plates hanging on the walls. All menu items—from the chips and salsa to the margarita mix—are made in-house, and the food is fresh and full of flavor. Try Grandma's classic chicken mole recipe, which packs more than 25 ingredients, or the creamy langostino enchiladas. If you can restrain yourself, save room for dessert—there's a small but savory dessert menu. Like any good Mexican restaurant, the bar is stocked with 40-plus tequila options. $ *Average main: $18* ⊠ *1279 S. Kihei Rd., Suite 122, Kihei* ☎ *808/868–4357.*

$$$$
ITALIAN
✕ **Sarento's on the Beach.** This upscale Italian restaurant's setting right on spectacular Keawakapu Beach, with views of Molokini and Kahoolawe, is irresistible. After years of serving dinner only, it now offers breakfast service, so diners can enjoy the extraordinary view in the morning too. The breakfast menu offers all the regular fare; dinner has a decidedly Italian bent, with dishes like penne alla vodka, spaghetti with Kobe meatballs, and osso buco. The food is very good if a bit old-fashioned, and the portions are quite large. $ *Average main: $38* ⊠ *2980 S. Kihei Rd., Kihei* ☎ *808/875–7555* ⊕ *www. sarentosonthebeach.com* ☺ *No lunch.*

$
AMERICAN
✕ **South Shore Tiki Lounge.** Come on, how can you come to Hawaii and *not* go to a tiki bar? And this one—tucked into Kihei Kalama Village—is consistently voted "Best Bar" (and "Best Pizza") by locals. During the day, sit on the shaded lanai to enjoy a burger, sandwich, or, better yet, one of those delicious specialty pizzas, crafted from scratch with sauces made from fresh roma tomatoes and Maui herbs. Seven nights a week, the tiny bar area lights up with a lively crowd, as DJs spin dance tunes under the glowing red eyes of the lounge's namesake tiki. And you can order food right up until 10 pm. $ *Average main: $15* ⊠ *Kihei Kalama Village, 1913-J S. Kihei Rd., Kihei* ☎ *808/874–6444* ⊕ *www. southshoretikilounge.com.*

$
THAI
✕ **Thailand Cuisine.** Fragrant tea and coconut-ginger chicken soup begin a satisfying meal at this excellent Thai restaurant, set unassumingly in the middle of a shopping mall. The care and expense that has gone into the interior—glittering Buddhist shrines, elaborate hardwood facades, fancy napkin folds, and matching blue china—also applies to the cuisine. Take an exotic journey with the fantastic pad thai, special house noodles, curries, and crispy fried chicken. Can't decide? Try the family dinners for two or four. The fried bananas with ice cream are wonderful. There's a second location in Kahului's Maui Mall, a perfect choice before or after a movie at the megaplex. $ *Average main: $15* ⊠ *Kukui Mall, 1819 S. Kihei Rd., Kihei* ☎ *808/875–0839* ⊕ *www. thailandcuisinemaui.net* ☺ *No lunch Sun.*

$$
ECLECTIC
✕ **Three's Bar & Grill.** The name of the restaurant comes from the three young chefs who met working at a Wailea restaurant, only to decide in 2010 to strike out on their own. Each has a distinctive style (Hawaiian, Southwestern, and Pacific Rim), but somehow it all works. The food is good, with a large selection of salads, burgers, and flatbreads for lunch; fresh fish and steaks are served at dinner. There's also a raw bar, sushi, ceviche, and poke. Their daily happy hour offers some killer deals. The space is as big as the menu with three separate dining areas, plus an outdoor patio. $ *Average main: $25* ⊠ *1945-G S. Kihei Rd., Kihei* ☎ *808/879–3133* ⊕ *www.threesbarandgrill.com.*

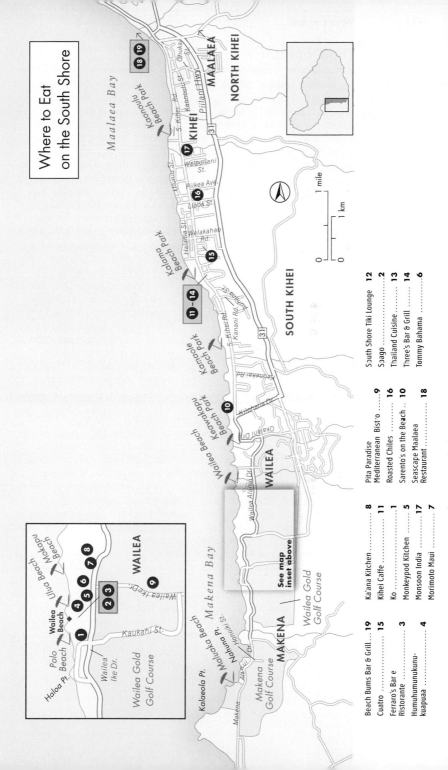

Where to Eat on the South Shore

Maalaea Bay

MAALAEA

NORTH KIHEI

KIHEI

Koonoulu
Beach Park

Waipuilani
St.

Piikea Ave.

Lipoa St.

Kalama
Beach Park

Welakahao
Rd.

Kamaole
Beach Park

SOUTH KIHEI

Wailea Beach

Keawakapu
Beach Park

WAILEA

Makena Bay

MAKENA

Wailea Gold
Golf Course

Makena
Golf Course

See map
inset above

1 mile
1 km

Polo Beach
Ulua Beach
Mokapu Beach
Wailea Beach

WAILEA

Wailea Ike Dr.

Kaukahi St.

Wailea
Ike Dr.

Wailea Gold
Golf Course

Kalaeola Pt.
Maluaka Beach
Nahuna Pt.

Beach Bums Bar & Grill ... **19**
Cuatro **15**
Ferraro's Bar e
Ristorante **3**
Humuhumunukunu-
kuapuaa **4**

Ka'ana Kitchen **8**
Kihei Caffe **11**
Ko **1**
Monkeypod Kitchen **5**
Monsoon India **17**
Morimoto Maui **7**

Pita Paradise
Mediterranean Bist'o **9**
Roasted Chiles **16**
Sarento's on the Beach .. **10**
Seascape Maalaea
Restaurant **18**

South Shore Tiki Lounge ... **12**
Sgago **2**
Thailand Cuisine **13**
Three's Bar & Grill **14**
Tommy Bahama **6**

CLOSE UP

The Plate Lunch Tradition

To experience island history firsthand, take a seat at one of Hawaii's ubiquitous "plate lunch" eateries, where you'll be served a segmented Styrofoam plate piled with a protein—usually in an Asian-style preparation, like beef teriyaki—two scoops of rice, a scoop of macaroni salad, and maybe a pickled vegetable condiment. On the sugar plantations, immigrant workers from many different countries ate together in the fields, sharing food from their *kaukau* tins, the utilitarian version of the Japanese *bento* (a divided box filled with savory items). From this stir-fry of people came the vibrant pidgin language and its equivalent in food: the plate lunch.

At beaches and public parks you will probably see locals eating plate lunches from nearby restaurants, stands, or trucks. Favorite combos include deep-fried chicken *katsu* (rolled in Japanese panko flour and spices), marinated beef teriyaki, and miso butterfish. *Saimin,* a noodle soup with Japanese fish stock and Chinese red-tinted barbecue pork, is a distinctly local medley. Koreans have contributed spicy barbecue *kalbi* ribs, often served with chili-laden kimchi (pickled cabbage or, sometimes, cucumber). Portuguese bean soup and tangy Filipino *pinakbet* (a mixed-vegetable dish with eggplant, okra, and bitter melons in fish sauce) are also favorites. The most popular contribution to this genre is the Hawaiian plate, featuring *laulau,* a mix of meat and fish and young taro leaves, wrapped in *ti* leaves and steamed, *kalua* pork and cabbage, *lomilomi* salmon, and chicken long rice, and *haupia* (coconut pudding) for dessert.

MAALAEA

$ AMERICAN

🍴 **Beach Bums Bar & Grill.** Its proximity to the harbor and a good surf spot means that this joint is always jumping, and the look is funky, beachy, and kitschy. There's a major cocktail list, and drinks are prepared by experienced, excellent bartenders. But the draw here is definitely the barbecue—ribs, chicken, and prime rib, all smoked on-site. Try the Tuesday night lobster fest or the Wednesday night ribs fest for big portions at low prices. The sweet-potato fries drizzled with honey are an obvious must. [$] *Average main: $16* ✉ *300 Maalaea Rd., Maalaea* ☎ *808/243–2286* 🌐 *www.beachbumshawaii.com.*

$ SEAFOOD FAMILY

🍴 **Seascape Maalaea Restaurant.** A good choice for a seafood lunch, the Maui Ocean Center's signature restaurant (aquarium admission is not required to dine here) offers harbor and ocean views from its open-air perch. The restaurant promotes heart-healthy cuisine, using sustainable seafood and trans fat–free items. Fresh fish entrée, lunch-size salads, sandwiches, burgers, fish tacos, teriyaki tofu, fish-and-chips, chicken, ribs, and a full kids' menu are on offer. There's something for everyone here, and the view isn't bad either. [$] *Average main: $15* ✉ *Maui Ocean Center, 192 Maalaea Rd., Maalaea* ☎ *808/270–7068* 🌐 *www.mauioceancenter.com* 🕒 *No dinner.*

WAILEA

$$$$ ITALIAN

🍴 **Ferraro's Bar e Ristorante.** Overlooking the ocean from a bluff above Wailea Beach, this outdoor Italian restaurant at Four Seasons Resort Maui at Wailea is beautiful both day and night. For lunch, indulge in a lobster sandwich or one of a variety of stone-baked pizzas. At dinner, try the Italian-inspired salads and a house-made pasta. Not surprisingly, the wine list includes excellent Italian choices. Live classical music often adds to the atmosphere, and occasionally you can spot celebrities at the bar. [$] *Average main: $40* ✉ *Four Seasons Resort Maui at Wailea, 3900 Wailea Alanui Dr., Wailea* ☎ *808/874–8000* 🌐 *www.fourseasons.com/maui/dining/restaurants/ferraros_bar_e_ristorante.*

$$$ MODERN HAWAIIAN

🍴 **Humuhumunukunukuapuaa.** Dinner here is accompanied nightly by heavenly sunsets. The Polynesian-style thatch-roof, open-air restaurant "floats" atop a saltwater lagoon. It's exotic, romantic, and well suited for special occasions. When you order, you don't have to wrestle with the restaurant's formidable name (it's Hawaii's state fish); simply tell the valet or concierge you're going to "Hoo-moo-hoo-moo." Obviously, fresh fish dominates the menu here, but there's also Niman Ranch angus, lamb, and even a vegetarian plate. Order the "Growing Future Farmers Salad"—$1 of each one sold goes to the Maui County Farm Bureau program of the same name. For dessert, try an over-the-top Humu pie. [$] *Average main: $35* ✉ *Grand Wailea, 3850 Wailea Alanui Dr., Wailea* ☎ *808/875–1234* 🌐 *www.grandwailea.com/dine/humuhumunukunukuapuaa* 🕒 *No lunch.*

$$$$ MODERN HAWAIIAN

Fodor's Choice ★

🍴 **Ka'ana Kitchen.** This signature restaurant at the island's most stylish luxury resort, Andaz Maui at Wailea, has it all. The farm-to-table menu is truly market-based, with most ingredients sourced within the Islands. The wine list is marvelous, the service is stellar, and the views are spectacular from every table thanks to the tiered layout. But wait, there's still more. The whole space has been masterfully designed—there are dining seats available at the cocktail bar and at strategic locations around the gorgeous exhibition kitchen "counters." Interaction is part of the experience: guests are encouraged to walk around to see what the cadre of cooks are up to and ask questions. It's better than a beautiful restaurant with creative and carefully prepared food—it's fun. [$] *Average main: $40* ✉ *Andaz Maui at Wailea, 3550 Wailea Alanui Dr., Wailea* ☎ *808/573–1234* 🌐 *www.maui.andaz.hyatt.com.*

$$$$ MODERN HAWAIIAN

🍴 **Ko.** The renovations took a long time (almost nine months) and cost a lot of money (more than $5 million), but the result is spectacular. While the setting is anything but humble, the menu at Ko—which means "sugarcane" in Hawaiian—features dishes from the many cultures of the plantation era, some of which are local family recipes. Executive Chef Tylun Pang adds modern, innovative twists to the Hawaiian, Chinese, Filipino, Portuguese, Korean, and Japanese dishes. The cocktail and wine lists arrive via iPad. Take note of the tabletops—glassware, cutlery, plates, bowls, serving pieces—as they are among the most handsome anywhere. [$] *Average main: $45* ✉ *Fairmont Kea Lani, 4100 Wailea Alanui, Wailea* ☎ *808/875–2210* 🌐 *www.fairmont.com/kea-lani-maui.*

4

$$ ✕**Monkeypod Kitchen.** The wooden surfboards hanging above the bar
ECLECTIC and surf videos playing in the background set a decidedly chill vibe at
this buzzing restaurant, the creation of local celebrity-chef Peter Merriman. He offers a menu that highlights local bounty, with such standout dishes as poke tacos, pumpkin ravioli, and fish-and-chips. Just about any of the wood-fired pizzas is a smart choice, particularly the Bourgeois topped with lobster, wild mushrooms, and garlic white sauce. Dine outside and watch the sun dip into the Pacific or pull up a seat at the expansive bar and sip on the popular Monkeypod mai tai—you're on island time now. $ *Average main: $25* ⊠ *10 Wailea Ike Dr., Wailea* ☏ *808/891–2322* ⊕ *www.monkeypodkitchen.com/wailea.*

$$$$ ✕**Morimoto Maui.** If you're a fan of Iron Chef and Iron Chef America,
MODERN ASIAN rejoice. Maui now has an outpost of Masaharu Morimoto's eponymous
Fodor's Choice restaurant. Located at the Andaz Maui resort, it's as hip as hip can be,
★ in every way. Outdoor tables, a bustling dining room, and a sushi bar all make it a lively choice. But the reason to go is for the food. There's a long sushi-sashimi menu, and the fish is the freshest. The tuna pizza is scrumptious; the fresh fish, steak, and lobster dishes are big enough to share. $ *Average main: $43* ⊠ *Andaz Maui at Wailea, 3550 Wailea Alanui Dr., Wailea* ☏ *808/243–4766* ⊕ *www.morimotomaui.com.*

$$ ✕**Pita Paradise Mediterranean Bistro.** The restaurant, with its warm decor
MEDITERRANEAN and friendly staff, set the tone for a relaxed dining experience. But it's
Fodor's Choice the food that's the main event here. The owner is a fisherman himself, so
★ you know the fish here is the freshest available. Lunch features affordable and delicious Greek-Mediterranean appetizers, fresh salads, and, of course, the signature pita sandwiches. The spicy falafel and Greek burgers are standouts. In the evening it's transformed into an Italian-Greek bistro with entrées like chicken fettuccine and moussaka. Save room for the award-winning baklava ice-cream cake—yes, that's right!—made with Maui's own Roselani Hawaiian vanilla-bean ice cream. $ *Average main: $20* ⊠ *Wailea Gateway Center, 34 Wailea Ike Dr., A-108, Wailea* ☏ *808/879–7177* ⊕ *www.pitaparadisehawaii.com.*

$$$$ ✕**Spago.** It's a marriage made in Hawaii heaven: the California cuisine
MODERN of celebrity-chef Wolfgang Puck combined with Maui flavors and served
HAWAIIAN lobby-level and oceanfront at the luxurious Four Seasons Resort. Try the spicy ahi tuna poke in sesame-miso cones to start and then see what the chefs-in-residence can do with some of Maui's fantastic local fish. It will cost you, but the service is spot-on, and the smooth, Asian-inspired interior allows the food to claim the spotlight. $ *Average main: $42* ⊠ *Four Seasons Resort Maui at Wailea, 3900 Wailea Alanui Dr., Wailea* ☏ *808/879–2999* ⊕ *www.wolfgangpuck.com* ☺ *No lunch.*

$$$ ✕**Tommy Bahama.** It's more "Island-style" than Hawaii—and yes, it's
MODERN a chain—but the food is consistently great, the service is filled with
AMERICAN aloha, and the ambience is Island refined. Try the ahi poke napoleon
Fodor's Choice (with capers, sesame, guacamole, and flatbread), the Kalua pork sand-
★ wich, any of the generous salads, or the local fish preparations. The crab bisque is worthy of a cross-island drive, as are the desserts. The cocktails are among the best and most creative on the Island. $ *Average main: $35* ⊠ *The Shops at Wailea, 3750 Wailea Alanui Dr., Wailea* ☏ *808/875–9983* ⊕ *www.tommybahama.com.*

SHAVE ICE AND ICE CREAM

The two most critical components in the making of the Islands' favorite frosty treat—shave ice—are the fineness of the shave and the quality of the syrup. The shave should be almost powdery, like snow. Top that ice with tropical flavors like mango, lilikoi, or guava. For a multipart taste sensation, start with a scoop of vanilla ice cream in the bottom (and maybe some Japanese adzuki beans), add shave ice and flavoring, and then top it with a drizzle of cream or a sprinkle of *li hing mui* powder for a salty-pungent kick. A great pick is **Ululani's Hawaiian Shave Ice** (🌐 *www.ululanishawaiianshaveice.com*), which makes "gourmet" shave ice and has locations all over Maui.

Prefer ice cream on its own? Maui's own Roselani has been made from scratch in Wailuku since 1932. Look for the brand's line of Tropics flavors, available at all Maui supermarkets. *Haupia* (coconut pudding) is the best-selling flavor. Some of the best ice-cream parlors are **Puukolii General Store & Ice Cream Shoppe at the Westin Kaanapali Ocean Resort Villas** (✉ 6 *Kai Ala Dr., Kaanapali* ☎ *808/667–3200*), **Royal Scoop** (✉ 2780 *Kekaa Dr., Kaanapali* ☎ *808/661–3611*), **Peggy Sue's** (✉ *1279 S. Kihei Rd., No. 303, Kihei* ☎ *808/875–8944*), and **Makawao Sushi & Deli** (✉ *3647 Baldwin Ave., Makawao* ☎ *808/573–9044*).

CENTRAL MAUI

Central Maui is where the locals live, and the area where you can find just about every ethnic cuisine in the Islands. Savory saimin shops and small joints dishing up *loco moco*—hamburger patties set on top of two scoops of rice with rich brown gravy—are plentiful. Be sure to check out Wailuku: drive along Lower Main Street, and take a chance on any of the numerous mom-and-pop eateries—it's truly a culinary adventure. If you walk along historic Market Street, you can shop for antiques between bites.

Kahului offers more variety, because it's in the main traffic corridor and near the big-box stores; on a few menus you can even find potatoes instead of rice. If you want to eat like a local and, more importantly, at local prices, don't miss Central Maui.

KAHULUI

$ ASIAN FUSION 🍴 **Aria's.** Dinner and lunch items are affordable and delicious at this Asian bistro. At lunch, try the flavor-packed *char siu bao* (barbecue-pork-filled bun) sliders and the gigantic crab club sandwich. Favorite dinner options include the Asian-braised pork belly and the vegetarian putanesca. Breakfast is equally tempting and is served only on the weekends. [$] *Average main: $16* ✉ *2062 W. Vineyard St., Wailuku* ☎ *808/242–2742* 🌐 *ariasmaui.com* 🕒 *No dinner Sun.* 💳 *No credit cards.*

$$ MEDITERRANEAN 🍴 **Bistro Casanova.** The location of this Mediterranean restaurant is smack-dab in the middle of Kahului, making it a convenient choice for lunch or dinner. The menu features everything from salads and crêpes

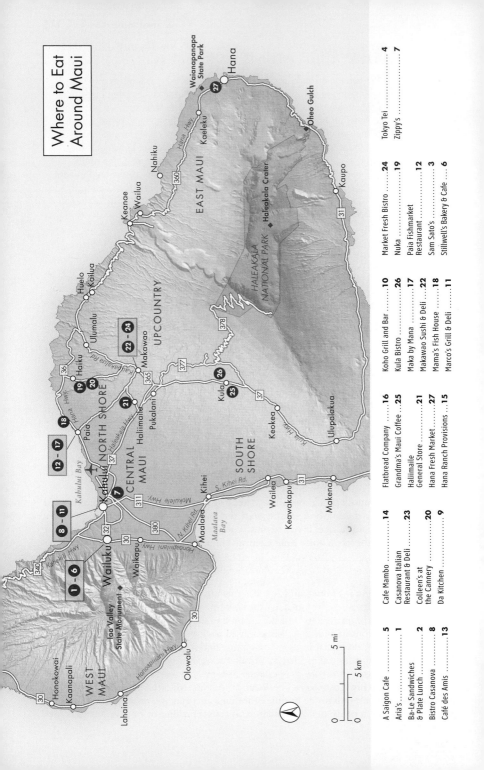

Where to Eat Around Maui

(both savory and sweet) to pastas and simple fish and meat preparations. A tapas menu (available after 3 pm) changes weekly and always has an excellent selection of dishes. If you're flying out on a red-eye, this is a perfect place for dinner before heading to the airport. $ *Average main: $26* ⊠ *33 Lono Ave., Kahului* ☎ *808/873–3650* ⊕ *www. bistrocasanova.com* ☾ *Closed Sun.*

$ ✕ **Da Kitchen.** This extremely popular purveyor of all food "local" is
ECLECTIC bright, shiny, comfortable, and able to accommodate at least 20 more
FAMILY hungry diners than before. But don't worry, the food is every bit as
Fodor'sChoice good as it's ever been. Try the signature mahimahi tempura, loco moco,
★ Hawaiian plate, chicken katsu, and daily mixed bentos; and rest assured that everything on the menu is delicious and portions are gigantic. The upbeat ambience is reflected in the service as well as the food. There's an "express" location in Kihei, but we recommend the happy, always-crowded Kahului location. $ *Average main: $14* ⊠ *425 Koloa St., Kahului* ☎ *808/871–7782* ⊕ *www.dakitchen.com* ☾ *Closed Sun.*

$ ✕ **Koho Grill and Bar.** If Hawaii had city-style diners, this would be Maui's
AMERICAN version. For those looking for a hearty breakfast, a business lunch, or a
FAMILY quick, simple dinner, this is a great choice. Burgers, sandwiches, salads, sizzling fajitas, and pastas are all menu staples. Year after year, Koho proves itself as a casual, family-friendly restaurant still worth recommending. $ *Average main: $12* ⊠ *Queen Kaahumanu Center, 275 W. Kaahumanu Ave., Kahului* ☎ *808/877–5588.*

$$ ✕ **Marco's Grill & Deli.** One of the go-to places for airport comers and
ITALIAN goers, this popular Italian restaurant also draws a steady crowd of local residents, mostly for "business" lunches. Meatballs, sausages, and sauces are all made in-house; the owner was a butcher in his former life. There's a long list of sandwiches that are available all day, and the salads are big enough to share. There are gluten-free options here, but note that substitutions or special requests are not recommended. $ *Average main: $18* ⊠ *444 Hana Hwy., Kahului* ☎ *808/877–4446.*

$ ✕ **Zippy's.** Hawaii's favorite casual, eat-in or takeout restaurant, Zippy's
ECLECTIC was founded more than 45 years ago. Today Oahu has more than two
FAMILY dozen locations from which to choose, and Maui waited a long time to get one. It's a diner-type place with a big menu and takeout is available 24 hours a day. Spaghetti with chili, oxtail soup, Korean chicken, chicken katsu, noodles, and burgers are just a few of the tasty menu options. Napoleon's Bakery counter up front serves its only-in-Hawaii-style turnovers, pies, cakes, and pastries, as well as made-to-order malasadas and andagi. $ *Average main: $10* ⊠ *15 Hookele St., Kahului* ☎ *808/856–7599* ⊕ *www.zippys.com.*

WAILUKU

$ ✕ **Ba-Le Sandwiches & Plate Lunch.** It began as a French-Vietnamese bakery
VIETNAMESE on Oahu and has branched into popular small restaurants sprinkled
Fodor'sChoice throughout the Islands. Some are kiosks in malls; others are stand-
★ alones with some picnic tables out front, as is the case at this location, which is one of four on Maui. Vietnamese *pho* (the famous soups laden with seafood or rare beef, fresh basil, bean sprouts, and lime) share menu space with local-style saimin and plates of barbecue or spicy

4

chicken, beef, pork, or local fish served with jasmine rice. The delicious sandwiches—*bánh mì* in Vietnamese—are perfect for lunch to stay or to go. There are a slew of tapioca flavors for dessert. $ *Average main: $9* ⊠ *1824 Oihana St., Wailuku* ☎ *808/249–8833* ⊕ *www.balemaui.com.*

$$ ╳ **A Saigon Cafe.** Locals have been flocking to this off-the-beaten path gem for years, lured in by the reliably delicious Vietnamese cuisine at decent prices. It's tucked behind a nondescript overpass, it doesn't have a website, and only recently did they put a sign on its building. The dishes are served family-style, and just about everything on the menu is a winner, but you can't go wrong with the green papaya salad, rice in a clay pot, and the make-your-own Vietnamese burritos. A recent renovation has freshened the place a bit, but the real reason to dine here is what's on the plate. $ *Average main: $19* ⊠ *1792 Main St., Wailuku* ☎ *808/243–9560* ▭ *No credit cards.*

VIETNAMESE

$ ╳ **Sam Sato's.** Every island has its noodle shrine, and this is Maui's. Dry mein, saimin, chow fun—they all come in different-size portions and with add-ins to satisfy every noodle craving. While you wait for your bowl, try a teriyaki beef stick or two. Save room for the popular turnovers (pineapple, coconut, apple, or peach) and traditional Japanese manju filled with either lima or adzuki beans. At busy times—which is almost always—you will likely have to wait for a table or a stool at the counter; write your name on the little yellow pad at the takeout window. $ *Average main: $8* ⊠ *The Millyard, 1750 Wili Pa Loop, Wailuku* ☎ *808/244–7124* ▭ *No credit cards* ⊘ *Closed Sun. No dinner.*

HAWAIIAN

Fodor's Choice

★

$ ╳ **Stillwell's Bakery & Cafe.** Roy Stillwell has been around Maui for a long time, and is unquestionably one of the best pastry chefs on the Island, so this is the place to come for coffee and an outrageously good macadamia-nut muffin or a renowned cream horn. At lunch time you'll rub elbows with local folks who work in the area; they come for the fresh sandwiches served, of course, on homemade breads (try the crab-cake sandwich), and for the Chinese chicken, tofu, and shrimp and crab salads. Be sure to order a macoco roll on the side. The desserts on display will surely make you drool—oh, go ahead, you're on vacation! And if you're celebrating a birthday (or any other special occasion) Roy is the guy you want to bake your cake. $ *Average main: $12* ⊠ *1740 Kaahumanu Ave., Wailuku* ☎ *808/243–2243* ⊕ *www.stillwellsbakery. com* ⊘ *No dinner.*

BAKERY

$ ╳ **Tokyo Tei.** Getting there is half—well, maybe a quarter—of the fun. Tucked in the back corner of a covered parking garage, Tokyo Tei is worth seeking out for wonderful local-style Japanese food. At lunch you can rub elbows with bankers and construction workers; at dinner, three generations might be celebrating *tutu's* (grandma's) birthday at the next table. This is a bona fide local institution where for more than six decades people have come for the food and the comfort of familiarity. Enjoy the freshest sashimi, feather-light yet crispy shrimp and vegetable tempura, and local-style bentos and plate lunches. $ *Average main: $12* ⊠ *1063 Lower Main St., Wailuku* ☎ *808/242–9630* ⊕ *www. tokyoteimaui.com* ⊘ *No lunch Sun.*

JAPANESE

Fodor's Choice

★

UPCOUNTRY

Take the drive up the slopes of magnificent Mt. Haleakala and you can find an abundance of restaurants catering to both locals and visitors. Haliimaile General Store is a landmark in the middle of rolling pineapple fields (Maui Gold Pineapple Company is still growing pineapple in this area), and in the *paniolo* (cowboy) town of Makawao you can sidle up to everything from an Italian restaurant to a farm-to-table standout. Upcountry also encompasses cool Kula, with a few mom-and-pops. Many visitors opt to check out nearby farm tours between meals.

$$$
ITALIAN

✕ **Casanova Italian Restaurant & Deli.** An authentic Italian dinner house and nightclub, this place is smack in the middle of Maui's paniolotown of Makawao. The brick wood-burning oven, imported from Italy, has been turning out perfect pies and steaming-hot focaccia for more than 20 years. You can pair a pie with a salad (they're all big enough to share) and a couple of glasses of wine without breaking the bank. The daytime deli is fabulous for breakfast, a cappuccino, croissants, and people-watching. The place turns positively raucous—in a good way—on Wednesday, Friday, and Saturday nights. $ *Average main:* $28 ✉ *1188 Makawao Ave., Makawao* ☎ *808/572–0220* ⊕ *www. casanovamaui.com.*

$
AMERICAN

✕ **Grandma's Maui Coffee.** If you're taking a drive through gorgeous Upcountry Maui, this is a great place to stop for a truly homegrown cup of coffee and a snack. All of the coffee is grown right on the slopes of Haleakala and roasted on the premises in a 100-year-old roaster proudly on display. The baked goods are fabulous—particularly the lemon bars—and the variety of menu items for breakfast and lunch is vast. Eggs, omelets, crêpes, and fantastic home fries are served for breakfast, while salads, sandwiches, lasagna, and more can be ordered at lunch. Enjoy your coffee and goodies on the lovely deck overlooking the central valley. $ *Average main:* $9 ✉ *9232 Kula Hwy., Kula* ☎ *808/878–2140* ⊕ *www.grandmascoffee.com.*

$$$$
MODERN
HAWAIIAN

✕ **Haliimaile General Store.** Chef-restaurateur Beverly Gannon's first restaurant remains a culinary destination after more than a quarter century. The big, rambling former plantation store has two dining rooms: sit in the front to be seen and heard; head on back for some quiet and privacy. Classic dishes like Bev's "Famous" Crab Pizza, Asian duck tostada, grilled rack of lamb, and many more are complemented with daily and nightly specials. To get here, take the exit on the left halfway up Haleakala Highway. $ *Average main:* $38 ✉ *900 Haliimaile Rd., Haliimaile* ☎ *808/572–2666* ⊕ *www.hgsmaui.com.*

$$
ITALIAN

✕ **Kula Bistro.** Dishing up home-style comfort food with an Italian accent, this out-of-the-way eatery is worth the drive to scenic Kula, no matter when you arrive. Start the day with their crab cake Benedict, grab any one of their outstanding panini around lunchtime, or come for dinner, when a dizzying array of choices await, including favorites such as vodka pomodoro with seafood, vegetable lasagna, and filet mignon. A spacious dining room and casual vibe make this place a great option for families and groups. $ *Average main:* $22 ✉ *4566 Lower Kula Rd., Kula* ☎ *808/871–2960* ⊕ *www.kulabistro.com* ▭ *No credit cards.*

4

$$ ECLECTIC 🍴 **Makawao Sushi & Deli.** It may seem an odd mix—sushi and deli—but this is a cute place on Makawao's main drag, where you can sip an espresso and snack on pastries, sandwiches, or any of the sushi rolls. The menu is much longer than you might expect, and the fish is always fresh. The most popular rolls are the 007, a spicy tuna roll topped with ebi, avocado, and unagi sauce, and the Rockin' Roll, a traditional California roll wrapped with tuna and covered with baked scallops. The baked mussels are divine and so is this place's version of ahi poke. [$] *Average main: $25* ✉ *3647 Baldwin Ave., Makawao* ☎ *808/573–9044.*

$$$ MODERN HAWAIIAN 🍴 **Market Fresh Bistro.** This hard-to-find restaurant tucked into a courtyard serves farm-to-table food prepared by chef Justin Pardo, formerly of Union Square Café in New York City. In addition to offering locally grown and produced ingredients, Pardo nods to healthful eating by using reductions and infused oils rather than butter. Representative dishes include the Upcountry vegetable salad and creative fresh fish preparations. Reservations are essential for the Thursday-night prix-fixe farm dinners, which are pricey. Lunch, however, is much less—around $12. Brunch is served on Sunday only. [$] *Average main: $75* ✉ *3620 Baldwin Ave., Makawao* ☎ *808/572–4877* 🌐 *www.marketfreshbistro.com* ⏲ *Closed Mon. No dinner Fri.–Wed.*

NORTH SHORE

The North Shore sets the dramatic stage for Maui's most famous—and most expensive—restaurant, Mama's Fish House in Kuau. The area also encompasses the great food town of Paia and the up-and-coming restaurant town of Haiku. Be sure to bring your bathing suit for a dip in the ocean at one of the nearby beaches.

HAIKU

$$ AMERICAN Fodor's Choice ★ 🍴 **Colleen's at the Cannery.** You'd never guess what's inside by the nondescript exterior and the location in an old pineapple cannery–cum–strip mall. Colleen's is one of the most overlooked restaurants on Maui. It's popular with locals for breakfast and lunch, but try it at dinner when the candles come out and it's time for martinis and fresh fish. The food is excellent, in particular the huge salads made with Upcountry's best produce, the fish specials, the burgers, and the simple roast chicken. When dining here, you'll feel like you're at a hip, urban eatery. [$] *Average main: $20* ✉ *Haiku Cannery Marketplace, 810 Haiku Rd., Haiku-Pauwela* ☎ *808/575–9211* 🌐 *www.colleensinhaiku.com.*

$$ ASIAN FUSION 🍴 **Nuka.** This off-the-beaten-path izakaya-style Japanese eatery is worth the trek to sleepy Haiku. The intimate restaurant is packed just about every night, and reservations aren't accepted, so it's a good idea to arrive early. Diners flock here for chef Hiro Takanashi's eclectic menu that includes everything from specialty French fries and fusion sushi rolls to fresh sashimi and some of the best tempura around. Ingredients are key, and the extensive menu and nightly specials take its cue from what's fresh from local farmers and fishermen. The homemade green tea and

black sesame ice cream flavors are too tempting to choose between—try a scoop of each. Ⓢ *Average main: $18* ✉ *780 Haiku Rd., Haiku-Pauwela* ☎ *808/575–2939* ⊕ *www.nukamaui.com* ⚞ *Reservations not accepted.*

KUAU

$$$$
SEAFOOD

✕ **Mama's Fish House.** For almost four decades, Mama's has been *the* Maui destination for special occasions. A path of gecko-shape stones leads through the coconut grove past the giant clamshell and under the banyan arch to an ever-changing fantasyland of Hawaiian kitsch. The setting couldn't be more spectacular, and the menu names the angler that reeled in your fresh catch. The savvy servers can explain the various fish types and preparations, and you'd be wise to heed their recommendation. Just be sure to save room for the deservedly famous Polynesian Black Pearl dessert. Ⓢ *Average main: $50* ✉ *799 Poho Pl., Kuau* ☎ *808/579–8488* ⊕ *www.mamasfishhouse.com.*

PAIA

$
ECLECTIC

✕ **Café des Amis.** The menu is a little neurotic—in a good way—featuring Mediterranean and Indian dishes, but the food is fresh and tasty. This budget-friendly café offers flavors and preparations not easily obtainable at other Island eateries, with a nice selection of sweet and savory crêpes, Indian wraps, and salads. Now, you can have a cocktail, wine, and beer, too. All in all, you get delicious, good-value food, as well as excellent people watching from the umbrella-shaded tables outside. Ⓢ *Average main: $16* ✉ *42 Baldwin Ave., Paia* ☎ *808/579–6323* ⊕ *www.cdamaui.com.*

$
ECLECTIC

✕ **Cafe Mambo.** Paia is one of Maui's most interesting food towns, and this Mediterranean-inspired joint is right in the thick of things. It's kind of frenetic in every way, from the menu to the style and the service. But the food is great and well priced, and the people-watching is fascinating. The husband and wife owners, from England and Spain respectively, decorated the place with Moroccan clay pieces; teak and coconut-wood tables are set in the middle of benches with Middle Eastern pillows. The menu goes all over the place, too, with all-American burgers, island fish, falafel and hummus, Spanish tapas, and paella. Ⓢ *Average main: $15* ✉ *30 Baldwin Ave., Paia* ☎ *808/579–8021* ⊕ *www.cafemambomaui.com.*

$$
PIZZA
FAMILY

✕ **Flatbread Company.** This Vermont-based company marched right in to Paia in 2007 and instantly became a popular restaurant and a valued addition to the community. As part of the company's mission, it started "giving back" to local nonprofits immediately. But it's not just good for its altruism; the food is fantastic. There's a big, primitive-looking, earthen, wood-fired oven from which emerge utterly delicious flatbread pizzas. The bustling restaurant uses organic, local, sustainable products, including 100% organically grown wheat for the made-fresh-daily dough. The place is a good spot to take the kids. There's a no-reservations policy, but there's "call-ahead seating," so you can put your name on the wait list before you arrive. Ⓢ *Average main: $22* ✉ *89 Hana Hwy., Paia* ☎ *808/579–8989* ⊕ *www.flatbreadcompany. com* ⚞ *Reservations not accepted.*

$$ ECLECTIC Fodor's Choice ★ 🍴 **Hana Ranch Provisions.** Modern farmhouse decor sets the tone for this chic eatery, a relative newcomer to Paia town. As its name suggests, the restaurant sources most ingredients from its ranch on Maui's rural east end. The eclectic rotating menu takes it cue from what's in season, but you'll always find made-from-scratch baked goods, house-smoked meats, and locally sourced organic produce. Can't decide? Simply close your eyes and point at the menu—yes, everything is that good. Make room for something from the inventive cocktail or dessert menus, which also changes depending on what's fresh. [$] *Average main: $19* ✉ *71 Baldwin Ave., Paia* ☎ *808/868–3688* 🌐 *www.hanaranchprovisions.com.*

$ VEGETARIAN 🍴 **Maka by Mana.** When the popular Mana Foods market opened this bright and airy restaurant a few blocks down the street, health-conscious foodies rejoiced. Dishing up raw and vegan food that's also gluten-free, their inventive offerings are tasty enough to tempt those who aren't accustomed to a plant-based diet. Try one of their fresh-squeezed juices or smoothies to start, plant your fork into one of their vibrant salads, or bite into one of their flavor-filled sandwiches. You'll want to save room for a slice of pie, which comes in flavors including lilikoi blueberry and raspberry mango. [$] *Average main: $12* ✉ *115 Baldwin Ave., Paia* ☎ *808/579–9125* 🌐 *www.makabymana.com.*

$ SEAFOOD Fodor's Choice ★ 🍴 **Paia Fishmarket Restaurant.** If you're okay with communal picnic tables, or taking your meal to a nearby beach, this place in funky Paia town serves, arguably, the best fresh fish for the best prices on this side of the island. Four preparations are offered and, on any given day, there are at least four fresh fishes from which to choose. For the non–fish fans, there are burgers, chicken, and pasta. The side dishes—Cajun rice, home fries, and the amazing hand-cut crunchy cole slaw—are all as delectable as the main event. You can have a beer or a glass of wine, too, as long as you stay inside, of course. There's a sister restaurant in Kihei. [$] *Average main: $15* ✉ *100 Hana Hwy., Paia* ☎ *808/579–8030* 🌐 *www.paiafishmarket.com.*

ROAD TO HANA

HANA

$ AMERICAN Fodor's Choice ★ 🍴 **Hana Fresh Market.** Directly in front of (and associated with) Hana Health, you'll find rows of tables laden with delicious and organic fresh salads and entrées worthy of any chic farm-to-table restaurant. Fresh fish plates, poke bowls, panini, and wraps are just a few of the always-changing choices. Early birds can enjoy made-to-order omelets and waffles, or sip on fresh fruit juices and smoothies. Best of all, the produce comes from the restaurant's own farm, directly behind the health center. If your accommodations include a kitchen, stock up here on bags of fresh veggies at incredibly reasonable prices. [$] *Average main: $10* ✉ *4590 Hana Hwy., Hana* ☎ *808/248–7515* 🌐 *www.hanafresh.org.*

WHERE TO STAY

Updated by
Christie Leon

Maui's accommodations run the gamut from rural bed-and-breakfasts to opulent megaresorts, and in between there's something for every vacation style and budget. The large resorts, hotels, and condominiums for which Maui is noted are on the sunny, leeward, southern, and western shores. They bustle with activity and are near plenty of restaurants, shopping, golf, and water sports. Those seeking a different experience can try the inns, B&Bs, and rentals in the small towns and quieter areas along the North Shore and Upcountry on the verdant slopes of Haleakala.

If the latest and greatest is your style, be prepared to spend a small fortune. Properties like the Ritz-Carlton, Kapalua; the Four Seasons Resort Maui at Wailea; the sparkling Andaz Maui at Wailea; and condo complexes such as the luxe Wailea Beach Villas may set you back at least $600 a night.

Although there aren't many of them, small B&Bs are charming. They tend to be in residential or rural neighborhoods around the island, sometimes beyond the resort areas of West Maui and the South Shore. The B&Bs offer both a personalized experience and a window into authentic local life. The rates tend to be the lowest available on Maui, sometimes less than $200 per night.

Apartment and condo rentals are ideal for families, groups of friends, and those traveling on modest budgets. Not only are the nightly rates lower than hotel rooms, but eating in—all have kitchens of some description—is substantially less expensive than dining out. There are literally hundreds of these units all over the island, ranging in size from studios to luxurious four-bedroom properties with multiple baths. The vast majority are found along the sunny coasts, from Makena to Kihei on the South Shore and Lahaina up to Kapalua in West Maui.

Rates depend on the size of the unit and its proximity to the beach, as well as the amenities and services offered. For about $250 a night, you can get a lovely one-bedroom apartment without many frills or flourishes, close to but probably not on the beach. Many rentals have minimum stays (usually three to five nights).

Most of Maui's resorts—several are megaresorts—have opulent gardens, fantasy swimming pools, championship golf courses, and full-service fitness centers and spas. Expect to spend at least $350 a night at the less posh resort hotels; they are all in the Wailea and Makena resort area on the South Shore and Kaanapali and Kapalua in West Maui. At all lodgings, ask about discounts and deals (free nights with longer stays, for example), which have proliferated.

MAUI LODGING PLANNER

PROPERTY TYPES

HOTELS AND RESORTS

Maui's resorts are clustered along the island's leeward (west and south) shores, so they offer near-perfect weather year-round. Kaanapali, in West Maui, has the most action. Kapalua, farther north, is more private and serene. Among the South Shore resort communities, posh Wailea has excellent beaches and golf courses. Most resorts charge parking and facility fees—a "resort fee." In Hawaii room prices can rise dramatically if a room has an ocean view. To save money, ask for a garden or mountain view.

CONDOS AND RENTALS

If you compromise on luxury, you can find convenient condos in West Maui in Napili, Honokowai, or Kahana, and on the South Shore in Kihei. Many are oceanfront and offer the amenities of a hotel without the cost, though central air-conditioning is rare. Be sure to ask about minimum stays. Besides the condos listed here, Maui has condos rented through central agents. They may represent an entire resort property, most of the units at one property, or even individually owned units. The companies listed here have a long history of excellent service to Maui visitors.

Contacts AA Oceanfront Rentals and Sales. ⊠ *1279 S. Kihei Rd., #107, Kihei* ☎ *808/879-7288, 800/488-6004* ⊕ *www.aaoceanfront.com.* **Bello Maui Vacations.** ⊠ *95 E. Lipoa, #201, Kihei* ☎ *808/879-3328, 800/541-3060* ⊕ *www. bellomaui.com.* **Chase 'n Rainbows.** ⊠ *118 Kupuohi St., Suite C6, Lahaina* ☎ *808/667-7088, 877/611-6022* ⊕ *www.westmauicondos.com.* **Destination Residences Hawaii.** ⊠ *34 Wailea Gateway Pl., Suite A102, Wailea* ☎ *808/891-6249, 800/367-5246* ⊕ *www.destinationresidenceshawaii.com.* **Maalaea Bay Realty and Rentals.** ⊠ *280 Hauoli St., Maalaea* ☎ *808/244-5627, 800/367-6084* ⊕ *www.maalaeabay.com.* **Maui Condo & Home Vacations.** ⊠ *1819 S. Kihei Rd., Suite D103, Kihei* ☎ *808/879-5445, 844/856-5841* ⊕ *www.mauicondo. com.* **Tropical Villa Vacations.** ⊠ *310 Ohukai Rd., Suite 304, Kihei* ☎ *808/875-2818, 888/875-2818* ⊕ *www.tropicalvillavacations.com.*

5

B&BS AND INNS

Maui County has updated its policies regarding the licensing of B&Bs and what are technically called TVRs (transient vacation rentals). New rules and permit policies have been enacted and, as of this writing, many new permits have been issued. In the past, glorious inns were lumped together—for the county's legal purposes—with what may have been nothing more than a bed set up in someone's garage. To avoid disappointment (some places have closed), the best advice is to ask whether the property is licensed by the county. You might even ask for the permit number, which should be posted on the property's website.

RESERVATIONS

The further in advance you book, the more likely you are to get the room you want. This is especially true at the big resort hotels December 20–April, and again during July and August, Maui's busiest times. For these times, booking a year in advance is not uncommon.

PRICES

There's no denying that Maui's lodging prices can be steep, but rates run the full range. Many hotels slash their rates significantly for promotions and web-only deals. Note that prices exclude 13.42% sales tax. *Hotel reviews have been shortened. For full information, visit Fodors.com.*

WHAT IT COSTS			
$	$$	$$$	$$$$
Hotels	under $181	$181–$260	$261–$340	over $340

Hotel prices are the lowest cost of a standard double room in high season. Prices for rentals are the lowest per-night cost for a one-bedroom unit in high season.

WEST MAUI

LAHAINA

Lahaina doesn't have a huge range of accommodations, but it does make a great headquarters for active families or those who want to avoid spending a bundle on resorts. One major advantage is the proximity of restaurants, shops, and activities—everything is within walking distance. It's a business district, however, and won't provide the same peace and quiet as resorts or secluded vacation rentals. Still, Lahaina has a nostalgic charm, especially early in the morning before the streets have filled with visitors and vendors.

$ **Best Western Pioneer Inn.** With some of the best prices around, this
HOTEL   small, heart-of-town hotel, built in 1901 when Lahaina was the bawdy heart of the Pacific's whaling industry, has been substantially remodeled and updated to offer clean and basic rooms. **Pros:** convenient location for the harbor, shops, and restaurants; children under 12 stay free; free parking and Wi-Fi. **Cons:** can be noisy, with Front Street on one side and the harbor on the other; two floors but no elevator; off-site parking. $ *Rooms from: $165 ⊠ 658 Wharf St., Lahaina ☎ 808/661–3636, 800/457–5457 ⊕ www.pioneerinnmaui.com ⤵ 34 rooms ⊙ No meals.*

WHERE TO STAY IN MAUI

	Local Vibe	Pros	Cons
West Maui	Popular and busy, West Maui includes the picturesque, touristy town of Lahaina and the upscale resort areas of Kaanapali and Kapalua.	A wide variety of shops, water sports, and historic sites provide plenty to do. To relax, there are great beaches and brilliant sunsets.	Traffic is usually congested; parking is hard to find; beaches can be crowded.
South Shore	The protected South Shore of Maui offers diverse experiences and accommodations, from comfortable condos to luxurious resorts—and golf, golf, golf.	Many beautiful beaches; sunny weather; great snorkeling.	Numerous strip malls; crowded with condos; there can be lots of traffic.
Upcountry	Country and chic come together in farms, ranches, and trendy towns on the cool, green slopes of Haleakala.	Cooler weather at higher elevations; panoramic views of nearby islands; distinctive shops, boutiques, galleries, and restaurants.	Fewer restaurants; no nightlife; can be very dark at night and difficult to drive for those unfamiliar with roads and conditions.
North Shore	A hub for surfing, wind-surfing, and kiteboarding. When the surf's not up, the focus is on shopping: Paia is full of galleries, shops, and hip eateries.	Wind and waves are terrific for water sports; colorful small towns to explore without the intrusion of big resorts.	Weather inland may not be as sunny as other parts of the island, and coastal areas can be windy; little nightlife; most stores in Paia close early, around 6 pm.
Road to Hana and East Maui	Remote and rural, laid-back and tropical Hana and East Maui are special places to unwind.	Natural experience; rugged coastline and lush tropical scenery; lots of waterfalls.	Accessed by a long and winding road; no nightlife; wetter weather; few places to eat or shop.

5

$

B&B/INN

⌂ **Garden Gate Bed & Breakfast Inn.** In an older neighborhood just outside of busy Lahaina town lies a quiet place that welcomes you with light and clean rooms featuring pleasant tropical furnishings and private entrances. **Pros:** free use of chairs, coolers, boogie boards, and other beach toys; knowledgeable hosts; convenient location—a two-block walk to Wahikuli Wayside Beach Park across the highways and the Maui Bus stops at the corner. **Cons:** not secluded; no resort amenities; no stores within safe, easy walking distance. $ *Rooms from: $149* ✉ *67 Kaniau Rd., Lahaina* ☎ *808/661–8800, 800/939–3217* ⊕ *www.gardengatebb.com* 🛏 *4 rooms* ⏐⊙⏐ *Breakfast.*

$$$

B&B/INN

Fodor's Choice

★

⌂ **Hooilo House.** A luxurious, intimate getaway without resort facilities, this stunning, 2-acre, Bali-inspired B&B in the foothills of the West Maui Mountains, just south of Lahaina town, exemplifies quiet perfection. **Pros:** friendly, on-site hosts (Amy and Dan Martin); beautiful furnishings; gazebo for weddings and special events. **Cons:** not good for families with younger children; three-night minimum. $ *Rooms from: $339* ✉ *138 Awaiku St., Lahaina* ☎ *808/667–6669* ⊕ *www.hooilohouse.com* 🛏 *6 rooms* ⏐⊙⏐ *Breakfast.*

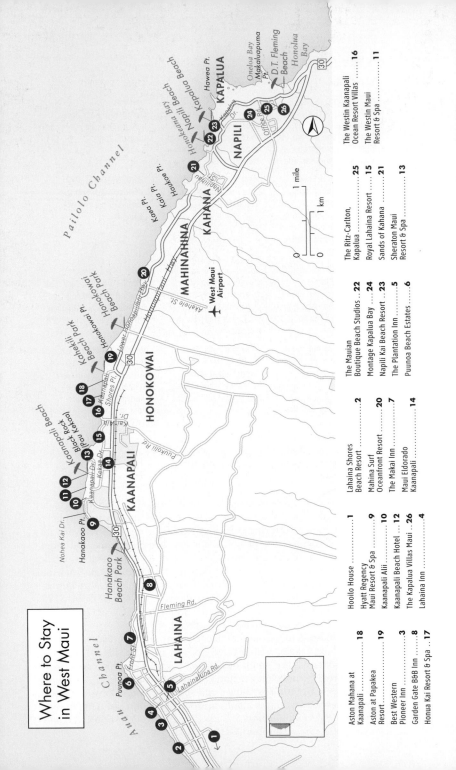

Where to Stay in West Maui

Aston Mahana at Kaanapali **18**
Aston at Papakea Resort **19**
Best Western Pioneer Inn **3**
Garden Gate B&B Inn **8**
Honua Kai Resort & Spa ... **17**

Hooilo House **1**
Hyatt Regency Maui Resort & Spa **9**
Kaanapali Alii **10**
Kaanapali Beach Hotel ... **12**
The Kapalua Villas Maui .. **26**
Lahaina Inn **4**

Lahaina Shores Beach Resort **2**
Mahina Surf Oceanfront Resort **20**
The Makai Inn **7**
Maui Eldorado Kaanapali **14**

The Mauian Boutique Beach Studios .. **22**
Montage Kapalua Bay **24**
Napili Kai Beach Resort .. **23**
The Plantation Inn **5**
Puunoa Beach Estates **6**

The Ritz-Carlton, Kapalua **25**
Royal Lahaina Resort **15**
Sands of Kahana **21**
Sheraton Maui Resort & Spa **13**

The Westin Kaanapali Ocean Resort Villas **16**
The Westin Maui Resort & Spa **11**

$ B&B/INN **Lahaina Inn.** An antique jewel in the heart of town, this two-story timbered building will transport romantics back to the turn of the 20th century. **Pros:** a half block off Front Street, the location is within easy walking distance of shops, restaurants, and attractions; lovely antique style; the price is right. **Cons:** rooms are small, bathrooms particularly so; some street noise; two stories, no elevator. [$] *Rooms from: $99* ✉ *127 Lahainaluna Rd., Lahaina* ☎ *808/661–0577, 800/222–5642* 🌐 *www.lahainainn.com* 🛏 *9 rooms, 3 suites* 🍴 *No meals.*

$$ RENTAL **Lahaina Shores Beach Resort.** You really can't get any closer to the beach than this lofty (by Lahaina standards), seven-story rental property that offers panoramic ocean and mountain views and fully equipped kitchens. **Pros:** right on the beach; historical sites, attractions, and activities are a short walk away. **Cons:** older property; no posh, resort-type amenities. [$] *Rooms from: $250* ✉ *475 Front St., Lahaina* ☎ *808/661–4835, 866/934–9176* 🌐 *www.lahainashores.com* 🛏 *199 rooms* 🍴 *No meals.*

$ B&B/INN **The Makai Inn.** Right on the ocean, though a bit of a stroll to the center of Lahaina, this breezy, two-story inn features small units with fully equipped kitchens and casual interiors all topped with a dollop of aloha. **Pros:** oceanfront location; reasonable rates include taxes, parking, and Wi-Fi. **Cons:** older building; no televisions, pool, elevator, or daily maid service; most units do not have a/c. [$] *Rooms from: $110* ✉ *1415 Front St., Lahaina* ☎ *808/870–9004* 🌐 *www.makaiinn.net* 🛏 *18 units* 🍴 *No meals.*

$ B&B/INN **The Plantation Inn.** Ten minutes from the beach, this tropical plantation-era inn is a fine value for those who want to be in the heart of the action—which means easy access to shops, sights, and restaurants, but also that there may be noise from the town. **Pros:** guests have full privileges at the sister Kaanapali Beach Hotel, 3 miles north; free parking; 24-hour access to pool and Jacuzzi. **Cons:** Wi-Fi connection is hit-or-miss (try the lanai); two-story inn has no elevator or bellman; no children under 13. [$] *Rooms from: $179* ✉ *174 Lahainaluna Rd., Lahaina* ☎ *808/667–9225, 800/433–6815* 🌐 *www.theplantationinn.com* 🛏 *14 rooms, 4 suites* 🍴 *Breakfast.*

$$$$ RENTAL **Puunoa Beach Estates.** High-end travelers tired of sharing their slice of vacation paradise with the noisy hordes will find privacy and luxury—and incredible views—at this 10-unit, beachfront enclave. **Pros:** gated driveway for security; no resort fee; free parking. **Cons:** stairs may pose an obstacle for some; a bit far to walk to Lahaina stores and tourist center. [$] *Rooms from: $1100* ✉ *45 Kai Pali Pl., Lahaina* ☎ *877/657–7909* 🌐 *www.puunoabeachestates.com* 🛏 *10 units* 🍴 *No meals.*

KAANAPALI

With its long stretch of beach lined with luxury resorts, shops, and restaurants, Kaanapali is a playground. Expect top-class service here, and everything you could want a few steps from your room, including the calm waters of sun-kissed Kaanapali Beach. Wandering along the beach path between resorts is a recreational activity unto itself. Weather is dependably warm, and for that reason as well as all the others, Kaanapali is a popular—at times, downright crowded—destination.

$$$$
RESORT
FAMILY

▦ **Hyatt Regency Maui Resort & Spa.** Fantasy landscaping with splashing waterfalls, swim-through grottoes, a lagoonlike swimming pool, and a 150-foot waterslide "wow" guests of all ages at this bustling Kaanapali resort in the midst of the Kaanapali Beach action. **Pros:** nightly on-site luau; contemporary restaurant and bar. **Cons:** can be difficult to find a space in self-parking; popular resort might not offer the most peaceful escape. $ *Rooms from: $429* ⊠ *200 Nohea Kai Dr., Kaanapali* ☎ *808/661–1234* ⊕ *www.maui.hyatt.com* ⤳ *806 rooms* ❄*No meals.*

$$$$
RENTAL

▦ **Kaanapali Alii.** Amenities like daily maid service, an activities desk, a small store with complimentary DVDs for guests to borrow, and a 24-hour front-desk service—and no pesky resort fees—make this a winning choice for families and those wanting to play house on Maui's most stunning shores. **Pros:** large, comfortable units on the beach; quiet compared to other hotels in the resort; good location in the heart of the action in Kaanapali Resort. **Cons:** parking can be crowded during high season; no on-site restaurant. $ *Rooms from: $495* ⊠ *50 Nohea Kai Dr., Kaanapali* ☎ *808/667–1400, 877/713–2844* ⊕ *www.kaanapalialii. com* ⤳ *264 units* ❄*No meals.*

$
HOTEL
Fodor's Choice
★

▦ **Kaanapali Beach Hotel.** From the Hawaiian artifacts in the garden to the tropical interiors, this charming beachfront hotel is full of aloha— locals say it's one of the few resorts on the island where you can get a true Hawaiian experience. **Pros:** no resort fee; friendly staff; weekly luau. **Cons:** the property is older than neighboring modern resorts; fewer amenities than other places along this beach. $ *Rooms from: $159* ⊠ *2525 Kaanapali Pkwy., Kaanapali* ☎ *808/661–0011, 800/262– 8450* ⊕ *www.kbhmaui.com* ⤳ *432 rooms* ❄*No meals.*

$
RENTAL
Fodor's Choice
★

▦ **Maui Eldorado Kaanapali.** The Kaanapali Golf Course's fairways wrap around this fine, well-priced, two-story condo complex that boasts spacious studios, one- and two-bedroom units with fully equipped kitchens, and access to a stocked beach cabana on a semiprivate beach. **Pros:** privileges at the Kaanapali Golf Courses; Wi-Fi in all units; friendly staff. **Cons:** not right on beach; some distance from attractions of the Kaanapali Resort; no housekeeping but checkout cleaning fee; additional resort fees. $ *Rooms from: $150* ⊠ *2661 Kekaa Dr., Kaanapali* ☎ *808/661–0021* ⊕ *www.mauieldorado.com* ⤳ *204 units* ❄*No meals.*

$$
RESORT

▦ **Royal Lahaina Resort.** Built in 1962, this grand property on the uncrowded, sandy shore in North Kaanapali has hosted millionaires and Hollywood stars, and today it pleases families and budget seekers as well as luxury travelers with a variety of lodging styles. **Pros:** on-site luau nightly; variety of lodgings and rates; tennis ranch with 11 courts and a pro shop; no resort fees. **Cons:** phased renovations of cottage underway. $ *Rooms from: $220* ⊠ *2780 Kekaa Dr., Kaanapali* ☎ *808/661–3611, 800/447–6925* ⊕ *www.hawaiianhotels.com* ⤳ *316 rooms, 17 suites, 114 cottage rooms* ❄*No meals.*

$$$$
RESORT

▦ **Sheraton Maui Resort & Spa.** Set among dense gardens on Kaanapali's best stretch of beach, the Sheraton offers a quieter, more low-key atmosphere than its neighboring resorts and sits next to and on top of the 80-foot-high Puu Kekaa, from which divers leap in a sunset torchlighting and cliff-diving ritual. **Pros:** luxury resort with terrific beach location; great snorkeling right off the beach. **Cons:** extensive property can mean a long walk from your room to the lobby, restaurants, and beach. [$] *Rooms from: $659* ✉ *2605 Kaanapali Pkwy., Kaanapali* ☎ *808/661–0031, 866/500–8313* 🌐 *www.sheraton-maui.com* 🛏 *464 rooms, 44 suites* 🍴 *No meals.*

$$$$ RESORT FAMILY 🏨 **The Westin Kaanapali Ocean Resort Villas.** Abundant resort amenities and pools are notable at these luxury villas just north of Black Rock (Puu Kekaa) along the beach in Kaanapali. **Pros:** Westin Kids Club with day and evening programs; complimentary shuttle to Westin Maui Resort and Spa, Sheraton Maui, and Lahaina town; no resort fee. **Cons:** large complex could be overwhelming; not within the boundaries of the Kaanapali Resort; $10 self-parking fee. [$] *Rooms from: $619* ✉ *6 Kai Ala Dr., Kaanapali* ☎ *808/667–3200, 866/716–8112* 🌐 *www.westinkaanapali.com* 🛏 *1,021 units* 🍴 *No meals.*

$$$$ RESORT FAMILY 🏨 **The Westin Maui Resort & Spa.** The cascading waterfall in the lobby of this hotel gives way to an aquatic playground with five heated swimming pools, abundant waterfalls (15 at last count), lagoons complete with pink flamingos and swans, and a premier location right on famed Kaanapali Beach—you could end up with fantasy overload. **Pros:** complimentary shuttle to Westin Kaanapali Ocean Resort Villas, Sheraton Maui, and to Lahaina (where parking can be difficult); activity programs for all ages; one adults-only pool. **Cons:** $30 daily resort fee (includes parking and Wi-Fi). [$] *Rooms from: $639* ✉ *2365 Kaanapali Pkwy., Kaanapali* ☎ *808/667–2525, 866/716–8112* 🌐 *www.westinmaui.com* 🛏 *731 rooms, 28 suites* 🍴 *No meals.*

5

KAPALUA AND NEARBY

The neighborhoods north of Kaanapali—Honokowai, Mahinahina, Kahana, Napili, and finally, Kapalua—blend almost seamlessly into one another along Lower Honoapiilani Highway. Each has a few shops and restaurants and a secluded bay or two to call its own. Many visitors have found a second home here, at one of the condominiums nestled between beach-access roads and groves of mango trees. You won't get the stellar service of a resort (except at Kapalua), but you'll be among the locals here, in a relatively quiet part of the island. Be prepared for a long commute, though, if you're planning to do much exploring elsewhere on the island. Kapalua is the area farthest north, but well worth all the driving to stay at the elegant Ritz-Carlton, which is surrounded by misty greenery and overlooks beautiful D.T. Fleming Beach.

HONOKOWAI

$$$ RENTAL FAMILY 🏨 **Aston Mahana at Kaanapali.** Though the name claims Kaanapali, this older, 12-story oceanfront condominium complex, where all units have unobstructed panoramic views of the ocean and nearby islands, is actually in quiet, neighboring Honokowai. **Pros:** the private lanai and floor-to-ceiling windows are great for watching Maui's spectacular sunsets and whales in the winter season; tennis courts; daily maid service. **Cons:** furnishings in some units may need updating; no shops or restaurants on property. [$] *Rooms from: $329* ✉ *110 Kaanapali Shores Pl., Honokowai* ☎ *808/661–8751, 866/774–2924* 🌐 *www.themahana.com* 🛏 *215 units* 🍴 *No meals.*

$$ RENTAL FAMILY 🏠 **Aston at Papakea Resort.** All studios and one- and two-bedroom units at this casual, oceanfront condominium complex face the ocean and, because the units are spread out among 11 low-rise buildings on about 13 acres of land, there is built-in privacy and easy parking. **Pros:** units have large rooms; lovely garden landscaping; such complimentary activities as yoga, putting greens, and tennis lessons. **Cons:** no beach in front of property; pool can get crowded. [$] *Rooms from: $225* ✉ *3543 Lower Honoapiilani Hwy., Honokowai* ☎ *808/669–4848, 866/774–2924* 🌐 *www.astonatpapakea.com* 🛏 *364 units* 🍴 *No meals.*

$$$$ RENTAL FAMILY 🏠 **Honua Kai Resort & Spa.** Two high-rise towers contain these individually owned, eco-friendly (and family-friendly) units combining the conveniences of a condo with the full service of a hotel. **Pros:** large units; upscale appliances and furnishings. **Cons:** can be windy here. [$] *Rooms from: $514* ✉ *130 Kai Malina Pkwy., Honokowai* ☎ *808/662–2800, 855/718–5789* 🌐 *www.honuakai.com* 🛏 *628 units* 🍴 *No meals.*

MAHINAHINA

$ RENTAL 🏠 **Mahina Surf Oceanfront Resort.** Of the many condo complexes lining the oceanside stretch of Honoapiilani Highway, this one offers friendly service, a saline oceanfront pool, and affordable units—some with million-dollar views. **Pros:** oceanfront barbecues; resident turtles hang out on the rocks below; no hidden fees. **Cons:** oceanfront but with rocky shoreline rather than a beach. [$] *Rooms from: $180* ✉ *4057 Lower Honoapiilani Hwy., Mahinahina* ☎ *808/669–6068, 800/367–6086* 🌐 *www.mahinasurf.com* 🛏 *56 units* 🍴 *No meals.*

KAHANA

$$$ RENTAL 🏠 **Sands of Kahana.** Meandering gardens, spacious rooms, and an on-site restaurant distinguish this large condominium complex—units on the upper floors benefit from the height, with unrivalled ocean views stretching away from private lanai. **Pros:** restaurant on the premises; amenities include a fitness center, tennis courts, and sand volleyball court. **Cons:** you may be approached about buying a unit; street-facing units can get a bit noisy. [$] *Rooms from: $295* ✉ *4299 Lower Honoapiilani Hwy., Kahana* ☎ *808/669–0400 property phone, 800/332–1137 for vacation rentals (Sullivan Properties)* 🌐 *www.mauiresorts.com* 🛏 *196 units* 🍴 *No meals.*

NAPILI

$$ RENTAL 🏠 **The Mauian Boutique Beach Studios.** If you're looking for a low-key place with a friendly staff, this small, delightful beachfront property on Napili Bay may be for you. **Pros:** reasonable rates; located on one of Maui's top swimming and snorkeling beaches; free parking and no resort fees. **Cons:** units are small; some may find the motel-like design reduces privacy; few amenities. [$] *Rooms from: $208* ✉ *5441 Lower Honoapiilani Hwy., Napili* ☎ *808/669–6205, 800/367–5034* 🌐 *www.mauian.com* 🛏 *44 rooms* 🍴 *Breakfast.*

$$$ RESORT FAMILY Fodor's Choice ★ 🏠 **Napili Kai Beach Resort.** Spread across 10 beautiful acres along one of the best beaches on Maui, the Napili Kai with its "old Hawaii" feel draws a loyal following to its Hawaiian-style rooms that open onto private lanai. **Pros:** kids' hula performances and weekly Hawaiian slack-key guitar concert; fantastic swimming and sunning beach; no resort

fees. **Cons:** not as modern as other resorts in West Maui. [$] *Rooms from: $310* ✉ *5900 Lower Honoapiilani Hwy., Napili* ☎ *808/669–6271, 800/367–5030* 🌐 *www.napilikai.com* 🛏 *163 units* 🍴 *No meals.*

KAPALUA

$$$$ RENTAL 🏨 **The Kapalua Villas Maui.** Set among the 22,000 sprawling acres of the Kapalua Resort, these posh condominiums are named for their locations: the Golf Villas line the fairways of Kapalua's Bay Golf Course; the Ridge Villas are perched along a cliff overlooking the ocean; and the Bay Villas are at the water's edge. **Pros:** large, well-appointed condos; amazing views; a network of walking and running trails. **Cons:** stores, beaches, restaurants are not within walking distance; Kapalua can be windy; complexes have small pools. [$] *Rooms from: $451* ✉ *2000 Village Rd., Kapalua* ☎ *808/665–9170, 800/545–0018* 🌐 *www.kapaluavillas.com* 🛏 *162 villas* 🍴 *No meals.*

$$$$ RESORT FAMILY 🏨 **Montage Kapalua Bay.** Maui's newest luxury resort in tony Kapalua caters to well-heeled travelers who want the comfort and privacy of a condo unit combined with resort-style service and amenities. **Pros:** Kapalua Bay offers prime snorkeling; truly top-drawer accommodations; large rooms are well appointed. **Cons:** $40 daily resort fee. [$] *Rooms from: $695* ✉ *1 Bay Dr., Kapalua* ☎ *808/662–6600* 🌐 *www.montagehotels.com/kapaluabay* 🛏 *50 units, 6 grand residences* 🍴 *No meals.*

$$$$ RESORT Fodor's Choice ★ 🏨 **The Ritz-Carlton, Kapalua.** One of Maui's most notable resorts, this elegant hillside property features luxurious service, upscale accommodations, a spa, restaurants, and a pool, along with an enhanced Hawaiian sense of place. **Pros:** luxury and service you'd expect from a Ritz; Banyan Tree restaurant will please dedicated locavores; many cultural and recreational programs. **Cons:** expensive; can be windy on the grounds and at the pool; not on the beach and far from major attractions such as Haleakala; daily parking and resort fees. [$] *Rooms from: $549* ✉ *1 Ritz-Carlton Dr., Kapalua* ☎ *808/669–6200, 800/262–8440* 🌐 *www.ritzcarlton.com/en/Properties/KapaluaMaui/Default.htm* 🛏 *321 rooms, 142 suites* 🍴 *No meals.*

SOUTH SHORE

The South Shore comprises two main communities: resort-filled Wailea and down-to-earth Kihei. In general, the farther south you go, the fancier the accommodations get. **■ TIP→ North Kihei tends to have great prices, but it also has some windy beaches scattered with seaweed. (This isn't a problem if you don't mind driving to another beach.)** As you travel down South Kihei Road, you can find condos both fronting and across the street from inviting beach parks and close to shops and restaurants. Once you hit Wailea, the opulence quotient takes a giant leap; this is the land of perfectly groomed resorts. Wailea and West Maui's Kaanapali continuously compete over which is more exclusive and which has better weather. In our opinion, it's a draw.

KIHEI

If you're a beach lover, you won't find many disadvantages to staying in Kihei. A string of welcoming beaches stretches from tip to tip. Snorkeling, body boarding, and barbecuing find their ultimate expression here. Affordable condos line South Kihei Road; however, some find the busy traffic and the strip-mall shopping distinctly un-Maui and prefer quieter hideaways.

$$ RENTAL **Hale Hui Kai.** This modest three-story condo complex of mostly two-bedroom units is just steps away from the beach. **Pros:** far enough from the noise and tumult of "central" Kihei; a hidden gem for bargain hunters; close enough to all the conveniences; free parking. **Cons:** nondescript 1970s architecture; some of the units are dated; no daily housekeeping. [$] *Rooms from: $250* ✉ *2994 S. Kihei Rd., Kihei* ☎ *808/879–1219, 800/809–6284* 🌐 *www.halehuikaimaui.com* 🛏 *40 units* 🍴 *No meals.*

$$ RENTAL FAMILY **Kamaole Sands.** This south Kihei property is a good choice for active families, with its swimming pool, tennis courts, and an ideal family beach (Kamaole III) just across the street. **Pros:** in the seemingly endless strip of Kihei condos, this stands out for its pleasant grounds and well-cared-for units; unlike many low-rise condos, this one has elevators. **Cons:** the complex of buildings may seem a bit too "citylike"; lack of diversity among the building facade. [$] *Rooms from: $249* ✉ *2695 S. Kihei Rd., Kihei* ☎ *808/874–8700, 800/367–5004* 🌐 *www.castleresorts.com* 🛏 *440 units* 🍴 *No meals.*

$ RENTAL Fodor's Choice ★ **Luana Kai Resort.** If you don't need everything to be totally modern, consider setting up house at this great value condominium-by-the-sea with individually owned units offered in two categories: standard and deluxe. **Pros:** meticulously landscaped grounds; excellent management team; free parking. **Cons:** no elevators; no maid service; not all units have air conditioning. [$] *Rooms from: $149* ✉ *940 S. Kihei Rd., Kihei* ☎ *808/879–1268, 800/669–1127* 🌐 *www.luanakai.com* 🛏 *113 units* 🍴 *No meals.*

$$$ RENTAL FAMILY **Mana Kai Maui.** You simply cannot get any closer to gorgeous Keawakapu Beach than this unsung hero of South Shore hotels, offering both renovated hotel rooms and condos that may be older than its competitors but are well-priced and have marvelous ocean views, especially during the winter humpback whale season. **Pros:** arguably the best beach on the South Shore; Maui Yoga Path is on the property and offers classes at an additional cost; free assigned parking. **Cons:** older property; interior design might not appeal to discerning travelers; four-night minimum. [$] *Rooms from: $312* ✉ *2960 S. Kihei Rd., Kihei* ☎ *808/879–2778, 800/367–5242* 🌐 *www.crhmaui.com* 🛏 *98 units* 🍴 *No meals.*

$$ RENTAL **Maui Kamaole.** These one- and two-bedroom condos—some with ocean views—lie across the street from one of Maui's best beach parks, Kamaole III. **Pros:** great location in sunny Kihei; nice grounds and pool; free parking. **Cons:** two-story buildings have no elevators; four-night minimum. [$] *Rooms from: $254* ✉ *2777 S. Kihei Rd, Kihei* ☎ *808/879–2778, 800/367–5242* 🌐 *www.crhmaui.com* 🛏 *310 rooms* 🍴 *No meals.*

FOOD SHOPPING FOR RENTERS

Condo renters in search of food and take-out meals should try these great places around Maui.

WEST MAUI

Foodland Farms. This large supermarket combines the best of gourmet selections and local products, with all the familiar staples you need to stock your vacation kitchen. They also make a mean *poke* (seafood salad). ✉ *Lahaina Gateway Shopping Center, 345 Keawe St., Lahaina* ☎ *808/662–7088.*

SOUTH SHORE

Safeway. Find everything you could possibly need at this supermarket, the largest on Maui, located in the Piilani Village Shopping Center. ✉ *277 Piikea Ave., Kihei* ☎ *808/891–9120.*

Times Supermarket. Watch for the parking lot barbecue on Wednesday and Friday, when chicken, teriyaki beef, steak, and shrimp are served plate lunch–style outside this supermarket. Hawaiian plates are served up on Thursday. ✉ *1310 S. Kihei Rd., Kihei.*

CENTRAL MAUI

Safeway. This 24-hour supermarket has a deli, a prepared-foods and seafood section, and a bakery that are all fantastic. There's a good wine selection, tons of produce, and a flower shop where you can treat yourself to a fresh lei. ✉ *170 E. Kaahumanu Ave., Kahului* ☎ *808/877–3377.*

Whole Foods Market. This busy supermarket carries local organic produce, and the wine, seafood, bakery, beer and wine, and meat offerings are exceptional. The pricey prepared foods, including pizza, sushi, a salad bar, Asian bowls, and Mexican fare, are the best. ✉ *70 E. Kaahumanu Ave., Kahului.*

UPCOUNTRY

Foodland. This member of a local supermarket chain is at Pukalani Terrace Center; it is a full-service store with prepared foods, a deli, fresh sushi, local produce, and a good seafood section in addition to the usual fare. On Friday and Saturday, the store sets up a grill in the parking to barbecue tender steak and teriyaki beef. Open 24 hours. ✉ *55 Pukalani St., Pukalani* ☎ *808/572–0674.*

Pukalani Superette. Stop at this family-owned store on your way up or down Haleakala for fresh Maui-grown produce and meat, flowers, chocolate *haupia* (coconut) cream pies, and a surprisingly refined selection of wine and beer. The hot prepared foods are another big draw. ✉ *15 Makawao Ave., Pukalani* ☎ *808/572–7616* 🌐 *www.pukalanisuperette.com.*

5

$ RENTAL 🏨 **Maui Sunseeker Resort.** Popular with a gay and lesbian clientele, this small, private, and relaxed North Kihei property is a great value for the area. **Pros:** impeccably maintained; friendly staff; no kids. **Cons:** no frills; most units are small; most rooms lack views. [$] *Rooms from: $159* ✉ *551 S. Kihei Rd., Kihei* ☎ *808/879–1261, 800/532–6284* 🌐 *www.mauisunseeker.com* 🛏 *26 units* 🍴 *No meals.*

$ B&B/INN 🏨 **Pineapple Inn.** Enjoy the amenities of a fine hotel with the peace and quiet of a small inn at a reasonable price. **Pros:** no resort fees; resort-quality furnishings; generous welcome gift baskets and well-stocked

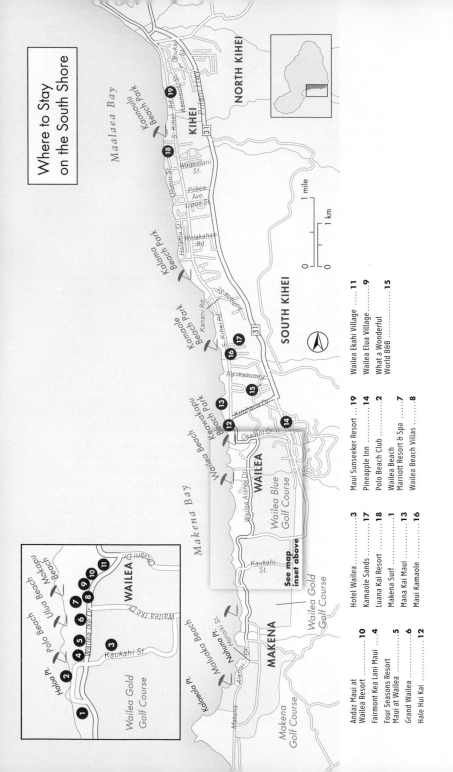

Where to Stay on the South Shore

Andaz Maui at
Wailea Resort **10**
Fairmont Kea Lani Maui 4
Four Seasons Resort
Maui at Wailea **5**
Grand Wailea **6**
Hale Hui Kai **12**

Hotel Wailea................. **3**
Kamaole Sands **17**
Luana Kai Resort **18**
Makena Surf **1**
Mana Kai Maui **13**
Maui Kamaole **16**

Maui Sunseeker Resort ... **19**
Pineapple Inn **14**
Polo Beach Club **2**
Wailea Beach
Marriott Resort & Spa **7**
Wailea Beach Villas **8**

Wailea Ekahi Village **11**
Wailea Elua Village **9**
What a Wonderful
World B&B **15**

minirefrigerator. **Cons:** although you don't see it from the inn, the rest of the neighborhood is not as well maintained; short drive to the beach. [$] *Rooms from: $159* ✉ *3170 Akala Dr., Kihei* ☎ *808/298–4403, 877/212–6284* 🌐 *www.pineappleinnmaui.com* 💳 *No credit cards* 🛏 *4 rooms, 1 cottage* 🍴 *No meals.*

$ B&B/INN 🏨 **What a Wonderful World B&B.** Convenient, comfortable, and affordable, this Polynesian-style pole house provides a good base for exploring the island. **Pros:** knowledgeable host (Eva); affordable rates. **Cons:** owner's dogs on the premises; a little hard to find in the neighborhood; no resort amenities. [$] *Rooms from: $145* ✉ *2828 Umalu Pl., Kihei* ☎ *800/943–5804* 🌐 *www.amauibedandbreakfast.com* 🛏 *3 suites, 1 room* 🍴 *Breakfast.*

WAILEA AND MAKENA

Warm, serene, and luxurious, Wailea properties offer less "action" than West Maui resorts. The properties here tend to focus on ambience, thoughtful details, and natural scenery. Nightlife is pretty much nil, save for a few swanky bars. However, you have your choice of sandy beaches with good snorkeling. Farther south, Makena is a little less developed. Expect everything—even bottled water—to double in price when you cross the line from Kihei to Wailea.

$$$$ RESORT Fodor's Choice ★ 🏨 **Andaz Maui at Wailea Resort.** Sophisticated travelers and romance seeking couples will swoon at the sleek luxury of this eco-friendly, beachfront resort. **Pros:** outstanding service and dining; a one-of-a-kind resort on Maui; free Wi-Fi and shuttle service around Wailea. **Cons:** expensive; not marketed to families; slick design style might be feel cold to some. [$] *Rooms from: $509* ✉ *3550 Wailea Alanui Dr., Wailea* ☎ *808/879–1234* 🌐 *www.andazmaui.com* 🛏 *255 rooms, 10 villas, 35 suites* 🍴 *No meals.*

$$$$ RESORT FAMILY Fodor's Choice ★ 🏨 **Fairmont Kea Lani Maui.** Gleaming white spires and tiled archways are the hallmark of this stunning resort that's particularly good for families. **Pros:** for families, this is one of the best of the South Shore luxury resorts; on-site bakery and deli are good for picnic fare. **Cons:** some feel the architecture and design scream anything *but* Hawaii; $35 resort fee daily. [$] *Rooms from: $549* ✉ *4100 Wailea Alanui Dr., Wailea* ☎ *808/875–4100, 800/798–4552* 🌐 *www.fairmont.com/kealani* 🛏 *413 suites, 37 villas* 🍴 *No meals.*

$$$$ RESORT Fodor's Choice ★ 🏨 **Four Seasons Resort Maui at Wailea.** "Impeccably stylish," "extravagant," and "relaxing" describe most Four Seasons properties, and this elegant one fronting award-winning Wailea Beach is no exception, with its poolside cabanas, beautiful courtyards, and luxuries such as 24-hour room service and twice-daily housekeeping. **Pros:** no resort fee; several activities (including children's program and tennis) are complimentary; exceptional service; great shopping and local crafts and artwork market. **Cons:** expensive; a bit ostentatious for some. [$] *Rooms from: $595* ✉ *3900 Wailea Alanui Dr., Wailea* ☎ *808/874–8000, 800/332–3442* 🌐 *www.fourseasons.com/maui* 🛏 *305 rooms, 75 suites* 🍴 *No meals.*

$$$$ RESORT FAMILY 🏨 **Grand Wailea.** "Grand" is no exaggeration for this opulent, sunny 40-acre resort—either astounding or over the top, depending on your point of view, and entertaining for kids either way—due to its elaborate water features such as a "canyon riverpool" with slides, caves, a Tarzan swing, and a water elevator. **Pros:** set on beautiful Wailea Beach; brides will love the stained glass wedding chapel; many shops. **Cons:** $30 daily valet parking fee in addition to resort fee; sometimes too much is just too much. [$] *Rooms from: $369* ✉ *3850 Wailea Alanui Dr., Wailea* ☎ *808/875–1234, 800/888–6100* 🌐 *www.grandwailea.com* 🛏 *728 rooms, 52 suites* 🍴 *No meals.*

$$$$ HOTEL 🏨 **Hotel Wailea.** This small, adults-only, boutique hotel, perched on a quiet hillside above the Wailea Resort, delivers romance with spectacular views of the ocean, sunsets, and stars from just about every suite, garden nook, and spacious public area. **Pros:** beautiful grounds with running water throughout; secluded location away from resort row; small, intimate setting. **Cons:** not on the beach; no elevator. [$] *Rooms from: $479* ✉ *555 Kaukahi St., Wailea* ☎ *808/874–0500, 866/970–4167* 🌐 *www.hotelwailea.com* 🛏 *72 suites* 🍴 *No meals.*

$$$$ RENTAL 🏨 **Makena Surf.** For travelers who've done all there is to do on Maui and just want simple but luxurious relaxation at a condo that spills onto a private beach, this is the spot. **Pros:** away from it all, yet still close enough to "civilization"; great snorkeling right off the beach; laundry facilities in every unit. **Cons:** too secluded and "locked-up" for some; split-level units may be difficult for guests with mobility issues; check-in is at a different location (34 Wailea Gateway Plaza). [$] *Rooms from: $449* ✉ *4820 Makena Alanui Rd., Makena* ☎ *808/891–6249, 800/367–5246* 🌐 *www.destinationresidenceshawaii.com* 🛏 *103 units* 🍴 *No meals.*

$$$$ RENTAL 🏨 **Polo Beach Club.** Lording over a hidden section of Polo Beach, this wonderful, older eight-story rental property's charm somehow manages to stay under the radar. **Pros:** herb garden you can pick from; beautiful beach fronting the building; superb management. **Cons:** some may feel isolated; split-level units potentially challenging for those with impaired mobility; check-in is at a different location (34 Wailea Gateway Plaza). [$] *Rooms from: $709* ✉ *4400 Makena Rd., Makena* ☎ *808/891–6249, 800/367–5246* 🌐 *www.drhmaui.com* 🛏 *71 units* 🍴 *No meals.*

$$$$ RESORT 🏨 **Wailea Beach Marriott Resort & Spa.** The Marriott's rooms sit closer to the crashing surf than the rooms at most resorts, and a stay here promises not only close proximity to the water but also luxurious amenities, spacious accommodations, and golf and tennis privileges nearby. **Pros:** spa is one of the most fanciful in Hawaii; near good shopping; luau four nights a week. **Cons:** not quite beachfront (has a rocky shore); there can be a lot of foot traffic on the beachwalk along the coast; $30 daily resort fee and $25 daily parking fee. [$] *Rooms from: $595* ✉ *3700 Wailea Alanui Dr., Wailea* ☎ *808/879–1922, 800/292–4532* 🌐 *www.waileamarriott.com* 🛏 *497 rooms, 47 suites* 🍴 *No meals.*

$$$$ RENTAL 🏨 **Wailea Beach Villas.** Wailea's hideaway for the rich and famous, these two- to five-bedroom villas are an immersion in luxury, with up to 3,100 square feet of living space, furnishings that inspire poetry, and gourmet kitchens fit for an Iron Chef. **Pros:** steps away from dining and

luxury stores at the Shops at Wailea; solid security with gated driveway and guard station; no resort fee. **Cons:** certainly not in most visitors' budgets; some units have limited views. [$] *Rooms from: $1259* ✉ *3800 Wailea Alanui Dr., Wailea* ☎ *808/891–6249, 800/367–5246* 🌐 *www.waileabeachvillas.com* 🛏 *98 units* 🍴 *No meals.*

$$$$ RESORT 🏨 **Wailea Ekahi Village.** Overlooking Keawakapu Beach, this family-friendly vacation resort features studios and one- and two-bedroom suites in low-rise buildings that span 34 acres of tropical gardens and won't cost your child's entire college fund. **Pros:** convenient access to a great beach; en-suite kitchen and laundry facilities; daily housekeeping; $155 in Wailea restaurant/spa credit. **Cons:** the large complex can be tricky to find your way around; check-in is at a different location (34 Wailea Gateway Plaza). [$] *Rooms from: $379* ✉ *3300 Wailea Alanui Dr., Wailea* ☎ *808/891–6249, 800/357–5246* 🌐 *www.drhmaui.com* 🛏 *289 units* 🍴 *No meals.*

$$$$ RESORT 🏨 **Wailea Elua Village.** Located on Ulua Beach, one of the Island's most beloved snorkeling spots, these upscale one-, two-, and three-bedroom condo suites have spectacular views and 24 acres of manicured lawns and gardens. **Pros:** easy access to the designer boutiques and upscale restaurants at The Shops at Wailea; daily housekeeping; $155 Wailea restaurant/spa credit. **Cons:** large complex; hard to find your way around; check-in is at a different location (34 Wailea Gateway Plaza). [$] *Rooms from: $429* ✉ *3600 Wailea Alanui Dr., Wailea* ☎ *808/891–6249, 800/367–5246* 🌐 *www.drhmaui.com* 🛏 *152 suites* 🍴 *No meals.*

CENTRAL MAUI

Kahului and Wailuku, the commercial, residential, and government centers that make up Central Maui, are not known for their lavish accommodations, but there are options that meet some travelers' needs perfectly.

KAHULUI

$$ HOTEL 🏨 **Courtyard by Marriott Maui Kahului Airport.** At the entrance to Kahului Airport, this hotel offers many amenities for business travelers as well as tourists. **Pros:** great for business and pleasure; central location; conference and banquet rooms available. **Cons:** not on the beach; airport and city noise; daily parking fee. [$] *Rooms from: $289* ✉ *532 Keolani Pl., Kahului* ☎ *808/871–1800, 877/852–1880* 🌐 *www.marriott.com* 🛏 *138 rooms* 🍴 *No meals.*

$ HOTEL 🏨 **Maui Beach Hotel.** Budget-friendly rates and a central location in the island's commercial, civic, transportation, and health-care hubs make this two-story bayfront hotel on a busy intersection a popular choice for local and business travelers as well as for frugal visitors who understand that they get what they pay for. **Pros:** shuttle to Kahului Airport and central area; great location for exploring all corners of the island; aloha-minded staff. **Cons:** in-room air-conditioners can be noisy; even with upgrades, some parts of the property may seem dated. [$] *Rooms from: $109* ✉ *170 Kaahumanu Ave., Kahului* ☎ *808/877–0051* 🌐 *www.mauibeachhotel.net* 🛏 *145 rooms, 2 suites* 🍴 *No meals.*

WAILUKU

$ B&B/INN Fodor'sChoice ★ **The Old Wailuku Inn at Ulupono.** Built in 1924 and listed on the State of Hawaii Register of Historic Places, this home with knowledgeable innkeepers offers the charm of old Hawaii, including authentic decor and architecture. **Pros:** walking distance to civic center, restaurants, historic Wailuku town; free Wi-Fi and parking; no resort fees. **Cons:** closest beach is a 15-minute drive away; you may hear traffic noise at certain times. [$] *Rooms from: $165* ✉ *2199 Kahookele St., Wailuku* ☎ *808/244–5897, 800/305–4899* 🌐 *www.mauiinn.com* 🛏 *10 rooms* 🍴 *Breakfast.*

UPCOUNTRY

Upcountry accommodations (those in Kula, Makawao, and Haliimaile) are generally on country properties and are privately owned vacation rentals. Situated at a high elevation, these lodgings offer splendid views of the island, temperate weather, and a "getting away from it all" feeling—which is actually the case, as most shops and restaurants are a fair drive away, and beaches even farther. You'll definitely need a car here.

$ B&B/INN FAMILY Fodor'sChoice ★ **The Banyan Tree Bed and Breakfast Retreat.** If a taste of rural Hawaii life in plantation days coupled with quiet time and privacy is what you crave, you can find it at this pastoral 2-acre property awash in tropical foliage, huge monkeypod, and banyan trees. **Pros:** two cottages and the pool are outfitted for travelers with disabilities; ample on-site parking; you can walk to quaint Makawao town for dining and shopping. **Cons:** cottages have pretty basic furniture and few amenities; some daytime traffic noise; not all units have air-conditioning. [$] *Rooms from: $175* ✉ *3265 Baldwin Ave., Makawao* ☎ *808/572–9021* 🌐 *www.bed-breakfast-maui.com* 🛏 *7 cottage suites* 🍴 *Breakfast.*

$ B&B/INN **G and Z Upcountry.** Just 20 minutes away from Kahului Airport but a world away from the heat and hustle of Maui's resort districts lies G and Z Upcountry, a new bed-and-breakfast run by retired tourism exec Marsha Wienert and husband John. **Pros:** close to Haleakala National Park and other rural attractions; free Wi-Fi and no cleaning fee; immaculate with new furnishing and appliances. **Cons:** permit allows only two adults and two children (extra $25 per night per child); two-night minimum. [$] *Rooms from: $149* ✉ *60 Kekaulike Ave., Kula* ☎ *808/224–6824* 🌐 *www.gandzmaui.com* 🛏 *1 suite* 🍴 *Breakfast.*

$ B&B/INN **Hale Hookipa Inn.** A handsome 1924 Craftsman-style house in the heart of Makawao town is on both the Hawaii and the National Historic Registers, and provides a great base for excursions to Haleakala, Hana, or North Shore beaches. **Pros:** genteel rural setting; price includes buffet breakfast with organic fruit from the garden. **Cons:** a 20-minute drive to the nearest beach; this is not the sun, sand, and surf surroundings of travel posters; no food allowed in rooms. [$] *Rooms from: $140* ✉ *32 Pakani Pl., Makawao* ☎ *808/572–6698, 877/572–6698, 808/281–2074* 🌐 *www.maui-bed-and-breakfast.com* 🛏 *3 rooms, 1 suite* 🍴 *Breakfast.*

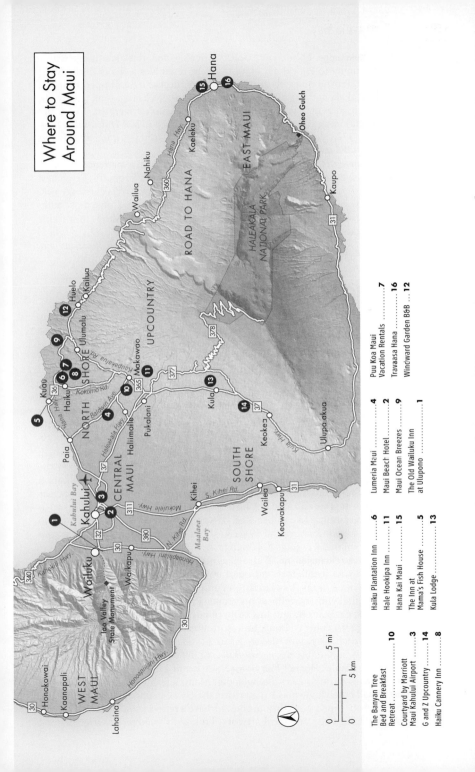

Where to Stay Around Maui

The Banyan Tree
Bed and Breakfast
Retreat **10**
Courtyard by Marriott
Maui Kahului Airport ...**3**
G and Z Upcountry **14**
Haiku Cannery Inn **8**

Haiku Plantation Inn **6**
Hale Hookipa Inn **11**
Hana Kai Maui **15**
The Inn at
Mama's Fish House **5**
Kula Lodge...............**13**

Lumeria Maui **4**
Maui Beach Hotel........**2**
Maui Ocean Breezes **9**
The Old Wailuku Inn
at Ulupono **1**

Puu Koa Maui
Vacation Rentals **7**
Travaasa Hana **16**
Windward Garden B&B ...**12**

$ HOTEL

🏨 **Kula Lodge.** Located at a 3,200-foot elevation, this older lodge within proximity to Haleakala National Park resembles a chalet in the Swiss Alps. **Pros:** a quiet place in the country; decent base of operations for Haleakala and Upcountry exploring. **Cons:** it's a long, long way to the beach; in winter, it can get downright cold; no refrigerator, TV, or air-conditioning in units. [$] *Rooms from: $175* ✉ *15200 Haleakala Hwy., Rte. 377, Kula* ☎ *808/878–1535, 800/233–1535* 🌐 *www.kulalodge.com* 🛏 *5 units* 🍴 *No meals.*

$$$$ B&B/INN

🏨 **Lumeria Maui.** Peace, tranquillity, and a healthful experience are what you will find at this beautifully restored historic property. **Pros:** new 1,700-square-foot Yoga Shala accommodates larger yoga classes, workshops, concerts, and meetings; a unique Maui retreat. **Cons:** most bathrooms have showers only; no beaches, restaurants, or shops in walking distance; no air-conditioning. [$] *Rooms from: $329* ✉ *1813 Baldwin Ave., Makawao* ☎ *808/579–8877, 855/579–8877* 🌐 *www.lumeriamaui.com* 🛏 *24 rooms, 2 suites* 🍴 *Breakfast.*

NORTH SHORE

You won't find any large resorts or condominium complexes along the North Shore, yet there's a variety of accommodations along the coastline from the surf town of Paia, through tiny Kuau, and along the rain-forested Hana Highway through Haiku. Some are oceanfront but not necessarily beachfront (with sand); instead, look for tropical gardens overflowing with ginger, bananas, papayas, and nightly bug symphonies. Some have breathtaking views or the type of solitude that seeps in, easing your tension before you know it. You may encounter brief, powerful downpours, but that's what makes this part of Maui green and lush. You'll need a car to enjoy staying on the North Shore.

$ B&B/INN

🏨 **Haiku Cannery Inn.** Hidden down a long driveway that winds through tall trees and hanging vines, this stately house-turned-B&B, on the Hawaii Register of Historic Places, offers a sense of Hawaii's plantation era. **Pros:** Hawaii-born and -raised hostess; off the beaten path but close to restaurants and stores. **Cons:** no pool or other resort amenities; a 10- to 15-minute drive to beaches. [$] *Rooms from: $140* ✉ *1061 Kokomo Rd., Haiku-Pauwela* ☎ *808/283–1274* 🌐 *www.haikucanneryinn.com* 🛏 *3 rooms, 1 cottage* 🍴 *Breakfast.*

$ B&B/INN

🏨 **Haiku Plantation Inn.** Water lilies and a shade tree bedecked in orchids greet you at this forested bend in the road, where a gracious estate, built in 1870 for the plantation-company doctor, continues the healing tradition with its wellness programs. **Pros:** quiet setting; close to restaurants, gas station, and bus stop; opportunities to experience authentic Hawaiian culture. **Cons:** no resort amenities; 10-minute drive to closest beach. [$] *Rooms from: $150* ✉ *555 Haiku Rd., Haiku-Pauwela* ☎ *808/575–7500* 🌐 *www.haikuleana.net* 🛏 *4 rooms* 🍴 *Breakfast.*

$ RENTAL FAMILY Fodor's Choice ★

🏨 **The Inn at Mama's Fish House.** Nestled in gardens adjacent to one of Maui's most popular dining spots (Mama's Fish House) and fronting a small beach known as Ku'au Cove, these well-maintained studios, suites, and one- and two-bedroom cottages have a retro-Hawaiian style with rattan furnishings and local artwork. **Pros:** daily maid service; free parking and Wi-Fi; next to Hookipa Beach and Paia town shops and restaurants. **Cons:** Mama's Fish House restaurant can get crowded during the evening (it's more mellow during the day). [$] *Rooms from: $175* ✉ *799 Poho Pl., Paia* ☎ *808/579–9764, 800/860–4852* 🌐 *www.innatmamas.com* 🛏 *12 units* 🍴 *No meals.*

$ RENTAL 🏨 **Maui Ocean Breezes.** The cool ocean breeze rolls through these pretty, eco-friendly rentals, making this a perfect spot to relax and enjoy the gorgeous scenery along the ocean side of the famed Road to Hana. **Pros:** one of few licensed rentals in area; located in an upscale, rural subdivision with large lots; expansive lawn with ocean views. **Cons:** isolated from stores, beaches, activities, and public transportation, making a rental car a must; five-night minimum. [$] *Rooms from: $165* ✉ *240 N. Holokai Rd., Haiku-Pauwela* ☎ *808/283–8526* 🌐 *www.mauivacationhideaway.com* 🛏 *3 units* 🍴 *No meals.*

$ RENTAL 🏨 **Puu Koa Maui Vacation Rentals.** Off a peaceful cul-de-sac in a residential area, these two well-maintained and immaculately clean homes offer studio and one-bedroom accommodations with a yard. **Pros:** very clean; reasonable rates; good spot for a group. **Cons:** inconvenient location (nowhere near beaches, stores, activities, or public bus routes), so a rental car is a necessity. [$] *Rooms from: $100* ✉ *66 Puu Koa Pl., Haiku-Pauwela* ☎ *808/573–2884* 🌐 *www.vrbo.com/100414* 🛏 *7 units* 🍴 *No meals.*

$$ B&B/INN 🏨 **Windward Garden B&B.** Eco-conscious travelers will appreciate this tranquil, nearly off-the-grid bed-and-breakfast located on five secluded acres in rural Pauwela on Maui's dramatic northeastern coastline. **Pros:** friendly, local hosts (Chris and Susan Gebb); unique Maui experience. **Cons:** far from town, stores, beaches, and bus stop—a car is a must; two of the suites share a bathroom. [$] *Rooms from: $165* ✉ *435 Hoolawa Rd., Haiku-Pauwela* ☎ *808/268–3874* 🌐 *www.windwardgardenbandb.com* 🛏 *3 suites, 1 studio cottage, 1 1-bedroom cottage* 🍴 *Breakfast.*

SHOPPING IN HANA

Hasegawa General Store. Do stop at Hana's charming, filled-to-the-rafters, one-stop shopping option. Buy fishing tackle, hot dogs, ice cream, and eggs here. You also can buy the newspaper, although it may not always be delivered on time. Check out the bulletin board for local events. ✉ *5165 Hana Hwy., Haiku-Pauwela* ☎ *808/248-8231.*

5

ROAD TO HANA

Why stay in Hana when it's so far from everything? In a world where everything moves at high speed, Hana still travels on horseback, ambling along slowly enough to smell the flowers. But old-fashioned and remote do not mean tame—this is a wild coast, known for heart-stopping scenery and frequent downpours. Leave city expectations behind: the single grocery may run out of milk, and the only videos to rent may be several years old. Be advised that dining options are slim. ■ **TIP→ If you're staying for several days or at a vacation rental, stock up on groceries before you head out to Hana.** Even with these inconveniences, Hana is a place you'll remember for a lifetime.

$$

RENTAL

Fodor'sChoice

★

⊡ Hana Kai Maui. Perfectly situated on Hana Bay, this two-story "condotel" has a long history and an excellent reputation for cleanliness and visitor hospitality—and the ocean views are stunning. **Pros:** a 10-minute walk to Hana Bay, where you can take a swim or enjoy a local-style plate lunch or snack at the café operated by a Hawaiian family; one-night rentals are accepted; daily housekeeping. **Cons:** early to bed and early to rise—no nightlife or excitement in Hana town; no elevator. $ *Rooms from: $210* ⊠ *4865 Uakea Rd., Hana* ☎ *808/248–8426, 800/346–2772* ⊕ *www.hanakaimaui.com* ➷ *18 units* ⎮◯⎮ *No meals.*

$$$$

RESORT

⊡ Travaasa Hana. A destination in itself, the former Hotel Hana-Maui might have a new name, but this secluded and quietly luxurious property still delivers the tropical Hawaii of your dreams. **Pros:** no resort or parking fees; no-tipping policy for everything except spa and food and drinks; a truly unique property in a special place. **Cons:** mobile service is spotty; it's oceanfront but doesn't have a sandy beach (however, free shuttle to Hamoa Beach). $ *Rooms from: $400* ⊠ *5031 Hana Hwy., Hana* ☎ *808/248–8211, 888/820–1043* ⊕ *www.travaasa.com/hana* ➷ *47 cottages, 25 suites* ⎮◯⎮ *All-inclusive; All meals.*

6

NIGHTLIFE AND PERFORMING ARTS

Looking for wild island nightlife? This island has little of Waikiki's after-hours decadence, and the club scene can be quirky, depending on the season and the day of the week. But Maui will surprise you with a big-name concert or world-class DJ, and local block parties are always entertaining. Outdoor music festivals are usually held at the Maui Arts & Cultural Center, or even a randomly scouted performance space in Hana.

Block parties in each town happen on Friday, with Wailuku leading the pack. Main streets are blocked for local bands, food vendors, and street performers, and it's a family-friendly affair. Lahaina, Paia, and Kihei are your best bets for action. Lahaina tries to uphold its reputation as a party town, and succeeds every Halloween when thousands of masqueraders converge for a Mardi Gras–style party on Front Street. Kihei has more club venues for live music but can attract something of a rough-and-tumble crowd in parts. On the right night, the towns stir with activity, and if you don't like one scene, there's always next door.

Outside Lahaina and Kihei, you might be able to hit an "on" night in Paia (North Shore) or Makawao (Upcountry). Charley's in Paia is the go-to venue for mainland and international DJs looking to play an intimate set. But generally these towns are on the mellow side. Your best option? Pick up the free *Maui Time Weekly,* or Thursday's edition of the *Maui News,* where you can find a listing of all your after-dark options islandwide.

NIGHTLIFE

Your best bet when it comes to bars on Maui? If you walk by and it sounds like it's happening, go in. If you want to scope out your options in advance, check the free *Maui Time Weekly,* available at most stores and restaurants, to find out who's playing where. The resorts and their bars and restaurants often have a good scene, too. The *Maui News* also publishes

an entertainment schedule in its Thursday edition of the "Maui Scene." With an open mind (and a little luck), you can usually find some fun.

WEST MAUI

With a few exceptions, West Maui's Lahaina nightlife is mellow. To find entertainment from local musicians to contemporary DJs, hop around town for your choice of scene.

LAHAINA
BARS AND RESTAURANTS

Cheeseburger in Paradise. A chain joint on Front Street, this place is known for—what else?—big beefy cheeseburgers, not to mention a great spinach-nut burger. It's a casual place to start your evening, as they have live music (usually classic or contemporary rock) until 10:30 pm. The second-floor balcony gives you a bird's-eye view of Lahaina's Front Street action. ⊠ *811 Front St., Lahaina* ☎ *808/661–4855* ⊕ *www.cheeseburgernation.com.*

Cool Cat Café. You could easily miss this casual 1950s-style diner while strolling through Lahaina. Tucked in the second floor of the Wharf Cinema Center, its semi-outdoor area plays host to rockin' local music nightly until 9:30 pm. The entertainment lineup covers jazz, contemporary Hawaiian, and traditional island rhythms. It doesn't hurt that the kitchen dishes out specialty burgers, fish that's fresh from the harbor, and delicious homemade sauces from the owner's family recipes. ⊠ *658 Front St., Lahaina* ☎ *808/667–0908* ⊕ *www.coolcatcafe.com.*

Spanky's Riptide. A casual sports-bar crowd gravitates here for *pau hana* (after-work get-together) and a game of pool. The bottle shop offers more than 30 beers and there are at least six on tap. There's no cover, the 11 televisions throughout the bar play all the sports packages, and you can help yourself to the condiment stand when you order a dawg. ⊠ *505 Front St., Lahaina* ☎ *808/667–2337* ⊕ *www. spankysmaui.com.*

KAPALUA
BARS AND RESTAURANTS

Alaloa Lounge. When ambience weighs heavy on the priority list, this spot at the Ritz-Carlton, Kapalua, might just be the ticket. Nightly performances range from jazz to island rhythms Thursday–Monday. The menu includes a fantastic seared filet mignon on a pretzel roll, and Kai Sushi's artisanal creations are available to order. Step onto the lanai for that plumeria-tinged Hawaiian air and gaze at the deep blue of the Pacific. ⊠ *The Ritz-Carlton, Kapalua, 1 Ritz-Carlton Dr., Kapalua* ☎ *808/669–6200* ⊕ *www.ritzcarlton.com.*

> ### WHAT'S A LAVA FLOW?
>
> Can't decide between a piña colada and a strawberry daiquiri? Go with a Lava Flow—a mix of light rum, coconut and pineapple juice, and a banana, with a swirl of strawberry purée. Add a wedge of fresh pineapple and a paper umbrella, and mmm . . . good.

Sansei Seafood Restaurant & Sushi Bar. Sansei has stayed a favorite among locals and visitors for years. The atmosphere is always spirited, and if you're more prone to doing the entertaining yourself, you can indulge in some mai tai–induced karaoke on Thursday and Friday nights and get 50% off fresh sushi at the same time. ✉ *600 Office Rd., Kapalua* ☎ *808/669–6286* ⊕ *www.sanseihawaii.com* ⊘ *5:15 pm–1 am, karaoke at 10 pm.*

SOUTH SHORE

If you're staying on the South Shore, you can find some great casual venues for live music but only a few options for dancing.

KIHEI

BARS AND RESTAURANTS

Fodor'sChoice
★
Ambrosia Martini Lounge. A South Maui favorite, Ambrosia is a lively hangout for house music and old-school jams, as well as the occasional absinthe drink. It's the size of a living room, but mixology is given more consideration here than at other venues. ✉ *1913 S. Kihei Rd., Kihei* ☎ *808/891–1011* ⊕ *www.ambrosiamaui.com* ⊘ *Mon.–Wed. 7 pm–1:30 am, Thurs.–Sun. 7 pm–1:45 am.*

Kahale's Beach Club. A friendly, festive dive bar, Kahale's hosts live music nightly (including funk, country, and rock) and greasy grub until the early morning hours. ✉ *36 Keala Pl., Kihei* ☎ *808/875–7711.*

Life's a Beach. This place brings in a young bunch looking to par-tay. Wednesday and Friday nights feature classic rock; a DJ presides over Thursday night; and Sunday, Monday, and Tuesday nights are for karaoke. Wednesday is also open-mike night, when aspiring local musicians come to jam. ✉ *1913 S. Kihei Rd., Kihei* ☎ *808/891–8010* ⊕ *www.mauibars.com.*

Sansei Seafood Restaurant & Sushi Bar. The fun atmosphere here is just as popular among locals and visitors, and the feel of the place is brighter and more casual than the resort-style polish of its sister restaurant in Kapalua. It always draws a good crowd on karaoke nights (Thursday–Saturday) when sushi and appetizers are half off 10 pm–1 am. ✉ *1881 S. Kihei Rd., Kihei* ☎ *808/879–0004* ⊕ *www.sanseihawaii.com.*

South Shore Tiki Lounge. Good eats are paired with cool tunes in this breezy, tropical tavern. Local acts and DJs are featured most evenings; if you're craving reggae, Tuesday is your night. Thursday features Top 40 hits. Happy hour specials run 11 am–6 pm. ✉ *Kihei Kalama Village, 1913-J S. Kihei Rd., Kihei* ☎ *808/874–6444* ⊕ *www.southshoretikilounge.com.*

WAILEA

BARS AND RESTAURANTS

Fodor'sChoice
★
Lobby Lounge at the Four Seasons Resort Maui. This lofty resort's lobby lounge is perfect when you want live Hawaiian music, a bit of hula, and freshly prepared sushi all in one sitting. If you're not in the mood for a ceremonius sit-down meal but still crave something out of the ordinary, the place is perfect for a quick bite. The artisanal cocktails are well done and highlight locally distilled spirits. Gorgeous orange ceilings, stark-white stone columns, and modern wicker furnishing pull off the

6

understated look quite well. The fiery sunset over Lanai isn't too shabby either. ✉ *Four Seasons Resort Maui at Wailea, 3900 Wailea Alanui Dr., Wailea* ☎ *808/874–8000* ⊕ *www.fourseasons.com.*

Mulligan's on the Blue. Frothy pints of Guinness and late-night fish-and-chips—who could ask for more? Sunday nights feature foot-stomping Irish jams that will have you dancing a jig, and singing something about "a whiskey for me-Johnny." Local favorite Willie K. performs most Wednesdays; other nights bring in various local bands. ✉ *Wailea Old Blue Golf Course, 100 Kaukahi St., Wailea* ☎ *808/874–1131* ⊕ *www. mulligansontheblue.com.*

UPCOUNTRY

This part of Maui is quite mellow, with a more local scene.

MAKAWAO
BARS AND RESTAURANTS
Casanova Italian Restaurant & Deli. Casanova sometimes brings big acts and electronic dance music DJs from the mainland. Most Friday and Saturday nights attract a hip, local scene with live bands and eclectic DJs spinning house, funk, and world music. Wednesday is for Wild Wahine (code for "ladies get in free"), which can be on the smarmy side, but hey, vacation is a no-udgment zone. There's a $5–$20 cover. ✉ *1188 Makawao Ave., Makawao* ☎ *808/572–0220* ⊕ *www.casanovamaui.com.*

Stopwatch Bar & Grill. This friendly dive bar hosts karaoke nights on Thursday and Saturday, and books favorite local bands on Friday for a $4 admission. ✉ *1127 Makawao Ave., Makawao* ☎ *808/572–1380.*

NORTH SHORE

On the North Shore, Paia gets a bit more action and a vibrant crowd.

PAIA
BARS AND RESTAURANTS
Fodor's Choice **Charley's Restaurant & Saloon.** The closest thing to country Maui has to
★ offer, Charley's is a down-home dive bar in the heart of Paia. It hosts reggae, house, Latin soul, and jazz nights, as well as one-off events with sought-after DJs. Live bands are featured throughout the week. And, despite its robust nightly offerings—or because of them?—Charley's is also known for its great breakfasts. ✉ *142 Hana Hwy., Paia* ☎ *808/579–8085* ⊕ *www.charleysmaui.com.*

PERFORMING ARTS

Before 10 pm there's a lot to offer by way of luau shows, dinner cruises, and tiki-lighted cocktail hours. Aside from that, you should at least be able to find some down-home DJ-spinning or the strum of acoustic guitars at your nearest watering hole or restaurant.

CLOSE UP

Slack-Key Guitars and Ukuleles

You may not think about Hawaii's music until you step off a plane on the Islands, and then there's no escaping it. It's a unique blend of the strings and percussion favored by the early settlers and the chants and rituals of the ancient Hawaiians.

Hawaiian music today includes a stylistic technique on acoustic guitar—slack-key and steel guitar—along with the celebrated *ukulele* (a four-string guitar about the size of a violin), and vocals that vary from traditional chants to euphoric falsettos, or more reggae-inspired compositions.

This is one of the few folk-music traditions in the United States that is fully embraced by the younger generation, with no prodding from their parents or grandparents. Many of the radio stations on Maui play plenty of Hawaiian music, and concerts performed by island favorites fill with fans of all ages.

A couple of don't-miss opportunities to hear Hawaiian music on Maui: the annual **Hawaiian Slack Key Guitar Festival** (☎ 888/226–2697 ⊕ www. slackkeyfestival.com) usually free to the public and held at the Maui Arts

& Cultural Center, and the outstanding **George Kahumoku Jr.'s Slack Key Show: Masters of Hawaiian Music** (☎ 888/669–3858 ⊕ www.slackkey. com), a weekly concert held at the Napili Kai Beach Resort. You can catch Grammy-winning slack-key legends in an intimate setting. The mellow *ki hoalu* (slack-key) music will show you a bit of Hawaii's *paniolo* (cowboy) history and knee-slapping banter among the musicians as they tune their guitars.

May is a month-long celebration of music, hula, and Hawaiian culture through Mele Mei events. *Mele* is Hawaiian for "song" and *Mei* refers to the month. The islands rev up the festivities with concerts, workshops, and festivals that lead to a major soirée on Oahu, **Na Hoku Hanohano Awards**, where the state's legendary and rising musicians are honored. (⊕ www.melemei.com)

Check ads and listings in local papers, and the Maui Arts & Cultural Center, for information on island concerts, which take place in indoor and outdoor theaters, hotel ballrooms, and nightclubs.

6

ARTS CENTERS

Maui Arts & Cultural Center (MACC). This hub of all highbrow arts features everything from hip-hop and reggae performances and Hawaiian slack-key guitar shows to international dance and circus troupes. On selected evenings, the MACC hosts movie from the Maui Film Festival. The complex includes the 350-seat McCoy Theater, the 1,200-seat Castle Theater, the Schaefer International Gallery, and the elegant Yokouchi Pavilion, used for outdoor concerts. There's also a courtyard café for preshow dining and drinks. ⊠ *1 Cameron Way, Kahului* ☎ *808/242–7469* ⊕ *www.mauiarts.org.*

DINNER CRUISES AND SHOWS

There's no better place to see the sun set on the Pacific than from one of Maui's many boat tours. You can find a tour to fit your mood, as the options range from a quiet, sit-down dinner to a festive, beer-swigging booze cruise. Note, however, that many cocktail cruises have put a cap on the number of free drinks offered with open bars, instead including a limited number of drinks per ticket.

Tours leave from Maalaea or Lahaina harbors. Be sure to arrive at least 15 minutes early (count in the time it will take to park). The dinner cruises typically feature music and are generally packed, which is great if you're feeling social but you might have to fight for a good seat. You can usually get a much better meal at one of the local restaurants, and then opt for a different type of tour. Most nondinner cruises offer *pupu* (appetizers) and sometimes a chocolate-and-champagne toast.

Winds are consistent in summer but variable in winter—sometimes making for a rocky ride. If you're worried about seasickness, you might consider a catamaran, which is much more stable than a monohull. Keep in mind that the boat crews are experienced in dealing with such matters. A Dramamine before the trip should keep you in tip-top shape, but if you feel seasick, you should sit in the shade, place a cold rag or ice on the back of your neck, and *breathe* as you look at the horizon.

George Kahumoku Jr.'s Slack Key Show: Masters of Hawaiian Music. Beloved musician George Kahumoku Jr. hosts this program on Wednesday, which features the Islands' most renowned slack-key artists as well as other traditional forms of Hawaiian music. The setup at Aloha Pavilion is humble, but you get to enjoy legendary Grammy-winning musicians. ⊠ *Napili Kai Beach Resort, 5900 Lower Honoapiilani Rd., Lahaina* ☎ *808/669–3858* ⊕ *www.slackkeyshow.com.*

FAMILY
Fodor's Choice
★

Hula Girl Dinner Cruise. This custom catamaran is one of the slickest and best-equipped boats on the island, complete with a VIP lounge for 12 people by the captain's fly bridge. Trips are on the pricier side, mainly because the initial cost doesn't include the cooked-to-order meals. But if you're willing to splurge a little for live music, an onboard chef, and upscale service, it's absolutely worth it. From mid-December to early April the cruise focuses on whale-watching. Check-in is in front of Leilani's restaurant at Whalers Village. ⊠ *2435 Kaanapali Pkwy., Kaanapali* ☎ *808/665–0344, 808/667–5980* ⊕ *www.sailingmaui.com* ⊡ *$78* ◷ *Tues., Thurs., and Sat. 3:30–6 and 4:30–7.*

Maui Princess Dinner Cruise. This 120-foot yacht is set up with a dance floor, open-air deck, snack bar, and cocktail lounge. Unlike other sunset dinner cruises, there's no need to rush to get a good seat—the upper-deck

MAUI MIDNIGHT

If you want to see any action on Maui, head out early. Otherwise, you might be out past what locals call "Maui Midnight," where as early as 9 pm the restaurants close and the streets empty. What can you expect, though, when most people wake up with the sun? After a long, salty day of sea and surf, you might be ready for some shut-eye yourself.

tables are reserved. There's a rotating lineup of live music, and dinner is prepared fresh daily by the onboard staff, who also provide tableside service. You have a choice of roasted chicken, a 12-ounce prime rib au jus with horseradish, macadamia-crusted mahimahi, or a vegetarian patty served with steamed veggies and marinara sauce. Three alcoholic beverages are included in the price; soda and juices are unlimited. ⊠ *Lahaina Harbor, Front St., Lahaina* ☎ *877/500–6284, 808/667–6165* ⊕ *www.hawaiioceanproject.com* ✉ *$85.55* ☉ *Daily 5–8.*

Pacific Whale Foundation Island Rhythms. If you're going out on a Friday, opt for a cocktail cruise with local reggae artist Marty Dread—because what's more perfect than ocean cruising and reggae during sunset? The barbecued pulled-pork sandwiches and fresh-baked brownies are totally satisfying, and Marty's classic reggae covers and original tunes will have you dancing your way back to the harbor. ⊠ *Maalaea Harbor, 101 Maalaea Boat Harbor Rd., Maalaea* ☎ *808/249–8811* ⊕ *www.pacificwhale. org* ✉ *$62.95* ☉ *Fri.; call for check-in times.*

Paragon Champagne Sunset Sail. You can spread out on deck and enjoy the gentle trade winds on this 47-foot catamaran. Cruises are limited to groups of 24, and children three and under are free. An easygoing, attentive crew will serve you hot and cold pupu, such as grilled chicken skewers, spring rolls, and a fruit platter, along with beer, wine, mai tais, and champagne at sunset. ⊠ *Lahaina Harbor, Front St., Lahaina* ☎ *808/244–2087* ⊕ *www.sailmaui.com* ✉ *$59* ☉ *Mon., Wed., and Fri.; call for check-in times.*

Pride of Maui Charters. A 65-foot catamaran built specifically for Maui's waters, the *Pride of Maui* has a spacious cabin for live entertainment, a dance floor, and a large upper deck for unobstructed sightseeing. Evening cruises include top-shelf cocktails and an impressive spread of baby-back ribs, grilled chicken, shrimp cocktail, Maui onion tartlets, and seasonal desserts. ⊠ *Maalaea Harbor, 101 Maalaea Boat Harbor Rd., Maalaea* ☎ *877/867–7433* ⊕ *www.prideofmaui.com* ✉ *$69.95* ☉ *Tues., Thurs., and Sat. 5:15–7:15.*

Teralani Sailing Charters. These catamarans are modern, spotless, and laid out nicely for dining and lounging. They head back shortly after sunset, which means there's plenty of light to savor dinner and the view. During whale-watching season, the best seats are the corner booths by the stern of the boat. Catered by local fave Pizza Paradiso, the meal outdoes most dinner-cruise spreads, with ratatouille, chipotle-citrus rôtisserie chicken, grilled fish, and potato gratin with sundried tomatoes. The trip departs from Kaanapali Beach in front of Leilani's at Whalers Village. ⊠ *2435 Kaanapali Pkwy., Kaanapali* ☎ *808/661–1230* ⊕ *www.teralani. net* ✉ *$83* ☉ *Daily, hrs vary.*

FESTIVALS

In addition to Mele Mei musical events during May, Maui also plays host to some exciting culinary, cultural, and eco-driven festivals. Residents and visitors gather to partake in great food and drink, as well as family-friendly cultural festivities that usually span multiple days.

WAILUKU FIRST FRIDAY

Wailuku sheds its reputation as a quiet, sleepy town for First Friday, a lively block party that shuts down all of Market Street 5:30–10 pm on the first Friday of each month. At last count about 4,000 people were turning out for good eats, local music, and a bit of retail therapy. Businesses hold wine-and-cheese receptions and other special events while performers appear on multiple stages set up along the charming block. Arrive early, as the nearby parking lot gets full by 6 pm. First Friday's success has prompted other towns to hold their own. The party is on Front Street in Lahaina on second Fridays and on Baldwin Avenue in Makawao on third Fridays, and fourth Fridays bring the festivities to Paia.

Celebration of the Arts Festival, The Ritz-Carlton, Kapalua. In March, cultural practitioners, community artisans, artists, and activists gather at the Ritz-Carlton, Kapalua, for a series of events that celebrate Hawaiian tradition and explore current societal topics. Visitors can partake in an *awa* (kava) ritual, observe *lauhala* (pandan or hala leaves) weaving, watch locally produced films, and listen to cultural panels. The festival concludes with a celebration luau. ⊠ *The Ritz-Carlton, Kapalua, 1 Ritz-Carlton Dr., Kapalua* ☎ *808/669–6200* ⊕ *www. kapaluacelebrationofthearts.com.*

Kapalua Wine and Food Festival. Kapalua Resort kicks off the summer in June with the Kapalua Wine and Food Festival. Events are held at various resorts and restaurants in Kapalua, and draw celebrated chefs, sommeliers, industry insiders, and foodies for themed tastings, wine seminars, and evening galas. Guests may book tickets to individual events or a festival package; tickets can be purchased online or, as the date of the event nears, at specific venues. ⊠ *Kapalua* ⊕ *www.kapaluawineandfoodfestival.com.*

FILM

In the heat of the afternoon, a movie theater can feel like paradise. There are megaplexes showing first-run movies in Maui Mall (Kahului) and Kaahumanu Shopping Center (Kahului).

Fodor's Choice **Maui Film Festival.** Held annually around mid-June, this international
★ festival attracts big-name celebrities, who come to Maui for cinema and soirées under the stars around Wailea and at the Maui Arts & Cultural Center. Throughout the year, the center presents art-house and indie films on selected evenings, often accompanied by live music, cocktails, and wine. ⊠ *1 Cameron Way, Kahului* ☎ *808/579–9244 for info, 808/242–7469 for box office* ⊕ *www.mauifilmfestival.com.*

LUAU

A trip to Hawaii isn't complete without a good luau. With the beat of drums and the sway of hula, a luau gives you a snippet of Hawaiian culture left over from a long-standing tradition. Early Hawaiians celebrated many occasions with a luau—weddings, births, battles, and

The small, four-string ukelele is part of Hawaiian music's unique sound.

more. The feasts originally brought people together as an offering to the gods, and to practice *hookipa,* the act of welcoming guests. The word *luau* itself refers to the taro root, a staple of the Hawaiian diet, which, when pounded, makes a gray, puddinglike substance called *poi.* You'll find poi at all the best feasts, along with platters of salty fish, fresh fruit, and *kalua* pork (baked underground).

Locals still hold luau to mark milestones or as informal, family-style gatherings. For tourists, luau are a major attraction and, for that reason, have become big business. Keep in mind—some are watered-down tourist traps just trying to make a buck; others offer a night you'll never forget. As the saying goes, you get what you pay for. ■ TIP➜ Many of the best luau book up weeks or months in advance, so reserve early. Plan your luau night early on in your trip to help you get into the Hawaiian spirit.

FAMILY **Drums of the Pacific Luau.** By Kaanapali Beach, this luau shines in every category—convenient parking, well-made food, smooth-flowing buffet lines, and a nicely paced program that touches on Hawaiian, Samoan, Tahitian, Fijian, Tongan, and Maori cultures. Some guests get tickled by the onstage audience hula tutorial. The finale features three fire-knife dancers. You'll feast on delicious Hawaiian delicacies like shoyu chicken, *lomilomi* salmon (tossed in a salad with tomatoes and Maui onions), and Pacific ahi *poke* (pickled raw tuna, tossed with herbs and seasonings). The dessert spread consists of chocolate, pineapple, and coconut indulgences. An open bar offers beer, wine, and standard tropical mixes. ⊠ *Hyatt Regency Maui, 200 Nohea Kai Dr., Kaanapali* ☎ *808/667–4727* ⊕ *www.drumsofthepacificmaui.com* ✐ *$95–$145* ☉ *Mon.–Sat. 5:30–8:30 (5–8 Oct.–Mar.).*

Fodor's Choice
★
Feast at Lele. This place redefines the luau by crossing it with island-style fine dining in an intimate beach setting. Each course of this succulent sit-down meal is prepared by chef James McDonald of the nearby Pacific'O restaurant, and coincides with the island cultures—Hawaiian, Samoan, Aotearoan, Tahitian—featured onstage. Wine, spirits, and cocktail options are copious and go beyond the usual tropical concoctions. Lahaina's gorgeous sunset serves as the backdrop to the show, which forgoes gimmicks and pageantry for an authentic expression of Polynesian chants and dances. Lele, by the way, is a more traditional name for Lahaina. ⊠ *505 Front St., Lahaina* ☎ *808/667–5353* ⊕ *www. feastatlele.com* ✉ *$120* ⊙ *Oct.–Jan., daily at 5:30; Feb.–Apr. and Sept., daily at 6; May–Aug., daily at 6:30* ⌧ *Reservations essential.*

FAMILY **Grand Luau at Honuaula.** This show captivates with a playful interpretation of Hawaiian mythology and folklore. Indulge in pre-luau fun with Hawaiian games, lei making, and photo ops with the cast, then witness the unearthing of the kalua pig from the underground oven. Traditional dances share a vision of the first Polynesian voyage to the island, and there are also dancers on stilts, an iridescent aerialist suspended by silk, and many elaborate costumes. As a finale, a champion fire-knife dancer brings the house down with a spectacular display. ⊠ *Grand Wailea Resort & Spa, 3850 Wailea Alanui Dr., Wailea* ☎ *808/875–7710* ⊕ *www.honuaula-luau.com* ✉ *$105 standard, $117 premium* ⊙ *Mon. and Thurs.–Sat. 4–8.*

FAMILY
Fodor's Choice
★
Old Lahaina Luau. Considered the best luau on Maui, it's certainly the most traditional. Immerse yourself in making *kapa* (bark cloth), weaving *lauhala* (coconut-palm fronds), and pounding *poi* at the various interactive stations. Sitting either at a table or on a lauhala mat, you can dine on Hawaiian cuisine such as pork *laulau* (wrapped with taro sprouts in *ti* leaves), ahi poke, lomi-lomi salmon, and haupia. At sunset, the historical journey touches on the arrival of the Polynesians, the influence of missionaries and, later, the advent of tourism. Talented performers will charm you with beautiful music, powerful chanting, and a variety of hula styles, from *kahiko,* the ancient way of communicating with the gods, to *auana,* the modern hula. You won't see fire dancers here, as they aren't considered traditional. ■**TIP→ This luau sells out regularly, so make reservations before your trip to Maui.** ⊠ *1251 Front St., near Lahaina Cannery Mall, Lahaina* ☎ *808/667–1998* ⊕ *www. oldlahainaluau.com* ✉ *$105* ⊙ *Oct.–Mar., dasily at 5:15; Apr.–Sept., daily at 5:45* ⌧ *Reservations essential.*

Wailea Beach Marriott Te Au Moana. Te Au Moana means "ocean tide," which is all you need to know about the simply breathtaking backdrop for this south Maui luau. The evening begins with lei making, local crafts, and an *imu* (underground oven) ceremony. The tasty buffet serves a plethora of local staples and desserts like haupia, macadamia-nut brownies, and key lime squares. The performance seamlessly intertwines ancient Hawaiian stories and contemporary songs with traditional hula and Polynesian dances, concluding with a jaw-dropping solo fire-knife dance. ⊠ *Wailea Beach Marriott, 3700 Wailea Alanui Dr., Wailea* ☎ *808/879–1922* ⊕ *www.marriotthawaii.com* ✉ *$110* ⊙ *Mon. and Thurs.–Sat. 4:30–8* ⌧ *Reservations essential.*

Westin Maui Resort & Spa Wailele Polynesian Luau. The oceanfront Aloha Pavilion at the Westin provides a picturesque setting for this Polynesian feast. Seating is family-style. A buffet of traditional dishes such as pickled ahi tuna, fire-roasted teriyaki beef, and Molokai sweet potato with coconut precede the dessert spread. The performances originate from the islands of Hawaii, Tahiti, New Zealand, and Samoa, and although the costumes may not be as elaborate as elsewhere, the pulse-raising five-member fire-knife dance is a thrilling highlight. ⊠ *Westin Maui Resort & Spa, 2365 Kaanapali Pkwy., Kaanapali* ☎ *808/661–2992* ⊕ *www.westinmaui. com* ⊠ *$110 standard, $125 premium* ☉ *Tues.–Thurs. at 5:30; call for updates.*

> **MAI TAI**
>
> Don't let your sweet tooth fool you. Maui's favorite drink—the mai tai—can be as lethal as it is sweet. The Original Trader Vic's recipe calls for two ounces of aged dark rum, mixed with almond syrup, orange curaçao, the juice of one lime, and (wouldn't you know it) rock-candy syrup.

STARGAZING

FAMILY **Tour of the Stars.** For nightlife of the celestial sort, children and astronomy buffs can try Tour of the Stars, a one-hour stargazing program on the roof or patio of the Hyatt Regency Maui. The Romance of the Stars version of the program provides extra twinkle for adults; it's held nightly at 10 pm, and champagne and chocolate-covered strawberries are served. Check in at the hotel lobby 15 minutes prior to starting time. ⊠ *Lahaina Tower, Hyatt Regency Maui Resort & Spa, 200 Nohea Kai Dr., Kaanapali* ☎ *808/661–1234* ⊕ *www.maui.hyatt.com* ⊠ *$25–$45* ☉ *Nightly at 8, 9, and 10.*

THEATER

For live theater, check local papers for events and show times.

Burn'n Love. The fiercely talented ensemble in Burn'n Love takes Elvis Presley aficionados on a whirlwind journey through the King's most memorable Hawaii moments. Pompadour or not, Elvis impersonator Darren Lee has major pipes, and the back-up musicians and dancers give dynamic performances. ⊠ *Maui Theatre, 878 Front St., Lahaina* ☎ *808/856–7900* ⊕ *www.burnnlove.com* ⊠ *$59.99–$109.99* ☉ *Mon., Tues., Thurs., and Fri. at 7:30.*

FAMILY **Maui Academy of Performing Arts.** Founded in 1974, this nonprofit performing arts group offers productions, as well as dance and drama classes for children and teens. Recent shows have included *Evita, Fiddler on the Roof,* and *The Emperor and the Nightingale.* ⊠ *81 N. Church St., Wailuku* ☎ *808/244–8760* ⊕ *www.mauiacademy.org* ⊠ *$10–$35.*

Maui OnStage. Located at the Historic Iao Theater in central Maui, this nonprofit theater group stages five shows each season. Recent productions include *Guys and Dolls, Elf,* Neil Simon's *Brighton Beach Memoirs,* and *The Addams Family.* Each October, it holds a haunted-theater experience in honor of Halloween. The audience is mostly locals, but visitors are warmly welcomed. ⊠ *Historic Iao Theater, 68 N. Market St., Wailuku* 📞 *808/242–6969* ⊕ *www.mauionstage.com* ✉ *$10–$45.*

FAMILY **Ulalena at Maui Theatre.** One of Maui's hottest tickets, *Ulalena* is a

Fodor'sChoice musical extravaganza that has received accolades from audiences and

★ Hawaiian culture experts. The powerful ensemble (20 singer-dancers and five musicians) use creative stage wizardry to give an enchanting portrayal of island history and mythology. Native rhythms from authentic and rare instruments are blended with heart-wrenching chants and aerialist precision, making the 75-minute production seem like a whirlwind. Beer and wine are for sale at the concession stand. ■TIP→ Call for details about dinner-theater packages in conjunction with local restaurants. ⊠ *Maui Theatre, 878 Front St., Lahaina* 📞 *808/661–9913,* ⊕ *www.mauitheatre.com* ✉ *$59.99–$79.99* ⊙ *Mon., Tues., Thurs., and Fri. at 5 (check-in at 4:15)* ⚠ *Reservations essential.*

Warren & Annabelle's. This is a hearty comedy with amazing sleight of hand. Magician Warren Gibson entices guests into his swank nightclub with a gleaming mahogany bar, a grand piano, and a resident ghost named Annabelle who tickles the ivories. Servers efficiently ply you with appetizers (coconut shrimp, crab cakes), desserts (chocolate pots de crème, assorted pies and cheesecakes, crème brûlée), and cocktails, while obliging a few impromptu song requests. Then, guests are ushered into a small theater where magic hilariously ensues. Because this is a nightclub act, no one under 21 is allowed. ⊠ *Lahaina Center, 900 Front St., Lahaina* 📞 *808/667–6244* ⊕ *www.warrenandannabelles.com* ✉ *$64 ($104.50 with food and drinks)* ⊙ *Mon.–Sat. at 5 and 7:30* ⚠ *Reservations essential.*

SHOPS AND SPAS

Updated by
Lehia Apana

We hope you've saved room in your suitcase. With our shopping guide, you can find the top shops for everything "Maui-grown," from *lilikoi* (passion fruit) jams and fresh pineapples to koa wood bowls and swimwear. Style hunters can get their fill of bohemian-resort chic in Paia, luxury brands in Wailea, and *paniolo* (cowboy) threads in Upcountry's quiet Makawao town. And before packing up your plunder, conjure up some Zen by soaking in Maui's natural resources at one of the island's top spas.

If you're seeking authentic Hawaiian artistry, check out the hand-crafted instruments at Mele Ukulele and Maui Divers' jewelry designs. Splurge on an heirloom Niihau shell lei found in art galleries around the island or score pretty *puka* charms from the Maui Swap Meet in Kahului. Maxed out on your luggage weight? No problem. There's Hello Makana (⊕ *www.hellomakana.com*), a subscription service that curates food and gift items from high-quality local artisans and ships to your doorstep. Although the cost of basic goods might be higher on the Islands, keep in mind that the state has a much lower sales tax (4%) than the mainland.

Specialty food products—pineapples, coconuts, or Maui onions—and "Made in Maui" jams and jellies make great, less expensive souvenirs. Cook Kwee's Maui Cookies have gained a following, as have Maui Potato Chips. Coffee sellers now offer Maui-grown and roasted beans alongside the better-known Kona varieties. Remember that fresh fruit must be inspected by the U.S. Department of Agriculture before it can leave the state, so it's safest to buy a box that has already passed inspection.

Business hours for individual shops on the island are usually 9–5, seven days a week. Shops on Front Street and in shopping centers tend to stay open later (until 9 or 10 on weekends).

To unwind on your trip, you can rejuvenate in a yoga class and then enter one of the island's world-class spas. Most treatments use ingredients indigenous to the Valley Isle, like *kukui* nut, coconut, ginger, and eucalyptus. With coveted beauty lines like Eminence or Epicuren sharing the shelves with locally made Ola Hawaii, you're bound to find a spa product or two to bring home.

Traditional Swedish massage and European facials anchor most spa menus on the island, though you can also find shiatsu, ayurveda, aromatherapy, and other body treatments drawn from cultures across the globe. It can be fun to try some more local treatments or ingredients, though. *Lomilomi,* traditional Hawaiian massage involving powerful strokes down the length of the body, is a regional specialty passed down through generations. Many treatments incorporate local plants and flowers. *Awapuhi,* or Hawaiian ginger, and *noni,* a pungent-smelling fruit, are regularly used for their therapeutic benefits. *Limu,* or seaweed, and even coffee are employed in rousing salt scrubs and soaks.

> ## BEST MADE-ON-MAUI GIFTS
>
> ■ Koa jewelry boxes from **Maui Hands**
>
> ■ Sushi platters and bamboo chopsticks from the **Maui Crafts Guild**
>
> ■ Black pearl pendant from **Maui Divers**
>
> ■ Handmade Hawaiian quilt from **Hana Coast Gallery**
>
> ■ Jellyfish paperweight from **Hot Island Glass**
>
> ■ Ukulele from **Mele Ukulele**
>
> ■ Plumeria lei—made by you!

SHOPS

WEST MAUI

One of Maui's top resort areas, West Maui supports abundant shopping options both cheap and high-end, from weekend crafts fairs under Lahaina's historical banyan tree to golf apparel at Kapalua and the art galleries on Front Street. Souvenir tchotchkes can be found in local swap meets, and Hawaiian confectionery items are available in most grocery stores.

LAHAINA
BOOKSTORES

Fodor'sChoice ★ **Maui Friends of the Library.** Behind the Wharf Cinema Center, this nonprofit bookstore is run by volunteers who are happy to let you spend a few minutes (or hours) browsing shelves filled with mystery, sci-fi, fiction, military history, and "oddball" volumes. There's a nice section reserved for new Hawaiiana books. If you've finished with your vacation reading, donate it to benefit the island's public libraries. There's a second location at Queen Kaahumanu Center in Kahului. ⊠ *658 Front St., Lahaina* ☎ *808/667–2696* ⊕ *www.mfol.org* ☉ *Closed Sun.*

CLOTHING

Hilo Hattie. Hawaii's largest manufacturer of aloha shirts also carries brightly colored blouses, skirts, and children's clothing. You can pick up many trinkets and gifts here, but be aware that many are not made locally. ⊠ *The Outlets of Maui, 900 Front St., Lahaina* ☎ *808/667–7911* ⊕ *www.hilohattie.com.*

Honolua Surf Company. If you're in the market for colorful print shirts and sundresses, check out this surf shop. It's popular with young women and men for surf trunks, casual clothing, and accessories. There are two locations on Front Street, plus branches in Lahaina Cannery Mall, The Shops at Wailea, and Paia. ⊠ *845 Front St., Lahaina* ☎ *808/661–8848* ⊕ *www.honoluasurf.com.*

Maggie Coulombe. This local designer's day-to-evening pieces add glam to resort wear. Her printed silk caftans and kimono-style tunics are worth a look. ⊠ *2435 Kaanapali Pkwy., Lahaina* ☎ *808/344–6672* ⊕ *www.maggiecoulombe.com.*

Mahina. At this boutique you can snap up the latest styles without breaking the bank. A friendly staff, easy-breezy dresses, resort-perfect rompers, and loads of accessories await the smart shopper. There are branches in Kihei, The Shops at Wailea, and Paia. ⊠ *335 Keawe St., #208, Lahaina* ☎ *808/661–0383* ⊕ *www.shopmahina.com.*

Maui Vintage. This vibrant clothing store champions locally made products from vintage aloha wear to embroidered hats. Owner Roy Wemyss personally makes earth-friendly Kula Herbs Excellent Soap, which he infuses with local flowers, herbs, and even red clay. The soaps are used in local resorts and spas. ⊠ *121 Dickenson St., Lahaina* ☎ *808/661–0550.*

FOOD

Lahaina Square Shopping Center Foodland. This Foodland serves West Maui and is open daily 6 am–midnight. ⊠ *878 Front St., #6B, Lahaina* ☎ *808/661–0975.*

Safeway. The grocery chain has four stores on the island open 24 hours daily. ⊠ *Lahaina Cannery Mall, 1221 Honoapiilani Hwy., Lahaina* ☎ *808/667–4392.*

Take Home Maui. The folks at this colorful grocery and deli in West Maui will supply, pack, and deliver produce to your hotel. They can even ship pineapples, papayas, and sweet Maui onions straight from the farm to your door (U.S. mainland only). ⊠ *121 Dickenson St., Lahaina* ☎ *800/661–1550* ⊕ *www.takehomemaui.com.*

GALLERIES

Lik Lahaina. Fine art photographer Peter Lik is known all over the world. It's easy to understand why when you see his exquisite and hyper-real pictures of vast Maui landscapes displayed in this Lahaina gallery. ⊠ *712 Front St., Lahaina* ☎ *808/661–6623* ⊕ *www.lik.com/galleries/lahaina.html.*

Village Galleries Maui. This gallery houses the landscape paintings of popular local artists Betty Hay Freeland, George Allan, Joseph Fletcher, Pamela Andelin, Fred KenKnight, and Macario Pascual. There's a second location at the Ritz-Carlton, Kapalua. ⊠ *120 Dickenson St., Lahaina* ☎ *808/661–4402* ⊕ *www.villagegalleriesmaui.com.*

HOME DECOR

Hale Zen. If you're shopping for gifts in West Maui, don't miss this store packed with beautiful island-inspired pieces for the home. Most of the teak furniture and home accessories are imported from Bali, but local purveyors supply the inventory of clothing, jewelry, beauty products, kitchenware, and food. ⊠ *180 Dickenson St., Suite 111, Lahaina* ☎ *808/661–4802* ⊕ *www.halezen.com.*

JEWELRY

Lahaina Scrimshaw. Here you can buy brooches, rings, pendants, cuff links, tie tacks, and collector's items adorned with intricately carved sailors' art. The store sells a few antiques, but most pieces are modern creations. ⊠ *845 Front St., Lahaina* ☎ *808/661–8820* ⊕ *www. lahainascrimshawmaui.com.*

Maui Divers Jewelry. This company has been crafting pearls, coral, and traditional gemstones into jewelry for more than 55 years. ⊠ *658 Wharf St., Lahaina* ☎ *808/662–8666* ⊕ *www.mauidivers.com.*

MARKETS

Lahaina Civic Center Craft Fair. An eclectic mix of vendors and artists set up shop here, offering the whole gamut of souvenir shopping, from towels to aloha prints. ⊠ *1840 Honoapiilani Hwy., Lahaina* ⌧ *$1 suggested donation* ☉ *Most Sun. 9–4.*

SHOPPING CENTERS

Lahaina Cannery Mall. This building, housed inside an old pineapple cannery, has 50 shops. The mall hosts free events year-round like the Keiki Hula Festival and an annual ice-sculpting competition. Free ukulele lessons are available on Tuesday afternoon, and there are free hula shows throughout the week. Recommended stops include Na Hoku, purveyor of striking Hawaiian heirloom-quality jewelry and pearls, and Banana Wind, which carries ocean-inspired home decor. Whether you're searching for surf and skate threads or tropical resortwear, Crazy Shirt, Hawaiian Island Creations, Serendipity, and other retailers give you ample selections. ⊠ *1221 Honoapiilani Hwy., Lahaina* ☎ *808/661–5304* ⊕ *www.lahainacannerymall.com.*

Lahaina Gateway. Besides a pizza and burger joint, this plaza includes Barnes & Noble, Maui Dive Shop, and other stores selling sporting goods and beach-chic apparel. Also found here is Foodland Farms, the local grocery store with excellent Maui-grown, organic, and fine-foods sections. ⊠ *305 Keawe St., Lahaina* ☎ *808/661–5304* ⊕ *www. lahainagateway.com.*

The Outlets of Maui. If discounted designer brands don't entice you to visit this Lahaina retail spot, the dining options most definitely will. Once you're done perusing goods at Adidas, Gap, Calvin Klein, or Maui Jim sunglasses, refuel with wood-fired pizzas and crafted cocktails from Pi Artisan Pizzeria. Hard Rock Cafe, Ruth's Chris, and the ultrapopular Warren and Annabelle's Magic Show are also on the property. ⊠ *900 Front St., Lahaina* ☎ *808/661–8277* ⊕ *www.theoutletsofmaui.com.*

7

KAANAPALI

GALLERIES

Lahaina Printsellers Ltd. Available here are Hawaii's largest selection of original antique maps and prints of Hawaii and the Pacific. You can also buy museum-quality reproductions, plus paintings and photographs, many from local artists. Visit their production gallery at 1013 Limahana Place in Lahaina for an even greater selection. ☒ *764 Front St., Lahaina* ☎ *808/667–5815* ⊕ *www.printsellers.com.*

JEWELRY

Jessica's Gems. Specializing in black pearls, Jessica's Gems also has a sublime selection of Hawaiian heirloom jewelry and locally made sterling silver, including custom designs by David Welty, Dave Haake, and Cici Maui Designs. ☒ *Whalers Village, 2435 Kaanapali Pkwy., Kaanapali* ☎ *808/661–4223* ⊕ *www.jessicasgemsmaui.com.*

SHOPPING CENTERS

Fodor's Choice   **Whalers Village.** Chic Whalers Village has a whaling museum and won-
★ derful oceanfront restaurants and shops. Upscale haunts include Louis Vuitton, Barron & Leeds, and Kate Spade New York, and beautyphiles can get their fix at Sephora. Elegant home accessories at Martin and MacArthur and Totally Hawaiian Gift Gallery are perfect Hawaii-made souvenirs, while the many great surf and swimwear shops will prepare you for a day at the beach. The outdoor mall also offers free weekly entertainment, lei-making classes, and hula lessons; check their website for a complete schedule. ☒ *2435 Kaanapali Pkwy., Kaanapali* ☎ *808/661–4567* ⊕ *www.whalersvillage.com.*

SOUTH SHORE

The South Shore resort area is best known for expensive designer shopping, but you can find some cheaper, more local options. Browse ornate beaded accessories while listening to island rhythms at Kihei Kalama Village Marketplace, or splurge on high-end labels at The Shops at Wailea. Otherwise, turn to a strip mall—or seven—to fulfill your gifting needs.

KIHEI

FOOD

Foodland. In Kihei town center, this is the most convenient supermarket for those staying in Wailea. It's open daily 5 am–1 am. ☒ *1881 S. Kihei Rd., Kihei* ☎ *808/879–9350.*

Safeway. Open 24 hours a day, this store is a convenient place to stock up for South Maui stays. ☒ *277 Piikea Ave., Kihei* ☎ *808/891–9120.*

Tutu's Pantry. In the middle of Kihei Kalama Village is this humble nook with an abundant supply of coffees, teas, cookies, jams, and other specialty-food items made on Maui. You're encouraged to ask for samples. ☒ *1941 S. Kihei Rd., Kihei* ☎ *808/874–6400* ⊕ *www.tutuspantry.com.*

SHOPPING CENTERS

Azeka Place Shopping Center. Spread across two phases on either side of South Kihei Road, this no-frills shopping center in the heart of Kihei caters to locals and visitors alike. The mall is comprised of more than

With a central location almost midway between the Westin and Sheraton resorts in Kaanapali, Whaler's Village offers a mix of upscale shopping, dining, and even live entertainment.

50 stores, including a scuba shop for rentals and dive bookings, a gas station, several great take out and dine-in restaurants, a coffee shop and post office. Ample free parking make this an easy stop to fulfill your basic needs. ⊠ *1279 and 1280 S. Kihei Rd., Kihei* ☎ *808/879–5000.*

Kihei Kalama Village. Encompassing more than 40 specialty shops and restaurants, this area known as "the Triangle" attracts visitors and locals alike. In addition to the brick-and-mortar establishments, there are shaded outdoor stalls selling everything from printed and hand-painted T-shirts and sundresses to jewelry, pottery, wood carvings, fruit, and gaudily painted coconut husks—some, but not all, made by local craftspeople. ⊠ *1941 S. Kihei Rd., Kihei* ☎ *808/879–6610.*

Rainbow Mall. Condo guests can do some one-stop shopping at this mall—it offers spa treatments, Hawaiian gifts, local art, plate lunches, snorkel rental, and a liquor store. There's also a henna tattoo shop and another doing the real thing. ⊠ *2439 S. Kihei Rd., Kihei* ☎ *808/879–1145* ⊕ *www.rainbowmall-maui.com.*

WAILEA
CLOTHING

Cruise. Sundresses, swimwear, sandals, bright beach towels, and stylish resort wear fill this upscale resort boutique. There is a second location in Whalers Village. ⊠ *Grand Wailea Resort, 3850 Wailea Alanui Dr., Wailea* ☎ *808/874–3998.*

Enchantress Boutique. Painted silk gowns and glittering tiaras command attention in the window of the Enchantress—the only boutique on the island where you can buy a fantasy wedding gown off the rack. Indulge the feminine whims with a woven leather handbag from Isabella Fiore, or Swarovski-studded sandals. ⊠ *The Shops at Wailea, 3750 Wailea Alanui Dr., Wailea* ☎ *808/891–6360* ⊕ *www.mauienchantress.com.*

Tommy Bahama. It's hard to find a man on Maui who *isn't* wearing a TB–logo aloha shirt. For better or worse, here's where you can get yours. And just to prove you're on vacation, grab a postshopping drink or dessert at the restaurant attached to the shop. ⊠ *The Shops at Wailea, 3750 Wailea Alanui Dr., Wailea* ☎ *808/879–7828* ⊕ *www.tommybahama.com.*

SHOPPING CENTERS

The Shops at Wailea. Stylish, upscale, and close to most of the resorts, this mall brings high fashion to Wailea. Luxury boutiques such as Gucci, Cos Bar, and Tiffany & Co. are represented, as are less expensive chains like Gap, BCBG Max Azria, and Tommy Bahama. Several good restaurants face the ocean, and regular Wednesday-night events include live entertainment, art exhibitions, and fashion shows. Island Gourmet Markets offers everything from grocery essentials to locally made food products, plus a wide selection of takeaway food options. Don't miss the wonderful galleries here, including Mouche Gallery, where you can find legendary Melvin Sokolsky prints. ⊠ *3750 Wailea Alanui Dr., Wailea* ☎ *808/891–6770* ⊕ *www.shopsatwailea.com.*

Wailea Gateway Center. Although lunch at chef Peter Merriman's Monkeypod is reason enough to venture to Wailea Gateway Center, you might also be enticed by the artisanal confections from Sweet Paradise Chocolate, fine foods at Market by Capische, and all things lovely, local, and stylish at Otaheite Hawaii. ⊠ *34 Wailea Gateway Pl., Wailea.*

CENTRAL MAUI

Locals come here in droves for their monthly Costco run or to catch the latest flick at Queen Kaahumanu Center, but Central Maui can also be an ideal shopping destination for visiting families who are passing time on their way to or from the airport. Most of the stores here can be found on the mainland; however, some specialty shops are worth a peek for Hawaiiana or water-sports goods.

KAHULUI

CLOTHING

Fodor'sChoice   **Hi-Tech.** Stop here immediately after deplaning to stock up on surf
★   trunks, windsurfing gear, bikinis, or sundresses. You can also rent a surfboard or sign up for windsurfing or kitesurfing lessons while you're at it. You'll find additional branches Kihei and Paia. ⊠ *425 Koloa St., Kahului* ☎ *808/877–2111* ⊕ *www.surfmaui.com.*

FOOD

Maui Coffee Roasters. The best stop on Maui for Kona and Island coffees is this café and roasting house near Kahului Airport. Salespeople give good advice and will ship items, and you even get a free cup of joe in a signature to-go cup when you buy a pound of coffee. ⊠ *444 Hana Hwy., Kahului* ☎ *808/877–2877* ⊕ *www.mauicoffeeroasters.com.*

Safeway. If you're coming from the airport, this grocery store (one of three on the island) may be a useful stop. It's open 24 hours daily. ⊠ *170 E. Kamehameha Ave., Kahului* ☎ *808/877–3377.*

MARKETS

Maui Swap Meet. Crafts, souvenirs, fruit, shells, and aloha attire make this flea market in a college parking lot the island's biggest bargain. Maui's food trucks and specialty doughnuts are an added draw. ⊠ *Off Kahului Beach Rd., Kahului* ☎ *808/244–3100* ⊕ *www.mauiexposition. com* ≊ *50¢* ⊗ *Sat. 7 am–1 pm.*

SHOPPING CENTERS

Maui Mall. Longs Drugs anchors the mall, which also has a Whole Foods where you can put together a great picnic lunch. There's a decent ramen house, Oritsu Ramen, and the cult fave Tasaka Guri Guri Shop—it's been around for nearly a hundred years, selling an ice cream–like confection called *guri guri.* The mall also has a whimsically designed 12-screen megaplex. ⊠ *70 E. Kaahumanu Ave., Kahului* ☎ *808/877– 8952* ⊕ *www.mauimall.com.*

Maui Marketplace. On the busy stretch of Dairy Road, this behemoth mall near Kahului Airport couldn't be more conveniently located. The 20-acre complex houses several outlet stores and big retailers, such as Pier One Imports, Sports Authority, and Old Navy. Sample local and ethnic cuisines at the Kau Kau Corner food court. ⊠ *270 Dairy Rd., Kahului* ☎ *808/873–0400.*

Queen Kaahumanu Center. Maui's largest mall has more than 100 stores and restaurants, a movie theater, and a food court. The mall's interesting rooftop, composed of a series of manta ray–like umbrella shades, is easily spotted. Stop at Camellia Seeds for what locals call "crack seed," a snack made from dried fruits, nuts, and lots of sugar. Fresh Hawaii-based streetwear like 808 All Day or In4mation can be found at 180 Boardshop. Other stops include mall standards such as Macy's, Pacific Sunwear, and American Eagle Outfitters. ⊠ *275 W. Kaahumanu Ave., Kahului* ☎ *808/877–3369* ⊕ *www.queenkaahumanucenter.com.*

WAILUKU

ARTS AND CRAFTS

Fodor's Choice ★ **Mele Ukulele.** For a professional quality, authentic ukulele, skip the souvenir shops. Mele's handcrafted beauties are made of koa or mahogany and strung and finished by the store's owner, Michael Rock. There is a second location in The Shops at Wailea. ⊠ *1750 Kaahumanu Ave., Wailuku* ☎ *808/244–3938* ⊕ *www.meleukulele.com.*

Fodor's Choice ★ **Native Intelligence.** This store in the heart of Wailuku champions cultural traditions and craftsmanship. It has curated Hawaiian and Polynesian works of art that include traditional wear, weaponry, photography, books, music, and even surfboards. ⊠ *1980 Main St., Wailuku* ☎ *808/249–2421* ⊕ *www.native-intel.com.*

CLOTHING

Ha Wahine. At this clothing store, statement Polynesian prints are redefined in vibrantly colored blouses, *pareos* (beach wraps), dresses, and aloha shirts. All clothing is designed and made locally, as is most of the jewelry. ⊠ *53 N. Market St., Wailuku* ☎ *808/344–1642.*

UPCOUNTRY

Beyond the resort areas and the airport retail strip you can find some of Maui's most distinctive shops. Discover Upcountry Maui's treasures like gourmet cheeses from Surfing Goat Dairy, and traipse around Makawao for fashion-forward tropical pieces and paniolo gear.

MAKAWAO

ARTS AND CRAFTS

Hot Island Glass. With furnaces glowing bright orange and loads of mesmerizing sculptures on display, this glassworks is an exciting place to visit. The studio, set back from Makawao's main street in a little courtyard, is owned by a family of glassblowers. There's one day each week when the furnace is at rest, so call the studio if you're visiting to see the artists at work. ⊠ *3620 Baldwin Ave., #101-A, Makawao* ☎ *808/572–4527* ⊕ *www.hotislandglass.com.*

MAUI'S BEST OMIYAGE

Omiyage is the Japanese term for food souvenirs.

■ Lavender-salt seasoning from **Alii Kula Lavender**

■ Maui Gold Pineapple from **Take Home Maui**

■ Peaberry beans from **Maui Coffee Company**

■ Nicky Beans from **Maui Coffee Roasters**

■ Jeff's Jams and Jellies from **Paia Gelato**

■ Hot Sauces from **Adoboloco**

■ Hawaiian spice blends from **Volcano Spice Co. Store**

CLOTHING

Collections. This eclectic boutique is brimming with clothing, pretty jewelry, humorous gift cards, housewares, leather goods, yoga wear, Asian-inspired silk shirts, and local beauty products. ⊠ *3677 Baldwin Ave., Makawao* ☎ *808/572–0781* ⊕ *www.collectionsmauiinc.com.*

Designing Wahine Emporium. At this Upcountry haven for Hawaiian merchandise and Balinese imports, you can find endless gift options like authentic aloha shirts, jams and jellies, children's clothes and books, bath and beauty products, and home decor crafted from wood. ⊠ *3640 Baldwin Ave., Makawao* ☎ *808/573–0990.*

Pink By Nature. Owner Desiree Martinez knows what the modern bohemian wants to wear. She keeps her rustic store stocked with local jewelry and feminine pieces from Indah, Bella Dahl, and Novella Royalle. Versatile plaid shirts from Rails are popular, as are their selections of Toms sunglasses and Frye boots. An equally stylish men's and home branch is located a few shops down. ⊠ *3663 Baldwin Ave., Makawao* ☎ *808/572–9576.*

FOOD

Volcano Spice Co. Store. This family operation sells spice blends and hot sauces. Try the fiery Hawaiian Style sea salt with local chilies. The store also carries locally made artwork, jewelry, and bath products. ⊠ *3621 Baldwin Ave., Suite 2, Makawao* ☎ *808/572–7729* ⊕ *www. volcanospicecompany.com.*

GALLERIES

Sherri Reeve Gallery and Gifts. Watercolor enthusiasts rave about Sherri Reeve's pastel expressions of Maui's landscapes, flora, and fauna. Her origami-like sculpted works are sublime, and her designs have been applied to houseware goods that make for ideal gifts. ⊠ *3669 Baldwin Ave., Makawao* ☎ *808/572–8931* ⊕ *www.sreeve.com.*

Viewpoints Gallery. This friendly gallery is co-owned by six local artists and offers eclectic paintings, sculptures, photography, ceramics, and glass, along with locally made jewelry and quilts. In a courtyard across from Market Fresh Bistro, its monthly exhibits feature artists from various disciplines. ⊠ *3620 Baldwin Ave., Makawao* ☎ *808/572–5979* ⊕ *www.viewpointsgallerymaui.com.*

JEWELRY

Maui Master Jewelers. The shop's exterior is as rustic as all the old buildings of Makawao and belies the elegance of the handcrafted jewelry displayed within. The store has added a diamond collection to its designs. ⊠ *3655 Baldwin Ave., Makawao* ☎ *808/573–5400* ⊕ *www.mauimasterjewelers.com.*

NORTH SHORE

Shops in the North Shore's Paia are as diverse as the town's history and eclectic as its residents.

PAIA

CLOTHING

Biasa Rose. The whole family can shop for stylish threads at this boutique. Charming items—including pillows, shoes, and earth-friendly bags—are on display along with comfy Splendid and James Perse cotton tees, airy tunics, Mother Denim jeans, and statement Joya necklaces. The store has a great menswear selection that include Velvet and vintage Aloha shirts. Repurposed kids' clothing and home accessories are locally made. At Rose's Closet, the women's consignment area in the back, you can score designer pieces on a dime. ⊠ *104 Hana Hwy., Paia* ☎ *808/579–8602* ⊕ *www.biasarose.com.*

Letarte. These sultry swimsuits and cover-ups have graced countless magazine covers and wowed celebrities. Letarte's eco-friendly Maui flagship store carries cool gift items, including local jewelry by Maui Mari and Taurus Moon. Founders and sisters Michele and Lisa have also opened locations in California, New York, Palm Beach, and other coastal hotspots. ⊠ *24 Baldwin Ave., Paia* ☎ *808/579–6022* ⊕ *www.letarteswimwear.com.*

Moonbow Tropics. If you're looking for an aloha shirt that won't look out of place on the mainland, make a stop at this store, which sells nicely designed pieces by Nat Nast. The women's store across the street carries work-friendly casual wear in luxurious and breatheable fabrics. If you can't make it to the North Shore, there are branches in Lahaina and Wailea. ⊠ *27 Baldwin Ave., Paia* ☎ *808/579–3131* ⊕ *www.moonbowtropics.com.*

7

Nuage Bleu. Los Angeles meets Maui at Nuage Bleu, a good spot for the coveted resort collections of Mara Hoffman, the downtown flair of Rebecca Minkoff and J Brand, and beachy Joie A La Plage sandals. The entrance emanates exotic scents from Comptoir Sud Pacifique, a fragrance line from Paris. If you're looking for something Maui-made, grab some Shaka Street Soap Works, Annie Fischer clutches, Hula Hoops jewelry, or stylish children's clothing by Bitty Bambu. ⊠ *76 Hana Hwy., Paia* ☎ *808/579–9792.*

Fodor'sChoice ★ **Tamara Catz.** This Maui designer has a worldwide following, and her superstylish threads have appeared in many fashion magazines. If you're looking for ethereal tunics, delicately embroidered maxis, or beaded wedge sandals, this is the place. Catz also has a bridal line that is elegant and beach-perfect. Her pieces cost a pretty penny, but if you visit around May or December, you might luck out on one of her sample sales. ⊠ *83 Hana Hwy., Paia* ☎ *808/579–9184* ⊕ *www.tamaracatz.com.*

FOOD

Fodor'sChoice ★ **Mana Foods.** At this bustling health food store you can stock up on local fish and grass-fed beef for your barbecue. You'll find the best selection of organic produce on the island, as well as a great bakery and deli. The healthy and beauty room has a dizzying selection of products that promise to keep you glowing. ⊠ *49 Baldwin Ave., Paia* ☎ *808/579–8078* ⊕ *www.manafoodsmaui.com.*

Paia Gelato. Fresh gelato made with organic fruit is the draw here. Try the lilikoi quark cheese flavor and thank us later. You'll also find jams, jellies, and dressings from Jeff Gomes, coffees from Maui Oma Roasters, and treats from the Maui Culinary Academy. ⊠ *115 Hana Hwy., Paia* ☎ *808/579–9201* ⊕ *www.paiagelato.com.*

GALLERIES

Art Project Paia. Photographer and gallerist Tatiana Botton brings a stark and fresh perspective to the Maui art community with a well-curated selection of contemporary photography, sculptures, ceramics, and paintings. ⊠ *77 Hana Hwy., Paia* ☎ *808/214–6949* ⊕ *www.artprojectpaia.com.*

Fodor'sChoice ★ **Maui Crafts Guild.** The island's only artist cooperative, Maui Crafts Guild is crammed with treasures. Resident artists produce lead-glazed pottery, basketry, glass and feather art, photography, ceramics, and pressed-flower art. The prices are surprisingly low. ⊠ *120 Hana Hwy., Paia* ☎ *808/579–9697* ⊕ *www.mauicraftsguild.com.*

Maui Hands. This gallery shows work by hundreds of local artists: exquisite woodwork, lovely ceramics, authentic Niihau shell lei, wave metal etchings by Richard DiGiacomo, and famous wave photography by Clark Little. There are locations in Lahaina, Makawao, and at the Hyatt Regency in Kaanapali. ⊠ *84 Hana Hwy., Paia* ☎ *808/579–9245* ⊕ *www.mauihands.com.*

SWIMWEAR

Fodor'sChoice ★ **Maui Girl.** This is *the* place on Maui for swimwear, cover-ups, beach hats, and sandals. Maui Girl designs its own suits, which have been spotted in *Sports Illustrated* fashion shoots, and imports tinier versions from Brazil as well. Tops and bottoms can be purchased separately, increasing your chances of finding the perfect fit. You can also find Tori Praver Swimwear designs here. ⊠ *12 Baldwin Ave., Paia* ☎ *808/579–9266* ⊕ *www.maui-girl.com.*

Pakaloha Bikinis. These Maui-designed bikinis are manufactured in Brazil and come in itty-bitty cuts that stay put during surfing or beach-volleyball sessions. There is a second branch in Lahaina. ⊠ *123 Hana Hwy., Paia* ☎ *808/579–8882* ⊕ *www.pakalohamaui.com.*

ROAD TO HANA

Hana's shopping scene consists mainly of flower and fruit stands, but you won't want to miss the fine art collection at Hana Coast Gallery.

HANA

ARTS AND CRAFTS

Hana Cultural Center. The center preserves ancient Hawaiian artifacts like distinctive quilts, fishing nets, and *kapas* (traditional cloth made from the beaten bark of a tree). It also sells books, jewelry boxes, and other cultural crafts. A small donation is requested at the museum entrance. ⊠ *4974 Uakea Rd., Hana* ☎ *808/248–8622* ⊕ *www.hanaculturalcenter.org.*

GALLERIES

Fodor's Choice
★
Hana Coast Gallery. One of the most well-curated galleries on the island, this 3,000-square-foot facility has handcrafted koa furniture, marble sculptures, photography, and jewelry on consignment from local artists. ⊠ *Travaasa Hana, 5031 Hana Hwy., Hana* ☎ *808/248–8636, 800/637–0188* ⊕ *www.hanacoast.com.*

SPAS

WEST MAUI

LAHAINA

Kamahao a Marilyn Monroe Spa, Hyatt Regency Maui. The spa's ocean-front salon has a million-dollar view and is a convenient beach stroll away from its adjacent parking lot. The facility is spacious and well appointed, offering traditional Hawaiian lomilomi and hot stone massage, in addition to refreshing treatments such as the detoxifying volcanic clay body wrap, and the Marilyn *kopa'a* scrub, a sugar scrub infused with lilikoi. Tap into the powers of aromatherapy with the Marilyn Signature Massage and Best of Both Worlds options; the latter also includes reflexology techniques. Facial treatments use the Marilyn Monroe organic skin care line. ⊠ *Hyatt Regency Maui, 200 Nohea Kai Dr., Lahaina* ☎ *808/667–4500* ⊕ *www.maui.hyatt.com* ☞ *$135 for 50-min massage, $200 spa packages.*

7

KAANAPALI

Heavenly Spa by Westin. Reward yourself at this oceanfront spa with an exquisite lime-sugar body scrub for better circulation or a green-papaya milk bath in a hydrotherapy tub to ease sore muscles. Other options include a cabana massage (for couples, too) and sunburn relief with a nurturing aloe and dilo blend. Facial and body treatments use eco-friendly emerginC organic products. The retail space also carries chic resort wear and locally made Ola products. While you wait for your treatment, sip on ambrosia tea or pineapple-mint water in the spacious, ocean-view relaxation lounge. ✉ *The Westin Maui Resort & Spa, 2365 Kaanapali Pkwy., Kaanapali* ☎ *808/661–2588* ⊕ *www.westinmaui.com* ☞ *$145 for 50-min massage, $270 day spa packages.*

KAPALUA

Fodor's Choice ★

Spa Montage, Kapalua Bay. This spa's nondescript entrance opens onto an airy, modern beach house with a panoramic view of Kapalua Bay. With amenities including a gym, a saltwater infinity pool, and outdoor hydrotherapy circuits, you can easily spend a day meandering about the spa's three floors without feeling cooped up. The menu includes some ancient Hawaiian healing practices. The 'awa and cacao cocoon, designed by Big Island resident and healer Darrell Lapulapu, begins with a special kava tea for instant relaxation, is followed by a body wrap of cacao and kukui oil, and finishes with lomilomi. ✉ *100 Bay Dr., Kapalua* ☎ *808/662–8282* ⊕ *www.spamontage.com* ☞ *$195 for 60-min massage; 15% discount on 3 or more treatments.*

Fodor's Choice ★

Waihua Spa, Ritz-Carlton, Kapalua. At this gorgeous 17,500-square-foot spa, you enter a blissful maze where floor-to-ceiling riverbed stones lead to serene treatment rooms, couples' *hales* (cabanas), and a rain forest–like grotto with a Jacuzzi, dry cedar sauna, and eucalyptus steam rooms. Hang out in the coed waiting area, where sliding-glass doors open to a whirlpool overlooking a taro-patch garden. Exfoliate any rough spots with a pineapple-papaya or alaea salt (Hawaiian red sea salt) and coconut oil scrub, then wash off in a private outdoor shower garden before indulging in a lomilomi massage. High-end beauty treatments include advanced oxygen technology to tighten and nourish mature skin. The boutique has a highly coveted collections of organic, local, and high-end beauty products, fitness wear, and Maui-made Nina Kuna jewelry and natural skin-care lines. The fitness center is handsomely appointed. ✉ *The Ritz-Carlton, Kapalua, 1 Ritz-Carlton Dr., Kapalua* ☎ *808/669–6200, 800/262–8440* ⊕ *www.ritzcarlton.com* ☞ *$175 for 50-min massage, $315 spa packages.*

SOUTH SHORE

WAILEA

Awili Spa and Salon, Andaz Maui at Wailea Resort. The Japanese term *omakase* means to trust the chef to create a fulfilling dining experience. The Awilii Spa and Salon uses this concept at its apothecary or blending bar (*awili* means "to mix"), where freshly dehydrated organic and local fruits and herbs are made into oils and blended together according to a guest's preferences. Papaya or pineapple pulp are made into powder for scrubs, and local chilies are made into a warming a massage oil. Set aside an extra hour to fully indulge in the blending bar, or opt for ready-made concoctions like the kava, noni, and aloe combo for body exfoliation. The cool, soothing interior of this spa is an extension of the minimalist, monochromatic style of the Andaz Maui at Wailea Resort. Relaxation lounges are stocked with thoughtful amenities like tea, coconut macaroons, and edamame hummus. ⊠ *Andaz Maui at Wailea Resort, 3550 Wailea Alanui Dr., Wailea* ☎ *808/573–1234* ⊕ *maui. andaz.hyatt.com* ⟟ *$175 for 60-min massage.*

Fodor'sChoice **The Spa at Four Seasons Resort Maui.** The resort's hawklike attention
★ to detail and genuine hospitality are reflected here. Thoughtful gestures like fresh flowers beneath the massage table, organic ginger tea in the relaxation room, and your choice of music ease your mind and muscles before the treatment even begins. The spa is romantic yet modern, and the therapists are superb. The Lomi Mohala massage uses muscle-relaxing oils blended exclusively for the treatment. Shop for sustainable and organic beauty products like ISUN and Ola Hawaii from the Big Island, or book an appointment at the Ajne blending bar to customize a scent according to your body chemistry. For the ultimate indulgence, reserve one of the seaside open-air *hale hau* (traditional thatch-roof houses). You can have two therapists realign your body and spirit with a lomilomi massage. Taking wellness to heart, the spa partnered with a clinical nutritionist, Dr. Mark Emerson, who gives a complimentary consultation and then designs a "Wellness Your Way" program befitting the guest's health needs. Offerings include noninvasive laser body shaping treaments, indoor or outdoor fitness activities, and a nourishing menu created by the hotel's culinary team. ⊠ *Four Seasons Resort Maui, 3900 Wailea Alanui Dr., Wailea* ☎ *808/874–8000* ⊕ *www.fourseasons.com/maui* ⟟ *$165 for 50-min massage.*

Fodor'sChoice **Willow Stream Spa, Fairmont Kea Lani.** This spa makes meticulous use of
★ Hawaii's natural elements to replenish your Zen. Give a full hour to enjoy the fascinating amenities, two if you plan to work out. At the mud bar, small bowls of volcanic ash eucalyptus clay or white lavender and taro clay can be applied to the body before you head to the steam room. From there, rinse off in a high-tech shower that combines color, sound, and hydrotherapy to mimic different types of Hawaiian rain. A heated stone bench awaits to deepen the relaxation before the treatment. The spa has advanced technology like a wave massage table to simulate floating or LED light and microcurrent electric pulse to tighten the skin. ⊠ *4100 Wailea Alanui, Wailea* ☎ *808/875–2229* ⊕ *www.willowstreamspamaui. com* ⟟ *$165 for 60-min massage, $345 spa package.*

7

ROAD TO HANA

HANA

The Spa at Travaasa Hana. A bamboo gate opens into an outdoor sanctuary with a lava-rock basking pool and hot tub. At first glimpse, this spa seems to have been organically grown, not built. The sprawling garden that overlooks Hana Bay. Ferns still wet from Hana's frequent downpours nourish the spirit as you rest with a cup of Hawaiian herbal tea, or take an invigorating dip in the cold plunge pool, or have a therapist stretch your limbs as you soak in the warm waters of the aquatic therapy pool. Luxurious skin-care treatments feature organic products from Amala, and body treatments incorporate organic Maui-made Ala Lani Bath and Body products. ⊠ *Travaasa Hana, 5031 Hana Hwy., Hana* 🕾 *808/270–5290* ⊕ *www.travaasa.com/hana* ⌕ *$130 for 60-min massage, $200 spa package.*

WATER SPORTS
AND TOURS

Updated by
Lehia Apana

Getting into (or onto) the water may well be the highlight of your Maui trip. The Valley Isle is an aquatic wonderland where you can learn to surf, stand-up paddle, or scuba dive. Vibrant snorkel sites can be explored right off the shore, or easily accessed aboard a kayak, motorized raft, or power catamaran. From December into May, whale-watching adventures are a top draw as humpbacks escaping Alaska's frigid winter arrive in Maui's warm, protected waters to frolic, mate, and birth.

Along Maui's leeward coastline, from Kaanapali on the West Shore all the way down to Waiala Cove on the South Shore, you can discover great spots for snorkeling and swimming, some more crowded than others. On a good day, you might encounter dozens of green sea turtles at an underwater cleaning station, a pod of dolphins riding by the catamaran's bow, and an abundance of colorful fish hovering by bright cauliflower coral reefs.

When your preferred sport calls for calm, glassy waters, get an early start when visibility is best; plus the trade winds begin to roll through the valleys in the late morning and pick up speed in the afternoon. For those thrill seekers who flock to Hawaii for the wind, it's best to head out to the North Shore's Hookipa, where consistent winds keep kiteboarders flying and windsurfers jibing; or Peahi (aka Jaws) where surfers seasonally get towed in to glide on 30- to 60-foot waves.

Treat the ocean with respect and for your safety, choose activities that suit your skill level and health condition. If in doubt, skip the rental and pay for a lesson so that you can have proper instructions in navigating swells and wind, and someone with you in case you get in a bind. The ocean might be beautiful but it can be unpredictable.

Surf can be enjoyed all year, and avid surfers live for the winter swells when the north and west coasts get really "lit up." Whale season on Maui is nothing short of majestic at its peak, late January–mid-March. You can spot them from the shore, or get up close from a motorized raft or catamaran.

BODY BOARDING AND BODYSURFING

Bodysurfing and "sponging" (as body boarding is called by the regulars; "boogie boarding" is another variation) are great ways to catch some waves without having to master surfing—and there's no balance or coordination required. A body board (or "sponge") is softer than a hard, fiberglass surfboard, which means you can ride safely in the rough-and-tumble surf zone. If you get tossed around—which is half the fun—you don't have a heavy surfboard nearby to bang your head on but you do have something to hang onto. Serious spongers invest in a single short-clipped fin to help propel them into the wave.

BEST SPOTS

In West Maui, **D.T. Fleming Beach** offers great surf almost daily along with some nice amenities: ample parking, restrooms, a shower, grills, picnic tables, and a daily lifeguard. Caution is advised, especially during winter months, when the current and undertow can get rough.

Between Kihei and Wailea on the South Shore, **Kamaole III** is a good spot for bodysurfing and body boarding. It has a sandy floor, with 1- to 3-foot waves breaking not too far out. It's often crowded late in the day, especially on weekends when local kids are out of school. Don't let that chase you away; the waves are wide enough for everyone.

If you don't mind public nudity (officially illegal but practiced nonetheless), **Little Beach** on the South Shore is the best break on the island for body boarding and bodysurfing. The shape of the sandy shoreline creates waves that break a long way out and tumble into shore. Because it's sandy, you only risk stubbing a toe on the few submerged rocks. Don't try body boarding at neighboring Big Beach—waves will slap you onto the steep shore. To get to Little Beach, take the first entrance to Makena State Beach Park; climb the rock wall at the north end of the beach.

On the North Shore, **Paia Bay** has waves suitable for spongers and body surfers. The beach is just before Paia town, beyond the large community building and grass field.

EQUIPMENT

Most condos and hotels have body boards available to guests—some in better condition than others (beat-up boards work just as well for beginners). You can also pick up a body board from any discount shop, such as Kmart or Longs Drugs (now owned by CVS), for upward of $30.

Auntie Snorkel. You can rent decent body boards here for $6 a day or $18 a week. ⊠ *2439 S. Kihei Rd., Kihei* ☎ *808/879–6263* ⊕ *www. auntiesnorkel.com.*

West Maui Sports and Fishing Supply. This old country store has been around since 1987 and has some of the best prices on the west side. Surf boards go for $15 a day or $70 a week. Snorkel and fishing gear, beach chairs, and umbrellas are also available. ⊠ *843 Wainee St., Lahaina* ☎ *808/661–6252* ⊕ *www.westmauisports.com.*

HOW TO CATCH A WAVE

The technique for catching waves is the same with or without a board. Swim out to where the swell is just beginning to break, and position yourself toward shore. When the next wave comes, lie on your body board (if you have one), kick like crazy, and catch it. You'll feel the push of the wave as you glide in front of the gurgling, foamy surf. When bodysurfing, put your arms over your head, bring your index fingers together (so you look like the letter "A"), and stiffen your body like a board to achieve the same effect.

If you don't like to swim too far out, stick with body boarding and bodysurfing close to shore. Shore break (if it isn't too steep) can be exhilarating to ride. You'll know it's too steep if you hear the sound of slapping when the waves hit the sand. You're looking for waves that curl over and break farther out, then roll, not slap onto the sand. Always watch first to make sure the conditions aren't too strong.

DEEP-SEA FISHING

If fishing is your sport, Maui is your island. In these waters you'll find ahi, *aku* (skipjack tuna), barracuda, bonefish, *kawakawa* (bonito), mahimahi, Pacific blue marlin, ono, and *ulua* (jack crevalle). You can fish year-round and you don't need a license.

Plenty of fishing boats run out of Lahaina and Maalaea harbors. If you charter a private boat, expect to spend in the neighborhood of $700 to $1,000 for a thrilling half day in the swivel seat. You can share a boat for much less if you don't mind close quarters with a stranger who may get seasick, drunk, or worse: lucky! Before you sign up, you should know that some boats keep the catch. Most will, however, fillet a nice piece for you to take home. And if you catch a real beauty, you might even be able to have it professionally mounted. ■ TIP→ Because boats fill up fast during busy seasons, make reservations before coming to Maui.

You're expected to bring your own lunch and beverages in unbreakable containers. (Shop the night before; it's hard to find snacks at 6 am.) Boats supply coolers, ice, and bait. A 7% tax is added to the cost of a trip, and a 10%–20% tip for the crew is suggested.

BOATS AND CHARTERS

Finest Kind Sportfishing. An 1,118-pound blue marlin was reeled in by the crew aboard *Finest Kind*, a lovely 37-foot Merritt kept so clean you'd never guess the action it's seen. Captain Dave has been around these waters for about 40 years, long enough to befriend other expert fishers. This family-run company operates four boats and specializes in skilled trolling. Shared charters start at $150 for four hours and go up to $195 for a full day. Private trips run $675–$1,500. No bananas on board, please; the captain thinks they're bad luck for

fishing. ✉ *Lahaina Harbor, Slip 7, Lahaina* ☎ *808/661–0338* ⊕ *www.
finestkindsportfishing.com.*

Hinatea Sportfishing. This family-run company has built an excellent
reputation. The active crew aboard the 41-foot *Hatteras* has one motto:
"No boat rides here—we go to catch fish!" Charters run $190–$210 for
a shared boat and $850–$1,100 for a private charter. ✉ *Lahaina Harbor, Slip 27, Lahaina* ☎ *808/667–7548* ⊕ *www.fishmaui.com/hinatea.*

Jayhawk Charters. This ultraluxe, 48-foot Cabo is available for private
charters and takes a maximum of six passengers. It's equipped with air-
conditioning, two bathrooms, a salon, and three comfy staterooms with
the latest music, video, and satellite TV channels. For serious anglers,
the boat also has Shimano rods and reels, a black-box sonar, and the
latest in fish finders, GPS, and chart plotters. Rates are $855 an hour,
and a full day runs last up to eight hours. ✉ *Lahaina Harbor, Slip 63,
Lahaina* ☎ *808/870–5492* ⊕ *www.jhawkyacht.com.*

Kai Palena Sportfishing. Captain Fuzzy Alboro runs a highly recommended operation on the 33-foot *Die Hard.* Check-in is at 1:45 am,
returning around noon. He takes a minimum of four and a maximum
of six people. The cost is from $220 for a shared boat to $1,175 for a
private charter. ✉ *Lahaina Harbor, Slip 10, Lahaina* ☎ *808/878–2362*
⊕ *www.diehardsportfishing.com.*

Start Me Up Sportfishing Charters. With more than 20 years in business,
Start Me Up has a fleet of seven boats, all impeccably maintained.
These 42-foot Bertram Sportfishers offer some of the most comfortable fishing trips around. The company provides an ice chest, tackle,
and equipment. A two-hour shared boat is $129 per person, while a
private charter runs from $399 for two hours to $1,399 for eight hours.
There's a six-person maximum. ✉ *Lahaina Harbor, Slip 12, Lahaina*
☎ *808/667–2774* ⊕ *www.sportfishingmaui.com.*

Strike Zone. This is one of the few charter companies to offer both morning bottom-fishing trips (for smaller fish like snapper) and deep-sea trips
(for the big ones—ono, ahi, mahimahi, and marlin). *Strike Zone* is a
43-foot Delta that offers plenty of room for up to 16 people. Lunch
and soft drinks are included. The catch is shared with the entire boat.
A six-hour trip is $168 per person for a pole; spectators can ride for
$78. Four-hour charters are offered on Tuesday, Thursday, and Sun-
day. Six-hour trips leave at 6:30 am, while four-hour trips depart at 7
am. ✉ *Maalaea Harbor, Slip 40, Maalaea* ☎ *808/879–4485* ⊕ *www.
strikezonemaui.com.*

KAYAKING

Kayaking is a fantastic and eco-friendly way to experience Maui's coast
up close. Floating aboard a "plastic Popsicle stick" is easier than you
might think, and allows you to cruise out to vibrant, living coral reefs
and waters where dolphins and even whales roam. Kayaking can be
a leisurely paddle or a challenge of heroic proportions, depending on
your ability, the location, and the weather. ∎TIP➔ Although you can
rent kayaks independently, we recommend hiring a guide.

An apparently calm surface can hide extremely strong ocean currents. Most guides are naturalists who will steer you away from surging surf, lead you to pristine reefs, and point out camouflaged fish, like the stalking hawkfish. Not having to schlep your gear on top of your rental car is a bonus. A half-day tour runs around $75.

If you decide to strike out on your own, tour companies will rent kayaks for the day with paddles, life vests, and roof racks, and many will meet you near your chosen location. Ask for a map of good entries and plan to avoid paddling back to shore against the wind (schedule extra time for the return trip regardless). Read weather conditions, bring binoculars, and take a careful look from the bay before heading in. For beginners, get there early in the day before the trade wind kicks in, and try sticking close to the shore. When you're ready to snorkel, secure your belongings in a dry pack on board and drag your kayak by its bowline behind you. (This isn't as hard as it sounds.)

BEST SPOTS

Makena Landing is an excellent starting point for a South Shore adventure. Enter from the paved parking lot or the small sandy beach a little south. The shoreline is lined with million-dollar mansions. The bay itself is virtually empty, but the right edge is flanked with brilliant coral heads and juvenile turtles. If you round the point on the right, you come across Five Caves, a system of enticing underwater arches. In the morning you may see dolphins, and the arches are havens for lobsters, eels, and spectacularly hued butterfly fish.

In West Maui, past the steep cliffs on the Honoapiilani Highway, there's a long stretch of inviting coastline that includes **Ukumehame Beach**. This is a good spot for beginners; entry is easy, and there's much to see in every direction. Pay attention if trade winds pick up from the late morning onward; paddling against them can be challenging. If you want to snorkel, the best visibility is farther out at Olowalu Beach. Watch for sharp kiawe thorns buried in the sand on the way into the water. Water shoes are recommended.

EQUIPMENT, LESSONS, AND TOURS

Kelii's Kayak Tours. One of the highest-rated kayak outfitters on the island, Kelii's offers kayaking trips and combo adventures where you can also surf, snorkel, or hike to a waterfall. Leading groups of up to eight people, the guides show what makes each reef unique. Trips are available on the island's north, south, and west shores, and run $69–$160. ⊠ *1993 S. Kihei Rd., Suite 12, Kihei* ☎ *888/874–7652, 808/874–7652* ⊕ *www.keliiskayak.com.*

Fodor's Choice **South Pacific Kayaks.** These guys pioneered recreational kayaking on
★ Maui, so they know their stuff. Guides are friendly, informative, and eager to help you get the most out of your experience; we're talking true, fun-loving, kayak geeks who will maneuver away from crowds when exploring prime snorkel spots. South Pacific stands out as adventurous *and* environmentally responsible, plus their gear and equipment are well

maintained. They offer a variety of trips leaving from both West Maui and South Shore locations. ⊠ *95 Halekuai St., Kihei* ☎ *800/776–2326, 808/875–4848* ⊕ *www.southpacifickayaks.com* 💲 *From $74.*

KITEBOARDING

Catapulting up to 40 feet above the breaking surf, kiteboarders hardly seem of this world. Silken kites hold these athletes aloft for precious seconds—long enough for the execution of mind-boggling tricks—then deposit them back in the sea. This new sport is not for the weak-kneed. No matter what people might tell you, it's harder to learn than windsurfing. The unskilled (or unlucky) can be caught in an upwind and carried far out in the ocean, or worse—dropped smack on the shore. Because of insurance (or the lack thereof), companies are not allowed to rent equipment. Beginners must take lessons and then purchase their own gear. Devotees swear that after your first few lessons, committing to buying your kite is easy.

BEST SPOTS

The steady tracks on **Kanaha Beach** make this North Shore spot primo for learning. Specific areas are set aside for different water activities, so launch and land only in kiteboarding zones, and kindly give way to swimmers, divers, anglers, and paddlers.

LESSONS

Aqua Sports Maui. A local favorite of kiteboarding schools, Aqua Sports is conveniently located near Kite Beach, at the west end of Kanaha Beach, and offers basic to advanced kiteboarding lessons. Rates start at $225 for a three-hour basics course taught by certified instructors. Students enjoy a 10% discount at several Maui kite and surf shops. ⊠ *111 Hana Hwy., Suite 110, near Kite Beach, Kahului* ☎ *808/242–8015* ⊕ *www.mauikiteboardinglessons.com.*

Fodor'sChoice
★ **Hawaiian Sailboarding Techniques.** Pro kiteboarder and legendary windsurfer Alan Cadiz will have you safely ripping in no time at lower Kanaha Beach Park. A "Learn to Kitesurf" package starts at $255 for a three-hour private lesson, equipment included. Instead of observing from the shore, instructors paddle after students on a chaseboard to give immediate feedback. The company is part of Hi-Tech Surf Sports, in the Triangle Square shopping center. ⊠ *Triangle Square, 425 Koloa St., Kahului* ☎ *808/871–5423, 800/968–5423* ⊕ *www.hstwindsurfing.com.*

Kiteboarding School of Maui. One of the first kiteboarding schools in the United States, KSM offers one-on-one "flight lessons." Pro kiteboarders will induct you at Kite Beach, at the west end of Kanaha Beach, providing private instruction with Cabrinha sponsored equipment. Rates start at $199 for three hours. ⊠ *400 Hana Hwy., Kahului* ☎ *808/873–0015* ⊕ *www.ksmaui.com.*

8

PARASAILING

Parasailing is an easy, exhilarating way to earn your wings: just strap on a harness attached to a parachute, and a powerboat pulls you up and over the ocean from a launching dock or a boat's platform. ■TIP➜ Parasailing is limited to West Maui, and "thrill craft"—including parasails—are prohibited in Maui waters during humpback-whale calving season, December 15–May 15.

LESSONS AND TOURS

UFO Parasail. This cheekily named company offers single, tandem, and triple rides at 800 feet ($75) or 1,200 feet ($85). Rides last 8–12 minutes, depending on headcount. It's more fun to take the "dip" (when the boat slows down to let the parachute descend slowly in the water). You'll get a little wet, though you'll probably catch more water while on the boat watching the others take flight. Observers are welcome aboard for $35. Trips leave from Kaanapali Beach, which fronts Whalers Village shopping center. ⊠ *12 Ulupono St., Lahaina* ☎ *808/661–7836* ⊕ *www.ufoparasail.net.*

West Maui Parasail. Soar at 800 feet above the ocean for a bird's-eye view of Lahaina, or be daring at 1,200 feet for smoother rides and even better views. The captain will be glad to let you experience a "toe dip" or "freefall" if you request it. Hour-long trips departing from Lahaina Harbor and Kaanapali Beach include 8- to 10-minute flights and run from $75 for the 800-foot ride to $85 for the 1,200-foot ride. Observers pay $35 each. ⊠ *Lahaina Harbor, Slip 15, Lahaina* ☎ *808/661–4060* ⊕ *www.westmauiparasail.com.*

RAFTING

The high-speed, inflatable rafts you find on Maui are nothing like the raft that Huck Finn used to drift down the Mississippi. While passengers grip straps, these rafts fly, skimming and bouncing across the sea. Because they're so maneuverable, they go where the big boats can't— secret coves, sea caves, and remote beaches. Two-hour trips run around $50, half-day trips upward of $100. ■TIP➜ Although safe, these trips are not for the faint of heart. If you have back or neck problems or are pregnant, you should reconsider this activity.

TOURS

Blue Water Rafting. One of the few ways to get to the stunning Kanaio Coast (the roadless southern coastline beyond Ahihi-Kinau), this rafting tour begins conveniently at the Kihei boat ramp on the South Shore. Dolphins, turtles, and other marine life are the highlight of this adventure, along with majestic sea caves, lava arches, and views of Haleakala. The Molokini stop is usually timed between the bigger catamarans, so you can enjoy the crater without the usual massive crowd. If conditions permit, you'll be able to snorkel the back wall, which has much more marine life than the inside. ✉ *Kihei Boat Ramp, S. Kihei Rd., Kihei* ☎ *808/879–7238* ⊕ *www.bluewaterrafting.com* ✐ *From $55.*

Ocean Riders. Start the day with a spectacular view of the sun rising above the West Maui Mountains, then cross the Auauu Channel to Lanai's Kaiolohia (commonly referred to as Shipwreck Beach). After a short swim at a secluded beach, this tour circles Lanai, allowing you to view the island's 70 miles of remote coast. The "back side" of Lanai is one of Hawaii's unsung marvels, and you can expect to stop at three protected coves for snorkeling. You might chance upon sea turtles, monk seals, and a friendly reef shark, as well as rare varieties of angelfish and butterflyfish. Guides are knowledgeable and slow down long enough for you to marvel at sacred burial caves and interesting rock formations. Sit toward the back bench if you are sensitive to motion sickness. Tours include snorkel gear, a fruit breakfast, and a satisfying deli lunch. ✉ *Mala Wharf, Front St., Lahaina* ☎ *808/661–3586* ⊕ *www. mauioceanriders.com* ✐ *From $139.*

Fodor's Choice
★
Redline Rafting. This company's raft tours begin with a trip to Molokini Crater for some snorkeling. If weather permits, the raft explores the crater's backwall, too. There's a quick stop at La Perouse Bay to spot dolphins, and then it's off to Makena for more underwater fun and a deli lunch. The rafts provide great seating comfort and shade. Whale-watching excursions are $40, and snorkel trips are $125. ✉ *Kihei Boat Ramp, 2800 S. Kihei Rd., Kihei* ☎ *808/757–9211* ⊕ *www. redlinerafting.com.*

SAILING

8

With the islands of Molokai, Lanai, Kahoolawe, and Molokini a stone's throw away, Maui waters offer visually arresting backdrops for sailing adventures. Sailing conditions can be fickle, so some operations throw in snorkeling or whale-watching, and others offer sunset cruises. Winds are consistent in summer but variable in winter, and afternoons are generally windier throughout the year. Prices range from around $40 for two-hour trips to $80 for half-day excursions. ■TIP→ **You won't be sheltered from the elements on the trim racing boats, so be sure to bring a hat that won't blow away, a light jacket, sunglasses, and sunscreen.**

BOATS AND CHARTERS

Paragon Sailing Charters. If you want to snorkel and sail, this is your boat. Many snorkel cruises claim to sail but actually motor most of the way—Paragon is an exception. Both Paragon vessels (one catamaran in Lahaina, the other in Maalaea) are ship-shape, and crews are accommodating and friendly. Its mooring in Molokini Crater is particularly good, and tours will often stay after the masses have left. The Lanai trip includes a picnic lunch at Manele Bay, snorkeling, and a quick afternoon blue-water swim. Extras on the trips to Lanai include mai tais, sodas, dessert, and champagne. Hot and cold appetizers come with the sunset sail, which departs from Lahaina Harbor every Monday, Wednesday, and Friday. Sunset sail starts at $65, snorkel at $70. ⊠ *Maalaea Harbor, Maalaea* ☎ *808/244–2087, 800/441–2087* ⊕ *www.sailmaui.com.*

Scotch Mist Charters. Follow the wind aboard this 50-foot Santa Cruz sailing yacht. The four-hour snorkeling excursion, and two-hour whale-watching and sunset sail trips usually carry fewer than 18 passengers. Two-hour sunset sails start at $70 and include soft drinks, wine, beer, champagne, and chocolate-covered macadamia nuts. ⊠ *Lahaina Harbor, Slip 2, Lahaina* ☎ *808/661–0386* ⊕ *www.scotchmistsailingcharters.com.*

Fodor'sChoice ★ **Trilogy Excursions.** With more than four decades of experience and some good karma from their reef-cleaning campaigns, Trilogy has a great reputation in the community. It's one of only two companies that sail, rather than motor, to Molokini Crater. A two-hour sail starts at $69. The sunset trip includes appetizers, beer, wine, champagne, margaritas, and mai tais. Boarding the catamaran from shore can be tricky—timing is everything and getting wet is inevitable, but after that it's smooth sailing. Tours depart from Lahaina Harbor; Maalaea Harbor; and, in West Maui, in front of the Kaanapali Beach Hotel. ⊠ *Lahaina Harbor, Lahaina* ☎ *808/874–5649, 888/225–6284* ⊕ *www.sailtrilogy.com.*

PRIVATE CHARTERS

Hiring a private charter for a sail will cost you more, but it's one way to avoid crowds. Although almost all sailing vessels offer private charters, a few cater to them specifically.

Cinderella. This swift and elegant 51-foot Peterson costs $400 per hour for regular charter and includes beverages and light appetizers (two-hour minimum), while a snorkel sail with lunch is $1,800 for the day, roughly five hours. Sunset sails run at $900 for two hours. The yacht takes up to six passengers. ⊠ *Maalaea Harbor, 101 Maalaea Rd.* ☎ *808/244–0009* ⊕ *www.cinderellasailing.com.*

Island Star. This 57-foot Columbia offers customized trips out of Maalaea. It's equipped with a galley for on-board food preparation and a master stateroom with a king-size bed. The rate is $600 per hour with a minimum of two hours. ⊠ *Maalaea Harbor, Slip 42, Maalaea* ☎ *888/677–7238* ⊕ *www.islandstarexcursions.com.*

Shangri-La. A 65-foot catamaran, *Shangri-La* is the largest and most luxurious boat catering to private charters. This gorgeous yacht can accommodate up to 49 guests, with a starting hourly rate of $1,533 for a group of 24 or less. A chef and premium alcohol are available for additional fees. ⊠ *Lahaina* ☎ *808/665–0077* ⊕ *www.sailingmaui.com.*

SCUBA DIVING

Maui, just as scenic underwater as it is on dry land, has been rated one of the top 10 dive spots in the United States. It's common on any dive to see huge sea turtles, eagle rays, and small reef sharks, not to mention many varieties of angelfish, parrotfish, eels, and octopuses. Most of the species are unique to this area, making it unlike other popular dive destinations. In addition, the terrain itself is different from other dive spots. Here you can find ancient and intricate lava flows full of nooks where marine life hide and breed. Although the water tends to be a bit rougher—not to mention colder—divers are given a great thrill during humpback-whale season, when you can actually hear whales singing underwater.

Some of the finest diving spots in all of Hawaii lie along the Valley Isle's western and southwestern shores. Dives are best in the morning, when visibility can hold a steady 100 feet. If you're a certified diver, you can rent gear at any Maui dive shop simply by showing your PADI or NAUI card. Unless you're familiar with the area, however, it's probably best to hook up with a dive shop for an underwater tour. Tours include tanks and weights and start around $130. Wet suits and buoyancy compensators are rented separately, for an additional $15–$30. Shops also offer introductory dives ($100–$160) for those who aren't certified. ■TIP➔ Before signing on with any outfitter, it's a good idea to ask a few pointed questions about your guide's experience, the weather outlook, and the condition of the equipment.

Before you head out on your dive, be sure to check conditions. Check the Glenn James weather site (⊕ *www.hawaiiweathertoday.com*) for a breakdown of the weather, wind, and visibility conditions.

BEST SPOTS

Honolua Bay, a marine preserve in West Maui, is alive with many varieties of coral and tame tropical fish, including large *ulua* (jack crevalle), kahala, barracuda, and manta rays. With depths of 20–50 feet, this is a popular summer dive spot, good for all levels. ■TIP➔ High surf often prohibits winter dives.

On the South Shore, one of the most popular dive spots is **Makena Landing** (also called Nahuna Point, Five Graves, or Five Caves). You can revel in underwater delights—caves, ledges, coral heads, and an outer reef home to a large green–sea turtle colony called Turtle Town. ■TIP➔ Entry is rocky lava, so be careful where you step. This area is for more experienced divers.

Three miles offshore from Wailea on the South Shore, **Molokini Crater** is world renowned for its deep, crystal clear, fish-filled waters. A crescent-shape islet formed by the eroding top of a volcano, the crater is a marine preserve ranging 10–80 feet deep. The numerous tame fish and brilliant coral within the crater make it a popular introductory dive site. On calm days, the back side of Molokini Crater (called Back Wall) can be a dramatic sight for advanced divers, with visibility of up to 150 feet. The enormous drop-off into the Alalakeiki Channel offers awesome seascapes, black coral, and chance sightings of larger fish and sharks.

Some of the southern coast's best diving is at **Ahihi Bay,** part of the Ahihi-Kinau Natural Area Reserve. The area has been closed for several years to allow the coral to recover from overuse. At the time of writing, the closure continues. The area is best known for its "Fishbowl," a small cove right beside the road, next to a hexagonal house. Here you can find excellent underwater scenery, with many types of fish and coral.

8

Snorkelers can see adorable green sea turtles around Maui.

TIP→ Be careful of the rocky-bottom entry (wear reef shoes if you have them). The Fishbowl can get crowded, especially in high season. If you want to steer clear of the crowds, look for a second entry ½ mile farther down the road—a gravel parking lot at the surf spot called Dumps. Entry into the bay here is trickier, as the coastline is all lava.

Formed from the last lava flow two centuries ago, **La Perouse Bay** brings you the best variety of fish—more than any other site. The lava rock provides a protective habitat, and all four types of Hawaii's angelfish can be found here. To dive the spot called Pinnacles, enter anywhere along the shore, just past the private entrance to the beach. Wear your reef shoes, as entry is sharp. To the right, you'll be in the Ahihi-Kinau Natural Area Reserve; to the left, you're outside. Look for the white, sandy bottom with massive coral heads. Pinnacles is for experienced divers only.

EQUIPMENT, LESSONS, AND TOURS

Fodor's Choice ★ **Ed Robinson's Diving Adventures.** Ed Robinson wrote the book, literally, on Molokini. Because he knows so much, he includes a "Biology 101" talk with every dive. An expert marine photographer, he leads dives to south Maui and the back side of Molokini Crater. There's a discount if you book multiple dives. Prices start at $129.95, plus $20 for the gear. ✉ *165 Halekuai St., Kihei* ☎ *808/879–3584* ⊕ *www.mauiscuba.com.*

Extended Horizons. This eco-friendly dive boat stands apart by being the only commercial vessel on Maui to run on 100% locally made biodiesel. Its popular Lanai charter has divers swimming through dramatic

DIVING 101

If you've always wanted gills, Hawaii is a good place to get them. Although the bulky, heavy equipment seems freakish on shore, underwater it allows you to move about freely, almost weightlessly. As you descend into another world, you slowly grow used to the sound of your own breathing and the strangeness of being able to do so 30-plus feet down.

Most resorts offer introductory dive lessons in their pools, which allow you to acclimate to the awkward breathing apparatus before venturing out into the great blue. If you aren't starting from a resort pool, no worries. Most intro dives take off from calm, sandy beaches, such as Ulua or Kaanapali. If you're bitten by the deep-sea bug and want to continue diving, you should get certified. Only certified divers can rent equipment or go on more adventurous dives, such as night dives, open-ocean dives, and cave dives.

There are several certification companies, including PADI, NAUI, and SSI. PADI, the largest, is the most comprehensive. A child must be at least 10 to be certified. Once you begin your certification process, stick with the same company. The dives you log will not apply to another company's certification. (Dives with a PADI instructor, for instance, will not count toward SSI certification.) Remember that you will not be able to fly or go to the airy summit of Haleakala within 24 hours of diving. Open-water certification will take three to four days and cost around $350. From that point on, the sky—or rather, the sea—is the limit!

archways and lava structures, while other trips venture along west Maui. Shore and night dives are also available. Tours are run by enthusiastic and professional guides who are keen at not only identifying underwater creatures, but also interpreting their behavior. ⊠ *Mala Wharf, Lahaina* ☎ *808/667–0611* ⊕ *www.extendedhorizons.com* ✉ *From $109.*

Lahaina Divers. With nearly 40 years of diving experience, this West Maui shop offers tours of Maui, Molokini, Molokai, and Lanai. Big charter boats (which can be crowded, with up to 25 divers per boat) leave daily for Molokini Crater, Back Wall, Lanai, Turtle Reef, and other destinations. Breakfast pastries and deli lunch are included. For uncertified divers, there's a daily "Discover Scuba" lesson off one of the Turtle Reef sites or the Mala ramp wreckage, depending on conditions. ⊠ *143 Dickenson St., Lahaina* ☎ *808/667–7496, 800/998–3483* ⊕ *www.lahainadivers.com* ✉ *Diving packages from $375.*

Maui Dive Shop. With four locations islandwide, Maui Dive Shop offers scuba charters, diving instruction, and equipment rental. Excursions go to Molokini, Shipwreck Beach, and Cathedrals on Lanai. The West Maui manta ray dives have a 70% success rate. Intro dives are done offshore. Night dives, scooter dives, and customized trips are available, as are full SSI and PADI certificate programs. ⊠ *1455 S. Kihei Rd., Kihei* ☎ *808/879–3388, 800/542–3483* ⊕ *www.mauidiveshop.com.*

Mike Severns Diving. This company has been around for nearly four decades and takes groups of up to 12 certified divers with two dive

8

masters to both popular and off-the-beaten-path dive sites. Boat trips leave from Kihei Boat Ramp, and go wherever conditions are best: the Molokini Marine Life Conservation District, Molokini Crater's Back Wall, Makena, or beyond La Perouse Bay. ✉ *Kihei Boat Ramp, S. Kihei Rd., Kihei* 🕾 *808/879–6596* ⊕ *www.mikesevernsdiving.com* ✎ *Dives from $154; charters from $1,670.*

Shaka Divers. Since 1983, owner Doug Corbin has led personalized dives, including great four-hour intro dives, refresher courses, scuba certifications, and south shore dives to Ulua, Nahuna Point or Turtle Town (also called Five Caves or Five Graves), and Bubble Cave. Typical dives last about an hour. Dives can be booked on short notice, with afternoon tours available (hard to find on Maui). Shaka also offers night dives and torpedo-scooter dives. The twilight two-tank dive is nice for day divers who want to ease into night diving. ✉ *24 Hakoi Pl., Kihei* 🕾 *808/250–1234* ⊕ *www.shakadivers.com* ✎ *From $69.*

Tiny Bubbles Scuba. Owner and dive master Tim Rollo has led customized, private shore dives along West Maui since 1998. He'll take only four to six divers at a time, and can cater to the most novice diver. Intro dives include gear, air, and shuttle service. Night dives, scooter dives, and scuba certifications are also offered. ✉ *104 Kaanapali Shores, Lahaina* 🕾 *808/870–0878* ⊕ *www.tinybubblesscuba.com* ✎ *Dives from $109.*

SNORKELING

No one should leave Maui without ducking underwater to meet a sea turtle, moray eel, or the tongue-twisting *humuhumunukunukuapuaa*—the state fish. ■TIP→ Visibility is best in the morning, before the trade winds pick up.

There are two ways to approach snorkeling—by land or by sea. At around 7 am daily, a parade of boats heads out to Lanai or to Molokini Crater, that ancient cone of volcanic cinder off the coast of Wailea. Boat trips offer some advantages—deeper water, seasonal whale-watching, crew assistance, lunch, and gear. But much of Maui's best snorkeling is found just steps from the road. Nearly the entire leeward coastline from Kapalua south to Ahihi-Kinau offers opportunities to ogle fish and turtles. If you're patient and sharp-eyed, you may glimpse eels, octopuses, lobsters, eagle rays, and even a rare shark or monk seal.

BEST SPOTS

Snorkel sites here are listed from north to south, starting at the northwest corner of the island.

Just north of Kapalua, the **Honolua Bay Marine Life Conservation District** has a superb reef for snorkeling. ■TIP→ Bring a fish key with you, as you're sure to see many species of triggerfish, filefish, and wrasses. The coral formations on the right side of the bay are particularly dramatic, with pink, aqua, and orange varieties. On a lucky day, you might even be snorkeling with a pod of dolphins nearby. Take care entering the water;

there's no beach, and the rocks and concrete ramp can be slippery. The northeast corner of this windward bay periodically gets hammered by big waves in winter. Avoid the bay then, as well as after heavy rains.

Minutes south of Honolua Bay, dependable **Kapalua Bay** beckons. As beautiful above the water as it is below, Kapalua is exceptionally calm, even when other spots get testy. Needle and butterfly fish dart just past the sandy beach, which is why it's sometimes crowded. ■TIP→ The sand can be particularly hot here—watch your toes!

Black Rock, in front of the Sheraton Maui Resort & Spa at the northernmost tip of **Kaanapali Beach,** is great for snorkelers of any skill level. The entry couldn't be easier—dump your towel on the sand and in you go. Beginners can stick close to shore and still see lots of action. Advanced snorkelers can swim to the tip of Black Rock to see larger fish and eagle rays. One of the underwater residents here is a turtle whose hefty size earned him the name Volkswagen. He sits very still, so you have to look closely. Equipment can be rented on-site. Parking, in a small lot adjoining the hotel, is the only hassle.

Along Honoapiilani Highway there are several favorite snorkel sites, including the area just out from the cemetery at **Hanakaoo Beach Park.** At depths of 5 and 10 feet, you can see a variety of corals, especially as you head south toward Wahikuli Wayside Park.

South of Olowalu General Store, the shallow coral reef at **Olowalu** is good for a quick underwater tour, but if you're willing to venture out about 50 yards, you'll have easy access to an expansive coral reef with abundant turtles and fish—no boat required. Swim offshore toward the pole sticking out of the reef. Except for during a south swell, this area is calm, and good for families with small children. Boats sometimes stop here (they refer to this site as Coral Gardens) when conditions in Honolua Bay are not ideal. During low tide, be extra cautious when hovering above the razor-sharp coral.

Excellent snorkeling is found down the coastline between Kihei and Makena on the South Shore. ■TIP→ The best spots are along the rocky fringes of Wailea's beaches—Mokapu, Ulua, Wailea, and Polo— off Wailea Alanui Drive. Find one of the public parking lots sandwiched between Wailea's luxury resorts (look for a blue sign reading "Shoreline Access" with an arrow pointing to the lot), and enjoy the sandy entries, calm waters with relatively good visibility, and variety of fish. Of the four beaches, Ulua has the best reef. You may listen to snapping shrimp and parrotfish nibbling on coral.

In South Maui, the end of the paved section of Makena Road is where you'll find the **Ahihi-Kinau Natural Area Reserve.** Despite its lava-scorched landscape, the area was so popular that it had to be temporarily closed in 2008. At this writing, it is scheduled to reopen on August 1, 2016. It's difficult terrain and the area did sometimes get crowded, but it's worth a visit to experience some of the reserve's outstanding treasures, such as the sheltered cove known as the Fish Bowl. ■TIP→ Be sure to bring water: this is a hot and unforgiving wilderness.

TIPS ON SAFE SNORKELING

- Snorkel with a buddy and stay together.

- Choose a location where lifeguards are present.

- Ask the lifeguard about conditions before getting in the water.

- Plan your entry and exit points prior to getting in the water.

- Swim into the current on entering and then ride the current back to your exit point.

- Pop your head above the water periodically to ensure you aren't drifting too far out or near rocks.

- Think of the ocean as someone else's home—don't take anything that doesn't belong to you or leave any trash behind.

- Don't touch any ocean creatures; they may reveal hidden stingers.

- Do not bump against or step on coral. Touching it can kill the delicate creatures that reside within the hard shell. Coral reefs grow only an inch or two a year.

- Wear a rash guard; it will keep you from being fried by the sun.

- Apply sunscreen at least 30 minutes before entering the water so less of it enters the water.

- When in doubt, don't go without a snorkeling professional; try a tour.

Between Maui and neighboring Kahoolawe you'll find the world-famous **Molokini Crater.** Its crescent-shape rim acts as a protective cove from the wind and provides a sanctuary for birds and colorful marine life. Most snorkeling tour operators offer a Molokini trip, and it's not unusual for your charter to share this dormant volcano with five or six other boats. The journey to this sunken crater takes more than 90 minutes from Lahaina, an hour from Maalaea, and less than half an hour from the South Shore.

EQUIPMENT

Most hotels and vacation rentals offer free use of snorkel gear. Beachside stands fronting the major resort areas rent equipment by the hour or day.

■TIP➔ Don't shy away from asking for instructions; a snug fit makes all the difference in the world. A mask fits if it sticks to your face when you inhale deeply through your nose. Fins should cover your entire foot (unlike diving fins, which strap around your heel).

If you're squeamish about using someone else's gear (or need a prescription lens), pick up your own at any discount shop. Costco and Longs Drugs have better prices than ABC stores; dive shops have superior equipment.

Maui Dive Shop. You can rent pro gear (including optical masks, body boards, and wet suits) from four locations islandwide. Pump these guys for weather info before heading out; they'll know better than last night's news forecaster, and they'll give you the real deal on conditions. ✉ *1455 S. Kihei Rd., Kihei* ☎ *808/879–3388* ⊕ *www.mauidiveshop.com.*

Snorkel Bob's. Here you can rent fins, masks, and snorkels, and Snorkel Bob's will throw in a carrying bag, map, and snorkel tips for as little as $9 per week. Avoid the circle masks and go for the split-level ($25 per week) or dry snorkel ($44 per week); it's worth the extra money. There are many Snorkel Bob's locations in Maui, including Napili, Wailea, and Lahaina. ⊠ *Napili Village Hotel, 5425 Lower Honoapiilani Hwy., Napili* ☎ *808/669–9603* ⊕ *www.snorkelbob.com.*

TOURS

The same boats that offer whale-watching, sailing, and diving also offer snorkeling excursions. Trips usually include visits to two locales, lunch, gear, instruction, and possible whale or dolphin sightings. Some captains troll for fish along the way.

Molokini Crater, a crescent about 3 miles offshore from Wailea, is the most popular snorkel cruise destination. You can spend half a day floating above the fish-filled crater for about $80. Some say it's not as good as it's made out to be, and that it's too crowded, but others consider it to be one of the best spots in Hawaii. Visibility is generally outstanding and fish are incredibly tame. Your second stop will be somewhere along the leeward coast, either Turtle Town near Makena or Coral Gardens toward Lahaina. ■TIP➔ On blustery mornings, there's a good chance the waters will be too rough to moor in Molokini Crater, and you'll end up snorkeling somewhere off the shore, where you could have driven for free.

If you've tried snorkeling and are tentatively thinking about scuba, you may want to try "snuba," a cross between the two. With snuba, you dive 20 feet below the surface, only you're attached to an air hose from the boat. Many boats now offer snuba (for an extra fee of $45–$65) as well as snorkeling.

Snorkel cruises vary—some serve mai tais and steaks whereas others offer beer and cold cuts. You might prefer a large ferryboat to a smaller sailboat, or vice versa. Be sure you know where to go to board your vessel; getting lost in the harbor at 6 am is a lousy start. ■TIP➔ Bring sunscreen, an underwater camera (they're double the price on board), a towel, and a cover-up for the windy return trip. Even tropical waters get chilly after hours of swimming, so consider wearing a rash guard. Wet suits can usually be rented for a fee. Hats without straps will blow away, and valuables should be left at home.

Alii Nui Maui. On this 65-foot luxury catamaran, you can come as you are (with a bathing suit, of course); towels, sunblock, and all your gear are provided. Because the owners also operate Maui Dive Shop, snorkel and dive equipment are top-of-the-line. Wet-suit tops are available to use for sun protection or to keep extra warm in the water. The boat, which holds a maximum of 60 people, is nicely appointed. A morning snorkel sail (there's a diving option, too) heads to Turtle Town or Molokini Crater and includes a continental breakfast, lunch, and postsnorkel alcoholic drinks. The three-, five-, or six-hour snorkel trip offers transportation from your hotel. Videography and huka (similar to snuba) are available for a fee. ⊠ *Maalaea Harbor, Slip 56, Maalaea* ☎ *800/542–3483, 808/875–0333* ⊕ *www.aliinuimaui.com* ⊟ *From $69.*

8

FAMILY **Gemini Sailing Charters.** One of the main draws of this snorkel excursion is its affordable rates. The vacation-friendly check-in time of 10:30 am is another plus. Honolua Bay is the primary destination, but Mala wharf in Lahaina and Olowalu are possible options in case of choppy waters. The hot buffet lunch is catered by the Westin Maui Resort & Spa. You can find the company on Kaanapali Beach near the Westin's activity desk. ✉ *Westin Maui Resort & Spa, 2365 Kaanapali Pkwy., Kaanapali* ☎ *808/669–0508* ⊕ *www.geminicharters.com* ⚓ *From $120.*

FAMILY **Hawaiian Sailing Canoe Adventure.** Few things could qualify as a more authentic Hawaiian experience than paddling in a sail canoe with this family-run outfit. Get a deep sense of history and mythology as you listen to your guide pray, chant, and bestow a wealth of knowledge about ancient Hawaii during this intimate excursion. The canoe makes a snorkel stop at a nearby reef. Refreshments and snorkel equipment are included. You meet at Polo Beach in front of the Fairmont Kea Lani. ✉ *Fairmont Kea Lani, 4100 Wailea Alanui Dr., Wailea* ☎ *808/281–9301* ⊕ *www.mauisailingcanoe.com* ⚓ *From $179.*

FAMILY **Maui Classic Charters.** Hop aboard the *Four Winds II,* a 55-foot, glass-bottom catamaran (great fun for kids), for one of the most dependable snorkel trips around. You'll spend more time than other charter boats at Molokini Crater and enjoy turtle-watching on the way home. The trip includes optional snuba ($59 extra), continental breakfast, barbecue lunch, beer, wine, and soda. With its reasonable price, the trip can be popular and crowded. The crew works hard to keep everyone happy, but if the trip is fully booked, you will be cruising with more than 100 new friends. For a more intimate experience, opt for the *Maui Magic,* Maalaea's fastest PowerCat, which holds fewer people than some of the larger vessels. ✉ *Maalaea Harbor, Slips 55 and 80, Maalaea* ☎ *808/879–8188, 800/736–5740* ⊕ *www.mauicharters.com* ⚓ *From $98.*

Queen's Treasure. This catamaran on the west side gets kudos for its attentive crew, who will nudge you to "walk the plank," a fun diving ledge off the side of the bow. Pricing is slightly lower than most half-day charters in Kaanapali. The spread includes a light breakfast, deli lunch, and an open bar (for an extra fee) for postsnorkel merriment. Check-in is in front of Hula Grill. ✉ *Whalers Village, 2435 Kaanapali Pkwy., Kaanapali* ☎ *808/667–2469* ⊕ *www.queenstreasure.com* ⚓ *From $99.*

EDUCATIONAL EXCURSIONS

Jean-Michel Cousteau's **Ambassadors of the Environment,** housed at the Ritz-Carlton, Kapalua, presents more of an educational excursion than a regular tour. The 2½-hour beginner's snorkel class and underwater photography session ($120), held in Kapalua Bay, is especially great for kids. An extensive youth program includes whale-watching, stargazing, and more, with all sessions led by naturalists who link Hawaiian culture with conservation. For information, call ☎ *808/665–7292.*

Teralani Sailing Charters. Choose between a standard snorkel trip with a deli lunch or a top-of-the-line excursion that's an hour longer and includes two snorkel sites and a barbecue-style lunch. The company's cats could hold well over 100 people, but 49 is the maximum per trip. The boats are kept in pristine condition. Freshwater showers are available, as is an open bar after the second snorkel stop. A friendly crew provides all your gear, a flotation device, and a quick course in snorkeling. During whale season, only the premier trip is available. Boarding is right off Kaanapali Beachfronting Whalers Village. ⊠ *Kaanapali Beach, Kaanapali* ☎ *808/661–7245* ⊕ *www.teralani. net* 🍴 *From $112.*

FAMILY
Fodor's Choice
★

Trilogy Excursions. Many people consider a trip with Trilogy Excursions to be a highlight of their vacation. Maui's longest-running operation has comprehensive offerings, with seven beautiful 50- to 64-foot sailing vessels at three departure sites. All excursions are staffed by energetic crews who will keep you well fed and entertained with local stories and corny jokes. A full-day catamaran cruise to Lanai includes a continental breakfast and barbecue lunch, a guided tour of the island, a "Snorkeling 101" class, and time to snorkel in the waters of Lanai's Hulopoe Marine Preserve (Trilogy Excursions has exclusive commercial access). The company also offers a Molokini Crater and Honolua Bay snorkel cruise that is top-notch. Tours depart from Lahaina Harbor; Maalaea Harbor; and, in West Maui, in front of the Kaanapali Beach Hotel. ⊠ *207 Kuopohi St., Lahaina* ☎ *808/874–5649, 888/225–6284* ⊕ *www. sailtrilogy.com* 🍴 *From $119.*

STAND-UP PADDLING

Also called stand-up paddle surfing or paddleboarding, stand-up paddling is the "comeback kid" of surf sports; you stand on a longboard and paddle out with a canoe oar. While stand-up paddling requires even more balance and coordination than regular surfing, it is still accessible to just about every skill level. Most surf schools now offer stand-up paddle lessons. Advanced paddlers can amp up the adrenaline with a downwind coastal run that spans almost 10 miles from North Shore's Maliko Gulch to Kahului Harbor, sometimes reaching speeds up to 30 mph.

8

The fun thing about stand-up paddling is that you can enjoy it whether the surf is good or the water is flat. However, as with all water sports, it's important to read the environment and be attentive. Look at the sky and assess the wind by how fast the clouds are moving. Note where the whitecaps are going and always point the nose of your board perpendicular to the wave. ■TIP→ Because of the size and speed of a longboard, stand-up paddling can be dangerous, so lessons are highly recommended, especially if you intend to surf.

LESSONS

Maui Surfer Girls. Owner and bona fide waterwoman Dustin Tester has been surfing since she was 7 and has been a multisport athlete ever since. Class sizes are limited to three guests per instructor to ensure highly personalized lessons. Board, paddle, rash guard, and booties are included. Locations vary, depending on wind conditions, but you'll most likely go to beginner-friendly Ukumehame Beach (Thousand Peaks) at mile marker 12. Rates begin at $100 per person for a group lesson, or $175 for a private lesson. ⊠ *Ukumehame Beach Park, Lahaina* ☎ *808/214–0606* ⊕ *www.mauisurfergirls.com.*

Stand-Up Paddle Surf School. Maui's first school devoted solely to stand-up paddling was founded by the legendary Maria Souza, the first woman to surf the treacherous waves of "Jaws" on Maui's North Shore. Although most surf schools offer stand-up paddling, Maria's classes are in a league of their own. They include a proper warm-up with a hula-hoop and balance ball and a cool-down with yoga. The cost is $165 per person for a group session, $199 for a private session. Locations vary depending on conditions. ⊠ *185 Paka Pl., Kihei* ☎ *808/579–9231* ⊕ *www.standuppaddlesurfschool.com.*

SURFING

Maui's coastline has surf for every level of waterman or -woman. Waves on leeward-facing shores (West and South Maui) tend to break in gentle sets all summer long. Surf instructors in Kihei and Lahaina can rent you boards, give you onshore instruction, and then lead you out through the channel, where it's safe to enter the surf. They'll shout encouragement while you paddle like mad for the thrill of standing on water—most will give you a helpful shove. These areas are great for beginners; the only danger is whacking a stranger with your board or stubbing your toe against the reef.

The North Shore is another story. Winter waves pound the windward coast, attracting water champions from every corner of the world. Adrenaline addicts are towed in by Jet Ski to a legendary, deep-sea break called Jaws. Waves here periodically tower upward of 40 feet. The only spot for viewing this phenomenon (which happens just a few times a year) is on private property. So, if you hear the surfers next to you crowing about Jaws "going off," cozy up and get them to take you with them.

Whatever your skill, there's a board, a break, and even a surf guru to accommodate you. A two-hour lesson is a good intro to surf culture.

You can get the wave report each day by checking page 2 of the *Maui News*, logging on to the Glenn James weather site (⊕ *www.hawaiiweathertoday. com*) or by calling ☏ *808/871–5054* (for the weather forecast) or ☏ *808/877–3611* (for the surf report).

BEST SPOTS

On the South Shore, beginners can hang ten at Kihei's **Cove Park,** a sometimes crowded but reliable 1- to 2-foot break. Boards can easily be rented across the street, or in neighboring Kalama Park's parking lot. The only bummer is having to balance the 9-plus-foot board on your head while crossing busy South Kihei Road.

For advanced wave riders, **Hookipa Beach Park** on the North Shore boasts several well-loved breaks, including "Pavilions," "Lanes," "the Point," and "Middles." Surfers have priority until 11 am, when windsurfers move in on the action.

■ TIP→ Competition is stiff here. If you don't know what you're doing, consider watching.

WATCHING SURFERS

Even if you aren't a surfer, watching is just as fun (well, almost). Near-perfect waves can be seen at Honolua Bay, on the northern tip of West Maui. To get here, continue 2 miles north of D. T. Fleming Park on Highway 30 and take a left onto the dirt road next to a pineapple field; a path leads down the cliff to the beach. In addition, Hookipa Beach Park, just outside of Paia, gives you the perfect overlook to see pro surfers, windsurfers, and kiters.

Long- or shortboarders in West Maui can paddle out at **Launiupoko State Wayside.** The east end of the park has an easy break, good for beginners.

Also called Thousand Peaks, **Ukumehame** is one of the better beginner spots in West Maui. You'll soon see how the spot got its name—the waves here break again and again in wide and consistent rows, giving lots of room for beginning and intermediate surfers.

Good surf spots in West Maui include "Grandma's" at **Papalaua Park,** just after the *pali* (cliff) where waves are so easy a grandma could ride 'em; **Puamana Beach Park** for a mellow longboard day; and **Lahaina Harbor,** which offers an excellent inside wave for beginners (called Breakwall), as well as the more advanced outside (a great lift if there's a big south swell).

EQUIPMENT AND LESSONS

Surf camps are becoming increasingly popular, especially with women. One- or two-week camps offer a terrific way to build muscle and self-esteem simultaneously.

Big Kahuna Adventures. Rent soft-top longboards here for $20 for two hours, or $30 for the day. Weekly rates are available. The shop also offers surf lessons starting at $60, and rents kayaks, plus snorkel and beach gear. The company is across from Cove Park. ✉ *1913-C S. Kihei Rd., Kihei* ☎ *808/875–6395* ∰ *www.bigkahunaadventures.com.*

Goofy Foot. Surfing "goofy foot" means putting your right foot forward. They might be goofy, but we like the right-footed gurus here. This shop is just plain cool and only steps away from "Breakwall," a great beginner's spot in Lahaina. A two-hour class with five or fewer students is $65, and you're guaranteed to be standing by the end or it's free. Owner and "stoke broker" Tim Sherer offers private lessons for $250 and will sometimes ride alongside to record video clips and give more thorough feedback. A private two-hour lesson with another instructor is $150. ✉ *505 Front St., Suite 123, Lahaina* ☎ *808/244–9283* ∰ *www. goofyfootsurfschool.com.*

Hi-Tech Surf Sports. Hi-Tech has some of the best boards, advice, and attitude around. It rents even its best surfboards—choose from longboards, shortboards, and hybrids—starting at $25 per day. ✉ *425 Koloa St., Kahului* ☎ *808/877–2111* ∰ *www.surfmaui.com.*

Maui Surfer Girls. Maui Surfer Girls started in 2001 with surf camps for teen girls, but quickly branched out to offer surfing lessons year round. Located away from the crowds, Maui Surfer Girls specializes in private lessons and small groups, and their ratio of four students per instructor is the smallest in the industry. The highly popular summer camps are still run for teen girls, and are now open to women as well. ✉ *Lahaina* ☎ *808/214–0606* ∰ *www.mauisurfergirls.com.*

FAMILY
Fodor's Choice
★
Maui Surf Clinics. Instructors here will get even the shakiest novice riding with the school's "Learn to Surf in One Lesson" program. A two-hour group lesson (up to five students) is $78. Private lessons with the patient and meticulous instructors are $165 for two hours. The company provides boards, rash guards, and water shoes, all in impeccable condition—and it's tops in the customer-service department. ✉ *505 Front St., Suite 201, Lahaina* ☎ *808/244–7873* ∰ *www.mauisurfclinics.com.*

Outrageous Surf School. If you're not too keen on shore lessons, Outrageous Surf School might be your best bet. After a quick demo in the shop, down to the Breakwall you go. Lessons start at $60 for a group lesson, $75 for a semiprivate lesson, and $120 for a private lesson. Repeat lessons are $40. ✉ *640 Front St., Lahaina* ☎ *808/669–1400* ∰ *www.youcansurf.com.*

Royal Hawaiian Surf Academy. Owner Kimo Kinimaka grew up rippin' it with his uncle, legendary surfer Titus Kinimaka, so it's no wonder his passion translates to a fun, memorable time at the novice-friendly Lahaina Breakwall. Private lessons are $150, and group lessons cost $65 per person. Rash guards and shoes are provided. ✉ *113-B Prison St., Lahaina* ☎ *808/276–7873* ∰ *www.royalhawaiiansurfacademy.com.*

Second Wind. Surfboard rentals at this centrally located shop are a deal—good boards go for $20 per day or $130 per week. The shop also rents and sells its own Elua Makani boards (which means "second wind" in Hawaiian). Although the staff don't offer lessons, they will book you with the best surfing, windsurfing, and kiteboarding lessons on the island. ✉ *111 Hana Hwy., Kahului* ☎ *808/877–7467* ∰ *www. secondwindmaui.com.*

Humpback whale calves are plentiful in winter; this one is breaching off West Maui.

WHALE-WATCHING

From December into May whale-watching becomes one of the most popular activities on Maui. During the season *all* outfitters offer whale-watching in addition to their regular activities, and most do an excellent job. Boats leave the wharves at Lahaina and Maalaea in search of humpbacks, allowing you to enjoy the awe-inspiring size of these creatures in closer proximity. From November through May, the Pacific Whale Foundation sponsors the Maui Whale Festival, a variety of whale-related events for locals and visitors; check the calendar at ⊕ *www.mauiwhalefestival.org.*

As it's almost impossible *not* to see whales in winter on Maui, you'll want to prioritize: is adventure or comfort your aim? If close encounters with the giants of the deep are your desire, pick a smaller boat that promises sightings. Those who think "green" usually prefer the smaller, quieter vessels that produce the least amount of negative impact to the whales' natural environment. For those wanting to sip mai tais as whales cruise by, stick with a sunset cruise ($40 and up) on a boat with an open bar and *pupu* (Hawaiian tapas). ■TIP➜ Afternoon trips are generally rougher because the wind picks up, but some say this is when the most surface action occurs.

Every captain aims to please during whale season, getting as close as legally possible (100 yards). Crew members know when a whale is about to dive (after several waves of its heart-shape tail) but rarely can predict breaches (when the whale hurls itself up and almost entirely out of the water). Prime viewing space (on the upper and lower decks, around the railings) is limited, so boats can feel crowded even when half

The Humpback's Winter Home

The humpback whales' attraction to Maui is legendary, and seeing them December–May is a highlight for many visitors. More than half the Pacific's humpback population winters in Hawaii, especially in the waters around the Valley Isle, where mothers can be seen just a few hundred feet offshore, training their young calves in the fine points of whale etiquette. Watching from shore, it's easy to catch sight of whales spouting, or even breaching—when they leap almost entirely out of the sea, slapping back onto the water with a huge splash.

At one time there were thousands of the huge mammals, but a history of overhunting and marine pollution reduced the world population to about 1,500. In 1966 humpbacks were put on the endangered-species list. Hunting or harassing whales is illegal in the waters of most nations, and in the United States boats and airplanes are restricted from getting too close. The jury is still out, however, on the effects of military sonar testing on the marine mammals.

Marine biologists believe the humpbacks (much like humans) keep returning to Hawaii because of its warmth. Having fattened themselves in subarctic waters all summer, the whales migrate south in the winter to breed, and a rebounding population of thousands cruise Maui waters. Winter is calving time, and the young whales probably couldn't survive in the frigid Alaskan waters. No one has ever seen a whale give birth here, but experts know that calving is their main winter activity, because the 1- and 2-ton youngsters suddenly appear while the whales are in residence.

The first sighting of a humpback whale spout each season is exciting for locals on Maui. A collective sigh of relief can be heard: "Ah, they've returned." In the not-so-far distance, flukes and flippers can be seen rising above the ocean's surface. It's hard not to anthropomorphize the tail waving; it looks like such an amiable gesture. Each fluke is uniquely patterned, like a human's fingerprint, and is used to identify the giants as they travel halfway around the globe and back.

full. If you don't want to squeeze in beside strangers, opt for a smaller boat with fewer bookings. Don't forget to bring sunscreen, sunglasses, a light long-sleeve cover-up, and a hat you can secure. Winter weather is less predictable and at times can be extreme, especially as the wind picks up. Arrive early to find parking.

BEST SPOTS

The northern end of **Keawakapu Beach** on the South Shore seems to be a whale magnet. Situate yourself on the sand or at the nearby restaurant and watch mamas and calves. From mid-December to mid-April, the Pacific Whale Foundation has naturalists at Ulua Beach and at the scenic viewpoint at **Papawai Point Lookout.** Like the commuting traffic, whales can be spotted along the pali of West Maui's Honoapiilani Highway all day long. Make sure to park safely before craning your neck out to see them.

BOATS AND CHARTERS

Gemini Sailing Charters. Morning and afternoon whale-watching trips off the Kaanapali coast are available on this well-maintained catamaran staffed by an experienced and fun crew. The cost is $60 per person for the morning trip and $70 for the afternoon trip. You can find Gemini on Kaanapali Beach near the Westin Maui resort's activity desk. ✉ *Westin Maui Resort & Spa, 2365 Kaanapali Pkwy., Lahaina* ☎ *800/820–7245, 808/669–0508* ⊕ *www.geminicharters.com.*

Maui Adventure Cruises. Whale-watching from this company's raft puts you right above the water surface and on the same level as the whales. You'll forego the cocktail in your hand but you won't have to deal with crowds, even if the vessel is at max capacity with 36 people. The whales can get up close if they like, and when they do it's absolutely spectacular. These rafts can move with greater speed than a catamaran, so you don't spend much time motoring between whales or pods. Refreshments are included. Prices are $45 for adults and $35 for kids 5–12 years old (children under 4 years old are not admitted). ✉ *Lahaina Harbor, Slip 11, Lahaina* ☎ *808/661–5550* ⊕ *www.mauiadventurecruises.com.*

FAMILY **Pacific Whale Foundation.** With a fleet of 10 boats, this nonprofit organization pioneered whale-watching back in 1979. The crew (including a certified marine biologist) offers insights into whale behavior and suggests ways for you to help save marine life worldwide. One of the best things about these trips is the underwater hydrophone that allows you to listen to the whales sing. Trips meet at the organization's store, which sells whale-theme and local souvenirs. You'll share the boat with about 100 people in stadium-style seating. If you prefer a smaller crowd, book their eco-friendly raft cruises instead. ✉ *612 Front St., Lahaina* ☎ *808/249–8811* ⊕ *www.pacificwhale.org.*

Trilogy Excursions. Whale-watching trips with Trilogy Excursions consist of smaller groups of 20–36 passengers and include beverages and snacks, an onboard marine naturalist, and hydrophones that detect underwater sound waves. Trips are $59 and depart from Lahaina Harbor, Maalaea Harbor, and West Maui's Kaanapali Beach Hotel. ✉ *Kaanapali Beach Hotel, 2525 Kaanapali Pkwy., Lahaina* ☎ *808/874–5649, 888/225–6284* ⊕ *www.sailtrilogy.com.*

WINDSURFING TOURNAMENTS

In March the **PWA Hawaiian Pro-Am Windsurfing** competition gets underway at Hookipa Beach. In June the **Da Kine Windsurfing Classic** lures windsurfers to Kanaha Beach, and in November the **Aloha Classic World Wave Sailing Championships** takes place at Hookipa. For windsurfing competitions featuring amateurs as well as professionals, check out the **Maui Race Series**, six events held at Kanaha Beach in Kahului in summer.

8

WINDSURFING

Windsurfing, invented in the 1950s, found its true home at Hookipa on Maui's North Shore in 1980. Seemingly overnight, windsurfing pros from around the world flooded the area. Equipment evolved, amazing film footage was captured, and a new sport was born.

If you're new to the action, you can get lessons from the experts island-wide. For a beginner, the best thing about windsurfing is that (unlike surfing) you don't have to paddle. Instead, you have to hold on like heck to a flapping sail as it whisks you into the wind. Needless to say, you're going to need a little coordination and balance to pull this off. Instructors start you out on a beach at Kanaha, where the big boys go. Lessons range from two-hour introductory classes to five-day advanced "flight school."

BEST SPOTS

After **Hookipa Bay** was discovered by windsurfers four decades ago, this windy North Shore beach 10 miles east of Kahului gained an international reputation. The spot is blessed with optimal wave-sailing wind and sea conditions, and offers the ultimate aerial experience.

In summer, the windsurfing crowd heads to **Kalepolepo Beach** on the South Shore. Trade winds build in strength, and by afternoon a swarm of dragonfly-sails can be seen skimming the whitecaps, with Mauna Kahalawai (often called the West Maui Mountains) as a backdrop.

A great site for speed, **Kanaha Beach Park** is dedicated to beginners in the morning hours, before the waves and wind really get roaring. After 11 am, the professionals choose from their quiver of sails the size and shape best suited for the day's demands. This beach tends to have smaller waves and forceful winds—sometimes sending sailors flying at 40 knots. If you aren't ready to go pro, this is a great place for a picnic while you watch from the beach. To get here, use any of the three entrances on Amala Place, which runs along the shore just north of Kahului Airport.

EQUIPMENT AND LESSONS

Action Sports Maui. The quirky, friendly professionals here will meet you at Kanaha Beach Park on the North Shore, outfit you with your sail and board, and guide you through your first "jibe," or turn. They promise your learning time for windsurfing will be cut in half. Lessons begin at 9 am every day except Sunday and cost $89 for a 2½-hour class. Three- and five-day courses cost $240 and $395, respectively. ⊠ 96 Amala Pl., Kahului ☎ 808/871–5857 ⊕ www.actionsportsmaui.com.

Fodor's Choice ★ **Hawaiian Sailboarding Techniques.** Considered Maui's finest windsurfing school, Hawaiian Sailboarding Techniques brings you quality instruction by skilled sailors. Founded by Alan Cadiz, an accomplished World Cup Pro, the school sets high standards for a safe, quality windsurfing experience. Intro classes start at $99 for 2½ hours, gear included. The company is inside Hi-Tech Surf Sports, which offers excellent

equipment rentals. ✉ *Hi-Tech Surf Sports, 425 Koloa St., Kahului* ☎ *808/871–5423* ⊕ *www.hstwindsurfing.com.*

Maui Paddle Sports. Glide atop the ocean inside a six-person outrigger canoe, as you spot turtles, marine life, and even humpback whales during their winter migration. Complimentary water and fresh pineapple is a nice touch, and the delightful guides are eager to share their local knowledge. ✉ *6 Kai Ala Dr., Kaanapali* ☎ *808/283–9344* ⊕ *www. mauipaddlesports.com* ⧉ *$85.*

Second Wind. Located in Kahului, this company rents boards with two sails for $55 per day (additional sails are $10 each). Intro classes start at $89. ✉ *111 Hana Hwy., Kahului* ☎ *808/877–7467* ⊕ *www. secondwindmaui.com.*

GOLF, HIKING, AND OUTDOOR ACTIVITIES

Updated by
Heidi Pool

We know how tempting it is to spend your entire vacation on the beach (many days we're tempted as well), but if you do, you'll miss out on the "other side of Maui": the eerie, moonlike surface of Haleakala Crater, the lush rain forests of East Maui, and the geological wonder that is Iao Valley State Monument, to name just a few. Even playing a round of golf on one of the world-class courses provides breathtaking vistas, reminding you just why you chose to come to Maui in the first place.

Maui's exceptional climate affords year-round opportunities for outdoor adventures, whether it's exploring cascading waterfalls on a day hike, riding horseback through verdant valleys, soaring across vast gulches on a zipline, or taking an exhilarating bicycle ride down Haleakala. When you take time to get off the beaten path, you'll discover just why Maui *no ka oi* (is the best). But make sure not to overbook yourself—one or two activities per day is plenty. You're on vacation, remember.

ADVENTURE SPORTS

Rappel Maui. If the idea of walking backward down waterfalls appeals to you, this company stands ready, willing, and able to accommodate. Their friendly, knowledgeable guides encourage and assist you literally every step of the way. You must be at least 10 years old to participate, have a waist size between 22 and 54 inches, and weigh between 70 and 249 pounds. Rappelling is a fairly strenuous activity, so be prepared for a workout that includes hiking and swimming in addition to rappelling. The tour price of $200 includes all gear, lunch, bottled water, mosquito repellent, and transportation to and from the site from their pickup point in Central Maui. Nonrappellers can go along for $150, and can

either swim or simply sit on a rock and take in the action. The pickup spot is at the intersections of Highways 310 and 30. ⊠ *10600 Hana Hwy., Haiku-Pauwela* ☎ *808/270–1500* ⊕ *www.rappelmaui.com.*

AIR TOURS

Helicopter flight-seeing excursions can take you over the West Maui Mountains, Haleakala Crater, or the island of Molokai. This is a beautiful, thrilling way to see the island, and the *only* way to see some of its most dramatic areas and waterfalls. Tour prices usually include a DVD of your trip so you can relive the experience at home. Prices run from about $175 for a half-hour rain-forest tour to more than $400 for a 90-minute experience that includes a midflight landing at an exclusive remote site, where you can enjoy refreshments along with the view. Generally the 45- to 50-minute flights are the best value; discounts may be available online or, if you're willing to chance it, by calling at the last minute.

Tour operators come under sharp scrutiny for passenger safety and equipment maintenance. Don't be shy; ask about a company's safety record, flight paths, age of equipment, and level of operator experience. Generally, though, if it's still in business, it's doing something right.

Air Maui Helicopters. Priding itself on a perfect safety record, Air Maui provides 30- to 90-minute flights covering the waterfalls of the West Maui Mountains, Haleakala Crater, Hana, and the spectacular sea cliffs of Molokai. Prices range from $200 for the Maui Lite tour, to $456 for their Sunset Dinner Landing, which includes an island-style meal at their private deck facility overlooking Lanai and Molokai. Discounts are available online. Charter flights are also available. ⊠ *1 Kahului Airport Rd., Hangar 110, Kahului* ☎ *877/238–4942, 808/877–7005* ⊕ *www.airmaui.com.*

Blue Hawaiian Helicopters. Since 1985, this company has provided aerial adventures in Hawaii and has been integral in some of the filming Hollywood has done on Maui. Its A-Star and Eco-Star helicopters are air-conditioned and have Bose noise-blocking headsets for all passengers. Flights are 30–120 minutes and cost $169–$563, with considerable discounts online. Charter flights are also available. ⊠ *1 Kahului Airport Rd., Hangar 105, Kahului* ☎ *808/871–8844, 800/745–2583* ⊕ *www. bluehawaiian.com.*

Sunshine Helicopters. Take a tour of Maui in Sunshine's FXStar or WhisperStar aircraft. Prices start at $260 for 40–50 minutes, with discounts available online. First-class seating is available for an additional fee. Sunshine also offers tours that combine helicopter flights with either a horseback ride or submarine adventure. Charter flights can be arranged. A pilot-narrated DVD of your actual flight is available for purchase. ⊠ *Kahului Heliport, Hangar 107, Kahului Airport Rd. and Keolani Blvd., Kahului* ☎ *808/270–3999, 866/501–7738* ⊕ *www. sunshinehelicopters.com.*

BIKING

Long distances and mountainous terrain keep biking from being a practical mode of travel on Maui. Still, painted bike lanes enable cyclists to travel all the way from Makena to Kapalua, and you'll see hardy souls battling the trade winds under the hot Maui sun.

Several companies offer guided bike tours down Haleakala. This activity is a great way to enjoy an easy, gravity-induced bike ride, but isn't for those not confident on a bike. The ride is inherently dangerous due to the slope, sharp turns, and the fact that you're riding down an actual road with cars on it. That said, the guided bike companies take every safety precaution. A few companies offer unguided (or, as they like to say, "self-guided") tours where they provide you with the bike and transportation to the mountain and then you're free to descend at your own pace. Most companies offer discounts for Internet bookings.

Haleakala National Park no longer allows commercial downhill bicycle rides within the park's boundaries. As a result, tour amenities and routes differ by company. Ask about sunrise viewing from the Haleakala summit (be prepared to leave *very* early in the morning), if this is an important feature for you. Some lower-price tours begin at the 6,500-foot elevation just outside the national park boundaries, where you will be unable to view the sunrise over the crater. Weather conditions on Haleakala vary greatly, so a visible sunrise can never be guaranteed. Sunrise is downright cold at the summit, so be sure to dress in layers and wear closed-toe shoes.

Each company has age and weight restrictions, and pregnant women are discouraged from participating, although they are generally welcome in the escort van. Reconsider this activity if you have difficulty with high altitudes, have recently been scuba diving, or are taking medications that may cause drowsiness.

BEST SPOTS

Thompson Road in Keokea and Poli Poli Spring State Recreation Area in Kula are popular areas for cycling in Maui, and two relatively new mountain biking courses—Bike Park Maui and Makawao Forest Reserve—are attracting riders of all ages and ability levels with their well-maintained, clearly marked trails.

Makawao Forest Reserve. Mountain bikers of all ages and ability levels will find something to please at this recreation area that features seven trails and three skill areas. Trails are well marked, and there are maps posted at each intersection. ⊠ *Kahakapao Rd., Makawao* ⊹ *To get here from Piiholo Rd., turn left on Waiahiwi Rd. and then right on Kahakapao Rd.*

Polipoli Spring State Recreation Area. Mountain bikers have favored the remote Polipoli Spring State Recreation Area for its bumpy trail through an unlikely forest of conifers. Polipoli Spring is often closed following heavy storms due to fallen trees and other damage. Check the Hawaii

State Parks website prior to making the drive up there. ⊠ *End of Waip-oli Rd., off Rte. 377, Kula* ⊕ *www.hawaiistateparks.org.*

Thompson Road. Street bikers will want to head out to scenic Thompson Road. It's quiet, gently curvy, and flanked by gorgeous views on both sides. Because it's at a higher elevation, the air temperature is cooler and the wind lighter. The coast back down toward Kahului on the Kula Highway is worth the ride up. ⊠ *Kula Hwy., off Rte. 37, Keokea.*

EQUIPMENT AND TOURS

Fodor's Choice
★
Bike It Maui. Small and family-owned, this company offers two guided sunrise tours down Haleakala each day. The price of $140 includes transfers from your hotel, a sunrise van tour of the summit, a guided 28-mile bicycle ride down the mountain, and a full sit-down breakfast at Cafe O'Lei at the Dunes in Kahului. Riders must be at least 12 and weigh no more than 260 pounds. ⊠ *Kula* ☎ *808/878–3364, 866/776–2453* ⊕ *www.bikeitmaui.com.*

Fodor's Choice
★
Cruiser Phil's Volcano Ridersr. In the downhill bicycle industry since 1983, "Cruiser" Phil Feliciano offers sunrise tours ($163) and morning tours ($147) that include hotel transfers, continental breakfast, a van tour of the summit, and a guided 28-mile ride down the mountain. Participants should be between 13 and 64, at least 5 feet tall, weigh less than 250 pounds, and have ridden a bicycle in the past year. Feliciano also offers structured independent bike tours ($109) and van-only tours ($125). Discounts are available for online bookings. ⊠ *58-A Amala Pl., Kahului* ☎ *808/893–2332, 877/764–2453* ⊕ *www.cruiserphil.com.*

Go Cycling Maui. Serious cyclists can join an exhilarating group ride with Donnie Arnoult, a fixture on the Maui cycling scene since 1999. Routes include Haiku to Keanae, Kula to Kahikinui, and the ultimate Maui cycling challenge: Paia to the top of Haleakala crater. One-day rides are $140 per person ($150 to go to the crater); custom multiday rides run $275–$650. You bring your own cycling shoes, pedals, and clothes, and Donnie provides the bicycle, helmet, gloves, water bottle, snacks, and energy drinks. His shop is also a full-service cycling store offering sales, rentals, and repairs. ⊠ *99 Hana Hwy., Unit A, Paia* ☎ *808/579–9009* ⊕ *www.gocyclingmaui.com.*

Haleakala Bike Company. If you're thinking about a Haleakala bike trip, consider Haleakala Bike Company. Meet at the Old Haiku Cannery and take the van shuttle to the summit. Along the way you can learn about the history of the island, the volcano, and other Hawaiiana. Food is not included, but there are several spots along the way down to stop, rest, and eat. The simple, mostly downhill route takes you right back to the cannery where you started. HBC also offers bike sales, rentals, and services, as well as van tours. Tour prices run $75–$135, with discounts available for online bookings. ⊠ *810 Haiku Rd., Suite 120, Haiku-Pauwela* ☎ *808/575–9575, 888/922–2453* ⊕ *www.bikemaui.com.*

Island Biker. Maui's premier bike shop for rentals, sales, and service offers standard front-shock bikes, road bikes, and full-suspension mountain bikes. Daily rental rates run $60–$70, and weekly rates are $210–$250. The price includes a helmet, pump, water bottle, cages, tire-repair kit, and spare tube. Car racks are $5 per day (free with weekly rentals). The staff can suggest routes appropriate for mountain or road biking. ✉ *415 Dairy Rd., Kahului* ☎ *808/877–7744* ⊕ *www.islandbikermaui.com.*

Krank Cycles. Krank Cycles is located in Upcountry Maui, close to both the Makawao Forest Reserve and Bike Park Maui. They offer half- and full-day rentals. Daily rental prices range from $35 for a GT Zaskar 20 to $90 for a GT Fury 27.5 650b. Owner Moose will provide you with maps and trail reports, in addition to your rental bike. ✉ *1120 Makawao Ave., Makawao* ☎ *808/572–2299* ⊕ *www.krankmaui.com.*

Maui Downhill. If biking down the side of Haleakala sounds like fun, Maui Downhill is ready to pick you up at your resort, shuttle you to the mountain, help you onto a bike, and follow you as you coast down through clouds and gorgeous scenery into the town of Pukalani. There is also a combination bike and winery tour that includes a visit to MauiWine at Ulupalakua Ranch, a combination bike and Maui Ocean Center tour, and a Bike N' Zip tour that includes a zipline experience at Skyline Eco-Adventures. Treks cost $149–$260 and include a simple continental breakfast. ✉ *201 Dairy Rd., Kahului* ☎ *808/871–6875, 800/535–2453* ⊕ *www.mauidownhill.com.*

Maui Mountain Cruisers. Guided sunrise and midday bike trips "cruise" down Haleakala to Makawao, where you get back on board the van for a tour down to Paia. The cost is $155 for the sunrise tour; $135 for midday tours. Meals not included. ✉ *381 Baldwin Ave., #C, Paia* ☎ *808/871–6014* ⊕ *www.mauimountaincruisers.com.*

West Maui Cycles. Serving the island's west side, West Maui Cycles offers cruisers for $15 per day, hybrids for $35 per day, and performance road bikes for $60–$130 per day. Per day rates are discounted for longer-term rentals. The shop also rents baby joggers and car racks. Sales and service are available. ✉ *1087 Limahana Pl., No. 6, Lahaina* ☎ *808/661–9005* ⊕ *www.westmauicycles.com.*

9

GOLF

Maui's natural beauty and surroundings offer some of the most jaw-dropping vistas imaginable on a golf course; add a variety of challenging, well-designed courses and it's easy to explain the island's popularity with golfers. Holes run across small bays, past craggy lava outcrops, and up into cool, forested mountains. Most courses have mesmerizing ocean views, some close enough to feel the salt in the air. Although many of the courses are affiliated with resorts (and therefore a little pricier), the general-public courses are no less impressive. Playing on Lanai is another option.

Greens Fees: Golf can be costly on Maui. Greens fees listed here are the highest course rates per round on weekdays and weekends for U.S. residents. (Some courses charge non-U.S. residents higher prices.) Rental clubs may or may not be included with the greens fee. Discounts are often available for resort guests, for twilight tee times, and for those who book online.

■**TIP→** Resort courses, in particular, offer more than the usual three sets of tees, so bite off as much or as little challenge as you like. Tee it up from the tips and you can end up playing a few 600-yard par 5s and see a few 250-yard forced carries.

DISCOUNTS AND DEALS
Maui Golf Shop. Discounted tee times and club rentals are offered here. ⊠ *1215 S. Kihei Rd., Kihei* ☎ *808/875–4653, 800/981–5512* ⊕ *www. golf-maui.com.*

MAUI GOLF TOURNAMENTS
Maui has a number of golf tournaments, most of which are of professional caliber and worth watching. Many are also televised nationally.

Hyundai Tournament of Champions. Held in January on Kapalua's Plantation Course, this tournament is an attention-getter—the first official PGA tour event. ⊠ *2000 Plantation Club Dr., Lahaina* ☎ *808/665–9160* ⊕ *www.golfatkapalua.com.*

Ka Lima O Maui Celebrity 100. Every May, self-proclaimed "lunatic" golfers play from sunrise to sunset in Wailea's annual Ka Lima O Maui Celebrity 100, a fund-raiser for a local charity. ⊠ *100 Wailea Golf Club Dr., Kihei* ☎ *808/875–7450* ⊕ *www.kalimaomaui.org.*

Kapalua Clambake Pro-Am. A clambake feast at the Ritz-Carlton tops off the Kapalua Clambake Pro-Am each June. ⊠ *300 Kapalua Dr., Lahaina* ☎ *808/669–8044* ⊕ *www.golfatkapalua.com.*

WEST MAUI

Kaanapali Golf Resort. The Royal Kaanapali (North) Course (1962) is one of three in Hawaii designed by Robert Trent Jones Sr., the godfather of modern golf architecture. The greens average a whopping 10,000 square feet, necessary because of the often-severe undulation. The par-4 18th hole (into the prevailing trade breezes, with out-of-bounds on the left and a lake on the right) is notoriously tough. Designed by Arthur Jack Snyder, the Kaanapali Kai (South) Course (1976) shares similar seaside-into-the-hills terrain, but is rated a couple of strokes easier, mostly because putts are less treacherous. ⊠ *2290 Kaanapali Pkwy., Lahaina* ☎ *808/661–3691, 866/454–4653* ⊕ *www.kaanapaligolfcourses.com* ⟐ *Royal Kaanapali (North) Course $255, Kaanapali Kai (South) Course $205* ⚑ *Royal Kaanapali (North) Course: 18 holes, 6500 yards, par 71; Kaanapali Kai (South) Course: 18 holes, 6400 yards, par 70.*

TIPS FOR GOLFING ON MAUI

Golf is golf and Hawaii is part of the United States, but island golf nevertheless has its own quirks. Here are a few tips to make your golf experience in the Islands more pleasant.

■ Sunscreen: Buy it, apply it (we're talking a minimum of 30 SPF). The subtropical rays of the sun are intense, even in December. Good advice is to apply sunscreen, at a minimum, on the 1st and 10th tees.

■ Stay hydrated. Spending four-plus hours in the sun and heat means you'll perspire away considerable fluids and energy.

■ All resort courses and many daily-fee courses provide rental clubs. In many cases, they're the latest lines from top manufacturers. This is true both for men and women, as well as for left-handers, which means you don't have to schlep clubs across the Pacific.

■ Pro shops at most courses are well stocked with balls, tees, and other accoutrements, so even if you bring your own bag, it needn't weigh a ton.

■ Come spikeless—few Hawaii courses still permit metal spikes. Also, most of the resort courses require a collared shirt.

■ Maui is notorious for its trade winds. Consider playing early if you want to avoid the breezes, and remember that although it will frustrate you at times and make club selection difficult, you may well see some of your longest drives ever.

■ In theory you can play golf in Hawaii 365 days a year, but there's a reason the Hawaiian Islands are so green: an umbrella and light jacket can come in handy.

■ Unless you play a muni or certain daily-fee courses, plan on taking a cart. Riding carts are mandatory at most courses and are included in the greens fee.

Fodor's Choice
★

Kapalua Golf. Perhaps Hawaii's best-known golf resort and the crown jewel of golf on Maui, Kapalua hosts the PGA Tour's first event each January: the Hyundai Tournament of Champions at the **Plantation Course** at Kapalua. On this famed course, Ben Crenshaw and Bill Coore (1991) tried to incorporate traditional shot values in a nontraditional site, taking into account slope, gravity, and the prevailing trade winds. The par-5 18th hole, for instance, plays 663 yards from the back tees (600 yards from the resort tees). The hole drops 170 feet in elevation, narrowing as it goes to a partially guarded green, and plays downwind and down-grain. Despite the longer-than-usual distance, the slope is great enough and the wind at your back usually brisk enough to reach the green with two well-struck shots—a truly unbelievable finish to a course that will challenge, frustrate, and reward the patient golfer.

The **Bay Course** (Arnold Palmer and Francis Duane, 1975) is the more traditional of Kapalua's courses, with gentle rolling fairways and generous greens. The most memorable hole is the par-3 fifth hole, with a tee shot that must carry a turquoise finger of Oneloa Bay. Each of the courses has a separate clubhouse. ⊠ *2000 Plantation Club Dr., Kapalua* ☎ *808/669–8044, 808/527–2582* ⊕ *www.golfatkapalua.com* ⊟ *$219 Bay Course, $299 Plantation Course* ⥉ *Bay Course: 18 holes, 6600 yards, par 72; 18 holes, 7411 yards, par 73.*

Kapalua Golf Academy. Along with 23 acres of practice turf and 11 teeing areas, an 18-hole putting course, and 3-hole walking course, the Kapalua Golf Academy also has an instructional bay with digital video analysis. ⊠ *1000 Office Rd., Kapalua* ☎ *808/665–5455, 877/527–2582* ⊕ *www.golfatkapalua.com.*

THE SOUTH SHORE

Maui Nui Golf Club. Maui Nui Golf Club is an exacting test. Fairways tend to be narrow, especially in landing areas, and can be quite a challenge when the trade winds come up in the afternoon. The course is lined with enough coconut trees to make them a collective hazard, not just a nutty nuisance. ⊠ *1345 Piilani Hwy., Kihei* ☎ *808/874–0777* ⊕ *www.mauinuigolfclub.com* ⊟ *$94* ⥉ *18 holes, 6404 yards, par 71.*

Wailea Blue Course. Wailea's original course, the Blue Course (1971), which is still referred to as the "Old Blue Course," is operated from a separate clubhouse from the Gold and Emerald courses, its newer siblings. Here, judging elevation change is key. Fairways and greens tend to be wider and more forgiving than on the newer Gold or Emerald courses, and they run through colorful flora that includes hibiscus, wiliwili, bougainvillea, and plumeria. ⊠ *100 Wailea Ike Dr., Wailea* ☎ *808/879–2530* ⊕ *www.waileagolf.com* ⊟ *$190* ⥉ *18 holes, 6765 yards, par 72.*

Fodor's Choice ★ **Wailea Golf Club.** Wailea is the only Hawaii resort to offer three different courses: Gold, Emerald, and Blue—the latter at a different location with a separate pro shop. Designed by Robert Trent Jones Jr. (Gold and Emerald) and Arthur Jack Snyder (Blue), these courses share similar terrain, carved into the leeward slopes of Haleakala. Although the ocean does not come into play, its beauty is visible on almost every hole. ■**TIP→** Remember, putts break dramatically toward the ocean.

Jones refers to the **Gold Course** at Wailea (1993) as the "masculine" course. It's all trees and lava, and regarded as the hardest of the three courses. The trick here is to note even subtle changes in elevation. The par-3 eighth, for example, plays from an elevated tee across a lava ravine to a large, well-bunkered green framed by palm trees, the blue sea, and tiny Molokini. The course demands strategy and careful club selection. The **Emerald Course** (1994) is the "feminine" layout with lots of flowers and bunkering away from greens. Although this may seem to render the bunker benign, the opposite is true. A bunker well in front of a green disguises the distance to the hole. Likewise, the Emerald's extensive flower beds are dangerous distractions because of their beauty. The Gold and Emerald courses share a clubhouse, practice facility, and 19th hole. ⊠ *100 Wailea Golf Club Dr., Wailea*

9

PLACES TO RELAX AFTER A ROUND

Among golf's great traditions is the so-called 19th hole. No matter how the first 18 go, the 19th is sure to offer comfort and cheer, not to mention a chilled beverage. Here's a look at some of the best.

Kapalua boasts three 19th holes with great fare and views: the **Plantation House** has a commanding view of the Plantation Course's 18th hole, the Pailolo Channel, and the island of Molokai beyond; the **Pineapple Grill** overlooks the Bay Course's 18th; and **Merriman's Kapalua** sits beside the ocean at Kapalua Bay.

At Wailea's Gold and Emerald courses, **Gannon's** overlooks the sea in a lovely garden setting and serves excellent food. The restaurant, with its elegant Red Bar, is owned and managed by famed chef Beverly Gannon of Haliimaile General Store.

The **Kahili Restaurant,** a plantation-style clubhouse at the King Kamehameha Golf Club's Kahili Course, offers commanding views of the ocean on both sides of the island and of 10,000-foot Haleakala.

Café O'Lei at the Dunes at Maui Lani offers indoor and outdoor seating overlooking the golf course, as well as a stunning view of the West Maui Mountains. Kono's on the Green at Maui Nui Golf Club has a welcoming lanai for sunset watching or just generally kicking back.

☎ *808/875–7450, 888/328–6284* ⊕ *www.waileagolf.com* ✉ *Gold Course $235, Emerald Course $235* ⚡ *Gold Course: 18 holes, 6653 yards, par 72; Emerald Course: 18 holes, 6407 yards, par 72.*

CENTRAL MAUI

Fodor's Choice ★ **The Dunes at Maui Lani.** Robin Nelson is at his minimalist best here, creating a bit of British links in the middle of the Pacific. Holes run through ancient, lightly wooded sand dunes, 5 miles inland from Kahului Harbor. Thanks to the natural humps and slopes of the dunes, Nelson had to move very little dirt and created a natural beauty. During the design phase he visited Ireland, and not so coincidentally the par-3 third looks a lot like the Dell at Lahinch: a white dune on the right sloping down into a deep bunker and partially obscuring the right side of the green—just one of several blind to semiblind shots here. ✉ *1333 Maui Lani Pkwy., Kahului* ☎ *808/873–0422* ⊕ *www.dunesatmauilani.com* ✉ *$79* ⚡ *18 holes, 6841 yards, par 72.*

Kahili Golf Course. The former Sandalwood Course (1991) was completely redone in 2005 by Robin Nelson and is now one of two 18-hole courses—one private (King Kamehameha) and one public (Kahili)—that make up the King Kamehameha Golf Club. Course holes run along the slopes of the West Maui Mountains, overlooking Maui's central plain, and feature panoramic ocean views of both the North and South shores. Consistent winds negate the course's shorter length. ✉ *2500 Honoapiilani Hwy., Wailuku* ☎ *808/242–4653* ⊕ *www.kahiligolf.com* ✉ *$85* ⚡ *18 holes, 6570 yards, par 72.*

Waiehu Golf Course. Maui's lone municipal course and undoubtedly the best bargain on the island, Waiehu is really two courses in one. The front nine, dating to 1930, feature authentic seaside links that run along Kahului Bay. The back nine, which climb up into the lower reaches of the West Maui Mountains through macadamia orchards, were designed by Arthur Jack Snyder and opened in 1963. ⊠ *200 Halewaiu Rd., Wailuku* ☎ *808/243–7400* ⊕ *www.mauicounty.gov/Facilities/Facility/Details/157* ⊑ *$55; $20 for golf cart* ⅄ *18 holes, 6330 yards, par 72.*

UPCOUNTRY

Pukalani Golf Courseu. At 1,110 feet above sea level, Pukalani (Bob E. Baldock and Robert L. Baldock, 1970) provides one of the finest vistas in all Hawaii. Holes run up, down, and across the slopes of Haleakala. The trade winds tend to come up in the late morning and afternoon. This, combined with frequent elevation change, makes club selection a test. The fairways tend to be wide, but greens are undulating and quick. ⊠ *360 Pukalani St., Pukalani* ☎ *808/572–1314* ⊕ *www.pukalanigolf. com* ⊑ *$63* ⅄ *18 holes, 6962 yards, par 72.*

HANG GLIDING AND PARAGLIDING

If you've always wanted to know what it feels like to fly, hang gliding or paragliding might be your perfect Maui adventure. You'll get open-air, bird's-eye views of the Valley Isle that you'll likely never forget. And you don't need to be a daredevil to participate.

EQUIPMENT AND LESSONS

Hang Gliding Maui. Armin Engert will take you on an instructional powered hang-gliding trip out of Hana Airport in East Maui. With more than 13,000 hours in the air and a perfect safety record, Armin flies you 1,000 feet over Maui's most beautiful coast. A 30-minute flight lesson costs $170, a 45-minute lesson costs $230, and a 60-minute lesson is $280. Snapshots of your flight from a wing-mounted camera cost an additional $40, and a 34-minute DVD of the flight from a wing-mounted camera is available for $80. Reservations are required. ⊠ *Hana Airport, Alalele Pl., off Hana Hwy., Hana* ☎ *808/572–6557* ⊕ *www.hangglidingmaui.com.*

Proflyght Paragliding. This is the only paragliding outfit on Maui to offer solo, tandem, and instruction at Polipoli Spring State Recreation Area. The leeward slope of Haleakala lends itself to paragliding with breathtaking scenery and air currents that increase during the day. Polipoli creates tremendous thermals that allow you to peacefully descend 3,000 feet to land. Tandem instruction prices run $95–$185. Solo paragliding certification is also available. ⊠ *Polipoli Spring State Recreation Area, Waipoli Rd., Kula* ☎ *808/874–5433* ⊕ *www.paraglidemaui.com.*

9

Cinder cones, deposits formed around a volcanic vent, are a striking feature in Haleakala Crater.

HIKING

Hikes on Maui include treks along coastal seashore, verdant rain forest, and alpine desert. Orchids, hibiscus, ginger, heliconia, and anthuriums grow wild on many trails, and exotic fruits like mountain apple, *lilikoi* (passion fruit), and strawberry guava provide refreshing snacks for hikers. Much of what you see in lower-altitude forests is alien, brought to Hawaii at one time or another by someone hoping to improve on nature. Plants like strawberry guava and ginger may be tasty, but they grow over native plants and have become problematic weeds.

The best hikes get you out of the imported landscaping and into the truly exotic wilderness. Hawaii possesses some of the world's rarest plants, insects, and birds. Pocket field guides are available at most grocery or drug stores and can really illuminate your walk. If you watch the right branches quietly, you can spot the same honeycreepers or happy-face spiders scientists have spent their lives studying.

BEST SPOTS

HALEAKALA NATIONAL PARK

Fodor's Choice ★ **Haleakala Crater.** Undoubtedly the best hiking on the island is at Haleakala Crater. If you're in shape, do a day hike descending from the summit along **Keonehe̒ehe̒e Trail** (aka Sliding Sands Trail) to the crater floor. You might also consider spending several days here amid the cinder cones, lava flows, and all that loud silence. Entering the crater is like landing on a different planet. In the early 1960s NASA actually brought moon-suited astronauts here to practice what it would be like to "walk on the moon." On the 30 miles of trails you can traverse black sand and wild lava formations, follow the trail of blooming *ahinahina* (silverswords), and take in tremendous views of big sky and burned-red cliffs.

The best time to go into the crater is in the summer months, when the conditions are generally more predictable. Be sure to bring layered clothing—and plenty of warm clothes if you're staying overnight. It may be scorching hot during the day, but it gets mighty chilly after dark. Bring your own drinking water, as potable water is only available at the two visitor centers. Overnight visitors must get a permit at park headquarters before entering the crater. *Moderate to difficult.* ⊠ *Haleakala Crater Rd., Makawao* ☎ *808/572–4400* ⊕ *www.nps.gov/hale.*

OHEO GULCH

A branch of Haleakala National Park, Oheo Gulch is famous for its pools (the area is sometimes called the Seven Sacred Pools). Truth is, there are more than seven pools and there's nothing sacred about them. A former owner of the Travaasa Hotel Hana started calling the area Seven Sacred Pools to attract the masses to sleepy old Hana. His plan worked and the name stuck, much to the chagrin of many Mauians.

The best time to visit the pools is in the morning, before the crowds and tour buses arrive. Start your day with a vigorous hike. Oheo has some fantastic trails to choose from, including our favorite, the Pipiwai Trail. When you're done, nothing could be better than going to the pools, lounging on the rocks, and cooling off in the freshwater reserves. (Keep in mind, however, that the park periodically closes the pools to swimming when the potential for flash flooding exists.)

You can find Oheo Gulch on Route 31, 10 miles past Hana town. To visit, you must pay the $15-per-car National Park fee, which is valid for three days and can be used at Haleakala's summit as well. For information about scheduled orientations and cultural demonstrations, be sure to visit Haleakala National Park's Kipahulu Visitor Center, 10 miles past Hana. Note that there is no drinking-water here.

Kahakai Trail. This quarter-mile hike (more like a walk) stretches between Kuloa Point and the Kipahulu campground. It provides rugged shoreline views, and there are places where you can stop to gaze at the surging waves below. *Easy.* ⊠ *Trailhead: Kuloa Point, Hana.*

Kuloa Point Trail. A half-mile walk, this trail takes you from the Kipahulu Visitor Center down to the pools of Oheo at Kuloa Point. On the trail you pass native trees and precontact Hawaiian sites. Don't forget to bring your swimsuit and a towel if you're planning a dip in the pools—but exercise extreme caution, as no lifeguards are on duty. Stick to the pools; don't even think about swimming in the ocean. The park periodically closes the pools when the potential for flash flooding exists. *Easy.* ⊠ *Trailhead: Kipahulu Visitor Center, Hana Hwy., Hana.*

Silverswords start as spiny-leaf rosettes, then grow stalks for 7–17 years; after they bloom once, they die.

Fodor's Choice
★

Pipiwai Trail. This 2-mile trek upstream leads to the 400-foot Waimoku Falls, pounding down in all its power and glory. Following signs from the parking lot, head across the road and uphill into the forest. The trail borders a sensational gorge and passes onto a boardwalk through a mystifying forest of giant bamboo. This stomp through muddy and rocky terrain takes around three hours to fully enjoy. Although this trail is never truly crowded, it's best done early in the morning before the tours arrive. Be sure to bring mosquito repellent. *Moderate.* ⊠ *Hana Hwy., near mile marker 42, Hana.*

POLIPOLI SPRING STATE RECREATION AREA

A hiking area with great trails for all levels—and something totally unexpected on a tropical island—is the Kula Forest Reserve at Polipoli Spring State Recreation Area in Upcountry Maui. During the Great Depression the government began a program to reforest the mountain, and soon cedar, pine, cypress, and even redwood took hold. The area, at an elevation of 6,200 feet, feels more like Vermont than Hawaii. It's cold and foggy, and often wet, but there's something about the enormity of the trees, quiet mist, and mysterious caves that makes you feel you've discovered an unspoken secret. Hikers should wear brightly colored clothing, as hunters may be in the area.

To reach the forest, take Route 37 all the way out to the far end of Kula, then turn left at Route 377. After about ½ mile, turn right at Waipoli Road. You'll encounter switchbacks; after that the road is bad but passable. Four-wheel-drive vehicles are strongly recommended, although standard cars have been known to make it. Use your best judgment.

Boundary Trail. This 4-mile trail begins just past the Kula Forest Reserve boundary cattle guard on Polipoli Road and descends into the lower boundary southward, all the way to the ranger's cabin at the junction of the Redwood and Plum trails. Combine them and you've got a hearty 5-mile day hike. The trail crosses many scenic gulches, with an overhead of tall eucalyptus, pine, cedar, and plum trees. Peep through the trees for wide views of Kula and Central Maui. Wear bright clothing, stay on the trail, and be aware you may encounter hunters who are hunting off the trail. *Moderate.* ■**TIP**➔ **Polipoli Spring is often closed following heavy storms due to fallen trees and other damage. Check the Hawaii State Parks website prior to making the drive up there.** ⊠ *Trailhead: Polipoli Campground, Polipoli Rd., Kula* ⊕ *www.hawaiistateparks.org.*

> ### KALAUPAPA TRAIL
>
> You can take an overnight trip to the island of Molokai for a day of hiking down to Kalaupapa Peninsula and back, by means of a 3-mile, 26-switchback trail. The trail is nearly vertical, traversing the face of some of the highest sea cliffs in the world. ⇨ *See Kalaupapa Peninsula in Chapter 10, Molokai, for more information.*

Redwood Trail. This colorful hike winds through redwoods and conifers past the short Tie Trail down to the old ranger's cabin. Although the views are limited, groves of trees and flowering bushes abound. At the end of the trail is an old cabin site and three-way junction with the Plum Trail and the Boundary Trail. Wear bright clothing, stay on the trail, and be aware you may encounter hunters who are hunting off the trail. *Moderate.* ■**TIP**➔ **Polipoli Spring is often closed following heavy storms due to fallen trees and other damage. Check the Hawaii State Parks website prior to making the drive up there.** ⊠ *Trailhead: Near Polipoli Campground, Polipoli Rd., Kula* ⊕ *www.hawaiistateparks.org.*

Upper Waiakoa Trail. Start this scenic albeit rugged trail at the Polipoli Access Road (look for trailhead signs) and proceed up Haleakala through mixed pine and past caves and thick shrubs. The path crosses the land of Kaonoulu to the land of Waiakoa, where it reaches its highest point (7,800 feet). Here you'll find yourself in barren, raw terrain with fantastic views. At this point, you can either turn around, or continue on to the 3-mile Waiakoa Loop for a 14-mile journey. Other than a cave shelter, there's no water or other facilities on these trails, so come prepared. Wear bright clothing, stay on the trail, and be aware you may encounter hunters who are hunting off the trail. *Difficult.* ■**TIP**➔ **Polipoli Spring is often closed following heavy storms due to fallen trees and other damage. Check the Hawaii State Parks website prior to making the drive up there.** ⊠ *Trailhead: Polipoli Access Rd., Kula* ⊕ *www.hawaiistateparks.org.*

IAO VALLEY STATE MONUMENT

Fodor's Choice
★

In Hawaiian, Iao means "supreme cloud." When you enter this mystical valley in the middle of an unexpected rain forest near Wailuku in West Maui, you'll know why. At 750 feet above sea level, the 10-mile valley clings to the clouds as if it's trying to cover its naked beauty. One of Maui's great wonders, the valley is the site of a famous battle to unite

9

the Hawaiian Islands. Out of the clouds, the **Iao Needle**, a tall chunk of volcanic rock, stands as a monument to the long-ago lookout for Maui warriors. Today, there's nothing warlike about it: the valley is a peaceful land of lush, tropical plants, clear pools and a running stream, and easy, enjoyable strolls.

To get to Iao Valley State Monument, head to the western end of Route 32. The road dead-ends into the parking lot ($5 per car). The park is open daily 7–7. Facilities are available, but there is no drinking water.

Fodor's Choice   **Iao Valley Trail.** Anyone (including grandparents) can handle this short
★   walk from the parking lot at Iao Valley State Monument. On your choice of two paved walkways, you can cross the Iao Stream and explore the junglelike area. Ascend the stairs up to the Iao Needle for spectacular views of Central Maui. Be sure to stop at the lovely Kepaniwai Heritage Gardens, which commemorate the cultural contributions of various immigrant groups. *Easy.* ⊠ *Trailhead: Iao Valley State Monument parking lot, Rte. 32, Wailuku* ⊕ *www. hawaiistateparks.org.*

THE SOUTH SHORE AND WEST MAUI

In addition to the trails listed below, the Kapalua Resort offers free access to 100 miles of self-guided hikes. Trail information and maps are available at the Kapalua Adventure Center.

Dragon's Teeth. The fascinating series of lava formations at Makaluapuna Point in Kapalua is nicknamed Dragon's Teeth. The forceful winds that sweep over the point caused the lava to harden upward into jagged points resembling giant teeth. To get there, park in the small paved lot to the right at the end of Office Road, and follow the path at the edge of the Bay Golf Course (watch for errant golf balls, and be respectful of the golfers). Along the way, there's a labyrinth where you can experience a meditative walk. ■ **TIP→** Wear sturdy shoes and bring water, as there are no facilities here. ⊠ *Office Rd., Kapalua.*

Hoapili Trail. A challenging hike through eye-popping scenery in southwestern Maui is this 5½-mile coastal trail beyond the Ahihi-Kinau Natural Area Reserve. Named after a bygone king, it follows the shoreline, threading through the remains of ancient villages. King Hoapili created an islandwide road, and this wide path of stacked lava rocks is a marvel to look at and walk on. (It's not the easiest surface for the ankles and feet, so wear sturdy shoes.) This is brutal territory with little shade and no facilities, and extra water is a must. To get here, follow Makena Road to La Perouse Bay. The trail can be a challenge to find—walk south along the ocean through the *kiawe* trees, where you'll encounter numerous wild goats (don't worry—they're tame), and past a scenic little bay. The trail begins just around the corner to the left. *Difficult.* ⊠ *Trailhead: La Perouse Bay, Makena Rd., Makena.*

Kapalua Coastal Trail. Meandering north from Kapalua Bay, Kapalua's Coastal Trail provides views of the ocean and wildlife as it crosses the golden sand dunes of Oneloa Bay and travels past the Ritz-Carlton,

TIPS FOR DAY HIKES

Hiking is a perfect way to see Maui. Just wear sturdy shoes to spare your ankles from a crash course in loose lava rock. At upper elevations the weather is guaranteed to be extreme—alternately chilly or blazing—so layers are good.

When hiking near streams or waterfalls, be cautious: flash floods can occur at any time. Don't drink stream water or swim in streams if you have open cuts; bacteria and parasites are not the souvenir you want to take home with you.

Here's a checklist for what to take for a great hike:

- Water (at least 2 quarts per person; drink even if you're not thirsty)
- Food—fruit, trail mix, and lunch
- Rain gear—especially if going into the crater
- Sturdy hiking shoes
- Layered clothing
- Wide-brimmed hat and sunglasses
- Sunscreen (SPF 30 or higher recommended)
- Mosquito repellent (a must around waterfalls and pools)

Kapalua, to its terminus at D.T. Fleming Beach Park. Spottings of green sea turtles, dolphins, and humpback whales (in season) are likely, along with nesting seabirds called *uau kani*. ⊠ *Kapalua*.

Kapalua Resort. The resort offers free access to 100 miles of hiking trails to guests and visitors as a self-guided experience. Trail information and maps are available at the Kapalua Adventure Center. Access most trails via a complimentary resort shuttle, which must be reserved in advance (only for resort guests). The Village Walking Trails offer a network of exercise opportunities, including the 3.6-mile Lake Loop, which features sweeping views and a secluded lake populated with quacking ducks. Guided hiking tours are also available through the Jean-Michel Cousteau Ambassadors of the Environment program at the Ritz-Carlton, Kapalua. ⊠ *2000 Village Rd., corner of Office Rd., Kapalua* ☎ *808/665–9110 Kapalua Resort Shuttle Reservations* ⊕ *www.kapaluamaui.com*.

Waihee Ridge. This 4¾-mile hike in West Maui offers a generous reward at the top: breathtaking panoramic views of the windward coast and the ridges that rise inland, as well as Mt. Lanilili, Puu Kukui, Eke Crater, and the remote village of Kahakuloa. Enjoy a comfortable lunch at the picnic table. In rainy conditions the trail can quickly turn into a muddy, slippery affair. To get here from Highway 340, turn left across the highway from Mendes Ranch and drive ¾ miles up a partially paved road to the signed trailhead. *Moderate.* ⊠ *Trailhead: Opposite Mendes Ranch, Hwy. 340, Wailuku*.

9

These horses on the less-developed North Shore seem to be taking in the ocean view.

GOING WITH A GUIDE

Guided hikes can help you see more than you might on your own. If the company is driving you to the site, be sure to ask about drive times; they can be fairly lengthy for some hikes.

Fodor's Choice ★ **Friends of Haleakala National Park.** This nonprofit offers overnight trips into the volcanic crater. The purpose of your trip, the service work itself, isn't too much—mostly native planting, removing invasive plants, and light cabin maintenance. But participants are asked to check the website to learn more about the trip and certify readiness for service work. An interpretive park ranger accompanies each trip, taking you to places you'd otherwise miss and teaching you about the native flora and fauna. ☎ *808/876–1673* ⊕ *www.fhnp.org.*

Fodor's Choice ★ **Hike Maui.** Started in 1983, the area's oldest hiking company remains extremely well regarded for waterfall, rain-forest, and crater hikes led by enthusiastic, highly trained guides who weave botany, geology, ethnobotany, culture, and history into the outdoor experience. Prices run $85–$254 for excursions lasting 3–11 hours (discounts for booking online). Hike Maui supplies day packs, rain gear, mosquito repellent, first-aid supplies, bottled water, snacks, lunch for the longer trips, and transportation to and from the site. Hotel transfers are available for most hikes (extra fee may apply). ⊠ *285 Hukilike St., Unit B-104, Kahului* ☎ *808/879–5270, 866/324–6284* ⊕ *www.hikemaui.com.*

Kipahulu 'Ohana. Native Hawaiian guides from this nonprofit organization lead cultural interpretive hikes and taro patch tours at Kipahulu near Hana through a cooperative agreement with Haleakala National

Park. The two-hour hike ($49) takes you to scenic overlooks and past remnants from the sugar-cane industry, culminating at an ancient taro farm that has been restored to active production. A three-hour hike ($79) includes a side trip to 400-foot Waimoku Falls. You can park at Kipahulu Visitor Center ($10 per car) and meet your guide at the Hale Kuai, the traditional thatched house near the center. ⊠ *Hana* ☎ *808/248–8558* ⊕ *www.kipahulu.org.*

Sierra Club. One great avenue into the island's untrammeled wilderness is Maui's chapter of the Sierra Club. Join one of the club's hikes into pristine forests, along ancient coastal paths, to historic sites, and to Haleakala Crater. Some outings require volunteer service, but most are just for fun. Bring your own food and water, rain gear, sunscreen, sturdy shoes, and a suggested donation of $5 for hikers over age 14 ($3 for Sierra Club members). This is a true bargain. ✑ *webmaster@ mauisierraclub.org* ⊕ *www.hi.sierraclub.org/maui.*

HORSEBACK RIDING

Several companies on Maui offer horseback riding far more appealing than the typical hour-long trudge over a dull trail with 50 other horses.

GOING WITH A GUIDE

Mendes Ranch. Family-owned and run, Mendes operates out of the beautiful ranchland of Kahakuloa on the windward slopes of the West Maui Mountains. Morning and afternoon trail rides lasting 1½ hours ($110) are available. Cowboys take you cantering up rolling pastures into the lush rain forest, and then you'll descend all the way down to the ocean for a photo op with a dramatic backdrop. Don't expect a Hawaiian cultural experience here—it's all about the horses and the ride. ⊠ *3530 Kahekili Hwy., Wailuku* ☎ *808/244–7320 for office, 800/871–5222 for reservations* ⊕ *www.mendesranch.com.*

Piiholo Ranch. The local wranglers here lead you on a rousing ride through family ranchlands—up hillside pastures, beneath a eucalyptus canopy, and past many native trees. Two-hour private rides ($229; minimum 2 guests) are offered three times daily. Three-hour private rides ($349) are offered twice daily, and include lunch at a private cabin. Their well-groomed horses navigate the challenging terrain easily—but hold on when axis deer pass by. ⊠ *End of Waiahiwi Rd., Makawao* ☎ *808/270–8750* ⊕ *www.piiholo.com.*

Pony Express Tours. This outfit offers 1½- and 2-hour rides ($95 and $125) on the slopes of the Haleakala Ranch, the largest working cattle ranch on Maui. ⊠ *Kula* ☎ *808/667–2200* ⊕ *www.ponyexpresstours.com.*

POLO

Paniolos show off their skills at three major annual events: the **Piiholo Cowboy Classic** in September; the **Oskie Rice Memorial Rodeo** in December; and Maui's biggest event, the **4th of July Rodeo**, which comes with a full parade in Makawao town and festivities that last for days.

Polo is popular with the Upcountry paniolos. From April through June, Haleakala Ranch hosts "indoor," or arena, contests on a field flanked by side boards. The field is on Route 377, 1 mile from Route 37. During the "outdoor" polo season (September–mid-November) matches are held at Kaonoulu Ranch Field, 1 mile above Makawao on Olinda Road. There's a $10 admission for most games, which start at 1:30 pm on Sunday.

Manduke Baldwin Memorial Tournament. Held over Memorial Day weekend, the Manduke Baldwin Memorial Tournament is a popular two-day polo event. It draws challengers from Argentina, England, South Africa, New Zealand, and Australia. ☎ 808/877–7744 ⊕ *www.mauipoloclub.com.*

TENNIS

Most courts charge by the hour but will let players continue after their initial hour for free, provided no one is waiting. Many hotels and condos charge a fee for nonguests.

BEST SPOTS

Kapalua Tennis Garden. Home to the Kapalua Tennis Club, this complex has 10 courts (four lighted for night play) and a pro shop. The fee is $15 per person per day. Private and group (3–6 persons) instruction is also available. ✉ *Kapalua Resort, 100 Kapalua Dr., Kapalua* ☎ *808/662–7730* ⊕ *www.golfatkapalua.com.*

Lahaina Civic Center. The best free courts are the nine at the Lahaina Civic Center, near Wahikuli State Park. They all have overhead lighting for night play and are available on a first-come, first-served basis. ✉ *1840 Honoapiilani Hwy., Lahaina* ☎ *808/661–4685* ⊕ *www.co.maui.hi.us/ facilities/Facility/Details/209.*

Makena Tennis Club. This club features six Plexipave courts, two of which are lighted for night play. Private lessons, ball machines, racquet stringing, and daily clinics are available. Rates are $20 per day. ✉ *5415 Makena Alanui Dr., Makena* ☎ *808/891–4050* ⊕ *www. makenaresortmaui.com.*

Wailea Tennis Club. Featuring 11 Sportsmaster courts (two lighted for night play), this club also offer lessons, rentals, and ball machines. Daily clinics help you improve your ground strokes, serve, volley, or doubles strategy. The daily court fee, which guarantees one hour of reserved time for singles and 1½ hours for doubles, is $20 per player. ✉ *131 Wailea Ike Pl., Wailea* ☎ *808/879–1958* ⊕ *www.waileatennis.com.*

TOURNAMENTS

Kapalua Open Tennis Tournament. Over Labor Day weekend, the Kapalua Open Tennis Tournament calls Hawaii's hitters to Kapalua's Tennis Garden. ✉ *100 Kapalua Dr., Kapalua* 🕾 *808/662–7730* ⊕ *www.golfatkapalua.com.*

Wailea Open Tennis Championship. This annual championship is held at the Wailea Tennis Club in May. ✉ *131 Wailea Ike Pl., Kihei* 🕾 *808/879–1958* ⊕ *www.waileatennis.com.*

ZIPLINE TOURS

Ziplining on one of Maui's several courses lets you satisfy your inner Tarzan by soaring high above deep gulches and canyons—for a price that can seem steep. A harness keeps you fully supported on each ride. Each course has its own age minimums and weight restrictions, but generally, you must be at least 10 years old and weigh a minimum of 60–80 pounds and a maximum of 250–275 pounds. You should wear closed-toe athletic-type shoes and expect to get dirty. ■TIP➔ **Reconsider this activity if you are pregnant, uncomfortable with heights, or have serious back or joint problems.**

Fodor's Choice ★ **Flyin' Hawaiian Zipline.** These guys have the longest line in the state (a staggering 3,600 feet), as well as the most unique course layout. You build confidence on the first line, then board a four-wheel-drive vehicle that takes you 1,500 feet above the town of Waikapu to seven more lines that carry you over 11 ridges and nine valleys. The total distance covered is more than 2½ miles, and the views are astonishing. The price ($185) includes water and snacks. You must be able to hike over steep, sometimes slippery terrain while carrying a 10-pound metal trolley. ✉ *Waikapu* 🕾 *808/463–5786* ⊕ *www.flyinhawaiianzipline.com.*

Kapalua Ziplines. Begin with a 20-minute ride in a four-wheel-drive van through pineapple fields to the Mountain Outpost, a 3,000-square-foot observation deck boasting panoramic ocean and mountain views. If you're on the seven-line zip ($207), you'll climb even higher above the Pacific Ocean in a Polaris Ranger to experience 2 miles of parallel zipping plus lunch. The shorter four-line zip ($176) and Sunset Zip Tour ($66) are great if you're on a time budget. ✉ *500 Office Rd., Kapalua* 🕾 *808/756–9147* ⊕ *www.kapaluaziplines.com.*

Fodor's Choice ★ **Piiholo Ranch Zipline.** Two zipline courses are on this gorgeous 900-acre family ranch. The original course consists of five lines—one quadruple and four side by side. Access to the fifth and longest line is via a four-wheel-drive vehicle to the top of Piiholo Hill, where you are treated to stunning bicoastal views. Guides do a good job of weaving Hawaiian culture into the adventure. You must be able to climb three steep suspension bridges while hefting a 12-pound trolley over your shoulder. Prices range from $140 for four lines to $190 for five. Zipline canopy tours keep you in the trees the entire time ($135–$145). For the

9

ultimate adventure, try the Zipline/Waterfall Hike ($229), for which the company has partnered with Hike Maui, the oldest land company in Hawaii. Piiholo offers significant discounts for online bookings. ⊠ *Piiholo Rd., Makawao* ☎ *800/374–7050* ⊕ *www.piiholozipline.com.*

Skyline Eco Adventures. The first company to open a zipline course in the United States, Skyline operates in two locations on Maui: the original course on the slope of Haleakala (five lines ranging 50–720 feet) and its west side venue at 1,000 feet above Kaanapali (eight lines ranging 50–1,000 feet). Tours at Haleakala range in price from $120 for the five-zipline tour to $250 for the Haleakala Sunrise Bike N' Zip tour, which combines a downhill bicycle safari with a five-line zip. Tours in Kaanapali range in price from $150 for the eight-line tour to $180 for the Zip & Dip tour, which combines a dip in a natural mountain pool with an eight-line zip. Advance reservations are suggested, and discounts are available for online bookings. ⊠ *Original Course, 8303 Haleakala Hwy., Kula* ☎ *808/518–4189* ⊕ *www.zipline.com.*

MOLOKAI

WELCOME TO MOLOKAI

TOP REASONS TO GO

★ **Kalaupapa Peninsula:** Hike or take a mule ride down the world's tallest sea cliffs to a fascinating historic community that still houses a few former Hansen's disease patients.

★ **A waterfall hike in Halawa:** A fascinating guided hike through private property takes you past ancient ruins, restored taro patches, and a sparkling cascade.

★ **Deep-sea fishing:** Sport fish are plentiful in these waters, as are gorgeous views of several islands. Fishing is one of the island's great adventures.

★ **Closeness to nature:** Deep valleys, sheer cliffs, and the untamed ocean are the main attractions on Molokai.

★ **Papohaku Beach:** This 3-mile stretch of golden sand is one of the most sensational beaches in all of Hawaii. Sunsets and barbecues are perfect here.

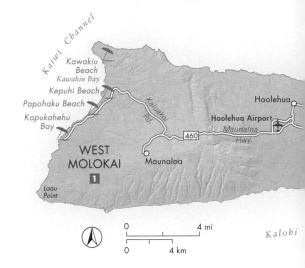

1 West Molokai. The most arid part of the island, known as the west end, has two inhabited areas: the coastal stretch includes a few condos and luxury homes, and the largest beaches on the island; nearby is the fading hilltop hamlet of Maunaloa.

2 Central Molokai. The island's only true town, Kaunakakai, with its mile-long wharf, is here. Nearly all the island's eateries and stores are in or close to Kaunakakai. Highway 470 crosses the center of the island, rising to the top of the sea cliffs and the Kalaupapa overlook. At the base of the cliffs is Kalaupapa National Historical Park, a top attraction.

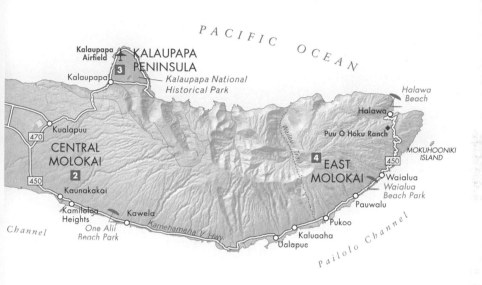

3 Kalaupapa Peninsula.
The most remote area in
the entire Hawaiian Islands
is accessible only by air,
on foot, or on a mule. It's
a place of stunning beauty
with a tragic history.

4 East Molokai. The scenic
drive on Route 450 around
this undeveloped area,
also called the east end,
passes through the green
pastures of Puu O Hoku
Ranch and climaxes with a
descent into Halawa Valley.
As you continue east, the
road becomes increasingly
narrow and the island ever
more lush.

GETTING ORIENTED

Molokai is about 10 miles
wide on average and four
times that long. The north
shore thrusts up from the
sea to form the tallest sea
cliffs on Earth, while the
south shore slides almost flat
into the water, then fans out
to form the largest shallow-
water reef system in the
United States. Kaunakakai,
the island's main town,
has most of the stores and
restaurants. Surprisingly, the
highest point on Molokai
rises to only 4,970 feet.

KALAUPAPA PENINSULA: TRAGEDY AND TRIUMPH

Today, it's hard to picture how for over a century Molokai's remote Kalaupapa Peninsula was "the loneliest place on earth," a feared place of exile for those suffering from leprosy (now known as Hansen's disease).

But for visitors who crave drama, there is no better destination than this remote strip, where the scenery blends with quintessential facets of small-town life.

The world's tallest sea cliffs, rain-chiseled valleys, and tiny islets dropped like exclamation points along the coast emphasize the passionate history of the Kalaupapa Peninsula. You'll likely be tugged by emotions—awe and disbelief, for starters. It's impossible to visit this stunning National Historical Park and view the evidence of human ignorance and heroism without responding.

Getting to the peninsula is still not easy, and there are only three ways: you can hike or take a guided mule trip down the dizzying switchback trail, or you can fly into the small Kalaupapa Airstrip. The strenuous hike takes about an hour down and 90 minutes up; the mule trip takes even longer—about two hours each way. Once on the ground, you must join a guided tour.

Daily tours are offered Monday–Saturday through Damien Tours or on the Kalaupapa Guided Mule Tour; be sure to reserve in advance. Visitors under 16 are not allowed at Kalaupapa, and photographing patients without their written permission is forbidden. Whatever your experience here may be, chances are you'll return home feeling that the journey to present-day Kalaupapa is one you'll never forget.

THE SETTLEMENT'S EARLY DAYS

In 1865, pressured by foreign residents, the Hawaiian Kingdom passed "An Act to Prevent the Spread of Leprosy." Anyone showing symptoms of the disease was to be permanently exiled to Kalawao, the north end of Kalaupapa Peninsula—a spot walled in on three sides by nearly impassable cliffs. The peninsula had been home to a fishing community for 900 years, but those inhabitants were evicted and the entire peninsula was declared settlement land.

The first 12 patients were arrested and sent to Kalawao in 1866. More banishments followed. People of all ages and many nationalities were taken from their homes and dumped on the isolated shore. Officials thought the patients could become self-sufficient, fishing and farming sweet potatoes in the stream-fed valleys. That was not the case. Settlement conditions were deplorable.

FATHER DAMIEN'S ARRIVAL

Belgian missionary Father Damien was one of four priests who volunteered to serve the leprosy settlement at Kalawao on a rotating basis. His turn came in 1873, and there were 600 patients on the island already. When his time was up, he refused to leave. Father Damien is credited with turning the settlement from a merciless exile into a place where

hope could be heard in the voices of his recruited choir.

Sixteen years after his arrival, in 1889, he died from the effects of leprosy, having contracted the disease during his service. Renowned for his sacrifice, Father Damien was canonized in 2009.

KALAUPAPA TODAY

Kalaupapa today exudes bittersweet charm. Signs posted here and there remind residents when the bankers will be there (once monthly), when to place annual barge orders for nonperishable items, and what's happening around town. It has the nostalgic, almost naive ambience expected from a place that's essentially segregated from modern life.

About eight former patients remain at Kalaupapa (by choice, as the disease is controlled by drugs and the patients are no longer carriers), and all are now quite elderly. They never lost their chutzpah, however. Having survived a lifetime of prejudice and misunderstanding, Kalaupapa's residents haven't been willing to be pushed around any longer—in past years, several made the journey to Honolulu from time to time to testify before the state legislature about matters concerning them.

To get a feel for what residents' lives were like, visit the National Park Service website (⊕ *www.nps.gov/kala*) or buy one of several heartbreaking memoirs at the park's library-turned-bookstore.

10

Updated by
Heidi Pool

With sandy beaches to the west, sheer sea cliffs to the north, and a rainy, lush eastern coast, Molokai offers a bit of everything, including a peek at what the Islands were like 50 years ago. Large tracts of land from Hawaiian Homeland grants have allowed the people to retain much of their traditional lifestyle. A favorite expression is "Slow down, you're on Molokai." Exploring the great outdoors and visiting the historic Kalaupapa Peninsula, where Saint Damien and Saint Marianne Cope helped people with leprosy, are attractions for visitors.

Molokai is generally thought of as the last bit of "real" Hawaii. Tourism has been held at bay by the island's unique history and the pride of its predominantly native Hawaiian population. Only 38 miles long and 10 miles wide at its widest point, Molokai is the fifth-largest island in the Hawaiian archipelago. Eight thousand residents call Molokai home, nearly 60% of whom are Hawaiian.

Molokai is a great place to be outdoors. There are no tall buildings, no traffic lights, no streetlights, no stores bearing the names of national chains, and nothing at all like a resort. You will, however, find 15 parks and more than 100 miles of shoreline to play on. At night the whole island grows dark, creating a velvety blackness and a wonderful, rare thing called silence.

GEOGRAPHY

Molokai was created when two large volcanoes—Kamakou in the east and Mauna Loa in the west—broke the surface of the Pacific Ocean to create an island. Afterward, a third section of the island emerged when a much smaller caldera, Kauhako, popped up to form the Kalaupapa Peninsula. But it wasn't until an enormous landslide sent much of Kauhako Mountain into the sea that the island was blessed with the sheer sea cliffs—the world's tallest—that make Molokai's north shore so spectacularly beautiful.

HISTORY

Molokai is named in chants as the child of the moon goddess Hina. For centuries the island was occupied by native people, who took advantage of the reef fishing and ideal conditions for growing taro.

When leprosy broke out in the Hawaiian Islands in the 1840s, the Kalaupapa Peninsula, surrounded on three sides by the Pacific and accessible only by a steep trail, was selected as the place to exile people suffering from the disease. The first patients were thrown into the sea to swim ashore as best they could, and left with no facilities, shelter, or supplies. In 1873 a missionary named Father Damien arrived and began to serve the peninsula's suffering inhabitants. He died in 1889 from leprosy and was canonized as a saint by the Catholic Church in 2009. In 1888, a nun named Mother Marianne Cope moved to Kalaupapa to care for the dying Father Damien and continue his vital work. Mother Marianne stayed at Kalaupapa until her death in 1918 (not from leprosy), and was canonized in 2012.

Although leprosy, known now as Hansen's disease, is no longer contagious and can be remitted, the buildings and infrastructure created by those who were exiled here still exist, and some longtime residents have chosen to stay in their homes. Today the area is Kalaupapa National Historical Park. Visitors are welcome but must prebook a tour operated by Damien Tours of Kalaupapa. You can reach the park by plane, by hiking, or by taking a mule ride down the steep Kalaupapa Trail.

THE BIRTHPLACE OF HULA

Tradition has it that, centuries ago, Lailai came to Molokai and lived on Puu Nana at Kaana. She brought the art of hula and taught it to the people, who kept it secret for her descendants, making sure the sacred dances were performed only at Kaana. Five generations later, Laka was born into the family and learned hula from an older sister. She chose to share the art and traveled throughout the Islands teaching the dance, although she did so without her family's consent. The yearly Ka Hula Piko Festival, held on Molokai in May, celebrates the birth of hula at Kaana.

10

PLANNING

WHEN TO GO

If you're keen to explore Molokai's beaches, coral beds, or fishponds, summer is your best bet for nonstop calm seas and sunny skies. The weather mimics that of the other Islands: low to mid-80s year-round, slightly rainier in winter. As you travel up the mountainside, the weather changes with bursts of downpours. The strongest storms occur in winter, when winds and rain shift to come in from the south.

For a taste of Hawaiian culture, plan your visit around a festival. In January, islanders and visitors compete in ancient Hawaiian games at the Ka Molokai Makahiki Festival. The Molokai Ka Hula Piko, an annual daylong event in May, draws premier hula troupes, musicians, and storytellers. Long-distance canoe races from Molokai to Oahu are in late September and early October. Although never crowded, the island is busier during these events—book accommodations and transportation six months in advance.

GETTING HERE AND AROUND

AIR TRAVEL

If you're flying in from the mainland United States, you must first make a stop in Honolulu, Oahu; Kahului, Maui; or Kailua-Kona, the Big Island. From any of those, Molokai is just a short hop away. Molokai's transportation hub is Hoolehua Airport, a tiny airstrip 8 miles west of Kaunakakai and about 18 miles east of Maunaloa. An even smaller airstrip serves the little community of Kalaupapa on the north shore.

From Hoolehua Airport, it takes about 10 minutes to reach Kaunakakai and 25 minutes to reach the west end of the island by car. There's no public bus. A taxi will cost about $27 from the airport to Kaunakakai with Hele Mai Taxi. Shuttle service costs about $28 per person from Hoolehua Airport to Kaunakakai; call Molokai Outdoors. Keep in mind, however, that it's difficult to visit the island without a rental car.

Contacts Hele Mai Taxi. ☎ *808/336–0967, 808/646–9060* ⊕ *www.molokaitaxi. com.* **Molokai Outdoors.** ☎ *808/553–4477, 877/553–4477* ⊕ *www.molokai-outdoors.com.*

CAR TRAVEL

If you want to explore Molokai from one end to the other, you must rent a car. With just a few main roads to choose from, it's a snap to drive around here. The gas stations are in Kaunakakai. Ask your rental agent for a free *Molokai Drive Guide.*

Alamo maintains a counter at Hoolehua Airport and will pick you up at Kaunakakai Harbor. Make arrangements in advance, because the number of rental cars on Molokai is limited. Be sure to check that the vehicle's four-wheel drive is working before you depart from the agency. There is a $75 surcharge for taking a four-wheel-drive vehicle off-road.

Contacts Alamo. ☎ *888/233–8749* ⊕ *www.alamo.com.* **Molokai Car Rental.** ☎ *808/336–0670* ⊕ *www.molokai-car-rental.com.*

FERRY TRAVEL

The Molokai Ferry crosses the channel four days per week between Lahaina (Maui) and Kaunakakai. Boats depart from Lahaina at 6 am, and from Kaunakakai at 5 pm. The 1½-hour trip takes passengers but not cars, so arrange ahead of time for a car rental or tour at the arrival point. ■TIP➔ All voyages may be subject to cancellation if a minimum of 20 confirmed passenger reservations per voyage leg are not received 48 hours in advance.

Contact Molokai Ferry. ☎ *800/667–5553* ⊕ *www.molokaiferry.com.*

COMMUNICATIONS

There are many locations on the island where cell-phone reception is difficult, if not impossible, to obtain. Your best bet for finding service is in Kaunakakai.

HOTELS

Molokai appeals most to travelers who appreciate genuine Hawaiian ambience rather than swanky digs. Most hotel and condominium properties range from adequate to funky. Visitors who want to lollygag on the beach should choose one of the condos or home rentals in West Molokai. Travelers who want to immerse themselves in the spirit of the island should seek out a condo or cottage, the closer to East Molokai the better. *Hotel reviews have been shortened. For full information, visit Fodors.com.*

Destination Molokai Visitors Bureau. Ask about a brochure with up-to-date listings of vacation rentals operated by this agency's members. ⊠ *12 Kenoi St., Suite 200, Kaunakakai* ☎ *808/553–5221* ⊕ *www.gohawaii. com/molokai.*

Molokai Vacation Properties. This company handles condo rentals and can act as an informal concierge, including arranging for a rental car, during your stay. There is a three-night minimum on all properties. Private rental properties, from beach cottages to large estates, are also available. ☎ *800/367–2984, 808/553–8334* ⊕ *www.molokai-vacation-rental.net.*

RESTAURANTS

Dining on Molokai is simply a matter of eating—there are no fancy restaurants, just pleasant low-key places to eat out. Paddlers' Inn currently has the best dinner offerings. Other options include burgers, plate lunches, pizza, coffee shop–style sandwiches, and make-it-yourself fixings.

VISITOR INFORMATION

Contacts Destination Molokai Visitors Bureau. ⊠ *12 Kamoi St., Suite 200, Kaunakakai* ☎ *808/553–5221* ⊕ *www.gohawaii.com/molokai.* **Maui Visitors Bureau.** ☎ *808/244–3530, 800/525–6284* ⊕ *www.gohawaii.com/maui.*

EXPLORING

The first thing to do on Molokai is to drive everywhere. It's a feat you can accomplish comfortably in two days. Depending on where you stay, spend one day exploring the west end and the other day exploring the east end. Basically you have one 40-mile west–east highway (two lanes, no stoplights) with three side trips: the nearly deserted little west-end town of Maunaloa, the Highway 470 drive (just a few miles) to the top of the north shore and the overlook of Kalaupapa Peninsula, and the short stretch of shops in Kaunakakai town. After you learn the general lay of the land, you can return to the places that interest you most. Directions on the island—as throughout Hawaii—are often given as *mauka* (toward the mountains) and *makai* (toward the ocean).

10

■ TIP→ Most Molokai establishments cater to the needs of locals, not tourists, so you may need to prepare a bit more than if you were going to a more popular destination. Pick up a disposable cooler in Kaunakakai town, then buy supplies in local markets. Don't forget to carry some water, and bring sunscreen and mosquito repellent to the island with you.

Kapuaiwa Coconut Grove in central Molokai is a survivor of royal plantings from the 19th century.

WEST MOLOKAI

Papohaku Beach is 17 miles west of the airport; Maunaloa is 10 miles west of the airport.

The remote beaches and rolling pastures on Molokai's west end are presided over by Mauna Loa, a dormant volcano, and a sleepy little former plantation town of the same name. Papohaku Beach, the Hawaiian Islands' second-longest white-sand beach, is one of the area's biggest draws. *For information about Papohaku Beach, see Beaches.*

GETTING HERE AND AROUND

The sometimes winding paved road through West Molokai begins at Highway 460 and ends at Kapukahehu Bay. The drive from Kaunakakai to Maunaloa is about 30 minutes.

WORTH NOTING

Kaluakoi. Although the late-1960s Kaluakoi Hotel and Golf Club is closed and forlorn, some nice condos and a gift shop are operating nearby. Kepuhi Beach, the white-sand beach along the coast, is worth a visit. ⊠ *Kaluakoi Rd., Maunaloa.*

Maunaloa. Built in 1923, this quiet community at the western end of the highway once housed workers for the island's pineapple plantation. Many businesses have closed, but it's the last place you can buy supplies when exploring the nearby beaches. If you're in the neighborhood, stop at Maunaloa's Big Wind Kite Factory. You'll want to talk with Uncle Jonathan, who has been making and flying kites here for more than three decades. ⊠ *Maunaloa Hwy., Maunaloa.*

CENTRAL MOLOKAI

Kaunakakai is 8 miles southeast of the airport.

Most residents live centrally, near the island's one and only true town, Kaunakakai. It's just about the only place on the island to get food and supplies—it *is* Molokai. Go into the shops along and around Ala Malama Street. Buy stuff. Talk with people. Take your time, and you'll really enjoy being a visitor. Also in this area, on the north side, is Coffees of Hawaii, a 500-acre coffee plantation, and the Kalaupapa National Historical Park, one of the island's most notable sights.

MOLOKAI VIBES

Molokai is one of the last places in Hawaii where most of the residents are living an authentic rural lifestyle and wish to retain it. Many oppose developing the island for visitors or outsiders, so you won't find much to cater to your needs, but if you take time and talk to the locals, you will find them hospitable and friendly. Some may even invite you home with them. It's a safe place, but don't interrupt private parties on the beach or trespass on private property. Consider yourself a guest in someone's house, rather than a customer.

GETTING HERE AND AROUND

Central Molokai is the hub of the island's road system, and Kaunakakai is the commercial center. Watch for kids, dogs, and people crossing the street downtown.

TOP ATTRACTIONS

Coffees of Hawaii. Visit the headquarters of a 500-acre Molokai coffee plantation, where the espresso bar serves freshly made sandwiches, *lilikoi* (passion fruit) smoothies, and java in artful ways. The "Mocha Mama" is a special Molokai treat. This is the place to pick up additions to your picnic lunch if you're headed to Kalaupapa. Live music is performed on the covered lanai every Tuesday and Thursday at lunch time, and their Mocha Mama Gift Shop carries all things coffee. ⊠ *1630 Farrington Hwy., off Rte. 470, Kualapuu* ☎ *877/322–3276, 808/567–9490, 808/567–6830 for espresso bar* ⊕ *www.coffeesofhawaii.com* ⊗ *Café Mon.–Sat. 7–4, gift shop Mon.–Sat. 9–4.*

Kaunakakai. Central Molokai's main town looks like a classic 1940s movie set. Along the one-block main drag is a cultural grab bag of restaurants and shops, and many people are friendly and willing to supply directions. Preferred dress is shorts and a tank top, and no one wears anything fancier than a cotton skirt or aloha shirt. ⊠ *Rte. 460, 3 blocks north of Kaunakakai Wharf, Kaunakakai.*

NEED A BREAK?

Kamoi Snack-n-Go. Stop here for some of Dave's Hawaiian Ice Cream. Sit in the refreshing breeze on one of the benches outside for a "Molokai rest stop." Snacks, crack seed, water, and cold drinks are also available. ⊠ *28 Kamoi St., Kaunakakai* ☎ *808/553–3742.*

Molokai Plumerias. The sweet smell of plumeria surrounds you at this ten-acre orchard containing thousands of these fragrant trees. Purchase a lei to go, or for $25 owner Dick Wheeler will give you a basket,

10

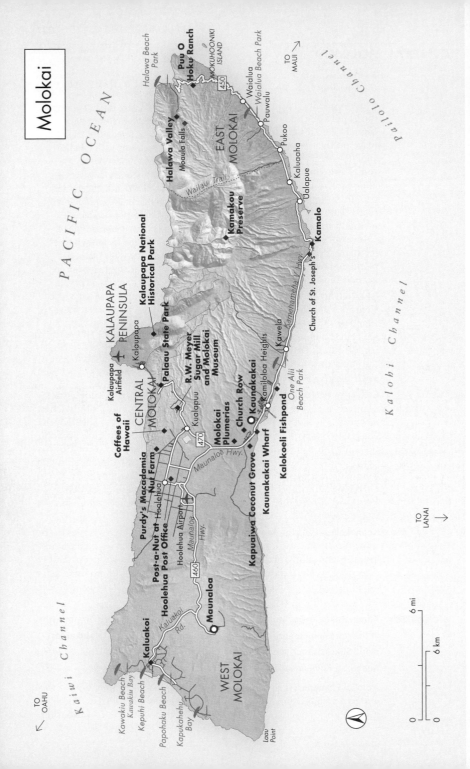

Molokai

PACIFIC OCEAN

Kaiwi Channel

TO OAHU

Kalohi Channel

Pailolo Channel

TO MAUI

TO LANAI

WEST MOLOKAI

CENTRAL MOLOKAI

EAST MOLOKAI

KALAUPAPA PENINSULA

MOKUHOONIKI ISLAND

Kawakiu Beach
Kawakiu Bay
Kepuhi Beach
Papohaku Beach
Kapukahehu Bay
Laau Point

Kaluakoi

Maunaloa

Kaluakoi Rd.
Maunaloa Hwy.
460
Maunaloa Hwy.

Hoolehua Post Office
Post-a-Nut at Hoolehua
Purdy's Macadamia Nut Farm
Hoolehua
Hoolehua Airport

Coffees of Hawaii
Kualapuu
470
R.W. Meyer Sugar Mill and Molokai Museum
Palaau State Park

Kalaupapa Airfield
Kalaupapa
Kalaupapa National Historical Park

Molokai Plumerias
Church Row
Kaunakakai
Kaunakakai Wharf
Kapuaiwa Coconut Grove
Kalokoeli Fishpond
Kamiloloa Heights
Kawela
One Alii Beach Park
Kamehameha V Hwy.
Church of St. Joseph's
Kamalo
Ualapue
Kaluaaha
Kaluapue
Pukoo
Pauwalu
Waialua
Waialua Beach Park
450

Wailau Trail
Kamakou Preserve

Halawa Valley
Moaula Falls
Halawa Beach Park
Puu O Hoku Ranch

0   6 mi
0   6 km

set you free to pick your own blossoms, then teach you how to string your own lei. For the latter, it's best to call first for an appointment. ☒ *1342 Maunaloa Hwy., Kaunakakai* ☎ *808/553–3391* ⊕ *www. molokaiplumerias.com* ☙ *Weekdays 9:30–noon.*

Palaau State Park. One of the island's few formal recreation areas, this 233-acre retreat sits at a 1,000-foot elevation. A short path through an ironwood forest leads to **Kalaupapa Lookout,** a magnificent overlook with views of the town of Kalaupapa and the 1,664-foot-high sea cliffs protecting it. Informative plaques have facts about leprosy, Saint Damien, and the colony. The park is also the site of **Kaule O Nanahoa** (Phallus of Nanahoa), where women in old Hawaii would come to the rock to enhance their fertility; it is said some still do. Because the rock is a sacred site, be respectful and don't deface the boulders. The park is well maintained, with trails, camping facilities, restrooms, and picnic tables. To get here, take Highway 460 west from Kaunakakai and then head mauka on Highway 470, which ends at the park. ☒ *Rte. 470, Kaunakakai* ☙ *Free* ☙ *Daily dawn–dusk.*

Purdy's Macadamia Nut Farm. Molokai's only working macadamia-nut farm is open for educational tours hosted by the knowledgeable and entertaining owner. A family business in Hoolehua, the farm takes up 1½ acres with a flourishing grove of 50 original trees that are more than 90 years old, as well as several hundred younger trees. The nuts taste delicious right out of the shell, home roasted, or dipped in macadamia-blossom honey. Look for Purdy's sign behind Molokai High School. ☒ *Lihi Pali Ave., Hoolehua* ☎ *808/567–6601* ⊕ *www.molokai-aloha. com/macnuts* ☙ *Free* ☙ *Weekdays 9:30–3:30, Sat. 10–2.*

R.W. Meyer Sugar Mill and Molokai Museum. Built in 1877, the fully restored, three-room sugar mill has been reconstructed as a testament to Molokai's agricultural history. It is located next to the Molokai Museum and is usually included in the museum tour. Several interesting machines from the past are on display, including a mule-driven cane crusher and a steam engine. The museum contains changing exhibits on the island's early history and has a gift shop. ☒ *Rte. 470, 2 miles southwest of Palaau State Park, Kualapuu* ☎ *808/567–6436* ☙ *$5* ☙ *Mon.–Sat. 10–2.*

HAWAII'S FIRST SAINT

A long-revered figure on Molokai and in Hawaii, Father Damien, who cared for the desperate patients at Kalaupapa, was elevated to sainthood in 2009. Plans call for a small museum and bookstore in his honor in Kaunakakai, and refurbishment of the three churches in the Catholic parish is currently under way. Visitors who cannot visit Kalaupapa can find information on Saint Damien at the Damien Center in Kaunakakai, and may worship at Our Lady of Seven Sorrows (just west of Kaunakakai) or at St. Vincent Ferrer in Maunaloa.

10

WORTH NOTING

Church Row. Standing together along the highway are several houses of worship with primarily native-Hawaiian congregations. Notice the unadorned, boxlike architecture so similar to missionary homes. ⊠ *Rte. 460, 5½ miles south of airport, Kaunakakai.*

Kapuaiwa Coconut Grove. From far away this spot looks like a sea of coconut trees. Closer up you can see that the tall, stately palms are planted in long rows leading down to the sea. This is a remnant of one of the last surviving royal groves planted for Prince Lot, who ruled Hawaii as King Kamehameha V from 1863 until his death in 1872. Watch for falling coconuts. ⊠ *Rte. 460, 5½ miles south of airport, Kaunakakai.*

Kaunakakai Wharf. Once bustling with barges exporting pineapples, these docks now host visiting boats, the ferry from Lahaina, and the twice-weekly barge from Oahu. The wharf is also the starting point for fishing, sailing, snorkeling, whale-watching, and scuba-diving excursions. It's a nice place at sunset to watch fish rippling the water. To get here, take Kaunakakai Place, which dead-ends at the wharf. ⊠ *Rte. 450, at Ala Malama St., Kaunakakai.*

Post-A-Nut at Hoolehua Post Office. At this small, rural post office you can mail a coconut to anywhere in the world. Postmaster Gary Lam provides the coconuts and colored markers. You decorate and address your coconut, and Gary affixes eye-catching stamps on it from his extensive collection. Costs vary according to destination, but for domestic addresses they start around $10. ⊠ *69-2 Puupeelua Ave., Hoolehua* ☎ *808/567–6144* ⊗ *Weekdays 8:30–noon and 12:30–4.*

KALAUPAPA PENINSULA

The Kalaupapa Airport is in the town of Kalaupapa.

The most remote area in the entire Hawaiian Islands is a place of stunning natural beauty coupled with a tragic past. It's here that residents of Hawaii who displayed symptoms of Hansen's disease (formerly known as leprosy) were permanently exiled beginning in 1866. Today, the peninsula is still isolated—it's accessible only by air, on foot, or on a mule. But a day spent here is, without a doubt, a profound, once-in-a-lifetime experience.

GETTING HERE AND AROUND

Unless you fly (through Makani Kai Air; ☎ *877/255–8532* ⊕ *www.makanikaiair.com*), the only way into Kalaupapa National Historical Park is to travel down a dizzying switchback trail, either on foot or by mule. Going down on foot takes at least an hour, but you must allow 90 minutes for the return; going down by mule is even slower, taking two hours and the same going back up. The switchbacks are numbered—26 in all—and descend 1,700 feet to sea level in just under 3 miles. The steep trail is more of a staircase, and most of the trail is shaded. Keep in mind, however, that the footing is uneven and there is little to keep you from pitching over the side. If you don't mind heights, you can stare straight down to the ocean for most of the way. It's strenuous regardless of which method you choose.

The Kalaupapa Trail and Peninsula are all part of Kalaupapa National Historical Park (☎ *808/567–6802* ⊕ *www.nps.gov/kala*), which is open every day but Sunday for tours only. Keep in mind, there are no public facilities (except an occasional restroom) anywhere in the park. Pack your own food and water, as well as light rain gear, sunscreen, and bug repellent.

TOURS

Damien Tours. The only way to explore Kalaupapa once you get there, this 3½-hour bus tour is operated by a resident family. You must bring your own snacks, lunch, and water if you travel by plane or hike in, and remain on the bus except for designated rest stops. No one may wander alone at Kalaupapa, and photographs are not allowed without prior permission of the subject. Remember this is home to the people here. No children under 16 are allowed. Both the mule ride and the plane meet this tour at Kalaupapa. The tour starts at 10 am; hikers must be down in the park by then. ⊠ *Kalaupapa* ☎ *808/567–6171* ⊠ *$60* ⊙ *Mon.–Sat. 10–1:45. Closed Sun.*

Fodor's Choice ★ **Kalaupapa Guided Mule Tour.** Mount a friendly, well-trained mule and wind along a thrilling 3-mile, 26-switchback trail to reach the town of Kalaupapa, which was once home to patients with leprosy who were exiled to this remote spot. The path was built in 1886 as a supply route for the settlement below. Once in Kalaupapa, you take a guided tour of the town and enjoy a light picnic lunch. The trail traverses some of the highest sea cliffs in the world, and views are spectacular. ■TIP➔ **Only those in good shape should attempt the ride, as two hours each way on a mule can take its toll.** You must be at least 16 years old and weigh no more than 250 pounds; pregnant women are not allowed. The entire event takes seven hours. Make reservations ahead of time, as space is limited. The same outfit can arrange for you to hike down or fly in. No one is allowed in the park or on the trail without booking a tour. ⊠ *100 Kalae Hwy., Kualapuu* ☎ *808/567–6088, 800/567–7550* ⊕ *www.muleride.com* ⊠ *$199* ⊙ *Mon.–Sat. check-in at 7:45 am (returns at 3:30 pm).*

TOP ATTRACTIONS

Kalaupapa National Historical Park. For 100 years, this remote strip of land was "the loneliest place on Earth," a beautiful yet feared place of exile for those suffering from leprosy (now known as Hansen's disease). Today, visitors to Molokai's **Kalaupapa Peninsula,** open every day but Sunday, can admire the tall sea cliffs, rain-chiseled valleys, and tiny islets along the coast. The park tells a poignant human story, as the Kalaupapa Peninsula was once a community of about 1,000 people who were banished from their homes in Hawaii. It also recounts the wonderful work of Father Damien, a Belgian missionary who arrived in 1873 to work with the patients. He died in 1889 from leprosy and was canonized as a saint by the Catholic Church in 2009. Mother Marianne Cope, who continued St. Damien's work after his death, was canonized in 2012.

DID YOU KNOW?

The Kalaupapa Guided Mule Tour down the 3-mile trail to Kalaupapa includes multiple switchbacks near high sea cliffs. The views are stunning, but this mule ride is not for the faint of heart or the out of shape.

The Truth About Hansen's Disease

■ A cure for leprosy has been available since 1941. Multidrug therapy, a rapid cure, has been available since 1981.

■ With treatment, none of the disabilities traditionally associated with leprosy need occur.

■ Most people have a natural immunity to leprosy. Only 5% of the world's population is even susceptible to the disease.

■ There are still more than 200,000 new cases of leprosy each year; the majority are in India.

■ All new cases of leprosy are treated on an outpatient basis.

■ The term "leper" is offensive and should not be used. It is appropriate to say "a person is affected by leprosy" or "by Hansen's disease."

Today there are about 8 patients still living in Kalaupapa—now by choice, as the disease is treatable. Out of respect to these people, visitors must be at least 16 years old, cannot stay overnight, and must be on a guided tour or invited by a resident. Photographing patients without their permission is forbidden. Guided tours of the settlement, which start at 10 am, are available by reservation only through Damien Tours if you're hiking or flying in, or the Kalaupapa Guided Mule Tour if you're riding. Reserve well in advance to avoid disappointment. Keep in mind that there are no public facilities (except an occasional restroom) anywhere in the park. Pack your own food and water, as well as light rain gear, sunscreen, and bug repellent.

Unless you fly with Makani Kai Air, the only way into Kalaupapa National Historic Park is on the dizzying switchback **Kalaupapa Trail.** The switchbacks are numbered—26 in all—and descend 1,700 feet to sea level in just under 3 miles. The steep trail is more of a staircase, and most of the trail is shaded. ⚠ Footing on the Kalaupapa Trail is uneven and there is little to keep you from pitching over the side. Hikers should be in good physical condition. If you don't mind heights, you can stare straight down to the ocean for most of the way. There is ample parking near the end of Highway 470. You can access Kalaupapa Trail off Highway 470 near Kalaupapa Overlook. ⊠ *Hwy. 470, Kualapuu* ☎ *808/567–6802* ⊕ *www.nps.gov/kala.*

EAST MOLOKAI

Halawa Valley is 36 miles northeast of the airport.

On the beautifully undeveloped east end of Molokai you can find ancient fishponds, a magnificent coastline, splendid ocean views, and a fertile valley that's been inhabited for 14 centuries. The eastern uplands are flanked by Mt. Kamakou, the island's highest point at 4,970 feet and home to The Nature Conservancy's Kamakou Preserve. Mist hangs over waterfall-filled valleys, and ancient lava cliffs jut out into the sea.

GETTING HERE AND AROUND

Driving the east end is a scenic adventure, but the road narrows and becomes curvy after the 20-mile marker. Take your time, especially in the seaside lane, and watch for oncoming traffic. Driving at night is not recommended.

TOP ATTRACTIONS

Fodor's Choice
★

Halawa Valley. The Solatorio Ohana (family) leads hikes through the valley, the oldest recorded habitation on Molokai. It is home to two sacrificial temples and many historic sites. Inhabitants grew taro and fished from 650 until the 1960s, when an enormous flood wiped out the taro patches and forced old-timers to abandon their traditional lifestyle. Now, a new generation of Hawaiians has begun the challenging task of restoring the taro fields. Much of this work involves rerouting streams to flow through carefully engineered level ponds called *loi*. Taro plants, with their big, dancing leaves, grow in the submerged mud of the loi, where the water is always cool and flowing. Hawaiians believe that the taro plant is their ancestor and revere it both as sustenance and as a spiritual necessity. The 3.4-mile round-trip valley hike, which goes to **Moaula Falls,** a 250-foot cascade, is rated intermediate to advanced and includes two moderate river crossings (so your feet will get wet). A $60 fee per adult supports restoration efforts. ✉ *Eastern end of Rte. 450* ☎ *808/542–1855* ⊕ *www.halawavalleymolokai.com* 💲 *$60.*

OFF THE
BEATEN
PATH

Kamakou Preserve. Tucked away on the slopes of Mt. Kamakou, Molokai's highest peak, this 2,774-acre rain-forest preserve is a dazzling wonderland full of wet *ohia* forests (hardwood trees of the myrtle family, with red blossoms called *lehua*), rare bogs, and native trees and wildlife. Guided educational tours, limited to eight people, are held one Saturday each month March–October. Reserve well in advance, as these excursions fill up several months in advance. ✉ *23 Pueo Pl., Kualapuu* ☎ *808/553–5236* ⊕ *www.nature.org* 💲 *Free.*

WORTH NOTING

Kalokoeli Fishpond. With its narrow rock walls arching out from the shoreline, Kalokoeli is typical of the numerous fishponds that define southern Molokai. Many were built around the 13th century under the direction of powerful chiefs. This early type of aquaculture, particular to Hawaii, exemplifies the ingenuity of native Hawaiians. One or more openings were left in the wall, where gates called *makaha* were installed. These gates allowed seawater and tiny fish to enter the enclosed pond but kept larger predators out. The tiny fish would then grow too big to get out. At one time there were 62 fishponds around Molokai's coast. ✉ *Rte. 450, 6 miles east of Kaunakakai, Kaunakakai.*

Kamalo. A natural harbor used by small cargo ships during the 19th century and a favorite fishing spot for locals, Kamalo is also the location of the **Church of St. Joseph's,** a tiny white church built by Saint Damien of the Kalaupapa colony in the 1880s. It's a state historic site and place of pilgrimage. The door is often open; if it is, slip inside and sign the guest book. The congregation keep the church in beautiful condition. ✉ *Rte. 450, 11 miles east of Kaunakakai, Kaunakakai.*

10

Lava ridges make Kepuhi Beach beautiful, but swimming is hard unless the water is calm.

NEED A BREAK?

Manae Goods & Grindz. The best place to grab a snack or picnic supplies is this store, 16 miles east of Kaunakakai. It's the only place on the east end where you can find essentials such as ice and bread, and not-so-essentials such as seafood plate lunches, bentos, burgers, and shakes. Try a refreshing smoothie while here. ✉ *Rte. 450, Kaunakakai* ☎ *808/558–8498, 808/558–8186.*

Puu O Hoku Ranch. A 14,000-acre private ranch in the highlands of East Molokai, Puu O Hoku was developed in the 1930s by wealthy industrialist Paul Fagan. Route 450 ambles right through this rural treasure with its pastures and grazing horses and cattle. As you drive slowly along, enjoy the splendid views of Maui and Lanai. The small island off the coast is Mokuhooniki, a favorite spot among visiting humpback whales, and a nesting seabird sanctuary. The ranch has limited accommodations, too. ✉ *Rte. 450, 25 miles east of Kaunakakai, Kaunakakai* ☎ *888/573–7775* ⊕ *www.puuohoku.com.*

BEACHES

Molokai's unique geography gives the island plenty of drama and spectacle along the shorelines but not so many places for seaside basking and bathing. The long north shore consists mostly of towering cliffs that plunge directly into the sea and is inaccessible except by boat, and even then only in summer. Much of the south shore is enclosed by a huge reef, which stands as far as a mile offshore and blunts the action of the waves. Within this reef you can find a thin strip of sand, but the water here is flat, shallow, and at times clouded with silt. This reef area is best suited to wading, pole fishing, kayaking, or learning how to windsurf. The big, fat, sandy beaches lie along the west end. The largest of these—the second largest in the Islands—is Papohaku Beach, which fronts a grassy park shaded by a grove of *kiawe* (mesquite) trees. These stretches of west-end sand are generally unpopulated. At the east end, where the road hugs the sinuous shoreline, you encounter a number of pocket-size beaches in rocky coves, good for snorkeling. Don't venture too far out, however, or you can find yourself caught in dangerous currents. The island's east-end road ends at Halawa Valley with its unique double bay, which is not recommended for swimming.

If you need beach gear, head to Molokai Fish & Dive at the west end of Kaunakakai's only commercial strip, or rent kayaks from Molokai Outdoors at Kaunakakai Wharf.

Department of Parks, Land and Natural Resources. All of Hawaii's beaches are free and public. None of the beaches on Molokai have telephones or lifeguards, and they're all under the jurisdiction of the Department of Parks, Land and Natural Resources. ☎ *808/587–0300* ⊕ *www. hawaiistateparks.org.*

WEST MOLOKAI

Molokai's west end looks across a wide channel to the island of Oahu. This crescent-shape cup of coastline holds the island's best sandy beaches as well as the sunniest weather. Remember: all beaches are public property, even those that front developments, and most have public access roads. *Beaches below are listed from north to south.*

Kawakiu Beach. Seclusion is yours at this remote, beautiful, white-sand beach, accessible by four-wheel-drive vehicle (through a gate that is sometimes locked) or a 45-minute walk. To get here, drive to Paniolo Hale off Kaluakoi Road and look for a dirt road off to the right. Park here and hike in or, with a four-wheel-drive vehicle, drive along the dirt road to beach. ⚠ Rocks and undertow make swimming extremely dangerous at times, so use caution. **Amenities:** none. **Best for:** solitude. ⊠ *Off Kaluakoi Rd., Maunaloa.*

Kepuhi Beach. The Kaluakoi Hotel is closed, but its half mile of ivory sand is still accessible. The beach shines against the turquoise sea, black outcroppings of lava, and magenta bougainvillea blossoms. When the sea is perfectly calm, lava ridges in the water make good snorkeling spots. With any surf at all, however, the water around these rocky places churns and foams, wiping out visibility and making it difficult to avoid being slammed into the jagged rocks. **Amenities:** showers; toilets. **Best for:** snorkeling; walking. ⊠ *Kaluakoi Rd., Maunaloa.*

Fodor's Choice ★ **Papohaku Beach.** One of the most sensational beaches in Hawaii, Papohaku is a 3-mile-long strip of light golden sand, the longest of its kind on the island. There's so much sand here that Honolulu once purchased bargeloads of the stuff to replenish Waikiki Beach. A shady beach park just inland is the site of the Ka Hula Piko Festival, held each year in May. The park is also a great sunset-facing spot for a

10

rustic afternoon barbecue. A park ranger patrols the area periodically. ■TIP➔ Swimming is not recommended, as there's a dangerous undertow except on exceptionally calm summer days. **Amenities:** showers; toilets. **Best for:** sunset; walking. ⊠ *Kaluakoi Rd., 2 miles south of the former Kaluakoi Hotel, Maunaloa.*

Kapukahehu Bay. The sandy protected cove is usually completely deserted on weekdays but can fill up when the surf is up. The water in the cove is clear and shallow with plenty of well-worn rocky areas. These conditions make for excellent snorkeling, swimming, and boogie boarding on calm days. Locals like to surf in a break called Dixie's or Dixie Maru. **Amenities:** none. **Best for:** snorkeling; surfing; swimming. ⊠ *End of Kaluakoi Rd., 3½ miles south of Papohaku Beach, Maunaloa.*

> ### BEACH SAFETY
>
> Unlike protected shorelines like Kaanapali on Maui, the coasts of Molokai are exposed to rough sea channels and dangerous rip currents. The ocean tends to be calmer in the morning and in summer. No matter what the time, however, always study the sea before entering. Unless the water is placid and the wave action minimal, it's best to stay on shore, even though locals may be in the water. Don't underestimate the power of the ocean.
>
> Protect yourself with sunblock; cool breezes make it easy to underestimate the power of the sun as well.

CENTRAL MOLOKAI

The south shore is mostly a huge, reef-walled expanse of flat saltwater edged with a thin strip of gritty sand and stones, mangrove swamps, and the amazing system of fishponds constructed by the chiefs of ancient Molokai. From this shore you can look out across glassy water to see people standing on top of the sea—actually, way out on top of the reef—casting fishing lines into the distant waves. This is not a great area for beaches but is a good place to snorkel or wade in the shallows.

One Alii Beach Park. Clear, close views of Maui and Lanai across the Pailolo Channel dominate One Alii Beach Park (*One* is pronounced "o-nay," not "won"), the only well-maintained beach park on the island's south-central shore. Molokai folks gather here for family reunions and community celebrations; the park's tightly trimmed expanse of lawn could almost accommodate the entire island's population. Swimming within the reef is perfectly safe, but don't expect to catch any waves. Nearby is the restored One Alii fishpond (it is appropriate only for native Hawaiians to fish here). **Amenities:** showers; toilets. **Best for:** parties; swimming. ⊠ *Rte. 450 east of Hotel Molokai, Kaunakakai.*

EAST MOLOKAI

The east end unfolds as a coastal drive with turnouts for tiny cove beaches—good places for snorkeling, shore fishing, or scuba exploring. Rocky little Mokuhooniki Island marks the eastern point of the island and serves as a nursery for humpback whales in winter and nesting seabirds in spring. The road loops around the east end, then descends and ends at Halawa Valley.

Halawa Beach Park. The vigorous water that gouged the steep, spectacular Halawa Valley also carved out two adjacent bays. Accumulations of coarse sand and river rock have created some protected pools that are good for wading or floating around. You might see surfers, but it's not wise to entrust your safety to the turbulent open ocean along this coast. Most people come here to hang out and absorb the beauty of Halawa Valley. The valley itself is private property, so do not wander without a guide. **Amenities:** toilets. **Best for:** solitude. ⌧ *End of Rte. 450, Kaunakakai.*

Waialua Beach Park. Also known as Twenty Mile Beach, this arched stretch of sand leads to one of the most popular snorkeling spots on the island. The water here, protected by the flanks of the little bay, is often so clear and shallow that even from land you can watch fish swimming among the coral heads. Watch out for traffic when you enter the highway. ■TIP➔ This is a pleasant place to stop on the drive around the east end. **Amenities:** none. **Best for:** snorkeling; swimming. ⌧ *Rte. 450 near mile marker 20.*

WHERE TO EAT

During a week's stay, you might easily hit all the dining spots worth a visit and then return to your favorites for a second round. The dining scene is fun, because it's a microcosm of Hawaii's diverse cultures. You can find locally grown vegetarian foods, spicy Filipino cuisine, or Hawaiian fish with a Japanese influence—such as tuna, mullet, and moonfish that's grilled, sautéed, or mixed with seaweed to make *poke* (salted and seasoned raw fish).

Most eating establishments are on Ala Malama Street in Kaunakakai. If you're heading to West Molokai for the day, be sure to stock up on provisions, as there is no place to eat there. If you are on the east end, stop by **Manae Goods & Grindz** (☎ *808/558–8186*) near mile marker 16 for good local seafood plates, burgers, and ice cream.

10

WHAT IT COSTS			
$	**$$**	**$$$**	**$$$$**
Restaurants			
under $18	$18–$26	$27–$35	over $35

Restaurant prices are the average cost of a main course at dinner or, if dinner is not served, at lunch.

CENTRAL MOLOKAI

Central Molokai offers most of the island's dining options.

$ CAFÉ Fodor's Choice ★ 🍴 **Kanemitsu's Bakery and Coffee Shop.** Stop at this Molokai institution for morning coffee and some of the round Molokai bread—a sweet, pan-style white loaf that makes excellent cinnamon toast. Take a few loaves with you for a picnic or a condo breakfast. You can also try a taste of *lavash*, a pricey flatbread flavored with sesame, taro, Maui onion, Parmesan cheese, or jalapeño. [$] *Average main: $6* ✉ *79 Ala Malama St., Kaunakakai* ☎ *808/553–5855* ▭ *No credit cards* ⏲ *Closed Tues.*

$ AMERICAN-HAWAIIAN 🍴 **Kualapuu Cookhouse.** The only restaurant in rural Kualapuu, this local favorite is a classic, refurbished, green-and-white plantation house with a shady lanai. Inside, local photography and artwork enhance the simple furnishings. Typical fare is an inexpensive plate of chicken or pork served with rice, but at dinner there's also the more expensive spicy crusted ahi. This laid-back diner sits across the street from the Kualapuu Market. [$] *Average main: $10* ✉ *Farrington Hwy., 1 block west of Rte. 470, Kualapuu* ☎ *808/567–9655* ▭ *No credit cards* ⏲ *No dinner Sun. and Mon.*

$ BURGER 🍴 **Molokai Burger.** Clean and cheery, Molokai Burger offers both drive-through and eat-in options. Burgers may be ordered on a whole wheat bun. Healthier items include breakfast sandwiches without cheese and mayonnaise, and salads featuring Kumu Farms-certified organic veggies. [$] *Average main: $6* ✉ *20 W. Kamehameha V Hwy., Kaunakakai* ☎ *808/553–3533* 🌐 *www.molokaiburger.com* ⏲ *Closed Sun.*

$ AMERICAN 🍴 **Molokai Pizza Cafe.** Cheerful and busy, this is a popular gathering spot for local families and a good place to pick up food for a picnic. Pizza, sandwiches, salads, pasta, and fresh fish are simply prepared and served without fuss. Kids keep busy at the nearby arcade, and art by local artists decorates the lavender walls. [$] *Average main: $15* ✉ *15 Kaunakakai Pl., at Wharf Rd., Kaunakakai* ☎ *808/553–3288.*

$ AMERICAN 🍴 **Paddlers' Inn.** There aren't many dinner options on Molokai, but this popular spot is a great place to grab a decent meal while rubbing elbows with locals. Hearty portions of ribs, pork chops, and chicken-fried steak come with two side dishes at a reasonable price. Fish options include salmon and mahimahi. There is live music on Tuesday, Thursday, and Saturday at 6:30 pm. Don't be surprised if the bass player is also a teacher at the local elementary school. [$] *Average main: $14* ✉ *10 N. Mohala St., Kaunakakai* ☎ *808/553–3300* 🌐 *www.molokaipaddlersinn.com.*

$ DELI 🍴 **Sundown Deli.** Small and clean, this deli focuses on freshly made takeout food. Sandwiches come on a half dozen types of bread, and the Portuguese bean soup and chowders are rich and filling. It's open weekdays 10:30–2. [$] *Average main: $8* ✉ *145 Ala Malama St., Kaunakakai* ☎ *808/553–3713* ▭ *No credit cards* ⏲ *Closed weekends. No dinner.*

WHERE TO STAY

The coastline along Molokai's west end has ocean-view condominium units and luxury homes available as vacation rentals. Central Molokai offers seaside condominiums. The only lodgings on the east end are some guest cottages in magical settings and the cottages and ranch lodge at Puu O Hoku. Note that room rates do not include 13.42% sales tax.

Note: Maui County has regulations concerning vacation rentals; to avoid disappointment, always contact the property manager or the owner and ask if the accommodations have the proper permits and are in compliance with local ordinances. *Hotel reviews have been shortened. For full information, visit Fodors.com.*

WHAT IT COSTS			
$	$$	$$$	$$$$
Hotels	under $181	$181–$260	$261–$340	over $340

Hotel prices are the lowest cost of a standard double room in high season. Condo price categories reflect studio and one-bedroom rates.

WEST MOLOKAI

If you want to stay in West Molokai so you'll have access to unspoiled beaches, your only choices are condos or vacation homes. Note that units fronting the abandoned Kaluakoi golf course present a bit of a dismal view.

$
RENTAL
Ke Nani Kai. These pleasant, spacious one- and two-bedroom condos near the beach have ocean views and nicely maintained tropical landscaping. **Pros:** on island's secluded west end; uncrowded pool; beach is across the road. **Cons:** amenities vary from unit to unit; far from commercial center; some units overlook abandoned golf course. ⓢ *Rooms from: $125* ✉ *50 Keuphi Beach Rd., Maunaloa* ☎ *808/553–8334, 800/367–2984* ⊕ *www.molokai-vacation-rental.net* ⛱ *120 units* ◯ *No meals.*

$
RENTAL
Fodor's Choice
★
Paniolo Hale. Perched high on a ridge overlooking a favorite local surfing spot, this is Molokai's best condominium property and boasts mature tropical landscaping and a private serene setting. **Pros:** close to beach; quiet surroundings; perfect if you are an expert surfer. **Cons:** amenities vary; far from shopping; golf course units front abandoned course. ⓢ *Rooms from: $125* ✉ *100 Lio Pl., Kaunakakai* ☎ *808/553–8334, 800/367–2984* ⊕ *www.molokai-vacation-rental.net* ⛱ *77 units* ◯ *No meals.*

CENTRAL MOLOKAI

There are two condo properties in this area, one close to shopping and dining in Kaunakakai, and the other on the way to the east end.

$
HOTEL
Hotel Molokai. At this local favorite, Polynesian-style bungalows are scattered around the nicely landscaped property, many overlooking the reef and distant Lanai. **Pros:** five minutes to town; some units have

kitchenettes; authentic Hawaiian entertainment. **Cons:** not many frills; lower-priced rooms are small and plain; late-night live music can be loud. [$] *Rooms from: $179* ✉ *1300 Kamehameha V Hwy., Kaunakakai* ☎ *808/660–3408, 877/553–5347* 🌐 *www.hotelmolokai.com* 🛏 *40 rooms* 🍴 *No meals.*

$ RENTAL 🏨 **Molokai Shores.** Many of the units in this three-story condominium complex have a view of the ocean, and there's a chance to see whales in season. **Pros:** convenient location; some units upgraded; near water. **Cons:** older accommodations; units close to highway can be noisy. [$] *Rooms from: $169* ✉ *1000 Kamehameha V Hwy., Kaunakakai* ☎ *808/553–8334, 800/367–2984* 🌐 *www.molokai-vacation-rental.net* 🛏 *100 units* 🍴 *No meals.*

$ RENTAL 🏨 **Wavecrest.** This 5-acre oceanfront condominium complex is convenient if you want to explore the east side of the island—it's 13 miles east of Kaunakakai—with access to a beautiful reef, excellent snorkeling, and kayaking. **Pros:** convenient location for divers; good value; nicely maintained grounds. **Cons:** amenities vary; far from shopping; area sometimes gets windy. [$] *Rooms from: $125* ✉ *Rte. 450, near mile marker 13, Kaunakakai* ☎ *800/367–2984, 808/553–8334* 🌐 *www.molokai-vacation-rental.net* 🛏 *126 units* 🍴 *No meals.*

EAST MOLOKAI

Puu O Hoku Ranch, a rental facility on East Molokai, is the main lodging option on this side of the island. The ranch is quite far from the center of the island.

$$ B&B/INN 🏨 **Puu O Hoku Ranch.** At the east end of Molokai, these ocean-view accommodations are on 14,000 isolated acres of pasture and forest—a remote and serene location for people who want to get away from it all or meet in a retreat atmosphere. **Pros:** ideal for large groups; authentic working ranch; great hiking. **Cons:** on remote east end of island; road to property is narrow and winding. [$] *Rooms from: $200* ✉ *Rte. 450 near mile marker 25, Kaunakakai* ☎ *888/573–7775, 808/558–8109* 🌐 *www.puuohoku.com* 🛏 *3 cottages, 1 lodge* 🍴 *No meals.*

WATER SPORTS AND TOURS

Molokai's shoreline topography limits opportunities for water sports. Sea cliffs dominate the north shore; the south shore is largely encased by a huge, taming reef. ■ **TIP→ Open-sea access at west-end and east-end beaches should be used only by experienced ocean swimmers, and then with caution because seas are rough, especially in winter.** Generally speaking, there's no one around—certainly not lifeguards—if you get into trouble. For this reason alone, guided excursions are recommended. At least be sure to ask for advice from outfitters or residents. Two kinds of water activities predominate: kayaking within the reef area, and open-sea excursions on charter boats, most of which tie up at Kaunakakai Wharf.

BODY BOARDING AND BODYSURFING

You rarely see people body boarding or bodysurfing on Molokai, and the only surfing is for advanced wave riders. The best spots for body boarding when conditions are safe (occasional summer mornings) are the west-end beaches. Another option is to seek out waves at the east end around mile marker 20.

DEEP-SEA FISHING

For Molokai people, as in days of yore, the ocean is more of a larder than a playground. It's common to see residents fishing along the shoreline or atop South Shore Reef, using poles or lines. Deep-sea fishing by charter boat is a great Molokai adventure. The sea channels here, though often rough and windy, provide gorgeous views of several islands. Big fish are plentiful in these waters, especially mahimahi, marlin, and various kinds of tuna. Generally speaking, boat captains will customize the outing to your interests, share a lot of information about the island, and let you keep some or all of your catch.

EQUIPMENT

Molokai Fish & Dive. If you'd like to try your hand at fishing, you can rent or buy equipment and ask for advice here. ⊠ *53 Ala Malama St., Kaunakakai* ☎ *808/553–5926* ⊕ *www.molokaifishanddive.com.*

BOATS AND CHARTERS

Alyce C. This 31-foot cruiser runs excellent sportfishing excursions in the capable hands of Captain Joe. The cost for the six-passenger boat is $550 for a full-day trip, $450 for four to five hours. Gear is provided. It's a rare day when you don't snag at least one memorable fish. ⊠ *Kaunakakai Wharf, Kaunakakai Pl., Kaunakakai* ☎ *808/558–8377* ⊕ *www.alycecsportfishing.com.*

Fun Hogs Sportfishing. Trim and speedy, the 27-foot flybridge boat named *Ahi* offers four-hour ($450), six-hour ($550), and eight-hour ($600) sportfishing excursions. Skipper Mike Holmes also provides one-way or round-trip fishing expeditions to Lanai, as well as sunset cruises and whale-watching trips in winter. ⊠ *Kaunakakai Wharf, Kaunakakai Pl., Kaunakakai* ☎ *808/567–6789* ⊕ *www.molokaifishing.com.*

Molokai Action Adventures. Walter Naki has traveled (and fished) all over the globe. He will create customized fishing expeditions and gladly share his wealth of experience. He will also take you to remote beaches for a day of swimming. If you want to explore the north side under the great sea cliffs, this is the way to go. His 21-foot *Boston Whaler* is usually seen in the east end at the mouth of Halawa Valley. Prices start at $300. ⊠ *Kaunakakai* ☎ *808/558–8184.*

KAYAKING

Molokai's south shore is enclosed by the largest reef system in the United States—an area of shallow, protected sea that stretches over 30 miles. This reef gives inexperienced kayakers an unusually safe, calm environment for shoreline exploring. ■TIP➔ Outside the reef, Molokai waters are often rough, and strong winds can blow you out to sea. Kayakers out here should be strong, experienced, and cautious.

BEST SPOTS

South Shore Reef. This reef's area is superb for flat-water kayaking any day of the year. It's best to rent a kayak from Molokai Outdoors in Kaunakakai and slide into the water from Kaunakakai Wharf. Get out in the morning before the wind picks up and paddle east, exploring the ancient Hawaiian fishponds. When you turn around to return, the wind will usually give you a push home. ⊠ *Kaunakakai.*

EQUIPMENT, LESSONS, AND TOURS

Molokai Fish & Dive. At the west end of Kaunakakai's commercial strip, this all-around outfitter offers guided kayak excursions inside the South Shore Reef. One excursion paddles through a mangrove forest and explores a hidden ancient fishpond. If the wind starts blowing hard, the company will tow you back with its boat. The fee is $69 for the half-day trip, which includes sodas and water. ⊠ *53 Ala Malama St., Kaunakakai* ☎ *808/553–5926* ⊕ *www.molokaifishanddive.com.*

Molokai Outdoors. This is the place to rent a kayak for exploring on your own. Kayaks rent for $42 per day or $210 per week, and extra paddles are available. ⊠ *9 Hio Pl., Kaunakakai* ☎ *808/553–4477, 877/553–4477* ⊕ *www.molokai-outdoors.com.*

SCUBA DIVING

Molokai Fish & Dive is the only PADI-certified dive company on Molokai. Shoreline access for divers is extremely limited, even nonexistent in winter. Boat diving is the way to go. Without guidance, visiting divers can easily find themselves in risky situations with wicked currents. Proper guidance, however, opens an undersea world rarely seen.

Molokai Fish & Dive. Owners Tim and Susan Forsberg can fill you in on local dive sites, rent you the gear, or hook you up with one of their PADI-certified guides to take you to the island's best underwater spots. Their 32-foot dive boat, the *Ama Lua,* can take eight divers and their gear. Two-tank dives lasting about five hours cost $145; three-tank dives lasting around six hours cost $295. They know the best blue holes and underwater-cave systems, and can take you swimming with hammerhead sharks. ⊠ *53 Ala Malama St., Kaunakakai* ☎ *808/553–5926* ⊕ *www.molokaifishanddive.com.*

10

SNORKELING

During the times when swimming is safe—mainly in summer—just about every beach on Molokai offers good snorkeling along the lava outcroppings in the island's clean and pristine waters. Although rough in winter, Kepuhi Beach is a prime spot in summer. Certain spots inside the South Shore Reef are also worth checking out.

BEST SPOTS

During the summer, **Kepuhi Beach,** on Molokai's west end, offers excellent snorkeling opportunities. The ½-mile-long stretch has plenty of rocky nooks that swirl with sea life. Take Kaluakoi Road all the way to the west end, park at the now-closed Kaluakoi Resort, and walk to the beach. Avoid Kepuhi Beach in winter, as the sea is rough here.

At **Waialua Beach Park,** on Molokai's east end, you'll find a thin curve of sand that rims a sheltered little bay loaded with coral heads and aquatic life. The water here is shallow—sometimes so shallow that you bump into the underwater landscape—and it's crystal clear. Pull off the road near mile marker 20.

EQUIPMENT AND TOURS

Rent snorkel sets from Molokai Fish & Dive in Kaunakakai. Rental fees are nominal ($7–$10 per day). All the charter boats carry snorkel gear and include dive stops.

Fun Hogs Sportfishing. Mike Holmes, captain of the 27-foot *Ahi,* knows the island waters intimately, likes to have fun, and is willing to arrange any type of excursion—for example, one dedicated entirely to snorkeling. His two-hour snorkel trips leave early in the morning and explore rarely seen fish and turtle sites outside the reef. Trips cost $70 per person; bring your own food and drink. ✉ *Kaunakakai Wharf, Kaunakakai Pl., Kaunakakai* ☎ *808/567–6789* ⊕ *www.molokaifishing.com.*

Molokai Fish & Dive. Climb aboard a 31-foot twin-hull PowerCat for a snorkeling trip to Molokai's pristine barrier reef. Trips cost $79 per person and include equipment, water, and soft drinks. ✉ *53 Ala Malama St., Kaunakakai* ☎ *808/553–5926* ⊕ *www.molokaifishanddive.com.*

WHALE-WATCHING

Although Maui gets all the credit for the local wintering humpback-whale population, the big cetaceans also come to Molokai December–April. Mokuhooniki Island at the east end serves as a whale nursery and courting ground, and the whales pass back and forth along the south shore. This being Molokai, whale-watching here will never involve floating amid a group of boats all ogling the same whale.

BOATS AND CHARTERS

Alyce C. Although this six-passenger sportfishing boat is usually busy hooking mahimahi and marlin, the captain will gladly take you on a three-hour excursion to admire the humpback whales. The price, around $75 per person, is based on the number of people in your group. ✉ *Kaunakakai Wharf, Kaunakakai Pl., Kaunakakai* ☎ *808/558–8377* ⊕ *www.alycecsportfishing.com.*

Ama Lua. The crew of this 31-foot dive boat, which holds up to 12 passengers, is respectful of the whales and the laws that protect them. A two-hour whale-watching trip is $79 per person; it departs from Kaunakakai Wharf at 7 am daily, December–April. Call Molokai Fish & Dive for reservations. ✉ *53 Ala Malama St., Kaunakakai* ☎ *808/553–5926* ⊕ *www.molokaifishanddive.com.*

Bikers on Molokai can explore the north-shore sea cliffs overlooking the Kalaupapa Peninsula.

Fun Hogs Sportfishing. The *Ahi*, a flybridge sportfishing boat, takes you on 2½-hour whale-watching trips in the morning, December–April. The cost is $70 per person; bring your own food and drink. ✉ *Kaunakakai Wharf, Kaunakakai Pl., Kaunakakai* ☎ *808/567–6789* ⊕ *www. molokaifishing.com.*

GOLF, HIKING, AND OUTDOOR ACTIVITIES

Activity vendors in Kaunakakai are a good source of information on outdoor adventures on Molokai. For a mellow round of golf, head to the island's only golf course, Ironwood Hills, where you'll likely share the greens with local residents. Molokai's steep and uncultivated terrain offers excellent hikes and some stellar views. Although the island is largely wild, all land is privately owned, so get permission before hiking.

BIKING

Cyclists who like to eat up the miles love Molokai, because its few roads are long, straight, and extremely rural. You can really go for it—there are no traffic lights and (most of the time) no traffic.

Molokai Bicycle. You can rent a bike here for $28–$32 per day, depending on the model, with reductions for additional days or week-long rentals. Bike trailers (for your drinks cooler, perhaps) are also available for $12 a day or $60 for a week. ✉ *80 Mohala St., Kaunakakai* ☎ *808/553–5740, 800/709–2453* ⊕ *www.mauimolokaibicycle.com.*

GOLF

Molokai is not a prime golf destination, but the sole 9-hole course makes for a pleasant afternoon.

Ironwood Hills Golf Course. Like other 9-hole plantation-era courses, Ironwood Hills is in a prime spot, with basic fairways and not always manicured greens. It helps if you like to play laid-back golf with locals and can handle occasionally rugged conditions. On the plus side, most holes offer ocean views. Fairways are *kukuya* grass and run through pine, ironwood, and eucalyptus trees. Carts and clubs are rented on the honor system; there's not always someone there to assist you. Bring your own water. Access is via a bumpy, unpaved road. ⊠ *Kalae Hwy., Kualapuu* ☎ *808/567–6000* ⊕ *www.molokaigolfcourse.com* ▪ *$18 for 9 holes, $24 for 18 holes* ♍ *9 holes, 3088 yards, par 34.*

HIKING

Rural and rugged, Molokai is an excellent place for hiking. Roads and developments are few. The island is steep, so hikes often combine spectacular views with hearty physical exertion. Because the island is small, you can come away with the feeling of really knowing the place. And you won't see many other people around. Much of what may look like deserted land is private property, so be careful not to trespass—seek permission or use an authorized guide.

BEST SPOTS

Kalaupapa Trail. You can hike down to the Kalaupapa Peninsula and back via this 3-mile, 26-switchback route. The trail is often nearly vertical, traversing the face of the high sea cliffs. You can reach Kalaupapa Trail off Highway 470 near Kalaupapa Overlook. Only those in excellent condition should attempt it. You must have made prior arrangements with **Damien Tours** (☎ *808/567–6171*) in order to access Kalaupapa via this trail. ⊠ *Off Hwy. 470, Kualapuu.*

GOING WITH A GUIDE

Fodor's Choice ★ **Halawa Valley Falls Cultural Hike.** This gorgeous, steep-walled valley was carved by two rivers and is rich in history. Site of the earliest Polynesian settlement on Molokai, Halawa is a sustained island culture with its ingeniously designed *loi*, or taro fields. Because of a tsunami in 1948 and changing cultural conditions in the 1960s, the valley was largely abandoned. The Solatorio Ohana (family) is restoring the loi and taking visitors on guided hikes through the valley, which includes two of Molokai's *luakini heiau* (sacred temples), many historic sites, and the trail to **Moaula Falls**, a 250-foot cascade. Bring water, food, and insect repellent, and wear sturdy shoes that can get wet. The 3½-mile round-trip hike is rated intermediate to advanced and includes two moderate river crossings. ☎ *808/542–1855* ⊕ *www.halawavalleymolokai.com* ▪ *$60.*

10

SHOPS AND SPAS

SHOPPING

Molokai has one main commercial area: Ala Malama Street in Kaunak-akai. There are no department stores or shopping malls, and the clothing is typical island wear. Local shopping is friendly, and you may find hidden treasures. A very few family-run businesses define the main drag of Maunaloa, a rural former plantation town. Most stores in Kaunakakai are open Monday–Saturday 9–6.

WEST MOLOKAI

ARTS AND CRAFTS

Big Wind Kite Factory and Plantation Gallery. The factory has custom-made kites you can fly or display. Designs range from Hawaiian petroglyphs to *pueo* (owls). Also in stock are paper kites, minikites, and wind socks. Ask to go on the factory tour, or take a free kite-flying lesson. The adjacent gallery carries an eclectic collection of merchandise, including locally made crafts, Hawaiian books and CDs, jewelry, handmade batik sarongs, and an elegant line of women's linen clothing. ⊠ *120 Maunaloa Hwy., Maunaloa* ☎ *808/552–2364* ⊕ *www.bigwindkites.com.*

FOOD

Maunaloa General Store. Stocking meat, produce, beverages, and dry goods, this shop is a convenient stop if you're planning a picnic at one of the west-end beaches. It's open Monday–Saturday 9–6 and Sunday 9 am to noon. ⊠ *200 Maunaloa Hwy., Maunaloa* ☎ *808/552–2346.*

CENTRAL MOLOKAI

ARTS AND CRAFTS

Molokai Art From the Heart. A small downtown shop, this arts and crafts co-op has locally made folk art like dolls, clay flowers, silk sarongs, and children's items. The shop also carries original art by Molokai artists and Giclée prints, jewelry, locally produced music, and Saint Damien keepsakes. Store hours are weekdays 10–4:30 and Saturday 9–2. ⊠ *64 Ala Malama St., Kaunakakai* ☎ *808/553–8018* ⊕ *www.molokaigallery. com.*

CLOTHING AND SHOES

Imports Gift Shop. Across from Kanemitsu Bakery, this one-stop shop offers fancy and casual island-style wear, including Roxy and Quick-silver for men, women, and children. The store is open Monday–Saturday 9–6 and Sunday 9–1. ⊠ *82 Ala Malama St., Kaunakakai* ☎ *808/553–5734.*

Molokai Island Creations. Try this shop for aloha wear, beach cover-ups, sun hats, and tank tops. ⊠ *53 Ala Malama St., Kaunakakai* ☎ *808/553–5926.*

FOOD

Friendly Market Center. The best-stocked supermarket on the island has a slogan ("Your family store on Molokai") that is truly credible. Sun-and-surf essentials keep company with fresh produce, meat, groceries, and liquor. Locals say the food is fresher here than at the other major supermarket. It's open weekdays 8:30–8:30 and Saturday 8:30–6:30. ⊠ *90 Ala Malama St., Kaunakakai* ☎ *808/553–5595.*

Home Town Groceries & Drygoods. For those staying at a condo on Molokai, this store will come in handy. It is like a mini-Costco, carrying bulk items. ⊠ *93 Ala Malama St., Kaunakakai* ☎ *808/553–3858.*

Kumu Farms. This is the most diverse working farm on Molokai, and *the* place to purchase fresh produce, herbs, and gourmet farm products. It's open Tuesday–Friday 9–4. ⊠ *Hua Ai Rd., off Mauna Loa Hwy., near Molokai Airport, Kaunakakai* ☎ *808/567–6480.*

Molokai Wines 'n' Spirits. Don't let the name fool you; along with a surprisingly good selection of fine wines and liquors, the store also carries cheeses and snacks. It's open Sunday–Thursday 9–7, and Friday and Saturday until 7:30 pm. ⊠ *77 Ala Malama St., Kaunakakai* ☎ *808/553–5009.*

JEWELRY

Imports Gift Shop. You'll find soaps and lotions, a small collection of 14-karat-gold chains, rings, earrings, and bracelets, and a jumble of Hawaiian quilts, pillows, books, and postcards at this local favorite. The shop also special orders (takes approximately one week) for Hawaiian heirloom jewelry, inspired by popular Victorian pieces and crafted here since the late 1800s. ⊠ *82 Ala Malama St., Kaunakakai* ☎ *808/553–5734.*

SPORTING GOODS

Molokai Bicycle. This bike shop rents and sells mountain and road bikes as well as helmets, racks, and jogging strollers. It supplies maps and information on biking and hiking and will pick up and drop off equipment nearly anywhere on the island. Call ahead for an appointment, or stop by Wednesday 3–6 or Saturday 9–2 to arrange what you need. ⊠ *80 Mohala St., Kaunakakai* ☎ *808/553–5740, 800/709–2453* ⊕ *www.mauimolokaibicycle.com.*

Molokai Fish & Dive. This is the source for your sporting needs, from snorkel rentals to free and friendly advice. This is also a good place to pick up original-design Molokai T-shirts, water sandals, books, and gifts. ⊠ *53 Ala Malama St., Kaunakakai* ☎ *808/553–5926* ⊕ *www.molokaifishanddive.com.*

10

SPAS

Molokai Acupuncture & Massage. This relaxing retreat offers acupuncture, massage, herbal remedies, wellness treatments, and private yoga sessions by appointment only. ⊠ *40 Ala Malama St., Suite 206, Kaunakakai* ☎ *808/553–3930* ⊕ *www.molokai-wellness.com.*

Molokai Lomi Massage. Allana Noury of Molokai Lomi Massage has studied natural medicine for more than 35 years and is a licensed massage therapist, master herbalist, and master iridologist. She will come to your hotel or condo by appointment. ☎ *808/553–8034* ⊕ *www.molokaimassage.com.*

ENTERTAINMENT AND NIGHTLIFE

Local nightlife consists mainly of gathering with friends and family, sipping a few cold ones, strumming ukuleles and guitars, singing old songs, and talking story. Still, there are a few ways to kick up your heels. Pick up a copy of the weekly Molokai *Dispatch* and see if there's a concert, church supper, or dance.

The bar at the Hotel Molokai is always a good place to drink. The "Aloha Friday" weekly gathering here (4–6 pm) is a must-do event, featuring Na Kapuna, a group of accomplished *kupuna* (old-timers) with guitars and ukuleles.

For something truly casual, stop in at Kanemitsu Bakery on Ala Malama Street in Kaunakakai for the nightly hot bread sale (Tuesday–Sunday beginning at 8 pm). You can meet everyone in town and take some hot bread home for a late-night treat.

LANAI

WELCOME TO LANAI

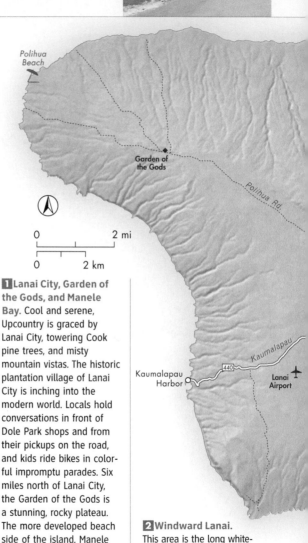

TOP REASONS TO GO

★ **Seclusion and serenity:** Lanai is small; local motion is slow motion. Get into the spirit and go home rested.

★ **Garden of the Gods:** Walk amid the eerie red-rock spires that Hawaiians still believe to be a sacred spot. The ocean views are magnificent, too; sunset is a good time to visit.

★ **A dive at Cathedrals:** Explore underwater pinnacle formations and mysterious caverns illuminated by shimmering rays of light.

★ **Dole Park:** Hang out in the shade of the Cook pines in Lanai City and talk story with the locals for a taste of old-time Hawaii.

★ **Hit the water at Hulopoe Beach:** This beach may have it all—good swimming, a shady park for perfect picnicking, great reefs for snorkeling, and sometimes schools of spinner dolphins.

Polihua Beach

Garden of the Gods

Polihua Rd.

0 ————— 2 mi

0 ————— 2 km

Kaumalapau

Kaumalapau Harbor

440

Lanai Airport

1 **Lanai City, Garden of the Gods, and Manele Bay.** Cool and serene, Upcountry is graced by Lanai City, towering Cook pine trees, and misty mountain vistas. The historic plantation village of Lanai City is inching into the modern world. Locals hold conversations in front of Dole Park shops and from their pickups on the road, and kids ride bikes in colorful impromptu parades. Six miles north of Lanai City, the Garden of the Gods is a stunning, rocky plateau. The more developed beach side of the island, Manele Bay is where it's happening: swimming, picnicking, off-island excursions, and boating are all concentrated in this accessible area.

2 **Windward Lanai.** This area is the long white-sand beach at the base of Lanaihale. Now uninhabited, it was once occupied by thriving Hawaiian fishing villages and a sugarcane plantation.

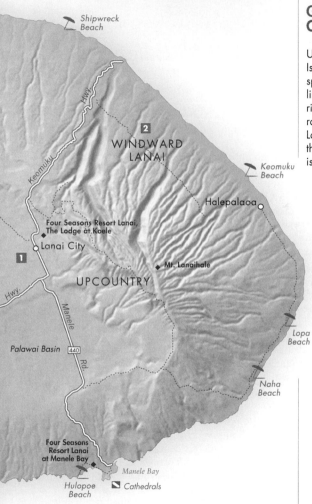

Shipwreck
Beach

2

**WINDWARD
LANAI**

Keomuku
Beach

Halepalaoa

Four Seasons Resort Lanai,
The Lodge at Koele

1

Lanai City

Mt. Lanaihale

UPCOUNTRY

Keomuku Hwy

Palawai Basin 440

Manele Rd.

Lopa
Beach

Naha
Beach

Four Seasons
Resort Lanai
at Manele Bay

Manele Bay

Hulopoe
Beach

Cathedrals

GETTING ORIENTED

Unlike the other Hawaiian Islands with their tropical splendors, Lanai looks like a desert: *kiawe* trees right out of Africa, red-dirt roads, and a deep blue sea. Lanaihale (house of Lanai), the mountain that bisects the island, is carved into deep canyons by rain and wind on the windward side, and the drier leeward side slopes gently to the sea, where waves pound against surf-carved cliffs. The town of Lanai City is in the center of the island, Upcountry. Manele Bay, on the south side of the island, is popular for swimming and boating.

Updated by
Heidi Pool

Mostly privately owned, Lanai is the smallest inhabited island in the Hawaiian Islands, and is a true getaway for slowing down and enjoying serenity amid world-class comforts.

With no traffic or traffic lights and miles of open space, Lanai seems suspended in time, and that can be a good thing. Small (141 square miles) and sparsely populated, it has just 3,500 residents, most of them living Upcountry in Lanai City. An afternoon strolling around Dole Park in historic Lanai City offers shopping, dining, and the opportunity to mingle with locals. Though it may seem a world away, Lanai is separated from Maui and Molokai by two narrow channels, and is easily accessed by commercial ferry from Maui.

FLORA AND FAUNA

Lanai bucks the "tropical" trend of the other Hawaiian Islands with African kiawe trees, Cook pines, and eucalyptus in place of palm trees, and deep blue sea where you might expect shallow turquoise bays. Abandoned pineapple fields are overgrown with drought-resistant grasses, Christmas berry, and lantana; native plants *aalii* and *ilima* are found in uncultivated areas. Axis deer from India dominate the ridges, and wild turkeys lumber around the resorts. Whales can be seen December–April, and a family of resident spinner dolphins rests and fishes regularly in Hulopoe Bay.

ON LANAI TODAY

Despite its fancy resorts, Lanai still has that languid Hawaii feel. The island is 97% owned by billionaire Larry Ellison, who is in the process of revitalizing the island. Old-time residents are a mix of just about everything: Hawaiian, Chinese, German, Portuguese, Filipino, Japanese, French, Puerto Rican, English, Norwegian—you name it. When Dole owned the island in the early 20th century and grew pineapples, the plantation was divided into ethnic camps, which helped retain cultural cuisines. Potluck dinners feature sashimi, Portuguese bean soup, *laulau* (morsels of pork, chicken, butterfish, or other ingredients steamed in *ti* leaves), potato salad, teriyaki steak, chicken *hekka* (a gingery Japanese chicken stir-fry), and Jell-O. The local language is pidgin, a mix of words as complicated and rich as the food. Newly arrived residents have added to the cultural mix.

PLANNING

WHEN TO GO

Lanai has an ideal climate year-round, hot and sunny at the sea and a few delicious degrees cooler Upcountry. In Lanai City and Upcountry, the nights and mornings can be almost chilly when a fog or harsh trade winds settle in. Winter months are known for *slightly* rougher weather—periodic rain showers, occasional storms, and higher surf.

Because higher mountains on Maui capture the trade-wind clouds, Lanai receives little rainfall and has a near-desert ecology. Consider the wind direction when planning your day. If it's blowing a gale on the windward beaches, head for the beach at Hulopoe or check out Garden of the Gods. Overcast days, when the wind stops or comes lightly from the southwest, are common in whale season. At that time, try a whale-watching trip or the windward beaches.

Whales are seen off Lanai's shores December–April. A Pineapple Festival on the July 4 Saturday in Dole Park features traditional entertainment, a pineapple-eating contest, and fireworks. Buddhists hold their annual outdoor Obon Festival, honoring departed ancestors with joyous dancing, local food, and drumming, in early July. During hunting-season weekends, mid-February–mid-May and mid-July–mid-October, watch out for hunters on dirt roads even though there are designated safety zones. Sunday is a day of rest in Lanai City, and shops and most restaurants are closed.

GETTING HERE AND AROUND

AIR TRAVEL

Hawaiian Airlines and Island Air are the only commercial airlines serving Lanai City. Direct flights are available from Oahu; if you're flying to Lanai from any other Hawaiian island, you'll make a stop in Honolulu.

If you're staying at the Hotel Lanai or the Four Seasons Resort Lanai at Manele Bay, or renting a vehicle from Lanai City Service, you'll be met at the airport or ferry dock by a bus that shuttles between the resort and Lanai City (and there may be an additional fee).

Contacts Hawaiian Airlines. ☎ *800/367–5320* ⊕ *www.hawaiianairlines.com.* **Island Air.** ☎ *800/652–6541* ⊕ *www.islandair.com.*

CAR TRAVEL

Lanai has only 30 miles of paved roads. Keomuku Highway starts just past The Lodge at Koele and runs northeast to the dirt road that goes to Shipwreck Beach and Lopa Beach. Manele Road (Highway 440) runs south down to Manele Bay, the Four Seasons Resort Lanai at Manele Bay, and Hulopoe Beach. Kaumalapau Highway (also Highway 440) heads west to Kaumalapau Harbor. The rest of your driving takes place on bumpy, dusty roads that are unpaved and unmarked. Driving in thick mud is not recommended, and the rental agency will charge a stiff cleaning fee. Watch out for blind curves on narrow roads.

Renting a four-wheel-drive vehicle is expensive but almost essential if you'd like to explore beyond the resorts and Lanai City. Make reservations far in advance of your trip, because Lanai's fleet of vehicles is limited. Lanai City Service, where you'll find a branch of Dollar Rent A Car, is open daily 7–7.

Stop from time to time to find landmarks and gauge your progress. Never drive or walk to the edge of lava cliffs, as rock can give way under you. Directions on the island are often given as *mauka* (toward the mountains) and *makai* (toward the ocean).

If you're visiting for the day, Rabaca's Limousine Service will take you wherever you want to go.

Contacts Lanai City Service. ✉ *1036 Lanai Ave., Lanai City* ☎ *808/565–7227, 800/533–7808* ⊕ *www.dollarlanai.com.* **Rabaca's Limousine Service.** ✉ *552 Alapa St., Lanai City* ☎ *808/565–6670.*

FERRY TRAVEL

Ferries operated by Expeditions cross the channel five times daily between Lahaina on Maui to Manele Bay Harbor on Lanai. The crossing takes 45 minutes and costs $30. Be warned: passage can be rough, especially in winter.

Contact Expeditions. ☎ *808/661–3756, 800/695–2624* ⊕ *www.go-lanai.com.*

SHUTTLE TRAVEL

A shuttle transports you to your hotel from the harbor or the airport (a nominal fee may apply). If you're renting a vehicle from Lanai City Service, their shuttle will pick you up at the harbor or airport for a nominal fee.

RESTAURANTS

Lanai has a wide range of choices for dining, from simple plate-lunch local eateries to fancy, upscale, gourmet resort restaurants.

HOTELS

The range of lodgings is limited on Lanai. Essentially there are only a few options: the Four Seasons Lanai at Manele Bay and The Lodge at Koele, and the historic Hotel Lanai; however, the Lodge at Koele is closed for renovation until the end of 2016. An alternative is a house rental, which will give you a feel for everyday life on the island; make sure to book far in advance. Maui County has strict regulations concerning vacation rentals; to avoid disappointment, always contact the property manager or owner and ask if the accommodation has the proper permits and is in compliance with local laws. *Hotel reviews have been shortened. For full information, visit Fodors.com.*

EXPLORING

You can easily explore Lanai City on foot. To access the rest of this untamed island, rent a four-wheel-drive vehicle. Take a map, be sure you have a full tank, and bring a snack and plenty of water. Ask the rental agency or your hotel's concierge about road conditions before you set out. Although roads may be dry on the coast, they could be impassable upland. It's always good to carry a cell phone. The main road on Lanai, Highway 440, refers to both Kaumalapau Highway and Manele Road.

Ocean views provide a backdrop to the eroded rocks at Garden of the Gods.

LANAI CITY, GARDEN OF THE GODS, AND MANELE BAY

Lanai City is 3 miles northeast of the airport; Manele Bay is 9 miles southeast of Lanai City; Garden of the Gods is 6 miles northwest of Lanai City.

A tidy plantation town, built in 1924 by Jim Dole to accommodate workers for his pineapple business, Lanai City is home to old-time residents, recently arrived resort workers, and second-home owners. A simple grid of roads is lined with stately Cook pines. With its charming plantation-era shops and restaurants having received new paint jobs and landscaping, Lanai City is worthy of whiling away a lazy Lanai afternoon.

Despite recent growth, the pace is still calm and the people are friendly. **Dole Park**, in the center of Lanai City, is surrounded by small shops and restaurants and is a favorite spot among locals for sitting, strolling, and talking story. Try a picnic lunch in the park and visit the **Lanai Culture and Heritage Center** in the Old Dole Administration Building to glimpse this island's rich past, purchase historical publications and maps, and get directions to anywhere on the island.

Manele Bay is an ocean lover's dream: Hulopoe Beach offers top-notch snorkeling, swimming, picnicking, tide pools, and sometimes spinner dolphins. Off-island ocean excursions depart from nearby Manele Small Boat Harbor. Take the short but rugged hike to the Puu Pehe (Sweetheart Rock) overlook, and you'll enjoy a bird's-eye view of this iconic Lanai landmark.

GETTING HERE AND AROUND

Lanai City serves as the island's hub, with roads leading to Manele Bay, Kaumalapau Harbor, and windward Lanai. Garden of the Gods is usually possible to visit by car, but beyond that you will need four-wheel drive.

TOP ATTRACTIONS

Fodor'sChoice ★ **Garden of the Gods.** This preternatural plateau is scattered with boulders of different sizes, shapes, and colors, the products of a million years of wind erosion. Time your visit for sunset, when the rocks begin to glow—from rich red to purple—and the fiery globe sinks to the horizon. Magnificent views of the Pacific Ocean, Molokai, and, on clear days, Oahu, provide the perfect backdrop for photographs.

The ancient Hawaiians shunned Lanai for hundreds of years, believing the island was the inviolable home of spirits. Standing beside the oxide-red rock spires of this strange, raw landscape, you might be tempted to believe the same. This lunar savanna still has a decidedly eerie edge, but the shadows disappearing on the horizon are those of mouflon sheep and axis deer, not the fearsome spirits of lore. According to tradition, Kawelo, a Hawaiian priest, kept a perpetual fire burning on an altar at the Garden of the Gods, in sight of the island of Molokai. As long as the fire burned, prosperity was assured for the people of Lanai. Kawelo was killed by a rival priest on Molokai and the fire went out. The Hawaiian name for this area is Keahiakawelo, meaning the "fire of Kawelo."

Garden of the Gods is 6 miles north of Lanai City. From the Stables at Koele, follow a dirt road through a pasture, turn right at a crossroad marked by carved boulder, and head through abandoned fields and ironwood forests to an open red-dirt area marked by a carved boulder. ⊠ *Off Polihua Rd., Lanai City.*

Ka Lokahi o Ka Malamalama Church. Built in 1938, this picturesque painted wooden church provided services for Lanai's growing population. (For many people, the only other Hawaiian church, in coastal Keomuku, was too far away.) A classic structure of ranching days, the one-room church was moved from its original site when the Lodge at Koele was built. It's open all day and Sunday services are still held in Hawaiian and English; visitors are welcome but are requested to attend quietly. The church is north of the entrance to the Four Seasons Resort Lodge at Koele. ⊠ *1 Keomuku Hwy., Lanai City.*

Kanepuu Preserve. Hawaiian sandalwood, olive, and ebony trees characterize Hawaii's largest example of a rare native dryland forest. Thanks to the combined efforts of volunteers at the Nature Conservancy and Castle & Cooke Resorts, the 590-acre remnant forest is protected from the axis deer and mouflon sheep that graze on the land beyond its fence. More than 45 native plant species, including *nau*, the endangered Hawaiian gardenia, can be seen here. A short, self-guided loop trail, with eight signs illustrated by local artist Wendell Kahoohalahala, reveals this ecosystem's beauty and the challenges it faces. The reserve is adjacent to the sacred hill, Kane Puu, dedicated to the Hawaiian god of water and vegetation. ⊠ *Polihua Rd., 4.8 miles north of Lanai City, Lanai City.*

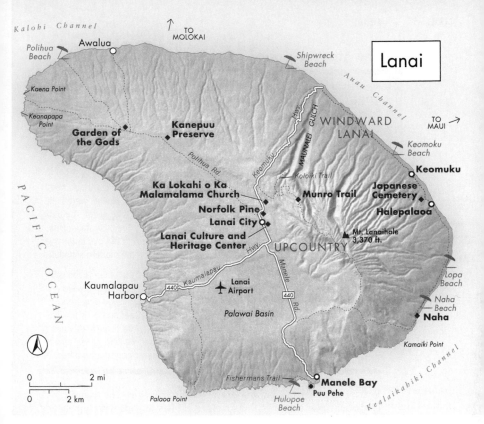

Manele Bay. The site of a Hawaiian village dating from AD 900, Manele Bay is flanked by lava cliffs hundreds of feet high. Ferries from Maui dock five times a day, and visiting yachts pull in here, as it's the island's only small boat harbor. Public restrooms, grassy lawns, and picnic tables make it a busy pit stop—you can watch the boating activity as you rest.

Just offshore to the west is **Puu Pehe.** Often called Sweetheart Rock, the isolated 80-foot-high islet carries a romantic Hawaiian legend that is probably not true. The rock is said to be named after Pehe, a woman so beautiful that her husband kept her hidden in a sea cave. One day, the surf surged into the cave and she drowned. Her grief-stricken husband buried her on this rock and jumped to his death. A more likely story is that the enclosure on the summit is a shrine to birds, built by bird-catchers. Protected shearwaters nest in the nearby sea cliffs July–November. ⊠ *Hwy. 440, Manele, Lanai City.*

WORTH NOTING

Lanai Culture and Heritage Center. Small and carefully arranged, this historical museum features artifacts and photographs from Lanai's varied and rich history. Plantation-era clothing and tools, ranch memorabilia, old maps, precious feather lei, poi pounders, and family portraits combine to give you a good idea of the history of the island and its people.

The Story of Lanai

Rumored to be haunted by hungry ghosts, Lanai was sparsely inhabited for many centuries. Most of the earliest settlers lived along the shore and made their living from fishing the nearby waters. Others lived in the Upcountry near seasonal water sources and traded their produce for seafood. The high chiefs sold off the land bit by bit to foreign settlers, and by 1910 the island was owned by the Gay family.

When the Hawaiian Pineapple Company purchased Lanai for $1.1 million in 1922, it built the town of Lanai City, opened the commercial harbor, and laid out the pineapple fields. Field workers came from overseas to toil in what quickly became the world's largest pineapple

plantation. Exotic animals and birds were imported for hunting. Cook pines were planted to catch the rain, and eucalyptus windbreaks anchored the blowing soil.

Everything was stable for 70 years, until the plantation closed in 1992. When the resorts opened their doors, newcomers arrived, homes were built, and other ways of life set in. The old pace, marked by the 6:30 am whistle calling everyone to the plantation, was replaced by a more modern schedule.

Because almost the entire island is now owned by Larry Ellison, vast areas remain untouched and great views abound. Deer and birds provide glimpses of its wild beauty. Although the ghosts may be long gone, Lanai still retains its ancient mysterious presence.

Postcards, maps, books, and pamphlets are for sale. The friendly staff can orient you to the island's historical sites and provide directions. This is the best place to start your explorations of the island. ⊠ *730 Lanai Ave., Lanai City* ☎ *808/565-7177* ⊕ *www.lanaichc.org* ✉ *Free* ☉ *Weekdays 8:30–3:30, Sat. 9–1.*

Norfolk Pine. Considered the "mother" of all the pines on the island, this 160-foot-tall tree was planted here, at the former site of the ranch manager's house, in 1875. Almost 30 years later, George Munro, the manager, observed how, in foggy weather, water collected on its foliage, dripping off rain. This led Munro to supervise the planting of Cook pines along the ridge of Lanaihale and throughout the town in order to add to the island's water supply. This majestic tree is just in front of the south wing of Four Seasons Resort Lodge at Koele. ⊠ *Four Seasons Resort Lodge at Koele, 1 Keomuku Hwy., Lanai City.*

WINDWARD LANAI

9 miles northeast of The Lodge at Koele to end of paved road.

The eastern shore of Lanai is mostly deserted. A few inaccessible *heiau*, or temples, rock walls and boulders marking old shrines, and a restored church at Keomuku reveal traces of human habitation. Four-wheel-drive vehicles are a must to explore this side of the isle. Be prepared for hot, rough conditions. Pack a picnic lunch, a hat and sunscreen, and plenty of drinking water. A mobile phone is also a good idea.

The calm crescent of Hulopoe Beach is perfect for swimming, snorkeling, or just relaxing.

GETTING HERE AND AROUND

Once you leave paved Keomuku Highway and turn left toward Shipwreck Beach or right to Naha, the roads are dirt and sand; conditions vary with the seasons. Mileage doesn't matter much here, but figure on 20 minutes from the end of the paved road to Shipwreck Beach, and about 45 minutes to Lopa Beach.

For information about Shipwreck Beach and Lopa Beach, see Beaches, below.

TOP ATTRACTIONS

Munro Trail. This 12.8-mile four-wheel-drive trail along a fern- and pine-clad narrow ridge was named after George Munro, manager of the Lanai Ranch Company, who began a reforestation program in the 1950s to restore the island's much-needed watershed. The trail climbs **Lanaihale** (House of Lanai), which, at 3,370 feet, is the island's highest point; on clear days you'll be treated to a panorama of canyons and almost all the Hawaiian Islands. ■TIP→ The road gets very muddy, and trade winds can be strong. Watch for sheer drop-offs, and keep an eye out for hikers. You can also hike the Munro Trail, although it's steep, the ground is uneven, and there's no water. From the Four Seasons Resort Lodge at Koele, head north on Highway 440 for 1¼ miles, then turn right onto Cemetery Road. Keep going until you're headed downhill on the main dirt road. It's a one-way road, but you may meet jeeps coming from the opposite direction. ⊠ *Cemetery Rd., Lanai City.*

WORTH NOTING

Halepalaoa. Named for the whales that once washed ashore here, Halepalaoa, or the "House of Whale Ivory," was the site of the wharf used by the short-lived Maunalei Sugar Company in 1899. Some say the sugar company failed because the sacred stones of nearby **Kahea Heiau** were used for the construction of the cane railroad. The brackish well water turned too salty, forcing the sugar company to close in 1901, after just two years. The remains of the heiau, once an important place of worship for the people of Lanai, are now difficult to find through the kiawe overgrowth. There's good public-beach access here and clear shallow water for swimming, but no other facilities. Take Highway 440 (Keomuku Highway) to its eastern terminus, then turn right on the dirt road and continue south for 5½ miles. ⊠ *On dirt road off Hwy. 440, Lanai City.*

Japanese Cemetery. In 1899 sugarcane came to this side of Lanai. The 2,400-acre plantation promised to be a profitable proposition, but that same year disease wiped out the labor force. This Buddhist shrine commemorates the Japanese workers who died, and the local congregation comes down to clean this sacred place each year. Take Highway 440 to its eastern terminus, then turn right on the dirt road and continue south for 6½ miles. The shrine is uphill on your right. ⊠ *On dirt road off Hwy. 440.*

Keomuku. There's a peaceful beauty about the former fishing village of Keomuku. During the late 19th century this small Lanai community served as the headquarters of Maunalei Sugar Company. After the company failed, the land was abandoned. Although there are no other signs of previous inhabitation, its church, **Ka Lanakila O Ka Malamalama,** built in 1903, has been restored by volunteers. Visitors often leave some small token, a shell or lei, as an offering. Take Highway 440 to its eastern terminus, then turn right onto a dirt road and continue south for 5 miles. The church is on your right in the coconut trees. ⊠ *On dirt road off Hwy. 440.*

Naha. An ancient rock-walled fishpond—visible at low tide—lies where the sandy shore ends and the cliffs begin their rise along the island's shores. Accessible by four-wheel-drive vehicle, the beach is a frequent dive spot for local fishermen. ■ TIP→ **Treacherous currents make this a dangerous place for swimming.** Take Highway 440 to its eastern terminus, then turn right onto a sandy dirt road and continue south for 11 miles. The shoreline dirt road ends here. ⊠ *On dirt road off Hwy. 440, Lanai City.*

BEACHES

Lanai offers miles of secluded white-sand beaches on its windward side, plus the moderately developed Hulopoe Beach, which is adjacent to the Four Seasons Resort Lanai at Manele Bay. Hulopoe is accessible by car or hotel shuttle bus; to reach the windward beaches you need a four-wheel-drive vehicle. Reef, rocks, and coral make swimming on the windward side problematic, but it's fun to splash around in the shallow water. Expect debris on the windward beaches due to the Pacific convergence of ocean currents. Driving on the beach itself is illegal and can be dangerous. *Beaches in this chapter are listed alphabetically.*

Fodor'sChoice **Hulopoe Beach.** A short stroll from
★ the Four Seasons Resort Lanai at Manele Bay, Hulopoe is one of the best beaches in Hawaii. The sparkling crescent of this Marine Life Conservation District beckons with calm waters safe for swimming almost year-round, great snorkeling reefs, tide pools, and sometimes spinner dolphins. A shady, grassy beach park is perfect for picnics. If the shore break is pounding, or if you see surfers riding big waves, stay out of the water. In the afternoon, watch Lanai High School students heave outrigger canoes down the steep shore break and race one another just offshore. To get here, take Highway 440 south to the bottom of the hill and turn right. The road dead-ends at the beach's parking lot. **Amenities:** parking (no fee); showers; toilets. **Best for:** snorkeling; surfing; swimming. ⊠ *Off Hwy. 440, Lanai City.*

> **THE COASTAL ROAD**
>
> Road conditions can change overnight and become impassable due to rain in the Upcountry. The car-rental agency will give you an update before you hit the road. Some of the spur roads leading to the windward beaches from the coastal dirt road cross private property and are closed off by chains. Look for open spur roads with recent tire marks (a fairly good sign that they are safe to drive on). It's best to park on firm ground and walk in to avoid getting your car mired in the sand.

Lopa Beach. A difficult surfing spot that tests the mettle of experienced locals, Lopa is also an ancient fishpond. With majestic views of West Maui and Kahoolawe, this remote white-sand beach is a great place for a picnic. ⚠ **Don't let the sight of surfers fool you: the channel's currents are too strong for swimming.** Take Highway 440 to its eastern terminus, turn right onto a dirt road, and continue south for 7 miles. **Amenities:** none. **Best for:** solitude; sunrise; walking. ⊠ *On dirt road off Hwy. 440.*

Polihua Beach. This often-deserted beach features long, wide stretches of white sand and unobstructed views of Molokai. The northern end of the beach ends at a rocky lava cliff with some interesting tide pools, and sea turtles that lay their eggs in the sand. (Do not drive on the beach and endanger their nests.) However, the dirt road leading here has deep, sandy places that are difficult in dry weather and impassable when it rains. In addition, strong currents and a sudden drop in the ocean floor make swimming dangerous, and strong trade winds can make walking uncomfortable. Thirsty wild bees sometimes gather around your car. To get rid of them, put out water some distance away and wait. The beach is in windward Lanai, 11 miles north of Lanai City. To get here, turn right onto the marked dirt road past Garden of the Gods. **Amenities:** none. **Best for:** solitude; sunrise; walking. ⊠ *East end of Polihua Rd., Lanai City.*

Shipwreck Beach. The rusting World War II tanker abandoned off this 8-mile stretch of sand adds just the right touch to an already photogenic beach. Strong trade winds have propelled vessels onto the reef since at least 1824, when the first shipwreck was recorded. Beachcombers come to this fairly accessible beach for shells and washed-up treasures, and photographers take great shots of Molokai, just across the Kalohi Channel. A deserted plantation-era fishing settlement adds to the charm. It's still possible to find glass-ball fishing floats as you wander along. Kaiolohia, its Hawaiian name, is a favorite local diving spot. Beyond the beach, about 200 yards up a trail past the Shipwreck Beach sign, are the Kukui Point petroglyphs, marked by reddish-brown boulders. ■TIP➜ An offshore reef and rocks in the water mean that it's not for swimmers, though you can play in the shallow water on the shoreline. To get here, take Highway 440 to its eastern terminus, then turn left onto a dirt road and continue to the end. **Amenities:** none. **Best for:** solitude; star gazing; windsurfing. ✉ *Off Hwy. 440, Lanai City.*

WHERE TO EAT

Lanai's own version of Hawaii regional cuisine draws on the fresh bounty provided by local farmers and fishermen, combined with the skills of well-regarded chefs. The upscale menus at the Four Seasons Resort Lanai at Manele Bay encompass European- and Asian-inspired cuisine as well as innovative preparations of international favorites and vegetarian delights. All Four Seasons Resort restaurants offer children's menus. Lanai City's eclectic ethnic fare runs from construction-worker-size local plate lunches to *poke* (raw fish), pizza, and pasta. ■TIP➜ Lanai "City" is really a small town; restaurants sometimes close their kitchens early, and only a few are open on Sunday.

WHAT IT COSTS			
$	$$	$$$	$$$$
Restaurants	under $18	$18–$26	$27–$35	over $35

Restaurant prices are the average cost of a main course at dinner or, if dinner is not served, at lunch.

MANELE BAY

Dining at Manele Bay offers the range of options provided by the Four Seasons Resort Lanai, from informal poolside meals to relaxed, eclectic dining.

$$ ✕ **Kailani.** Poolside at the Four Seasons Resort Lanai at Manele Bay, AMERICAN   Kailani offers casual dining with a stunning view of Hulopoe Bay. The big umbrellas are cool and cheerful, and the cushioned rattan chairs comfortable. Try the crunchy fish-and-chips, Italian farmers' market salad, or the grilled Angus beef burger. The service is the brand of cool aloha always offered by the Four Seasons. $ *Average main: $24* ✉ *Four Seasons Resort Lanai at Manele Bay, 1 Manele Bay Rd., Manele, Lanai City* ☎ *808/565–2092* ⊕ *www.fourseasons.com/manelebay* ⚐ *Reservations not accepted.*

$$$ JAPANESE 🍴 **Nobu.** Chef Nobuyuki "Nobu" Matsuhisa offers his signature new-style Japanese cuisine in this open-air, relaxed luxury venue. This is fine dining without the stress, as black-clad waiters present dish after dish of beautifully seasoned, raw and lightly cooked seafood flown in directly from Alaska and Japan. An *omakase* (chef's choice) multicourse menu makes it easy for first-timers. After a recent expansion, Nobu now features a lounge, teppanyaki stations, and sushi bar. This simple yet elegant establishment is as much about the experience as it is about the food itself, but brace yourself for a significant bill at meal's end. [$] *Average main: $32* ✉ *1 Manele Bay Rd., Manele, Lanai City* ☎ *808/565–2832* 🌐 *www.noburestaurants.com/lanai* 🕒 *No lunch* ✍ *Reservations essential.*

$$$$ AMERICAN 🍴 **One Forty.** Named after the island's 140 square miles, this ocean-view restaurant offers an extensive steak and seafood menu that emphasizes local ingredients. Prime cuts of beef and the freshest local fish are served in airy comfort on the hotel terrace, which overlooks the wide sweep of Hulopoe Bay. Retractable awnings provide shade on sunny days. Comfy rattan chairs, potted palms, and tropical decor create an inviting backdrop. At breakfast, fresh-baked pastries and made-to-order omelets ensure that your day starts well. [$] *Average main: $45* ✉ *Four Seasons Resort Lanai at Manele Bay, 1 Manele Bay Rd., Manele, Lanai City* ☎ *808/565–2290* 🌐 *www.fourseasons.com/manelebay* 🕒 *No lunch* ✍ *Reservations essential.*

$$ AMERICAN 🍴 **Views at Manele Clubhouse.** A stunning view of the legendary Puu Pehe rock only enhances the imaginative fare of this open-air restaurant. Spot frolicking dolphins from the terrace. Tuck into a Hulopoe Bay prawn BLT, or the crispy battered fish-and-chips with Meyer lemon tartar sauce. The Baja fish tacos are splendid, and specialty drinks add to the informal fun. [$] *Average main: $25* ✉ *Four Seasons Resort Lanai at Manele Bay, 1 Manele Bay Rd., Manele, Lanai City* ☎ *808/565–2230* 🌐 *www.fourseasons.com/manelebay* 🕒 *No dinner.*

LANAI CITY AND UPCOUNTRY

In Lanai City you can enjoy everything from local-style plate lunches to upscale gourmet meals. For a small area, there are a number of good places to eat and drink, but remember that Lanai City mostly closes down on Sunday.

$ AMERICAN-HAWAIIAN 🍴 **Blue Ginger Café.** Owners Joe and Georgia Abilay made this cheery place into a Lanai City institution with simply prepared, consistent, tasty food. Local paintings and photos line the walls inside, while townspeople parade by the outdoor tables. For breakfast, try the Lanai omelet with Portuguese sausage. Lunch selections range from burgers to local favorites such as saimin noodles. For dinner you can sample generous portions of shrimp tempura or roasted pork. Phone ahead for takeout. [$] *Average main: $12* ✉ *409 7th St., Lanai City* ☎ *808/565–6363* 🌐 *www.bluegingercafelanai.com* 💳 *No credit cards* ✍ *Reservations not accepted.*

$ AMERICAN-HAWAIIAN
🍴 **Café 565.** Named after the oldest telephone prefix on Lanai, Café 565 is a convenient stop for plate lunches, sandwiches like Palawai chicken breast on freshly baked focaccia, or platters of chicken *katsu* (Japanese-style breaded and fried chicken) to take along for an impromptu picnic. Phone ahead to order pizza. Bring your own beer or wine for lunch or dinner. The patio and outdoor tables are kid-friendly. [$] *Average main: $10* ✉ *408 8th St., Lanai City* ☎ *808/565–6622* 🕒 *Closed Sun.* ✍ *Reservations not accepted.*

$ AMERICAN
🍴 **Coffee Works.** A block from Dole Park, this Northern California–style café offers an umbrella-covered deck where you can sip cappuccinos and get in tune with the slow pace of life. Bagels with lox, deli sandwiches, and pastries add to the caloric content, while blended espresso shakes and gourmet ice cream complete the coffeehouse vibe. [$] *Average main: $8* ✉ *604 Ilima St., Lanai City* ☎ *808/565–6962* 🕒 *Closed Sun. No dinner* ✍ *Reservations not accepted.*

$ AMERICAN Fodor'sChoice ★
🍴 **Lanai City Grille.** Simple white walls hung with local art, lazily turning ceiling fans, and unobtrusive service provide the backdrop for a menu featuring fresh island ingredients prepared with bold flavors. The tapas-style menu features plates meant to be shared, like crab cakes, spicy chicken wings, and kalbi short ribs. The dining room is a friendly and comfortable alternative to the Four Seasons, and a convenient if sometimes noisy gathering place for large parties. [$] *Average main: $14* ✉ *Hotel Lanai, 828 Lanai Ave., Lanai City* ☎ *808/565–7211* 🌐 *www.hotellanai.com* 🕒 *Closed Mon. and Tues. No lunch* ✍ *Reservations essential.*

$ AMERICAN-HAWAIIAN
🍴 **Lanai Ohana Poke Market.** This is the closest you can come to dining on traditional cuisine on Lanai. Enjoy fresh food prepared by a Hawaiian family and served in a cool, shady garden. The emphasis is on poke, and Hawaiian plate lunches, take-out kimchi shrimp, and ahi and aku tuna steaks complete the menu. The place also caters picnics and parties. [$] *Average main: $9* ✉ *834A Gay St., Lanai City* ☎ *808/559–6265* 💳 *No credit cards* 🕒 *Closed weekends. No dinner* ✍ *Reservations not accepted.*

$ AMERICAN-HAWAIIAN FAMILY
🍴 **No Ka Oi Grindz Lanai.** A local favorite, this lunchroom-style café has a shaded picnic table in the landscaped front yard and five more tables in the no-frills interior. The innovative menu, which changes frequently, includes such delicacies as kimchi fried rice, pork-fritter sandwiches, and massive plate lunches. Sit outside and watch the town drive by. [$] *Average main: $10* ✉ *335 9th St., Lanai City* ☎ *808/565–9413* 💳 *No credit cards* 🕒 *Closed Sun.* ✍ *Reservations not accepted.*

$$ ITALIAN
🍴 **Pele's Other Garden.** Small and colorful, Pele's is a deli and bistro all in one. For lunch, sandwiches or daily hot specials satisfy hearty appetites. At night, it's transformed into a busy bistro, complete with tablecloths and soft jazz. Designer beers and fine wines enhance an Italian-inspired menu. Start with bruschetta, then choose from a selection of pizzas or pasta dishes. An intimate back-room bar add to the liveliness, and entertainers often drop in for impromptu jam sessions. [$] *Average main: $19* ✉ *811 Houston St., at 8th St., Lanai City* ☎ *808/565–9628, 888/764–3354* 🌐 *www.pelesothergarden.com* 🕒 *Closed Sun.* ✍ *Reservations essential.*

WHERE TO STAY

Though Lanai has few properties, it does have a range of price options. Four Seasons manages both The Lodge at Koele and Four Seasons Resort Lanai at Manele Bay. Although the room rates are different, guests can partake of all the resort amenities at both properties. If you're on a budget, consider the Hotel Lanai. Note that room rates do not include 13.42% sales tax. The Four Seasons Resort Lanai is scheduled to reopen in early 2016. The Lodge at Koele is closed until late 2016.

	WHAT IT COSTS			
	$	**$$**	**$$$**	**$$$$**
Hotels	under $181	$181–$260	$261–$340	over $340

Hotel prices are the lowest cost of a standard double room in high season. Condo price categories reflect studio and one-bedroom rates.

$$$$ RESORT FAMILY Fodor's Choice ★ **Four Seasons Resort Lanai at Manele Bay.** Overlooking Hulopoe Bay, this sublime retreat offering beachside urban chic with stunning views of the deep blue sea and astonishing rocky coastline has reopened after a major renovation. **Pros:** nearby beach; outstanding restaurants; newly renovated. **Cons:** 20 minutes from town; need a car to explore the area. [$] *Rooms from: $960* ✉ *1 Manele Rd., Manele, Lanai City* ☎ *808/565–2000, 800/321–4666* 🌐 *www.fourseasons.com/manelebay* *217 rooms, 51 suites* 🍴 *No meals.*

$ HOTEL **Hotel Lanai.** Built in 1923 to house visiting pineapple executives, this historic inn has South Pacific–style rooms with country quilts, ceiling fans, and bamboo shades. **Pros:** historic atmosphere; walking distance to town. **Cons:** rooms are a bit plain; noisy at dinnertime; no room phones or TVs. [$] *Rooms from: $174* ✉ *828 Lanai Ave., Lanai City* ☎ *808/565–7211, 800/795–7211* 🌐 *www.hotellanai.com* *10 rooms, 1 cottage* 🍴 *Breakfast.*

WATER SPORTS AND TOURS

The easiest way to enjoy the water on Lanai is to wade in at Hulopoe Beach and swim or snorkel. If you prefer an organized excursion, a fishing trip is a good bet (you keep some of the fish). Snorkel trips are a great way to see the island, above and below the surface, and scuba divers can marvel at one of the top cave-dive spots in the Pacific.

DEEP-SEA FISHING

Some of the best fishing grounds in Maui County are off the southwest shoreline of Lanai, the traditional fishing grounds of Hawaiian royalty. Pry your eyes open and go deep-sea fishing in the early morning, with departures at 6 or 6:30 am from Manele Harbor. Console yourself with the knowledge that Maui anglers have to leave an hour earlier to get to the same prime locations. Peak seasons are spring and summer, although good catches have been landed year-round. Mahimahi, *ono* (a mackerel-like fish; the word means "delicious" in Hawaiian), ahi, and marlin are prized catches and preferred eating.

Spinning Dolphin Charters of Lanai. The 36-foot Twin-Vee *Fish-n-Tips* with a tuna tower will get you to the fishing grounds in comfort. Friendly Captain Jason will do everything except reel in the big one for you. Plan on trolling along the south coast for ono and around the point at Kaunolu for mahimahi or marlin. A trip to the offshore buoy often yields skipjack tuna or big ahi. Whales are often spotted during the season. Fishing gear, soft drinks, and water are included. A four-hour charter (six-passenger maximum) is $700; each additional hour costs $110. Guests can keep a third of all fish caught. Shared charters on Sunday are $150 per person. ⊠ *Lanai City* ☎ *808/565–7676* ⊕ *www. sportfishinglanai.com.*

SCUBA DIVING

When you have a dive site such as Cathedrals—with eerie pinnacle formations and luminous caverns—it's no wonder that scuba-diving buffs consider exploring the waters off Lanai akin to a religious experience.

BEST SPOTS
Cathedrals. Just outside Hulopoe Bay, Cathedrals is the best cavern dive site in Lanai. Shimmering light makes the many openings resemble stained-glass windows. A current generally keeps the water crystal clear, even if it's turbid outside. In these unearthly chambers, large *ulua* and small reef sharks add to the adventure. Tiger sharks may appear in certain seasons. ⊠ *Manele, Lanai City.*

Sergeant Major Reef. Off Kamaiki Point, Sergeant Major Reef is named for big schools of yellow- and black-striped *manini* (sergeant major fish) that turn the rocks silvery as they feed. There are three parallel lava ridges separated by rippled sand valleys, a cave, and an archway. Depths range 15–50 feet. Depending on conditions, the water may be clear or cloudy. ⊠ *Lanai City.*

EQUIPMENT, LESSONS, AND TOURS
Trilogy Ocean Sports Lanai. Serious certified divers should go for Trilogy's four-hour, two-tank dive. Locations depend on the weather. The $189 fee includes a light breakfast of cinnamon rolls and coffee, wet suits, and all the equipment you need. Noncertified beginners over age 11 can try a one-tank introductory dive lasting 20–30 minutes for $102. You can wade into Hulopoe Bay with an instructor at your side. Certified divers can choose a 35- to 40-minute wade-in dive at Hulopoe, also for $102. ⊠ *Manele Small Boat Harbor, Manele Rd., Manele, Lanai City* ☎ *808/874–5649* ⊕ *www.scubalanai.com.*

SNORKELING

Snorkeling is the easiest ocean sport available on the island, requiring nothing but a snorkel, mask, fins, and good sense. Borrow equipment from your hotel or purchase some in Lanai City if you didn't bring your own. Wait to enter the water until you are sure no big sets of waves are coming, and observe the activity of locals on the beach. If little kids are playing in the shore break, it's usually safe to enter. ■ TIP➔ To get into the water safely, always swim in past the breakers, and in the comparative calm put on your fins, then mask and snorkel.

BEST SPOTS

The best snorkeling on Lanai is at **Hulopoe Beach** and **Manele Small Boat Harbor**. Hulopoe, which is an exceptional snorkeling destination, has schools of manini that feed on the coral and coat the rocks with flashing silver. You can also easily view *kala* (unicorn fish), *uhu* (parrot fish), and *papio* (small trevally) in all their rainbow colors. Beware of rocks and surging waves. At Manele Harbor, there's a wade-in snorkel spot beyond the break wall. Enter over the rocks, just past the boat ramp. ■ TIP➔ Do not enter if waves are breaking.

EQUIPMENT, LESSONS, AND TOURS

Trilogy Ocean Sports Lanai. A 3½-hour snorkeling trip aboard a spacious catamaran explores Lanai's pristine coastline with this company's experienced captain and crew. The trip includes lessons, equipment, and lunch served on board. Tours are offered Monday, Wednesday, Friday, and Saturday. ✉ *Manele Small Boat Harbor, Manele Rd., Manele, Lanai City* ☎ *808/874–5649* ⊕ *www.scubalanai.com* ✉ *From $181 per person.*

SURFING

Surfing on Lanai can be truly enjoyable. Quality, not quantity, characterizes this isle's few breaks. Be considerate of the locals and they will be considerate of you—surfing takes the place of megaplex theaters and pool halls here, serving as one of the island's few recreational luxuries.

BEST SPOTS

Don't try to hang 10 at **Hulopoe Bay** without watching the conditions for a while. When it "goes off," it's a tricky left-handed shore break that requires some skill. Huge summer south swells are for experts only. The southeast-facing breaks at **Lopa Beach** on the east side are inviting for beginners, but hard to get to. Give them a try in summer, when the swells roll in nice and easy.

EQUIPMENT AND LESSONS

Lanai Surf School. Nick Palumbo offers the only surf instruction on the island. Sign up for his 4x4 Safari—a four-hour adventure that includes hard- or soft-top boards, snacks, and transportation to windward "secret spots." Palumbo, who was born on Lanai, is a former Hawaii State Surfing Champion. Lessons are $200 (minimum of two people). Experienced riders can rent boards overnight for $58. Palumbo also has the only paddleboard permit for Hulopoe Bay, and gives lessons and rents equipment. He will pick you up at your hotel or at the ferry dock. ✉ *Lanai City* ☎ *808/649–0739* ⊕ *www.lanaisurfsafari.com.*

GOLF, HIKING, AND OUTDOOR ACTIVITIES

Manele Golf Course will certainly test your skill on the green. Experienced hikers can choose from miles of dirt roads and trails, but note that you're on your own—there's no water or support. Remember that Lanai is privately owned, and all land-based activities are at the owner's discretion.

BIKING

Many of the same red-dirt roads that invite hikers are excellent for biking, offering easy, flat terrain and long clear views. There's only one hitch: you will have to bring your own bike, as there are no rentals or tours available.

BEST SPOTS

A favorite biking route is along the fairly flat red-dirt road northward from Lanai City through the old pineapple fields to Garden of the Gods. Start your trip on Keomuku Highway in town. Take a left just before The Lodge at Koele's tennis courts, and then a right where the road ends at the fenced pasture, and continue on to the north end and the start of Polihua and Awalua dirt roads. If you're really hardy, you could bike down to Polihua Beach and back, but it would be a serious all-day trip. In wet weather these roads turn to mud and are not advisable. Go in the early morning or late afternoon, because the sun gets hot in the middle of the day. Take plenty of water, spare parts, and snacks.

For the exceptionally fit, it's possible to bike from town down the Keomuku Highway to the windward beaches and back, or to bike the Munro Trail (⇨ *see Hiking*). Experienced bikers also travel up and down the Manele Highway from Manele Bay to town.

GOLF

Lanai's main golf course, located at the Four Seasons Resort Lanai at Manele Bay, is one of the loveliest golf courses in the world—and one of the most challenging. Another course at the Four Seasons Resort, The Lodge at Koele, is closed for renovations.

Manele Golf Course. Designed by Jack Nicklaus in 1993, this course sits right over the water of Hulopoe Bay. Built on lava outcroppings, it features three holes on cliffs that use the Pacific Ocean as a water hazard. The five-tee concept challenges the best golfers—tee shots over natural gorges and ravines must be precise. Unspoiled natural terrain provides a stunning backdrop, and every hole offers ocean views. Early-morning tee times are recommended to avoid the midday heat. ⊠ *Four Seasons Resort Lanai at Manele Bay, Challenge Dr., Manele, Lanai City* ☎ *808/565–2222* ⊕ *www.fourseasons.com/lanai* ⊡ *$285 for resort guests, $325 for nonguests* ⅃. *18 holes, 7039 yards, par 72.*

Some holes at the Manele Golf Course use the Pacific Ocean as a water hazard.

HIKING

Only 30 miles of Lanai's roads are paved, but red-dirt roads and trails, ideal for hiking, will take you to sweeping overlooks, isolated beaches, and shady forests. Take a self-guided walk through Kane Puu, Hawaii's largest native dryland forest. You can also explore the Munro Trail over Lanaihale with views of plunging canyons, hike along an old coastal fisherman trail, or head out across Koloiki Ridge. Wear hiking shoes, a hat, and sunscreen, and carry a windbreaker, cell phone, and plenty of water.

BEST SPOTS

Koloiki Ridge. This marked trail starts behind The Lodge at Koele (closed indefinitely) and takes you along the cool and shady Munro Trail to overlook the windward side, with impressive views of Maui, Molokai, Maunalei Valley, and Naio Gulch. The average time for the 5-mile round trip is two hours. Bring snacks, water, and a windbreaker; wear good shoes; and take your time. *Moderate.* ⊠ *Lanai City.*

Lanai Fisherman Trail. Local anglers still use this trail to get to their favorite fishing spots. The trail takes about 1½ hours and follows the rocky shoreline below the Four Seasons Resort at Lanai Manele Bay. The marked trail entrance begins at the west end of Hulopoe Beach. Keep your eyes open for spinner dolphins cavorting offshore and the silvery flash of fish feeding in the pools below you. The condition of the trail varies with weather and frequency of maintenance; it can be slippery and rocky. Take your time, wear a hat and enclosed shoes, and carry water. *Moderate.* ⊠ *Manele, Lanai City.*

Fodor's Choice ★ **Munro Trail.** This is the real thing: a strenuous 12.8-mile trek that begins behind The Lodge at Koele (closed until late 2016) and follows the ridge of Lanaihale through the rain forest. The island's most demanding hike, it has an elevation gain of 1,400 feet and leads to a lookout at the island's highest point, Lanaihale. It's also a narrow dirt road; watch out for careening four-wheel-drive vehicles. The trail is named after George Munro, who supervised the planting of Cook pine trees and eucalyptus windbreaks. Mules used to wend their way up the mountain carrying the pine seedlings. Unless you arrange for someone to pick you up at the trail's end, you have a 3-mile hike back through the Palawai Basin to return to your starting point. The summit is often cloud-shrouded and can be windy and muddy, so check conditions before you start. *Difficult.* ⊠ *Four Seasons The Lodge at Koele, 1 Keomuku Hwy., Lanai City.*

Puu Pehe Trail. Beginning to the left of Hulopoe Beach, this trail travels a short distance around the coastline, and then climbs up a sharp, rocky rise. At the top, you're level with the offshore stack of Puu Pehe and can overlook miles of coastline in both directions. The trail is not difficult, but it's hot and steep. Be aware of nesting seabirds and don't approach their nests. ⚠ **Stay away from the edge, as the cliff can easily give way.** The hiking is best in the early morning or late afternoon, and it's a perfect place to look for whales in season (December–April). Wear a hat and enclosed shoes, and take water so you can spend some time at the top admiring the view. *Moderate.* ⊠ *Manele, Lanai City.*

SHOPS AND SPAS

SHOPPING

A cluster of Cook pines in the center of Lanai City surrounded by small shops and restaurants, Dole Park is the closest thing to a mall on Lanai. Except for high-end resort boutiques and pro shops, it's the island's only shopping. A morning or afternoon stroll around the park offers an eclectic selection of gifts and clothing, plus a chance to chat with friendly shopkeepers. Well-stocked general stores are reminiscent of the 1920s, and galleries and a boutique have original art and fashions for everyone.

ARTS AND CRAFTS
Island Treasures. This well-stocked boutique is chock-full of appealing souvenirs, including an array of vintage Lanai travel posters that owner Gail Allen will ship right to your door. Gail is always up for a bit of local conversation and advice as well. ⊠ *733 7th St., Lanai City* ☎ *808/565–6255.*

CLOTHING
Cory Labang Studio. This tiny studio shop near Dole Park reflects its owner's life-long love of vintage clothing. Cory Labang's old piano and her Hawaiian family photos are a nice backdrop for handmade bags and clutches in antique fabrics. Crystal glassware, glittering costume jewelry, and one-of-a-kind accessories complete this unique collection. ⊠ *431A 7th St., Lanai City* ☎ *808/315–6715.*

Fodor's Choice **The Local Gentry.** Spacious and classy, this store has clothing for every
★ need, from casual men's and women's beachwear to evening resort wear,
shoes, jewelry, and hats. There are fancy fashions for tots as well. A
selection of original Lanai-themed clothing is also available, including
the signature "What happens on Lanai everybody knows" T-shirts.
Proprietor Jenna Gentry Majkus will mail your purchases. ✉ *363 7th
St., Lanai City* ☎ *808/565–9130.*

FOOD

Pine Isle Market. One of Lanai City's two all-purpose markets, Pine Isle
stocks everything from beach toys and electronics to meats and vegetables. The staff are friendly, and it's the best place around to buy
fresh fish. The market is closed Sunday. ✉ *356 8th St., Lanai City*
☎ *808/565–6488.*

Richard's. Along with fresh meats, fine wines, and imported gourmet
items, Richard's stocks everything from camping gear to household
items. They're closed on Wednesday and during lunch (noon–1). ✉ *434
8th St., Lanai City* ☎ *808/565–3781.*

GALLERIES

Lanai Art Center. Local artists display their work at this dynamic center
staffed by volunteers. Workshops in pottery, photography, woodwork-
ing, and painting welcome visitors. The gift shop sells Lanai handicrafts
and special offerings like handmade Swarovski crystal bracelets, the
sale of which underwrites children's art classes. There are occasional
concerts and special events. It's closed on Sunday. ✉ *339 7th St., Lanai
City* ☎ *808/565–7503* ⊕ *www.lanaiart.org.*

Fodor's Choice **Mike Carroll Gallery.** The dreamy, soft-focus oil paintings of award-win-
★ ning painter Mike Carroll are inspired by island scenes. His work is
showcased along with those of other local artists and visiting plein air
painters. You can also find handcrafted jewelry and antiques. ✉ *443
7th St., Lanai City* ☎ *808/565–7122* ⊕ *www.mikecarrollgallery.com.*

GENERAL STORES

International Food and Clothing Center. This old-fashioned emporium stocks
everything from fishing and camping gear to fine wine and imported
beer. It's a good place to pick up last-minute items on Sunday, when
other stores are closed. ✉ *833 Ilima Ave., Lanai City* ☎ *808/565–6433.*

Lanai City Service. In addition to being Lanai's only gas station and auto-
parts store, this outfit sells resort wear, *manapua* (steamed buns with
pork filling), hot dogs, beer, soda, and bottled water. It's open daily
6:30–10. ✉ *1036 Lanai Ave., Lanai City* ☎ *808/565–7227.*

SPAS

The Spa at Manele. Granite floors, eucalyptus steam rooms, and private
cabanas set the scene for indulgence. State-of-the-art pampering enlists
a panoply of oils and lotions that would have pleased Cleopatra. The
Makai Ritual includes a full-body exfoliation, limu and sea clay body
wrap, and massage treatment with warm stones. The macadamia sugar
and pineapple-citrus polish treatments are delicious. Afterward, relax in
the sauna or steam room. Massages in private oceanfront *hale* (houses)

are available for singles or couples. ⊠ *Four Seasons Resort Lanai at Manele Bay, 1 Manele Bay Rd., Manele, Lanai City* ☎ *808/565–2088* ⊕ *www.fourseasons.com/manelebay/spa* ☞ *$180–$200 for 50-min massage, Makai Ritual $500 per person.*

NIGHTLIFE

Lanai's nightlife offerings are fairly limited. If you want to rub shoulders with locals, pull up a stool at the Hotel Lanai's bar. The Sports Bar at the Four Seasons Resort Lanai at Manele Bay features a lively, sophisticated atmosphere in which to take in ocean views while noshing with your favorite libations. The newly renovated Hale Keaka (Lanai Theater) screens recent releases five nights a week. An alternative is stargazing from the beaches or watching the full moon rise from secluded vantage points.

Hale Keaka (Lanai Theater). Hale Keaka's two 93-seat theaters and green room screen recent movie releases Wednesday–Sunday. ⊠ *465 7th St., Lanai City* ⊕ *www.lanai96763.com.*

Hotel Lanai. A visit to this small, lively bar lets you chat with locals and find out more about the island. Enjoy performances by local and visiting musicians in the big green tent two nights a week. Get here early—last call is at 9:30. ⊠ *Hotel Lanai, 828 Lanai Ave., Lanai City* ☎ *808/565–7211* ⊕ *www.hotellanai.com.*

Sports Bar. At the Four Seasons Resort Lanai at Manele Bay, the oceanfront Sports Bar is an open-air lounge serving casual fare such as kiawe-smoked chicken wings, burgers, and kalbi-beef short ribs. Pool tables, shuffleboard courts, and a 90-inch TV make for an amusing time out. An added bonus: dolphins play in the bay below. ⊠ *Four Seasons Resort Lanai at Manele Bay, 1 Manele Bay Rd., Manele, Lanai City* ☎ *808/565–2000* ⊕ *www.fourseasons.com.*

UNDERSTANDING MAUI

HAWAIIAN VOCABULARY

HAWAIIAN VOCABULARY

Although an understanding of Hawaiian is by no means required on a trip to the Aloha State, a *malihini*, or newcomer, will find plenty of opportunities to pick up a few of the local words and phrases. Traditional names and expressions are widely used in the Islands. You're likely to read or hear at least a few words each day of your stay.

With a basic understanding and some uninhibited practice, anyone can have enough command of the local tongue to ask for directions and to order from a restaurant menu. One visitor announced she would not leave until she could pronounce the name of the state fish, the *humuhumunukunukuāpua'a*.

Simplifying the learning process is the fact that the Hawaiian language contains only eight consonants—*H, K, L, M, N, P, W,* and the silent *'okina*, or glottal stop (written ')—plus one or more of the five vowels. All syllables, and therefore all words, end in a vowel. Each vowel, with the exception of a few diphthongized double vowels such as *au* (pronounced "ow") or *ai* (pronounced "eye"), is pronounced separately. Thus *'Iolani* is four syllables ("ee-oh-la-nee"), not three ("yo-la-nee"). Although some Hawaiian words have only vowels, most also contain some consonants, but consonants are never doubled.

Pronunciation is simple. Pronounce *A* "ah," as in father; *E* "ay," as in weigh; *I* "ee," as in marine; *O* "oh," as in no; *U* "oo," as in true.

Consonants mirror their English equivalents, with the exception of *W*. When the letter begins any syllable other than the first one in a word, it is usually pronounced as a *V*. *'Awa*, the Polynesian drink, is pronounced "ava"; *'ewa* is pronounced "eva."

Almost all long Hawaiian words are combinations of shorter words; they are not difficult to pronounce if you segment them. *Kalaniana'ole*, the highway running east from Honolulu, is easily understood as *Kalani-ana -ole*. Apply the standard pronunciation rules—the stress falls on the next-to-last syllable of most two- or three-syllable Hawaiian words—and Kalaniana'ole Highway is as easy to say as Main Street.

Now about that fish. Try *humu-humu nuku-nuku āpu a'a*.

The other unusual element in Hawaiian language is the *kahakō*, or macron, written as a short line (ˉ) placed over a vowel. Like the accent (´) in Spanish, the kahakō puts emphasis on a syllable that would normally not be stressed. The most familiar example is probably *Waikīkī*. With no macrons, the stress would fall on the middle syllable; with only one macron, on the last syllable, the stress would fall on the first and last syllables. Some words become plural with the addition of a macron, often on a syllable that would have been stressed anyway. No Hawaiian word becomes plural with the addition of an *s*, since that letter does not exist in the language.

What follows is a glossary of some of the most commonly used Hawaiian words. Hawaiian residents appreciate visitors who at least try to pick up the local language.

'a'ā: rough, crumbling lava, contrasting with *pāhoehoe*, which is smooth.

'ae: yes.

aikane: friend.

āina: land.

akamai: smart, clever, possessing savoir faire.

akua: god.

ala: a road, path, or trail.

ali'i: a Hawaiian chief, a member of the chiefly class.

aloha: love, affection, kindness; also a salutation meaning both greetings and farewell.

'ānuenue: rainbow.

'a'ole: no.

'apōpō: tomorrow.

'auwai: a ditch.

auwē: alas, woe is me!

'ehu: a red-haired Hawaiian.

'ewa: in the direction of 'Ewa plantation, west of Honolulu.

hala: the pandanus tree, whose leaves (*lau hala*) are used to make baskets and plaited mats.

hālau: school.

hale: a house.

hale pule: church, house of worship.

ha mea iki or **ha mea 'ole:** you're welcome.

hana: to work.

haole: ghost. Since the first foreigners were Caucasian, *haole* now means a Caucasian person.

hapa: a part, sometimes a half; often used as a short form of *hapa haole,* to mean a person who is part-Caucasian.

hau'oli: to rejoice. *Hau'oli Makahiki Hou* means Happy New Year. *Hau'oli lā hānau* means Happy Birthday.

heiau: an outdoor stone platform; an ancient Hawaiian place of worship.

holo: to run.

holoholo: to go for a walk, ride, or sail.

holokū: a long Hawaiian dress, somewhat fitted, with a yoke and a train. Influenced by European fashion, it was worn at court, and at least one local translates the word as "expensive mu'umu'u."

holomū: a post–World War II cross between a holokū and a mu'umu'u, less fitted than the former but less voluminous than the latter and having no train.

honi: to kiss; a kiss. A phrase that some tourists may find useful, quoted from a popular hula, is *Honi Ka'ua Wikiwiki:* Kiss me quick!

honu: turtle.

ho'omalimali: flattery, a deceptive "line," bunk, baloney, hooey.

huhū: angry.

hui: a group, club, or assembly. A church may refer to its congregation as a *hui* and a social club may be called a *hui.*

hukilau: a seine; a communal fishing party in which everyone helps to drive the fish into a huge net, pull it in, and divide the catch.

hula: the dance of Hawaii.

iki: little.

ipo: sweetheart.

ka: the. This is the definite article for most singular words; for plural nouns, the definite article is usually *nā.* Since there is no *s* in Hawaiian, the article may be your only clue that a noun is plural.

kahuna: a priest, doctor, or other trained person of old Hawaii, endowed with special professional skills that often included prophecy or other supernatural powers; the plural form is kāhuna.

kai: the sea, saltwater.

kalo: the taro plant from whose root *poi* (paste) is made.

kamā'aina: literally, a child of the soil. It refers to people who were born in the Islands or have lived there for a long time.

kanaka: originally a man or humanity, it is now used to denote a male Hawaiian or part-Hawaiian, but is occasionally taken as a slur when used by non-Hawaiians. *Kanaka maoli,* originally a full-blooded Hawaiian person, is used by some Native Hawaiian–rights activists to embrace part-Hawaiians as well.

kāne: a man, a husband. If you see this word on a door, it's the men's room. If you see *kane* on a door, it's probably a misspelling; that is the Hawaiian name for the skin fungus tinea.

kapa: also called by its Tahitian name, *tapa,* a cloth made of beaten bark and usually dyed and stamped with a repeat design.

kapakahi: crooked, cockeyed, uneven. You've got your hat on *kapakahi.*

kapu: keep out, prohibited. This is the Hawaiian version of the more widely known Tongan word *tabu* (taboo).

kapuna: grandparent; elder.

kēia lā: today.

keiki: a child; *keikikāne* is a boy, *keikiwahine* a girl.

kona: the leeward side of the Islands, the direction (south) from which the *kona* wind and *kona* rain come.

kula: upland.

kuleana: a homestead or small plot of ground on which a family has been installed for some generations without necessarily owning it. By extension, *kuleana* is used to denote any area or department in which one has a special interest or prerogative. You'll hear it used this way: "If you want to hire a surfboard, see Moki; that's his *kuleana.*"

lā: sun.

lamalama: to fish with a torch.

lānai: a porch, a balcony, an outdoor living room. Almost every house in Hawai'i has one. Don't confuse this two-syllable word with the three-syllable name of the island, Lāna'i.

lani: heaven, the sky.

lau hala: the leaf of the *hala,* or pandanus tree, widely used in handicrafts.

lei: a garland of flowers.

limu: sun.

lolo: stupid.

luna: a plantation overseer or foreman.

mahalo: thank you.

makai: toward the ocean.

malihini: a newcomer to the Islands.

mana: the spiritual power that the Hawaiian believed inhabited all things and creatures.

manō: shark.

manuwahi: free, gratis.

mauka: toward the mountains.

mauna: mountain.

mele: a Hawaiian song or chant, often of epic proportions.

Mele Kalikimaka: Merry Christmas (a transliteration from the English phrase).

Menehune: a Hawaiian pixie. The Menehune were a legendary race of little people who accomplished prodigious work, such as building fishponds and temples in the course of a single night.

moana: the ocean.

mu'umu'u: the voluminous dress in which the missionaries enveloped Hawaiian women. Now made in bright printed cottons and silks, it is an indispensable garment. Culturally sensitive locals have embraced the Hawaiian spelling but often shorten the spoken word to "mu'u." Most English dictionaries include the spelling "muumuu."

nani: beautiful.

nui: big.

ohana: family.

'ono: delicious.

pāhoehoe: smooth, unbroken, satiny lava.

Pākē: Chinese. "This Pākē carver makes beautiful things."

palapala: document, printed matter.

pali: a cliff, precipice.

pānini: prickly pear cactus.

paniolo: a Hawaiian cowboy, a rough transliteration of *español,* the language of the Islands' earliest cowboys.

pau: finished, done.

pilikia: trouble. The Hawaiian word is much more widely used here than its English equivalent.

puka: a hole.

pupule: crazy, like the celebrated Princess Pupule. This word has replaced its English equivalent in local usage.

pu'u: volcanic cinder cone.

waha: mouth.

wahine: a female, a woman, a wife, and a sign on the ladies' room door; the plural form is *wāhine.*

wai: freshwater, as opposed to saltwater, which is *kai.*

wailele: waterfall.

wikiwiki: to hurry, hurry up (since this is a reduplication of *wiki,* or quick, neither *w* is pronounced as a *v*).

Note: Pidgin is the unofficial language of Hawaii. It is a creole language, with its own grammar, evolved from the mixture of English, Hawaiian, Japanese, Portuguese, and other languages spoken in 19th-century Hawaii, and it is heard everywhere.

TRAVEL SMART
MAUI

GETTING HERE AND AROUND

▌ AIR TRAVEL

Flying time to Maui is about 10 hours from New York, 8 hours from Chicago, and 5 hours from Los Angeles.

Hawaii is a major destination link for flights traveling between the U.S. mainland, Asia, Australia, New Zealand, and the South Pacific. Island-hopping is easy, with several daily interisland flights connecting all the major islands. International travelers also have options: Oahu and the Big Island are gateways to the United States.

Although Maui's airports are smaller and more casual than Oahu's Honolulu International, during peak times they can also be quite busy. Allow extra travel time to either airport during morning and afternoon rush-hour traffic periods, and allow time if you are returning a rental car. Plan to arrive at the airport at least two hours before departure for interisland flights.

Plants and plant products are subject to regulation by the Department of Agriculture, both when entering and leaving Hawaii. Upon leaving the Islands, you're required to have your bags X-rayed and tagged at one of the airport's agricultural-inspection stations before you proceed to check-in. Pineapples and coconuts with the packer's agricultural-inspection stamp pass freely; papayas must be treated, inspected, and stamped. All other fruits are banned for export to the U.S. mainland. Flowers pass except for jade vine and mauna loa. Also banned are insects, snails, soil, cotton, cacti, sugarcane, and all berry plants, including fresh coffee berries.

Dogs and other pets must be left at home: a quarantine of up to 120 days is imposed to keep out rabies, which is nonexistent in Hawaii. However, if specific pre- and postarrival requirements are met, animals may qualify for 30-day or 5-day-or-less quarantine.

The Transportation Security Administration has answers for almost every question that might come up.

Airline-Security Issues Transportation Security Administration. ⊕ *www.tsa.gov.*

Air-Travel Resources in Maui State of Hawaii Airports Division Offices. ☎ *808/836–6413* ⊕ *hidot.hawaii.gov.*

AIRPORTS

All of Hawaii's major islands have their own airports, but Oahu's Honolulu International is the main stopover for most U.S. mainland and international flights. From Honolulu, daily flights to Maui leave almost every hour from early morning until evening. To travel interisland from Honolulu, you can depart from either the interisland terminal or the commuter-airline terminal, in two separate structures adjacent to the main overseas terminal building. A free bus service, the Wiki Wiki Shuttle, operates between terminals. In addition, several carriers offer nonstop service directly from the U.S. mainland to Maui. Flights from Honolulu into Lanai and Molokai are offered several times a day.

Maui has two major airports. Kahului Airport handles major airlines and interisland flights; it's the only airport on Maui that has direct service from the mainland. Kapalua–West Maui Airport is served by Mokulele Airlines. If you're staying in West Maui and you're flying in from another island, you can avoid the hour drive from the Kahului Airport by flying into Kapalua–West Maui Airport. Hana Airport in East Maui is small; Mokulele Airlines flies twice per day between Kahului and Hana.

Molokai's Hoolehua Airport is small and centrally located, as is Lanai Airport. Both rural airports handle a limited number of flights per day. There's a small airfield at Kalaupapa on Molokai (prebook your ground tour with Damien Tours

✆ 808/567–6171). Visitors coming from the U.S. mainland to these islands must first stop in Oahu or Maui and change to an interisland flight. Lanai Airport has a federal agricultural inspection station, so guests departing to the mainland can check luggage directly.

Airport Information Hana Airport (HNM).
☎ 808/248-4861 ⊕ www.hawaii.gov/hnm.
Honolulu International Airport (HNL).
☎ 808/836-6411 ⊕ www.hawaii.gov/hnl.
Kahului Airport (OGG). ☎ 808/872-3830
⊕ www.hawaii.gov/ogg. **Kalaupapa Airfield (LUP).** ☎ 808/838-8701 ⊕ www.hawaii.gov/lup. **Kapalua-West Maui Airport (JHM).**
☎ 808/665-6108 ⊕ www.hawaii.gov/jhm.
Lanai Airport (LNY). ☎ 808/565-7942 ⊕ www.hawaii.gov/lny. **Molokai Airport (MKK).**
☎ 808/567-9660 ⊕ www.hawaii.gov/mkk.

GROUND TRANSPORTATION

If you're not renting a car, you'll need to take a taxi, or SpeediShuttle if your hotel is along its route. Maui Airport Taxi serves the Kahului Airport and charges $3.50, plus $3 for every mile. Cab fares to locations around the island are estimated as follows: Kaanapali $87, Kahului town $13, Kapalua $105, Kihei town $33 to $55, Lahaina $78, Maalaea $33, Makena $65, Wailea $57, and Wailuku $20.

SpeediShuttle offers transportation between the Kahului Airport and hotels, resorts, and condominium complexes throughout Maui. There is an online reservation and fare-quote system for information and bookings. You can expect to pay around $67 per couple to Kaanapali, $47 to Wailea.

Contacts Maui Airport Taxi. ☎ 808/281-9533 ⊕ www.nokaoitaxi.com. **SpeediShuttle Hawaii.**
☎ 877/242-5777 ⊕ www.speedishuttle.com.

FLIGHTS

Service to Maui changes regularly, so it's best to check when you are ready to book. American has daily nonstop flights into Maui from Los Angeles and Dallas–Fort Worth. Alaska, Delta, United, and US Airways (now merged with American) also have daily nonstops into Maui from Los Angeles. United has one nonstop flight from Newark Liberty near New York to Honolulu. Alaska Airlines flies a daily nonstop to Maui from Portland, Seattle, San Diego, and San Jose. Virgin America has a daily nonstop flight to Maui from San Francisco.

Delta serves Maui from Atlanta, Los Angeles, Minneapolis–St. Paul, Portland, Salt Lake City, San Francisco, and Seattle. Hawaiian Airlines serves Maui from Las Vegas, Los Angeles, New York (the only nonstop flight from JFK to Honolulu), Oakland, Phoenix, Portland, Sacramento, San Diego, San Francisco, San Jose, and Seattle. In addition to offering competitive rates and online specials, all have frequent-flyer programs that will entitle you to rewards and upgrades the more you fly.

Airline Contacts Alaska Airlines.
☎ 800/252-7522 ⊕ www.alaskaair.com.
American Airlines. ☎ 800/433-7300 ⊕ www.aa.com. **Delta Airlines.** ☎ 800/221-1212 ⊕ www.delta.com. **Hawaiian Airlines.**
☎ 800/367-5320 ⊕ www.hawaiianairlines.com.
United Airlines. ☎ 800/864-8331 ⊕ www.united.com. **Virgin America.** ☎ 877/359-8474 ⊕ www.virginamerica.com.

CHARTER FLIGHTS

George's Aviation offers on-demand private air charters and cargo service between all the major Hawaiian Islands. Should you want to explore Maui, Kauai, Oahu, and the Big Island from the air and ground, you can book tours through Discover Hawaii Tours.

Charter Companies Discover Hawaii Tours.
☎ 808/690-9050 ⊕ www.discoverhawaiitours.com. **George's Aviation.** ✉ 18 Lagoon Dr.
☎ 808/834-2120, 866/834-2120 ⊕ www.georgesaviation.com.

INTERISLAND FLIGHTS

Hawaiian Airlines offers regular interisland service to Maui's Kahului airport. Island Air and Mokulele Airlines provide interisland service between Maui (Kahului), Lanai, Molokai (Hoolehua), Oahu, Kauai, and the Big Island. Makani Kai Air provides service between Maui (Kahului) and Molokai (Hoolehua and Kalaupapa). Mokulele also services Maui's Kapalua and Hana airports.

Be sure to compare prices offered by all the interisland carriers. Plan ahead and be flexible with your dates and times if you're looking for an affordable round trip.

Airline Contacts Hawaiian Airlines. ☎ 800/367–5320 ⊕ www.hawaiianairlines. com. **Island Air.** ☎ 800/652–6541 ⊕ www. islandair.com. **Makani Kai Air.** ☎ 808/834–1111, 877/255–8532 ⊕ www.makanikaiair. com. **Mokulele Airlines.** ☎ 808/495–4188, 866/260–7070 ⊕ www.mokuleleairlines.com.

▌BOAT TRAVEL

There is daily ferry service between Lahaina on Maui, and Manele Bay on Lanai, with Expeditions Lanai Ferry. The 9-mile crossing costs $60 round-trip and takes about 45 minutes or so, depending on ocean conditions (which can make this trip a rough one).

Molokai Ferry offers ferry service four times per week between Lahaina on Maui, and Kaunakakai on Molokai. Check their website for available travel dates. Travel time is about 90 minutes each way, and the one-way fare is $68.27. Reservations are essential. ▌TIP➔ All voyages may be subject to cancellation if a minimum of 20 confirmed passenger reservations per voyage leg are not received 48 hours in advance.

Ferry Contacts Expeditions Lanai Ferry. ☎ 800/695–2624 ⊕ www.go-lanai.com. **Molokai Ferry.** ☎ 808/667–5553 ⊕ www. molokaiferry.com.

CRUISES

⇨ For information about cruises, see Chapter 1, Experience Maui.

▌BUS TRAVEL

Maui Bus, operated by the tour company Roberts Hawaii, offers 13 routes in and between various Central, South, and West Maui communities. You can travel in and around Wailuku, Kahului, Lahaina, Kaanapali, Kapalua, Kihei, Wailea, Maalaea, the North Shore (Paia), and Upcountry (including Kula, Pukalani, Makawao, Haliimaile, and Haiku). The Upcountry and Haiku Islander routes include a stop at Kahului Airport. All routes cost $2 per boarding.

Bus Contact Maui Bus. ☎ 808/871–4838 ⊕ www.mauicounty.gov/bus.

▌CAR TRAVEL

Should you plan to do any sightseeing on Maui, it's best to rent a car. Even if all you want to do is relax at your resort, you may want to hop in the car to check out one of the island's popular restaurants.

Many of Maui's roads are two lanes, so allow plenty of time to return your vehicle to the airport. Traffic can be bad during morning and afternoon rush hours, especially between Kahului and Paia, Kihei, and Lahaina. Give yourself about 3½ hours before departure time to return your vehicle.

On Molokai and Lanai four-wheel-drive vehicles are recommended for exploring off the beaten path. Many of the roads are poorly paved or unpaved.

Make sure you've got a GPS or a good map. Free visitor publications containing high-quality road maps can be found at airports, hotels, and shops.

Asking for directions will almost always produce a helpful explanation from the locals, but you should be prepared for an island term or two. Hawaii residents refer to places as being either *mauka* (toward the mountains) or *makai* (toward the ocean).

Hawaii has a strict seat-belt law. Those riding in the front seat must wear a seat belt, and children under the age of 18 in the backseat must be belted. The fine for not wearing a seat belt is $92. Jaywalking is also common, so pay careful attention to pedestrians. Turning right on a red light is legal in the state, except where noted.

Your unexpired mainland driver's license is valid for rental cars for up to 90 days.

Morning (6:30–9:30 am) and afternoon (3:30–6:30 pm) rush-hour traffic around Kahului, Paia, Kihei, and Lahaina can be bad, so use caution.

GASOLINE

Gas costs more on Maui than on the U.S. mainland, up to $1–$1.50 more per gallon. Expect to pay more (sometimes significantly more) on Lanai and Molokai. The only gas station on Lanai is in Lanai City, at Lanai City Service.

In rural areas, it's not unusual for gas stations to close early. If you see that your tank is getting low, don't take any chances; fill up when you see a station.

PARKING

With a population of more than 155,000 and nearly 30,000 visitors on any given day, Maui has parking challenges. Lots sprinkled throughout West Maui charge by the hour. There are about 700 parking spaces at The Outlets of Maui in Lahaina; shoppers can get validated parking here, as well as at Whalers Village. Parking along many streets is curtailed during rush hours, and towing is widely practiced. Read curbside parking signs before leaving your vehicle.

RENTALS

While on Maui you can rent anything from a subcompact to a Ferrari. Rates are usually better if you reserve though a rental agency's website. All the big national rental-car agencies have locations on Maui, but Dollar (⊕ *www. dollar.com*) is the only major company on Lanai, and Alamo (⊕ *www.alamo.com*) is the only one on Molokai. There also are local rental-car companies, so be sure to compare prices before you book. It's wise to make reservations far in advance, especially if you're visiting during peak seasons or for major conventions or sporting events, as car rental companies often sell out completely during these times. *For more specifics about renting on Molokai and Lanai, see the planning sections of Chapters 10 and 11.*

Rates begin at $20–$31 a day for an economy car with air-conditioning, automatic transmission, and unlimited mileage, depending on your pickup location. This does not include the airport concession fee, general excise tax, rental-vehicle surcharge, or vehicle license fee. When you reserve a car, ask about cancellation penalties and drop-off charges should you plan to pick up the car in one location and return it to another. Many rental companies offer money-saving coupons for local attractions.

In Hawaii you must be 21 to rent a car, and you must have a valid driver's license and a major credit card. You can use a debit card at most rental agencies, but they will put a $500 hold on your account for the duration of the rental. Those under 25 will pay a daily surcharge of $10–$25. Request car seats and extras such as a GPS when you make your reservation. Hawaii's Child Restraint Law requires that all children under age four be in an approved child-safety seat in the backseat of a vehicle. Children ages four to seven, and those who are less than 4 feet 9 inches tall and weigh less than 80 pounds, must be seated in a rear booster seat or child restraint such as a lap and shoulder belt. Car seats and boosters run $7–$12 per day; some companies have a maximum charge per rental period.

Maui has some unusual rental options. Aloha Campers rents older VW Westfalia Campers and newer Honda Elements for $99–$149 per day, depending upon the season, with a three-day minimum. And if exploring the island on two wheels is more your speed, Hawaii Harley Rental rents motorcycles. Hawaiian Riders also rents luxury cars. Prefer an earth-friendly automobile that gets 35–50 miles to the gallon? Bio-Beetle Eco Rental Cars run on clean-burning diesel fuel that comes from renewable sources like recycled vegetable oil.

Car Rental Resources

Local Agencies		
AA Aloha Cars-R-Us	800/655-7989	www.hawaiicarrental.com
Adventure Lanai EcoCentre (Lanai)	808/565-7373	www.adventurelanai.com
Aloha Campers (Maui)	800/482-2070	www.alohacampers.com
Bio-Beetle Eco Rental Cars	808/873-6121	www.bio-beetle.com
Discount Hawaii	888/292-1930	www.discounthawaiicarrental.com
Hawaiian Discount Car Rentals	800/955-3142	www.hawaiidrive-o.com
Hawaiian Riders	800/440-7029	www.hawaiianriders.com
Hawaii Harley Rental	800/230-0021	www.hawaiiharleyrental.com

ROAD CONDITIONS

Getting around Maui is relatively easy, as only a few major roads hit the must-see sights. Honoapiilani Highway will get you from the central Maui towns of Wailuku and Kahului to the leeward coast and the towns of Lahaina, Kaanapali, Kahana, and Kapalua. Depending on traffic, it should take about 30–45 minutes to travel this route. Those gorgeous mountains that hug Honoapiilani Highway are the West Maui Mountains.

North and South Kihei Road will take you to the town of Kihei and the resort area of Wailea on the South Shore. The drive from the airport in Kahului to Wailea should take about 30 minutes, and the drive from Kaanapali in West Maui to Wailea on the South Shore will take about 45–60 minutes.

Your vacation to Maui must include a visit to Haleakala National Park, and you should plan on 2–2½ hours' driving time from Kaanapali or Wailea. The drive from Kaanapali or Wailea to the charming towns of Makawao and Kula will take about 45–60 minutes. And you must not miss the Road to Hana, a 55-mile stretch with one-lane bridges, hairpin turns, and breathtaking views. The Hawaii Visitors and Convention Bureau's red-caped King Kamehameha signs mark major attractions and scenic spots.

All major roads on Maui are passable with two-wheel-drive vehicles. You should exercise caution on Kahekili Highway between Waihee Point and Keawalua, which is somewhat treacherous due to sheer drop-offs, and the southern stretch of Piilani Highway between Ulupalakua and Kipahulu, which has sections of extremely rough and unpaved roadway. Both roads are remote, have no gas stations, and provide little or no cell-phone service, so plan accordingly.

In rural areas it's not unusual for gas stations to close early. Use caution during heavy downpours, especially if you see signs warning of falling rocks. If you're enjoying the views or need to study a map, pull over to the side. Remember the aloha spirit: allow other cars to merge, don't honk (it's considered rude), and use your headlights and turn signals.

Emergency Services AAA Help. ☎ 800/222-4357 ⊕ www.hawaii.aaa.com.

ESSENTIALS

▮ COMMUNICATIONS

INTERNET

If you've brought your laptop or tablet with you to Maui, you should have no problem checking email or connecting to the Internet. Most major hotels and resorts offer high-speed access in rooms or public areas. If you're staying at a small inn or bed-and-breakfast without Internet access, ask the proprietor for the nearest café or coffee shop with wireless access.

Most Maui hotels, restaurants, and tour companies have mobile-friendly websites. Reliable Internet access from your smartphone is available throughout the majority of Maui, but can be challenging in some rural areas.

PHONES

The area code for Hawaii is 808. For local calls on Maui, you need to dial only the seven-digit number (not the 808 area code). If you are calling numbers on neighboring islands while on Maui, you will need to use "1–808," followed by the number.

▮ HEALTH

Hawaii is known as the Health State. The life expectancy here is 81.3 years, the longest in the nation. Balmy weather makes it easy to remain active year-round, and the low-stress aloha attitude contributes to the general well-being. When visiting the Islands, however, there are a few health issues to keep in mind.

The Hawaii State Department of Health recommends that you drink 16 ounces of water per hour to avoid dehydration when hiking or spending time in the sun. Use sunblock, wear UV-reflective sunglasses, and protect your head with a visor or hat. If you're not used to warm, humid weather, allow plenty of time for rest stops and refreshments.

WORD OF MOUTH

Before your trip, be sure to check out what other travelers are saying in Travel Talk Forums on ⊕ www.fodors.com.

When visiting freshwater streams, be aware of the relatively rare tropical disease leptospirosis, which is spread by animal urine. Symptoms include fever, headache, nausea, and red eyes. To avoid leptospirosis, don't swim or wade in freshwater streams or ponds if you have open sores, and don't drink from any freshwater streams or ponds. If you do exhibit symptoms after exposure to freshwater streams, seek immediate medical assistance.

On the Islands, fog is a rare occurrence, but there can often be "vog," an airborne haze of gases released from volcanic vents on the Big Island. During certain weather conditions such as "Kona Winds," the vog can settle over the Islands and wreak havoc with respiratory conditions, especially asthma or emphysema. If susceptible, stay indoors and get emergency assistance if needed. Periodic sugarcane burning by Hawaiian Commercial & Sugar Company can also affect some people's respiratory systems. A burning schedule is posted on the company's website (⊕ www.hcsugar. com/sugarcane-burn-schedule).

The Islands have their share of insects. Most are harmless but annoying. When planning to spend time outdoors in hiking areas, wear long-sleeved clothing and long pants and use mosquito repellent containing DEET. In damp places you may encounter the dreaded local centipedes, which are brown and blue and measure up to eight inches long. Their painful sting is similar to those of bees and wasps. When camping, shake out your sleeping bag and check your shoes, as the centipedes like cozy places. When hiking in remote areas, always carry a first-aid kit.

■ HOURS OF OPERATION

Even people in paradise have to work. Generally, local business hours are weekdays 8–5. Banks are usually open Monday through Thursday 8:30–4 and until 6 on Friday. Some banks have Saturday-morning hours.

Many self-serve gas stations stay open around the clock, with full-service stations usually open 7 am–9 pm; stations in rural spots may close earlier. U.S. post offices generally open between 8:30 and 9:30 am on weekdays, and close between 3:30 and 4:30 pm. Saturday hours are generally short, and vary from office to office.

Most museums open their doors between 9 and 10 am and stay open until 4 or 4:30 pm. Many museums close on Sunday and Monday. Visitor-attraction hours vary throughout the state, but most sights are open daily with the exception of major holidays.

Stores in resort areas sometimes open as early as 8, with shopping-center opening hours varying from 9:30 to 10 on weekdays and Saturday, a bit later on Sunday. Bigger malls stay open until 9 weekdays and Saturday and close at 5 on Sunday. Boutiques in resort areas may stay open as late as 11.

■ MONEY

Prices in listings are given for adults. Substantially reduced fees are almost always available for children, students, and senior citizens.

CREDIT CARDS

It's a good idea to inform your credit-card company before you travel. Otherwise, the credit-card company might put a hold on your card owing to unusual activity—not a good thing halfway through your trip. Record all your credit-card numbers—as well as the phone numbers to call if your cards are lost or stolen—in a safe place, so you're prepared should something go wrong. Both MasterCard and Visa have general numbers you can call (collect if you're abroad) if your card is lost, but you're better off calling the number of your issuing bank, since MasterCard and Visa usually just transfer you to your bank; your bank's number is usually printed on your card.

Reporting Lost Cards American Express. ☎ 800/528–4800 ⊕ www.americanexpress. com. **Diners Club.** ☎ 800/234–6377 ⊕ www. dinersclub.com. **Discover.** ☎ 800/347–2683 ⊕ www.discover.com. **MasterCard.** ☎ 800/627–8372 ⊕ www.mastercard.com. **Visa.** ☎ 800/847–2911 ⊕ www.visa.com.

■ PACKING

Probably the most important thing to tuck into your suitcase is sunscreen. There are many tanning oils on the market in Hawaii, including coconut and *kukui* (the nut from a local tree) oils, but they can cause severe burns. Hats and sunglasses offer important sun protection, too.

Hawaii is casual: sandals, bathing suits, and comfortable, informal cotton clothing are the norm. In summer, synthetic slacks and shirts, although easy to care for, can be uncomfortably warm. The aloha shirt is accepted dress in Hawaii for business and most social occasions.

Shorts are acceptable daytime attire, along with a T-shirt or polo shirt. There's no need to buy expensive sandals on the mainland—here you can get flip-flops for a couple of bucks and off-brand sandals for $20 or less. Many golf courses have dress codes requiring a collared shirt. If you're visiting in winter or planning to visit a high-altitude area, bring a sweater, a light- to medium-weight jacket, or a fleece pullover.

If your vacation plans include an exploration of Maui's northeastern coast, including Hana and Upcountry Maui, pack a light rain jacket. And if you'll be exploring Haleakala National Park, make sure you pack appropriately, as weather at the summit can be very cold and windy. Bring good boots

LOCAL DO'S AND TABOOS

Hawaii was admitted to the Union in 1959, so residents can be sensitive when visitors refer to their own hometowns as "back in the States." Instead, refer to the contiguous 48 states as "the mainland." When you do, you won't appear to be such a *malihini* (newcomer).

GREETINGS

Hawaii is a friendly place, and this is reflected in the day-to-day encounters with friends, family, and even business associates. Women will often hug and kiss one another on the cheek, and men will shake hands and sometimes combine that with a friendly hug. When a man and woman are greeting each other and are good friends, it is not unusual for them to hug and kiss on the cheek. Children are taught to call any elders "auntie" or "uncle," even if they aren't related; it's a way to show respect.

When you walk off a long flight, nothing quite compares with a Hawaiian lei greeting. The casual ceremony ranks as one of the fastest ways to make the transition from the worries of home to the joys of your vacation. Though the tradition has created an expectation that everyone receives this floral garland when they step off the plane, the state of Hawaii cannot greet each of its nearly 8 million annual visitors.

If you've booked a vacation with a wholesaler or tour company, a lei greeting might be included in your package. If not, it's easy to arrange a lei greeting before you arrive at Kahului Airport with Kamaaina Leis, Flowers & Greeters. A dendrobium orchid lei is considered standard and costs about $25 per person.

Kamaaina Leis, Flowers & Greeters.
☎ *808/836–3246, 800/367–5183*
⊕ *www.alohaleigreetings.com.*

LANGUAGE

English is the primary language on the Islands. Making the effort to learn some Hawaiian words can be rewarding, however. Hawaiian words you are most likely to encounter during your visit to the Islands are *aloha* (hello and good-bye), *mahalo* (thank you), *keiki* (child), *haole* (Caucasian or foreigner), *mauka* (toward the mountains), *makai* (toward the ocean), and *pau* (finished, all done). If you'd like to learn more Hawaiian words, check out ⊕ *www.wehewehe.org.*

Hawaiian history includes waves of immigrants, each bringing their own language. To communicate with each other, they developed a language known as pidgin. If you listen closely, you will know what is being said by the inflections and by the body language. For an informative and sometimes hilarious view of things Hawaiian, check out *Pidgin to da Max* by Douglas Simonson and *Fax to da Max* by Jerry Hopkins. Both are available at most local bookstores in the Hawaiiana sections.

VISITING AND ALOHA

If you've been invited to the home of friends living in Hawaii (an ultimate compliment), bring a small gift and take off your shoes when you enter their house. Try to take part in a cultural festival during your stay in the Islands; there is no better way to get a glimpse of Hawaii's ethnic mosaic.

And finally, remember that *aloha* is not only the word for hello, good-bye, and love, but also stands for the spirit that is all around the Islands. Take your time (after all, you're on "Hawaiian time"). Respect the *aina* (land): that is not only a precious commodity here but also stands at the core of the Polynesian belief system. "Living aloha" will transform your vacation, fill you with the warmth that is unique to Hawaii, and have you planning your return.

for hiking at Haleakala Crater; sneakers will suffice for most other trails on Maui.

Transportation Security Administration (TSA). ⊕ *www.tsa.gov.*

▌ SAFETY

Hawaii is generally a safe tourist destination, but it's still wise to follow common-sense safety precautions. Don't leave any valuables inside your rental car, not even in a locked trunk. Avoid poorly lighted areas, beach parks, and isolated areas after dark. When hiking, stay on marked trails, no matter how alluring the temptation might be to stray. Weather conditions can cause landscapes to become muddy, slippery, and tenuous, so staying on marked trails will lessen the possibility of a fall or getting lost.

Women traveling alone are generally safe on the Islands, but always follow the safety precautions you would use in any major destination. When booking hotels, request rooms closest to the elevator and always keep your hotel-room door and balcony doors locked. Stay away from isolated areas after dark; camping and hiking solo are not advised. If you stay out late visiting nightclubs and bars, use caution when returning to your lodging.

▌ TAXES

There's a 4.17% state sales tax on all purchases, including food. A hotel room tax of 9.25%, combined with the sales tax of 4.17%, equals a 13.42% rate added onto your hotel bill. A $7.50-per-day road tax is also assessed on each rental vehicle.

▌ TIME

Hawaii is on Hawaiian standard time, 5 hours behind New York, 2 hours behind Los Angeles, and 10 hours behind London.

When the U.S. mainland is on daylight saving time, Hawaii is not, so add an extra hour of time difference between the Islands and U.S. mainland destinations. You may find that things generally move more slowly here. That has nothing to do with your watch—it's just the laid-back way called Hawaiian time.

▌ TIPPING

Tipping is not only common but expected: Hawaii is a major vacation destination and many of the people who work at the hotels and resorts rely on tips to supplement their wages.

TIPPING GUIDELINES FOR MAUI	
Bartender	$1–$5 per round of drinks, depending on the number of drinks
Bellhop	$1–$5 per bag, depending on the level of the hotel and whether you have bulky items like golf clubs, surfboards, etc.
Hotel Concierge	$5 or more, depending on the service
Hotel Doorman	$1–$5 if he helps you get a cab or helps with bags, golf clubs, etc.
Hotel Maid	$1–$3 per day (either daily or at the end of your stay, in cash)
Hotel Room-Service Waiter	$1–$2 per delivery, even if a service charge has been added
Porter at Airport	$1 per bag
Skycap at Airport	$1–$3 per bag checked
Spa Personnel	15%–20% of the cost of your service
Taxi Driver	15%–20%, but round up the fare to the next dollar amount
Tour Guide	10% of the cost of the tour
Valet-Parking Attendant	$2–$5, each time your car is brought to you
Waiter	15%–20%, with 20% being the norm at high-end restaurants; nothing additional if a service charge is added to the bill

▮ TOURS

Guided tours are a good option when you don't want to do it all yourself. You travel along with a group (sometimes large, sometimes small), stay in prebooked hotels, eat with your fellow travelers (the cost of meals is sometimes included in the price of your tour, sometimes not), and follow a schedule.

Tours can be just the thing for first-time travelers to Maui or those who enjoy the group-traveling experience. None of the companies offering general-interest tours in Hawaii include Molokai or Lanai. When you book a guided tour, find out what's included and what isn't. A "land-only" tour includes all your ground transportation but not necessarily your flights. Most prices in tour brochures don't include fees, taxes, and tips.

TOUR COMPANIES

Atlas Cruises & Tours. This escorted-tour operator, in business for more than 25 years, partners with major companies such as Collette, Globus, Tauck, and Trafalgar to offer a wide variety of travel experiences. Tours run 7–12 nights, and most include Maui. ☎ *800/942–3301* ⊕ *www. atlastravelweb.com* ✉ *From $2732.*

Globus. Founded in 1928 by a man who transported visitors across Lake Lugano, Switzerland, in a rowboat, this family-owned company grew to become the largest guided vacation operator in the world. Globus offers four Hawaii itineraries that include Maui, running 9–12 nights; two include a seven-night cruise on Norwegian Cruise Lines. ☎ *866/755–8581* ⊕ *www. globusjourneys.com* ✉ *From $2509.*

Tauck Travel. Begun in 1925 by Arthur Tauck with a tour through the back roads of New England, Tauck has since spread its offerings across the world. Its 11-night multi-island "Best of Hawaii" tour includes three nights on Maui and covers noteworthy sights such as Iao Valley and Haleakala National Park. ☎ *800/788–7885* ⊕ *www.tauck.com* ✉ *From $6190.*

Trafalgar. This company prides itself on its "Insider Experiences," defined as visiting hidden places not found in guidebooks, meeting local people, and sharing traditions you may not discover on your own. Trafalgar offers several itineraries that include Maui, runnin 7–12 nights. ☎ *866/513–1995* ⊕ *www.trafalgar.com* ✉ *From $2524.*

INSPIRATION

Driving & Discovering Hawaii: Maui and Molokai, by Richard Sullivan (Montgomery Ewing Publishing), has stunning photographs and more than 40 detailed maps of the two islands. In the book *Snorkel Maui and Lanai: Guide to the Underwater World of Hawaii* (Indigo Publications) authors Judy and Mel Malinowski share not only dozens of great snorkeling sites, but also a love of the Islands. *Maui Trailblazer: Where to Hike, Snorkel, Paddle, Surf, Drive,* by Jerry and Janine Sprout (Diamond Valley Company), features 137 hikes, 44 snorkel spots, 20 locations to kayak, and nearly 40 beaches for surfing, boogie boarding, or bodysurfing. There's also a Trailblazer Kids section for active families. If you're planning to do an abundance of exploring on foot, you'll want to get either *Maui Trails: Walks, Strolls and Treks on the Valley Island* (Wilderness Press) or *Hiking Maui, The Valley Isle* (Hawaiian Outdoor Adventures Publications).

For the most fascinating and concise history of the Hawaiian Islands, you should read the 1968 *Shoal of Time: A History of the Hawaiian Islands,* by Gavan Daws (University of Hawaii Press). And of course James Michener's 1959 novel *Hawaii* (Ballantine Books) is an epic, historical novel about the Islands that he dedicated to "all the people who came to Hawaii."

INDEX

PHOTO CREDITS

Front cover: Greg Vaughn / age fotostock [Description: Wailua Falls, Maui, Hawaii]. Back cover: from left to right: Kriss Russell/PhotoGen-X\LifeJourneys/iStockphoto; Molokai Ranch; Molokai Visitors Association. Spine: RonTech2000/iStockphoto. 1, Douglas Peebles/eStock Photo. 2-3, Douglas Peebles/ eStock Photo. Chapter 1: Experience Maui: 8-9, Hawaii Tourism Authority (HTA) / Tor Johnson. 16 (left), Danita Delimont/ Alamy. 16 (top center), Sekarb I Dreamstime.com. 16 (bottom center), David Fleetham/Alamy. 16 (right), Tomas del Amo/Alamy. 17 (top left), David Fleetham/Alamy. 17 (bottom left), Mitch Diamond/Alamy. 17 (bottom center), Ho'oilo House. 17 (right), Starwood Hotels & Resorts. 18 (top left), Jim Cazel/Photo Resource Hawaii/Alamy. 18 (bottom left), Robert Holmes/ Alamy. 18 (right), SuperStock/age fotostock. 19 (left), Jim Cazel/Photo Resource Hawaii/Alamy. 19 (top right), Andre Jenny/Alamy. 19 (bottom center), Hawaii Tourism Authority (HTA) / Tor Johnson. 19 (bottom right), Douglas Peebles Photography/Alamy. 36, Polynesian Cultural Center. 37 (top), Hawaii Tourism Authority (HTA) / Kirk Lee Aeder. 37 (bottom), iStockphoto 38, Linda Ching/HVCB. 39 (top), Hawaii Tourism Authority (HTA) / Dana Edmunds. 39 (bottom), Sri Maiava Rusden/HVCB. 40, HVCB. 41 (top), Hawaii Tourism Authority (HTA) / Sri Maiava Rusden Island. 41 (bottom), jhorrocks / iStockphoto. Chapter 2: Exploring Maui: 43, Ironrodart I Dreamstime.com. 44, The_seeker, Fodors. com member. 45, Chrishowey I Dreamstime.com. 50, Joelanai I Dreamstime.com. 54, Walter Bibikow/ age fotostock. 59, Douglas Peebles/eStock Photo. 79, SuperStock/age fotostock. Chapter 3: Beaches: 83, Brent Bergherm/age fotostock. 84, S. Greg Panosian/ iStockphoto. 90, Mike7777777 I Dreamstime. com 92, Robert Simon/iStockphoto. 95, Hawaii Tourism Authority (HTA) / Tor Johnson. Chapter 4: Where to Eat: 97, Douglas Peebles Photography/Alamy. 98, Eneri LLC/iStockphoto. Chapter 5: Where to Stay: 123, Courtesy of Four Seasons Resort Maui. 124, Ron Dahlquist. Chapter 6: Nightlife and Performing Arts: 145, Gaetano Images Inc./Alamy. 146, andy jackson/iStockhoto. 147, David Olsen/ Photo Resource Hawaii/Alamy. 155, Hawaii Convention & Visitors Bureau. Chapter 7: Shops and Spas: 159, Douglas Peebles Photography/Alamy. 160, Starwood Hotels & Resorts Worldwide, Inc. 165, CJ Anderson/Flickr, [CC BY-ND 2.0]. Chapter 8: Water Sports and Tours: 175, Eric Sanford/ age fotostock. 176, Kriss Russell/PhotoGenX\LifeJourneys/Stockphoto. 186, SUNNYphotography. com/Alamy. 197, Michael S. Nolan/age fotostock. 201, SuperStock/age fotostock. Chapter 9: Golf, Hiking and Outdoor Activities: 203, SuperStock/age fotostock. 204, Aimin Tang/iStockphoto. 205, Douglas Peebles/eStock Photo. 211, Ray Mains Photography /Wailea Golf Club. 216, Phil Degginger/Alamy. 218, 7Michael / iStockphoto. 222, SuperStock/age fotostock. Chapter 10: Molokai: 227, Molokai Visitors Association. 228, Douglas Peebles/age fotostock. 230, Greg Vaughn / Alamy. 231 (top), IDEA. 231 (bottom), Douglas Peebles Photography / Alamy. 232, Michael Brake/iStockphoto. 236, JS Callahan/tropicalpix/iStockphoto. 240, Aurora Photos. 243, David R. Frazier Photolibrary, Inc./Alamy. 246, Michael Brake/iStockphoto. 250, Tony Reed/Alamy. 257, Molokai Visitors Association. 258, Greg Vaughn/Alamy. Chapter 11: Lanai: 263, Lanai Image Library. 264, Lanai Visitors Bureau. 265, Michael S. Nolan/age fotostock. 266, Sheldon Kralstein/iStockphoto. 269, iStockphoto. 273, Pacific Stock/SuperStock. 283, Hawaii Tourism Japan (HTJ). About Our Writers: All photos are courtesy of the writers except for the following: Lehia Apana, courtesy of Brad Bayless; Christie Leon, courtesy of Honolulu Star-Advertiser.

NOTES

NOTES

NOTES

NOTES

NOTES

NOTES

NOTES

NOTES

NOTES

NOTES

NOTES

ABOUT OUR WRITERS

 Born and raised on Maui, **Lehia Apana** is an island girl with a wandering spirit. She has lived in Chicago, Rome, and Sydney, but always finds her way back home. Lehia has been writing about Maui for nearly a decade, beginning as a reporter, and later as special sections editor, at the *Maui News*. These days, when she's not flexing her writing muscles as the managing editor at *Maui Nō Ka 'Oi Magazine,* she can be found training for her next triathlon, surfing, or dancing hula.

 Christie Leon is an award-winning journalist who has covered volcanic eruptions, shark attacks, hurricanes, and all the other things not commonly written about in guidebooks. Raised in Honolulu, she has been living on Maui for 30 years and commutes by air to her job on Oahu with Hawaii's largest daily newspaper.

 Heidi Pool is a freelance writer and personal fitness trainer who moved to Maui in 2003 after having been a frequent visitor for the previous two decades. An avid outdoor enthusiast, Heidi enjoys playing tour guide when friends or family members come to visit.